GW00696827

THE HUGUENOTS

THE HUGUENOTS.

From the picture by Sir John Millais, P.R.A.

[Frontispiece.

THE HUGUENOTS

THEIR SETTLEMENTS, CHURCHES, AND INDUSTRIES, IN ENGLAND AND IRELAND

BY SAMUEL SMILES, LL.D.

AUTHOR OF "LIVES OF THE ENGINEERS,"
"SELF-HELP," "THRIFT," "CHARACTER," ETC.

LONDON

JOHN MURRAY, ALBEMARLE STREET, W.

1905

FIRST EDITION . . . *November* 1867
SECOND EDITION . . . *February* 1868
THIRD EDITION . . . *November* 1869
FOURTH EDITION . . . *November* 1869
FIFTH EDITION . . . *November* 1876
REPRINTED . . . *September* 1880
REPRINTED . . . *September* 1881
REPRINTED . . . *September* 1884
SIXTH EDITION . . . *December* 1889
SEVENTH EDITION . . . *December* 1894
POPULAR (3/6) EDITION . *July* 1905
REPRINTED . . . *October* 1905

PREFACE.

THE First Edition of this work was published in 1868, and it has since been frequently reprinted, with additions. It was stated in the First Edition that important names might have been omitted from the List of Huguenot Refugees and their Descendants at the close of the volume ; but the Author invited further contributions on the subject, which would be inserted in any future edition.

Numerous memoirs have accordingly been sent to the Author from England, Ireland, Scotland, and even India, in reply to his invitation. Many of these had never before been published, though they are of much interest. They are now included in the List of Distinguished Huguenots and their Descendants, and in the Appendix to the same list, at the end of this volume. The memoirs in the Appendix are the most recent additions.

The Author has also received numerous inquiries from descendants of Huguenots who had lost traces of their origin, requesting information as to their ancestors. Sometimes he was enabled to supply information, after consulting Haag's *La France Protestante*, Cooper's *Lists of Foreign Protestants and Aliens*, Burns' *History of the Foreign Refugees*, the *Ulster Journal of Archæology*, and Agnew's *Protestant Exiles from France*; but, in a large number of cases, he could give no information. During the last few years, however, a Huguenot Society has been established in London, from which all accessible facts can be easily ascertained.

The First Edition of this work was translated into French in 1870, with an excellent Preface by M. Athanase Coquerel fils. It was printed by Heitz, at Strasburg; and, while it was ready for transport to Paris, the city was surrounded and bombarded by the German army, when a considerable part of the edition was destroyed. After the conclusion of the Franco-German war, the book was eventually published by Cherbuliez, of Paris.

The surrenders of Bazaine at Metz, and of Napoleon III. at Sedan, will never be forgotten. Sedan, prior to the Revocation of the Edict of Nantes, was the renowned seat of Protestant learning; but after the university had been suppressed, and the Protestants driven away by persecution, Sedan withered, and had become almost forgotten. Now, however, it is known as the scene of the greatest military catastrophe which has happened in modern times.

" Cast thy bread upon the waters, and thou shalt

find it after many days," is a counsel which has received a significant realization in the relations between France and Prussia. A large number of the expatriated refugees took refuge in Prussia, which was then slowly emerging from the marshes of Brandenburg. France was the dominant power in Europe, while Prussia was of comparatively little moment. Now, Prussia, from a Dukedom has become a Kingdom, and, on the soil of France, an Empire.

What France lost by religious intolerance was forcibly expressed by M. Jules Simon, when Prime Minister. Discussing the ecclesiastical questions then perplexing French politicians, he recalled the fact that not less than eighty of the German staff, in the recent Franco-German war, were representatives of Protestant families who had been driven from France by the persecutions which followed the Revocation of the Edict of Nantes. It was meet that the descendants of the men whom Louis XIV., the despot of the seventeenth century, had cast out, should be conspicuous in dethroning the despot of the nineteenth.

LONDON: *October*, 1889.

CONTENTS.

CHAPTER IV.

THE DUKE OF ALVA IN FLANDERS—MASSACRE OF ST. BARTHOLOMEW.

CHAPTER V.

RELATIONS OF ENGLAND WITH FRANCE AND SPAIN.

CHAPTER VI.

SETTLEMENTS AND INDUSTRIES OF THE PROTESTANT REFUGEES IN ENGLAND.

CHAPTER VII.

EARLY WALLOON AND FRENCH CHURCHES IN ENGLAND.

CHAPTER VIII.

THE EDICT OF NANTES—COLBERT AND LOUIS XIV.

CHAPTER IX.

THE HUGUENOT PERSECUTIONS UNDER LOUIS XIV.

CHAPTER X.

RENEWED FLIGHT OF THE HUGUENOTS.

CHAPTER XI.

THE HUGUENOTS AND THE ENGLISH REVOLUTION OF 1688.

CHAPTER XII.

ADVENTURES OF DUMONT DE BOSTAQUET—IRISH CAMPAIGNS
OF 1689-90.

CHAPTER XIII.

HUGUENOT OFFICERS IN THE BRITISH SERVICE.

CHAPTER XIV.

HUGUENOT MEN OF SCIENCE AND LEARNING.

CHAPTER XV.

HUGUENOT SETTLEMENTS IN ENGLAND—MEN OF INDUSTRY.

CHAPTER XVI

THE HUGUENOT CHURCHES IN ENGLAND.

CHAPTER XVII.

HUGUENOT SETTLEMENTS IN IRELAND.

CHAPTER XVIII.

DESCENDANTS OF THE REFUGEES.

CHAPTER XIX.

CONCLUSION—THE FRENCH REVOLUTION.

INTRODUCTION.

THE geographical position of Britain has, from the earliest times, rendered it a country of refuge. Fronting Europe, yet separated from it by a deep sea-moat, the proscribed of other lands have by turns sought the protection of the island fortress, and made it their home. To the country of the Britons the Saxons brought their industry, the Northmen their energy, and the Flemings and French their skill and spirit of liberty; and out of the whole has come the English nation.

MICHELET, the French historian—though his observations in regard to England are usually conceived in a hostile spirit—has nevertheless acknowledged the free Asylum which this country has in all times afforded to foreigners flying from persecution abroad. "Hateful as England is," says he, "she appears grand indeed, as she faces Europe,—as she faces Dunkirk and Antwerp in ruins. All other countries—Russia, Austria, Italy, Spain, and France—have their capitals on the west, opposite the setting sun: the

great European vessel seems to float with her sails
bellied by the wind, which erst blew from Asia.
England alone has hers pointed to the east, as if in
defiance of that world—*unum omnia contra.* This
last country of the Old World is the heroical land;
the constant refuge of the exiled and the energetic.
All who have ever fled servitude,—Druids pursued
by Rome, Gallo-Romans chased by the barbarians,
Saxons proscribed by Charlemagne, famished Danes,
grasping Normans, the persecuted Flemish manufacturers, the vanquished French Calvinists,—all have
crossed the sea, and made the great island their country : *arva, beata petamus arva, divites et insulas . . .*
Thus England has thriven on misfortunes and grown
great out of ruins." [1]

The early industry of England was almost entirely
pastoral. Down to a comparatively recent period, it
was a great grazing country, and its principal staple
was Wool. The English people being as yet unskilled
in the arts of manufacture, the wool was bought up
by foreign merchants, and exported abroad in large
quantities, principally to Flanders and France, there
to be manufactured into cloth, and partly returned in
that form for sale in the English markets.

The English kings, desirous of encouraging home
industry, held out repeated inducements to foreign
artizans to come over and settle in this country for the

---

[1] *History of France*, Book III.

purpose of instructing their subjects in the industrial arts. This policy was pursued during many successive reigns, more particularly in that of Edward III. ; and, by the middle of the fourteenth century, large numbers of Flemish artizans, driven out of the Low Countries by the tyranny of the trades-unions as well as by civil wars, embraced the offers held out to them, settled in various parts of England, and laid the foundations of English skilled industry.

But by far the most important emigrations of skilled foreigners from Europe, were occasioned by the religious persecutions which prevailed in Flanders and France for a considerable period after the Reformation. Two great waves of foreign population then flowed over from the Continent into England,—probably the largest in point of numbers which have occurred since the date of the Saxon settlement. The first took place in the latter half of the sixteenth century, and consisted partly of French, but principally of Flemish Protestants; the second, towards the end of the seventeenth century, consisted almost entirely of French Huguenots.

The second of these emigrations, consequent on the religious persecutions which followed the Revocation of the Edict of Nantes by Louis XIV., was of extraordinary magnitude. According to Sismondi, the loss which it occasioned to France was not far short of a million of persons, and these were her best and most industrious subjects. Although the circumstances connected with this remarkable exodus, as well as the events which flowed from them, exercised an important influence on the political, religious, and industrial history of Northern Europe, they have as yet, viewed in this connection, received but slight notice at the hands of the historian.

It is the object of the following work to give an account of the causes which led to these great migrations of Flemish and French Protestants from Flanders and France into England, and to describe their effects upon English industry as well as English history. The author merely offers the book as a contribution to the study of the subject, which seems to be one well worthy of further investigation.

LIST OF ILLUSTRATIONS

THE HUGUENOTS.

CHAPTER I.

RISE OF THE HUGUENOTS.

A GENERAL ferment pervaded Europe about the beginning of the sixteenth century. The minds of men in all countries were fretting under the trammels which bound them. Privilege prevailed everywhere; the people could not breathe freely; they felt themselves enslaved, and longed for liberty.

At the same time intelligence was advancing. The leaders of thought were gradually adding to the domain of science. Important inventions had been made; a new world had just been discovered by Columbus; and great thinkers were casting their thoughts abroad on the world, stimulating other minds to action, and pointing the way to greater freedom.

But a great barrier stood in the way of all further advancement in the direction of human enfranchisement and liberty. The Papal Church upheld despotism, arrested science, suppressed thought, and barred progress. Wherever free inquiry showed itself, whether in religion or science, the Church endeavoured to crush it. For this purpose, the Inquisition was established. Savonarola was burnt at Florence, and Huss at Constance; whilst, at Rome, Bruno was condemned to the stake, and Galileo was imprisoned, if he was not even put to the torture, and compelled to recant his theory of the earth's motion round the sun.

1

Meanwhile, the Church itself was seen to be a mass of abuses; and the feeling of its intolerableness at length broke out into a general demand for its reformation. There were many eminent churchmen who sought to reform it from within. Amongst these, St. Bernard and others raised their voices long before the sixteenth century; but the corrupt influences which prevailed in the Church were too powerful to be overcome, and the reform was left to be done from without.

The profligacy and despotism of the Papal Church might, however, have continued for centuries longer, had not its agents proceeded to insult too audaciously the common sense and conscience of mankind, by the open sale of indulgences to commit sin, as well as absolutions for sins that had been committed. The young and voluptuous Pope Leo X., who succeeded the warlike Pope Julius II. in 1513, entertained the ambition of rearing an ecclesiastical fabric which should surpass in magnificence all that had preceded it. He surrounded himself with the greatest artists: Bramante, who designed it; Raphael, who painted 'its galleries; and Michael Angelo, who finished it; and the cathedral of St. Peter's at Rome was at length achieved. But it was at an enormous cost; for not only did it impoverish the Papal exchequer, but it split the Papal Church itself in pieces.

The sale of Indulgences was invented for the purpose of replenishing the Roman exchequer, and agents were sent all over Europe to raise funds by this means. Germany was then the great stronghold of the Papal treasury. In Spain and France it was the will of the King, rather than of the Pope, that ruled; but in Germany the civil authority was in a great measure left to the ecclesiastical power. In Germany, therefore, the first great efforts were made to fill the coffers of Rome by the sale of indulgences; and among the most zealous of all the agents who were so employed, was the Dominican monk, John Tetzel, who acted in subordination to Albert of Brandenburg, Elector of Mentz, the principal commissary of the Pope.

The traffic of indulgences was carried on openly. Indulgences were sold by auction, at beat of drum, in public places. They were sold by wholesale and retail. The traffic had its directors and sub-directors, —its officers, its tariffs, its travelling factors; and those agents were employed who best knew the art of deceiving and cozening the people.

Never had such privileges to commit sin been offered to the world, as those which were now openly hawked about by Tetzel. A regular tariff was fixed,[1] —so much for little sins, so much for great sins, so much for eating meat on Fridays, so much for lying, so much for theft, so much for adultery, so much for child-murder, so much for assassination. Bigamy cost only six ducats. This abominable traffic could not fail to rouse the indignation of good men, who saw, with affliction, people of all ranks running after Tetzel to buy indulgence for committing sin ; and at length the public conscience spoke through the voices of bold and earnest men, and, most loudly of all, through that of Martin Luther.

In the meantime a great invention had been made, which gave wings to Luther's words, and accelerated the coming Reformation in a remarkable degree.

Probably no invention has exercised a greater influence upon modern civilisation than that of Printing. While it has been the mother and preserver of many other inventions which have changed the face of society, it has also afforded facilities for the intercourse of mind with mind—of living men with each other, as

---

[1] The tariff of indulgences is set forth at length in the celebrated book entitled *Taxes of the Roman Chancery*. It is now repudiated by Roman Catholics ; but repeated editions of it (ten in number) were published at Rome, when the censorship was excessively strict, from the year 1471 downwards, under the eyes of the successive Popes, and doubtless with their sanction ; for no book could then be printed or published that had not been previously licensed.

well as with the thinkers of past generations,—which
have evoked an extraordinary degree of mental activity,
and exercised a powerful influence on the development
of modern history.

Although letters were diligently cultivated long
before the invention of printing, and many valuable
books existed in manuscript, and seminaries of learning
flourished in all civilised countries, knowledge was for
the most part confined to a comparatively small number of persons. The manuscripts which contained the
treasured thoughts of the ancient poets, scholars, and
men of science, were so scarce and dear that they were
frequently sold for double or treble their weight in
gold. In some cases they were considered so precious,
that they were conveyed by deed, like landed estates.
In the thirteenth century, a manuscript copy of the
Romance of the Rose was sold at Paris for over £33
sterling. A copy of the Bible cost from £40 to £60 for
the writing only; for it took an expert copyist about ten
months' labour to make one.[1] Such being the case, it
will be obvious that books were then for the most part
the luxury of the rich, and comparatively inaccessible
to the great body of the people.

---

[1] It is difficult to form an accurate idea of the relative value
of money to commodities in the
thirteenth century, compared
with present prices ; but it may
be mentioned that in 1445 (according to Fleetwood's *Chronicon
Pretiosum*, 1707) the price of
wheat was 4s. 6d. the quarter,
and oats 2s.; bullocks and heifers
sold for 5s., and sheep 2s. 5½d.
each. In 1460 a gallon of ale
sold for a penny, which was also
the ordinary day's wage of labourers and servants, in addition
to meat and drink. As late as
1558, a good sheep sold for 2s. 10d.
In 1414 the ordinary salary of
chaplains was five or six marks
a-year (the mark being equal to
13s. 4d.), and of resident parish-
priests eight marks ; so that for
about £5 10s. a-year, a single man
was expected to live cleanly and
decently. These prices multiplied by about twelve, would give
something approaching their
equivalent in modern money.
It is true, manuscripts were in
many cases sold at fancy prices,
as books are now. But copying
had become a regular branch of
business. At Milan, in the fourteenth century, about fifty persons earned their living by it.
The ordinary charge for making
a copy of the Bible was eighty
Bologna livres, or equal to fifty-
three gold florins.

Even the most advanced minds could exercise but little influence on their age. They were able to address themselves to only a very limited number of their fellow-men, and in most cases their influence died with them. The results of study, investigation, and experience remaining unrecorded, knowledge was for the most part transmitted orally, and often inaccurately. Thus many arts and inventions discovered by individuals became lost to the race, and a point of social stagnation was arrived at, beyond which further progress seemed improbable.

This state of things was entirely changed by the invention of printing. It gave a new birth to letters ; it enabled books to be perpetually renovated and multiplied at a comparatively moderate cost, and to diffuse the light which they contained over a much larger number of minds ; it gave a greatly increased power to individuals and to society, by facilitating the intercourse of educated men of all countries with each other. Active thinkers were no longer restricted by the limits of their town or parish, or even of their nation or epoch ; and the knowledge that their printed words would have an effect where their spoken words did not reach, could not fail to stimulate the highest order of minds into action. The permanency of invention and discovery was thus secured ; the most advanced point of one generation became the starting-point of the next ; and the results of the labours of one age were carried forward into all the ages that succeeded.[1]

The invention of printing, like most others, struggled slowly and obscurely into life. The wooden blocks or

---

[1] See C. BABBAGE's *Ninth Bridgewater Treatise*, pp. 52-6. Lord Bacon has observed,—" If the invention of ships was thought so noble, which carrieth riches and commodities from place to place, how much more are letters to be magnified, which, as ships, pass through the vast seas of time, and make ages so distant to participate of the wisdom, illuminations, and inventions, the one of the other !"

tablets of Laurence Coster were superseded by separate types of the same material. Gutenberg of Mentz next employed large types cut in metal, from which the impressions were taken. And, finally, Gutenberg's associate Schœffer cut the characters in a matrix, after which the types were cast, and thus completed the art as it now remains.

It is a remarkable circumstance, that the first book which Gutenberg undertook to print with his cut-metal types, was a folio edition of the Bible in the Latin Vulgate, consisting of 641 leaves. When the immense labour involved in carrying out such a work is considered—the cutting by hand, with imperfect tools, of each separate type required for the setting of a folio page, and the difficulties to be overcome with respect to vellum, paper, ink, and presswork—one cannot but feel astonished at the boldness of the undertaking; nor can it be matter of surprise that the execution of the work occupied Gutenberg and his associates a period of from seven to eight years.[1]

[1] The first Bible printed by Gutenberg is known as the Mazarin Bible, from a copy of it having been found in Cardinal Mazarin's library at Paris about the middle of last century. Johnson, in his *Typographia* (p. 17), says: "It was printed with large cut-metal types, and published in 1450." Others give the date of publication as five years later, in 1455. Mr. Hallam inclines to think that it was printed with cast-metal types; but there is reason to believe that the casting of the types by a matrix was invented at a subsequent period. Mr. Hallam says: "It is a very striking circumstance that the high-minded inventors of this great art tried at the very outset so bold a flight as the printing an entire Bible, and executed it with astonishing success. It was Minerva leaping on earth in her divine strength and radiant armour, ready at the moment of her nativity to subdue and destroy her enemies. The Mazarin Bible is printed, some copies on vellum, some on paper of choice quality, with strong, black, and tolerably handsome characters, but with some want of uniformity, which has led, perhaps unreasonably, to doubt whether they were cast in a matrix. We may see in imagination this venerable and splendid volume leading up the crowded myriads of its followers, and imploring, as it were, a blessing on the new art, by dedicating its first-fruits to the service of Heaven." — *Literary History,* edition 1864, pp. 156-7.

We do not, however, suppose that Gutenberg and
his associates were induced to execute this first printed
Bible through any more lofty motive than that of
earning a considerable sum of money by the enterprise.
They were, doubtless, tempted to undertake it by the
immense prices for which manuscript copies of the
Bible were then sold; and they merely sought to produce, by one set of operations, a number of duplicates
in imitation of the written character, which they hoped
to be able to sell at the manuscript prices. But, as
neither Gutenberg nor Schœffer were rich men, and as
the work involved great labour and expense while
in progress, they found it necessary to invite some
capitalist to join them; and hence their communication
of the secret to John Faust, the wealthy goldsmith of
Mentz, who agreed to join them in their venture, and
supply them with the necessary means for carrying
out the undertaking.

The first edition of the printed Bible having been
disposed of, without the secret having transpired, Faust
and Schœffer brought out a second edition in 1462,
which they again offered for sale at the manuscript
prices. Faust carried a number of copies to Paris to
dispose of, and sold several of them for 500 or 600
crowns,—the price then paid for manuscript Bibles.
But great was the astonishment of the Parisian copyists
when Faust, anxious to dispose of the remainder,
lowered his price to sixty and then to thirty crowns!
The copies sold having been compared with each other,
were found to be exactly uniform! It was immediately
inferred that these Bibles must be produced by magic,
as such an extraordinary uniformity was considered
entirely beyond the reach of human contrivance. Information was forthwith given to the police against
Faust as a magician. His lodgings were searched,
when a number of Bibles were found there complete.
The red ink, with which they were embellished, was
supposed to be his blood. It was seriously believed
that he was in league with the devil; and he was

carried off to prison, from which he was only delivered upon making a full revelation of the secret.[1]

Several other books, of less importance, were printed by Gutenberg and Schœffer at Mentz ; two editions of the Psalter, a Catholicon, a Codex Psalmorum, and an edition of Cicero's Offices ; but they were printed in such small numbers, and were sold at such high prices, that, like the manuscripts which they superseded, they were only purchasable by kings, nobles, collegiate bodies, and rich ecclesiastical establishments. It was only after the lapse of many years, when the manufacture of paper had become improved, and Schœffer had invented his method of cutting the characters in a matrix, and casting the type in quantity, that books could be printed in such forms as to be accessible to the great body of the people.

In the meanwhile, the printing establishments of Gutenberg and Schœffer were broken up by the sack and plunder of Mentz by the Archbishop Adolphus in 1462. Their workmen having thus become dispersed, and being no longer bound to secrecy, they shortly after carried with them the invention of the new art into nearly every country in Europe.

Wherever the printers set up their trade, they usually began by issuing an edition of the Latin Bible. There was no author class in those days to supply " copy " enough to keep their presses going. Accordingly, they fell back upon the ancient authors—issuing editions of Livy, Horace, Sallust, Cicero, and portions of Aristotle, with occasional devotional manuals ; but their favourite book, most probably because it was the one most in demand, was the Bible. Only twenty-four books were published in Germany during the ten years that followed the sack of Mentz ; but of these five were Latin and two were German Bibles. Translators were at the same time busily engaged upon it in different countries,

---

[1] Such is supposed to be the origin of the tradition of " The Devil and Dr. Faustus." It is believed that Faust died of the plague at Paris in 1466.

and year by year the Bible became more accessible. Thus an Italian version appeared in 1471, a Bohemian in 1475, a Dutch in 1477, a French in 1477, and a Spanish (Valencian) in 1478.[1]

The Bible, however, continued a comparatively scarce and dear book; being little known to the clergy generally, and still less to the people. By many of the former it was regarded with suspicion, and even with hostility. At length, the number of editions of the Bible which were published in Germany, as if heralding the approach of the coming Reformation, seriously alarmed the Church; and in 1486 the Archbishop of Mentz placed the printers of that city, which had been the cradle of the printing-press, under strict censorship. Twenty-five years later, Pope Alexander VI. issued a bull prohibiting the printers of Cologne, Mentz, Treves, and Magdeburg, from publishing any books without the express licence of their archbishops. Although these measures were directed against the printing of religious works generally, they were more particularly directed against the publication of the Scriptures in the vulgar tongue.[2]

The printers, nevertheless, continued to print the

---

[1] Lord Spencer's famous library contains twenty editions of the Bible in Latin, printed between the appearance of the Mazarin Bible in 1450-5, and the year 1480 inclusive. It also contains nine editions of the German Bible, printed before the year 1495.— See EDWARDS *on Libraries,* p. 430.

[2] HALLAM—*Literary History,* ed. 1864, i. 254. No translation of the Bible was permitted to appear in England during the fifteenth century ; and the reading of Wycliffe's translation was prohibited under penalty of *excommunication and death.* Tyndale's translation of the New Testament was first printed at Antwerp. The government tried to suppress the book, and many copies were seized and burnt. John Tyndale, a merchant of London, brother of the translator, having been convicted of reading the New Testament, was sentenced by the venerable Sir Thomas More " that he should be set upon a horse with his face to the tail, and have a paper pinned upon his head, and many sheets of New Testaments sewn to his cloak, to be afterwards thrown into a great fire kindled in Cheapside, and then pay to the king a fine which should ruin him."

Bible, regardless of these prohibitions—the Old Testament in Hebrew, the New in Greek, and both in Latin, German, French, and other modern languages. Finding that the reading of the Bible was extending, the priests began to inveigh against the practice from the pulpit. " They have now found out," said a French monk, " a new language called Greek ; we must carefully guard ourselves against it. That language will be the mother of all sorts of heresies. I see in the hands of a great number of persons a book written in this language, called ' The New Testament '; it is a book full of brambles, with vipers in them. As to the Hebrew, whoever learns that becomes a Jew at once." [1]

The fears of the priests increased as they saw their flocks becoming more intent upon reading the Scriptures, and hearing them read, than attending mass ; and they were especially concerned at the growing disposition of the people to call in question the infallibility of the Church and the sacred character of the priesthood. It was every day becoming clearer to them that if the people were permitted to resort to books, and pray to God direct in their vulgar tongue, instead of praying through the priests in Latin, the authority of the mass would fall, and the Church itself would be endangered.[2]

---

[1] SISMONDI — *Histoire des Français*, xvi. 364.

[2] Lord Herbert, in his *Life of Henry VII.* (p. 147), says that Cardinal Wolsey stated the effects of printing to the pope in the following terms :—" That his holiness could not be ignorant what diverse effects the new invention of printing had produced ; for it had brought in and restored books and learning ; so together it hath been the occasion of those sects and schisms which daily appear in the world, but especially in Germany ; where men begin now to call in question the present faith and tenets of the Church, and to examine how far religion is departed from its primitive institution. And that, which particularly was most to be lamented, they hath exhorted lay and ordinary men to read the Scriptures, and to pray in their vulgar tongue ; and if this was suffered, besides all other dangers, the common people at last might come to believe that there was not so much use of the clergy. For if men were persuaded once they could make their own way to God, and that prayers in their native and ordinary language might pierce heaven as well as Latin, how

A most forcible expression was given to this view by the Vicar of Croydon in a sermon preached by him at Paul's Cross, in which he boldly declared that " we must root out printing, or printing will root out us."

But printing could not be rooted out, any more than the hand of Time could be put back. This invention, unlike every other, contained within itself a self-preserving power which ensured its perpetuation. Its method had become known, and was recorded by itself. Printed books were now part of the inheritance of the human race ; and though Bibles might be burnt,—as vast numbers of them were, so that they might be kept out of the hands of the people,—so long as a single copy remained, it was not lost, but was capable of immediate restoration and of infinite multiplication.

The intense interest which the publication of the Bible excited, and the emotion which it raised in the minds of those who read it, are matters of history. At this day, when Bibles are common in almost every household, it is perhaps difficult to appreciate the deep feelings of awe and reverence with which men for the first time perused the sacred volume. We have become so familiar with it, that we are apt to look upon it merely as one amongst many books,—as part of the current literature of the day, or as a record of ancient history, to be checked off by the arithmetician or analysed by the critic.

It was far different in those early times, when the Bible was rare and precious. Printing had brought forth the Book, which had lain so long silent in manuscript beneath the dust of old libraries, and laid it before the people, to be read by them in their own tongue. It was known to be the charter and title-deed

much would the authority of the mass fall ! For this purpose, since printing could not be put down, it was best to set up learning against learning ; and by introducing all persons to dispute, to suspend the laity between fear and controversy. This at most would make them attentive to their superiors and teachers."

of Christianity—the revelation of God's will to man, and now, to read it, or hear it read, was like meeting God face to face, and listening to His voice speaking directly to them.

At first it could only be read to the people ; and in the English cathedrals, where single copies were placed, chained to a niche, eager groups gathered round to drink in its living truths. But as the art of printing improved, and copies of the Bible became multiplied in portable forms, it could then be taken home into the study or the chamber, and read and studied in secret. It was found to be an ever-fresh gushing spring of thought, welling up, as it were, from the Infinite. No wonder that men pondered over it with reverence, and read it with thanksgiving ! No wonder that it moved their hearts, influenced their thoughts, gave a colour to their familiar speech, and imparted a bias to their whole life ![1]

To the thoughtful, the perusal of the Bible gave new views of life and death. Its effect was to make those who pondered its lessons more solemn ; it made the serious more earnest, and impressed them with a deeper sense of responsibility and duty. To the poor, the suffering, and the struggling, it was the aurora of a new world. With this Book in their hands, what to them were the afflictions of time, which were but for a moment, working out for them " a far more exceeding and eternal weight of glory"?

It was the accidental sight of a copy of one of Gutenberg's Bibles in the library of the convent of Erfurt, where Luther was in training for a monk, that

---

[1] The perusal and study of the Bible in the fifteenth and sixteenth centuries exercised an important influence on literature in all countries. The great writers of the period unconsciously adopted Bible phraseology to a large extent—the thoughts of Scripture clothing themselves in language which became habitual to all who studied it closely. This tendency is noticeable in the early English writers — in Latimer, Bradford, Jewell, More, Brown, Bacon, Milton, and others. Coleridge has said, " Intense study of the Bible will keep any writer from being vulgar in point of style."

fixed his destiny for life.[1] He opened it, and read with inexpressible delight the history of Hannah and her son Samuel. " O God ! " he murmured, " could I but have one of these books, I would ask no other treasure ! " A great revolution forthwith took place in his soul. He read, and studied, and meditated, until he fell seriously ill. Dr. Staupitz, a man of rank in the Church, was then inspecting the convent at Erfurt, in which Luther had been for two years. He felt powerfully attracted towards the young monk, and had much confidential intercourse with him. Before leaving, Staupitz presented Luther with a copy of the Bible— a Bible all to himself, which he could take with him to his cell and study there. " For several years," said Luther afterwards, " I read the whole Bible twice in every twelvemonth. It is a great and powerful tree, each word of which is a mighty branch ; each of these branches have I shaken, so desirous was I to learn what fruit they every one of them bore, and what they could give me." [2]

This Bible of Luther's was, however, in the Latin Vulgate, a language known only to the learned. Several translations had been printed in Germany by the end of the fifteenth century ; but they were unsatisfactory versions, unsuited for popular reading, and were comparatively little known. One of Luther's first thoughts, therefore, was to translate the Bible into the popular speech, so that the people at large might have free access to the unparalleled Book. Accordingly, in 1521, he began the translation of the New Testament during

---

[1] " I was twenty years old," said Luther, " before I had ever seen the Bible. I had no notion that there existed any other Gospels or Epistles than those in the service. At last I came across a Bible in the library at Erfurt, and used often to read it to Dr. Staupitz with still increasing wonder."—TISCHREDEN—*Table Talk* (Frankfort, 1568), p. 255. And again: " Dr. Usinger, an Augustan monk, who was my preceptor at the convent of Erfurt, used to say to me, ' Ah, brother Martin ! why trouble yourself with the Bible ? Rather read the ancient doctors who have collected for you all its marrow and honey. The Bible itself is the cause of all our troubles.' "—TISCHREDEN, p. 7.

[2] TISCHREDEN, p. 311.

his imprisonment in what he called his Patmos—the castle of Wartburg. It was completed and published in the following year; and two years later, his Old Testament appeared.

None valued more than Luther did, the invention of printing. "Printing," said he, "is the latest and greatest gift by which God enables us to advance the things of the Gospel." Printing was, indeed, one of the prime agents of the Reformation. The ideas had long been born, but printing gave them wings. Had the writings of Luther and his fellow-labourers been confined only to such copies as could have been made by hand, they would have remained few in number, been extremely limited in their effects, and could easily have been suppressed and destroyed by authority. But the printing-press enabled them to circulate by thousands all over Germany.[1] Luther was the especial favourite of the printers and booksellers. The former took pride in bringing out his books with minute care, and the latter in circulating them. A large body of ex-monks lived by travelling about and selling them all over Germany. His books were also carried abroad,—into Switzerland, Bohemia, France, and England.[2]

The printing of the Bible was also carried on with great activity in the Low Countries. Besides versions in French and Flemish for the use of the people in the Walloon provinces, where the new views extensively

---

[1] At Nuremberg, at Strasburg, even at Mentz, there was a constant struggle for Luther's last pamphlets. The sheet, yet wet, was brought from the press under some one's cloak, and passed from shop to shop. The pedantic bookmen of the German trades' unions, the poetical tinmen, the literary shoemakers, devoured the good news. Worthy Hans Sachs raised himself above his wonted commonplace ; he left his shoe half-made, and with his most high-flown verses, his best pro-

ductions, he sang, in under-tones, "The Nightingale of Wittenberg," and the song was taken up and resounded all over the land.— MICHELET—*Life of Luther*, pp. 70, 71.

[2] Works printed in Germany or in the Flemish provinces, where at first the administration connived at the new religion, were imported into England, and read with that eagerness and delight which always compensate the risk of forbidden studies.—HALLAM—*Hist. of England*, i. p. 82,

prevailed, various versions in foreign tongues were printed for exportation abroad. Thus Tyndale, unable to get his New Testament printed in England, where its perusal was forbidden, had the first edition printed at Antwerp in 1526,[1] as well as two subsequent editions at the same place. Indeed, Antwerp seems at that time to have been the head-quarters of Bible-printing. No fewer than thirteen editions of the Bible and twenty-four editions of the New Testament, in the Flemish or Dutch language, were printed there within the first thirty-six years of the sixteenth century, besides various other editions in English, French, Danish, and Spanish.[2]

An eager demand for the Scriptures had by this time sprung up in France. Several translations of portions of the Bible appeared there towards the end of the fifteenth century; but these were all superseded by a version of the entire Scriptures, printed at Antwerp in successive portions, between the years 1512 and 1530. This translation was the work of Jacques le

---

[1] A complete edition of the English Bible, translated partly by Tyndale and partly by Coverdale, was printed at Hamburg in 1535; and a second edition, edited by John Rogers, under the name of "Thomas Matthew," was printed at Marlborow in Hesse, in 1537. Tyndale suffered martyrdom at Vilvorde, near Brussels, in 1536, yet he died in the midst of victory; for before his death no fewer than fourteen editions of the New Testament, several of them of two thousand copies each, had been printed; and at the very time when he died, the first edition of the Scriptures printed in England was passing through the press. Cranmer's Bible, so called because revised by Cranmer, was published in 1539-40. In the year 1542, Henry VIII. issued a proclama-

tion directing a large Bible to be set up in every parish-church, while at the same time Bibles were authorised to be publicly sold. The Spencer collection contains copies of fifteen English editions of the Bible printed between 1536 and 1581; showing that the printing-press was by that time actively at work in England. Wycliffe's translation, though made in 1380, was not printed until 1731.

[2] "There can be no sort of comparison," says Mr. Hallam, "between the number of these editions, and consequently the eagerness of the people of the Low Countries for biblical knowledge, considering the limited extent of their language, and anything that could be found in the Protestant states of the empire."
—*Literary History*, i. 387.

Fevre or Faber, of Etaples, and it formed the basis of all subsequent editions of the French Bible.

The effects were the same wherever the Book appeared, and was freely read by the people. It was followed by an immediate reaction against the superstition, indifferentism, and impiety, which generally prevailed. There was a sudden awakening to a new religious life, and an anxious desire for a purer faith,— less overlaid by the traditions, inventions, and corruptions, which impaired the efficacy, and obscured the simple beauty, of Christianity. The invention of printing had also its political effects. For men to be able to read books, and especially the Scriptures, in the common tongue, was itself a revolution. It roused the hearts of the people in all lands, producing commotion, excitement, and agitation. Society became electric, and was stirred to its depths. The sentiment of Right was created, and the long down-trodden peasants—along the Rhine, in Alsace, and Suabia— raised their cries on all sides, demanding freedom from serfdom, and to be recognised as Men. Indeed, this electric fervour and vehement excitement throughout society was one of the greatest difficulties that Luther had to contend with, in guiding the Reformation in Germany to a successful issue.

The ecclesiastical abuses, which had first evoked the indignation of Luther, were not confined to Germany, but prevailed all over Europe. There were Tetzels also in France, where indulgences were things of common traffic. Money had to be raised by the Church; for the building of St. Peter's at Rome must be paid for. Each sin had its price, each vice its tax. There was a regular tariff for peccadilloes of every degree, up to the greatest crimes. The Bible, it need scarcely be said, was at open war with this monstrous state of things; and the more extensively it was read and its precepts became known, the more strongly were these practices condemned. Hence the alarm occasioned at Rome by the rapid extension of the art of printing and the increasing circulation of the Bible. Hence also the prohibition of printing which shortly followed, and the burning of the printers who printed the Scriptures, as well as of the persons who were found guilty of reading them.

The first signs of the Reformation in France showed themselves in the town of Meaux, about fifty miles north-east of Paris—not far distant from the then Flemish frontier. It was a place full of working-people—mechanics, wool-carders, fullers, cloth-makers, and artizans. Their proximity to Flanders, and the similarity of their trade to that of the larger Flemish towns, occasioned a degree of intercourse between them, which doubtless contributed to the propagation of the new views at Meaux, where the hearts of the poor artizans were greatly moved by the tidings of the Gospel which reached them from the north.

At the same time men of learning in the Church had long been meditating over the abuses which prevailed in it, and devising the best means of remedying them. Among the most earnest of these was Jacques Lefevre, a native of Etaples in Picardy. He was a man of great and acknowledged learning, one of the most distinguished professors in the university of Paris. The study of the Bible produced the same effect upon his mind as it had done on that of Luther ; but he was a man of far different temperament,—gentle, retiring, and timid, though not less devoted to the cause of truth. He was, however, an old man of seventy. His life was fast fleeting; but yet there was a world lying all in wickedness about him. He translated the four Gospels into French in 1523; had them printed at Antwerp ; and put them into circulation. He found a faithful follower in Guillaume Farel—a young, energetic, and active man,—who abounded in those qualities in which the aged Lefevre was so deficient. Another coadjutor shortly joined them—Guillaume Briçonnet, Count of Montbrun and Bishop of Meaux, who also became a convert to the new doctrines.

The bishop, on taking charge of his diocese, had been shocked by the disorders which prevailed there,—by the licentiousness of the clergy, and their general disregard for religious life and duty. As many of them were non-resident, he invited Lefevre, Farel, and others, to occupy their pulpits and preach to the people—the bishop preaching in his turn; and the people flocked to hear them. The bishop also distributed the four Gospels gratuitously among the poor, and very soon a copy was to be found in almost every workshop in Meaux. A reformation of manners shortly followed. Blasphemy, drunkenness, and disorder disappeared; and the movement spread far and near.

It must not be supposed, however, that the supporters of the old Church were indifferent to these proceedings. At first they had been stunned by the sudden spread of the new views and the rapid increase of the "Gospellers," as they were called throughout the northern provinces; but they speedily rallied from their stupor. They knew that power was on their side,—the power of kings and parliaments, and their agents; and they loudly called them to their help, to prevent the spread of heresy. At the same time, Rome, roused by her danger, availed herself of all methods for winning back her wandering children, by force if not by suasion. The Inquisition was armed with new powers; and wherever heresy appeared, it was crushed, unsparingly, unpityingly. No matter what the rank or learning of the suspected heretic might be, he must satisfy the tribunal before which he was brought, or die at the stake.

The priests and monks of Meaux, though mostly absentees, finding their revenues diminishing, appealed for help to the Sorbonne, the Faculty of Theology at Paris; and the Sorbonne called upon parliament at once to interpose with a strong hand. The result was, that the Bishop of Meaux was heavily fined; and he shrank thenceforward out of sight, and ceased to give any further cause for offence. But his disciples were less

pliant, and continued boldly to preach the Gospel.
Jean Leclerc was burnt alive at Metz, and Jacques
Pavent and Louis de Berguin on the Place de Grève
at Paris.   Farel escaped into Switzerland, and there
occupied himself in printing copies of Lefevre's New
Testament, thousands of which he caused to be dis-
seminated throughout France by the hands of pedlars.
The Sorbonne then proceeded to make war against
books, and the printers of books.   Bibles and New
Testaments were seized and burnt.   But more Bibles
and Testaments seemed to rise, as if by magic, from
their ashes.   The printers who were convicted of
printing Bibles were next seized and burnt.   The
Bourgeois de Paris[1] gives a detailed account of the
human sacrifices offered up to ignorance and intolerance in that city during the six months ending June
1534, from which it appears that twenty men and one
woman were burnt alive.   One was a printer of the
Rue St. Jacques, found guilty of having "printed the
books of Luther."   Another, a bookseller, was burnt
for "having sold Luther."   In the beginning of the
following year, the Sorbonne obtained from the King
an ordinance, which was promulgated on the 26th of
February 1535, for the suppression of printing !
It was too late !   The art was now full born, and
could no more be suppressed than light, or air, or life.
Books had become a public necessity ; they supplied
a great public want ; and every year saw them multiplying more abundantly.[2]

---

[1] MICHELET says the *Bourgeois de Paris* (Paris, 1854) was
not the publication of a Protestant, which might be called in
question, but of a "very zealous
Catholic."— *Histoire de France
au Seizième Siècle*, viii., p. 411.

[2] It has been calculated (by
Daunon, Petit, Rudel, Taillandier,
and others) that by the end of the
fifteenth century four millions of

volumes had been printed, the
greater part in folio; and that
between 1500 and 1536 eighteen
more millions of volumes had
been printed. After that it is
impossible to number them. In
1533 there had already been
eighteen editions of the German
Bible printed at Wittemberg,
thirteen at Augsburg, thirteen at
Strasburg, twelve at Basle, and
so on. Schœffer, in his *Influence*

The same scenes were enacted all over France, wherever the Bible had penetrated and found followers. In 1545, the massacre of the Vaudois of Provence was perpetrated, accompanied by horrors which it is impossible to describe. This terrible persecution, however, did not produce its intended effect; but, on the other hand, it was followed by a strong reaction in the public mind against the fury of the persecutors. The king, Francis I., complained that his orders had been exceeded; but he was sick and almost dying at the time, and had not the strength to prosecute the assassins.

There was, however, a lull for a time in the violence of the persecutions, during which the new views made rapid progress; and men of rank, of learning, and ot arms, ranged themselves on the side of "The Religion." Then arose the Huguenots or French Protestants,[1] who shortly became so numerous as to constitute a considerable power in the state, and to exercise, during the next hundred years, a most important influence on the political history of France.

The origin of the term *Huguenot* is extremely obscure. It was at first applied to them as a nickname; and, like the *Gueux* of Flanders, they assumed and bore it with pride. Some suppose the term to be derived from *Huguon*, a word used in Touraine to signify persons who walk at nights in the streets,—the early Protestants, like the early Christians, having chosen that time for their religious assemblies. Others are of opinion that it was derived from a French and faulty pronunciation of the German word *Eidgenossen*,

---

of *Luther on Education*, says that Luther's Catechism soon ran to 100,000 copies. Printing was at the same time making rapid strides in France, England, and he Low Countries.

[1] The followers of the new views called themselves at first *Gospellers* (from their religion being based on the reading of the Gospel), *Religionaries*, or *Those of the Religion*. The name *Pro₁ɫ testant* was not applied to them until the end of the seventeenth century—that term originally characterising the disciples of the Lutheran Reformation in Germany.

or confederates—the name given to those citizens of
Geneva who entered into an alliance with the Swiss
cantons to resist the attempts of Charles ¡III., Duke
of Savoy, against their liberties. The confederates
were called *Eignots*; and hence, probably, the deriva-
tion of the word Huguenots. A third surmise is, that
the word was derived from one *Hugues*, the name of a
Genevese Calvinist.[1]

Further attempts continued to be made by Rome to
check the progress of printing. In 1599, Pope Paul IV.
issued the first *Index Expurgatorius*, containing a list
of the books expressly prohibited by the Church. It
included all Bibles printed in modern languages—of
which forty-eight editions were enumerated ; while
sixty-one printers were put under a general ban, and
all works of every description issuing from their presses
were forbidden. Notwithstanding, however, these and
similar measures—such as the wholesale burning of
Bibles wherever found—the circulation of the Scriptures
rapidly increased, and the principles of the Reformation
prevailed more and more throughout the northern
nations.

---

[1] MAHN, in his *Etymologische
Untersuchungen auf dem Gebiete
der Romanischen Sprachen*, gives
no fewer than fifteen supposed
derivations of the word *Huguenot*,
but inclines to the opinion that
it was originally used as a nickname, and derived from the word
Hughues—" the name of some
heretic or conspirator "—and the
French diminutive *ot*—as Jacot,
Margot, Jeannot, etc.

CHAPTER II.

EPISODE IN THE LIFE OF PALISSY.

At the time when the remarkable movement we have rapidly sketched, was sweeping round the frontiers of France, from Switzerland to Brabant—and men were everywhere listening with eagerness to the promulgation of the new ideas,—there was wandering along the Rhine a poor artizan, then obscure, but afterwards famous, who was seeking to earn a living by the practice of his trade. He could glaze windows, mend furniture, paint a little on glass, draw portraits rudely, gild and colour images of the Virgin, or do any sort of work requiring handiness and dexterity. On an emergency he would even undertake to measure land, and was ready to turn his hand to anything that might enable him to earn a living, and at the same time add to his knowledge and experience. This wandering workman was no other than Bernard Palissy,—afterwards the natural philosopher, the chemist, the geologist, and the artist,—but more generally known as the great Potter.

Fortunately for our present purpose, Palissy was also an author; and though the works he left behind him are written in a quaint and simple style, it is possible to obtain from certain passages in them a more vivid idea of the times in which he lived, and of the trials and sufferings of the Gospellers, of whom he was one of the most illustrious, than from any other contemporary record. The life of Palissy, too, is eminently illustrative of his epoch; and provided we can but accurately portray the life of any single man in rela-

tion to his epoch, then biography becomes history in its
truest sense ; for history, after all, is but accumulated
biography.

From the writings of Palissy,[1] then, we gather the
following facts regarding this remarkable man's life
and career. He was born about the year 1510, at La
Chapelle Biron, a poor village in Perigord, where his
father brought him up to his own trade of a glazier.
The boy was by nature quick and ingenious, with a
taste for drawing, designing, and decoration, which he
turned to account in painting glass and decorating
images for the village churches in his immediate
neighbourhood. Desirous of improving himself, at
the same time that he earned his living, he resolved
to travel into other districts and countries, according to the custom of skilled workmen in those days.
Accordingly, so soon as his term of apprenticeship had
expired, he set out upon his " wanderschaft," at about
the age of twenty-one. He first went into the country
adjacent to the Pyrenees ; and his journeyings in those
mountain districts awoke in his mind that love for
geology and natural history which he afterwards pursued with so much zeal. After settling for a time at
Tarbes, in the High Pyrenees, he proceeded northward,
through Languedoc, Dauphiny, part of Switzerland,
Alsace, the Duchies of Cleves and Luxemburg, and
the provinces of the Lower Rhine, to Ardennes and
Flanders.

It will be observed that Palissy's line of travel lay
precisely through the provinces in which the people
had been most deeply moved by the recent revolt of
Luther from Rome. In 1517 the Reformer had publicly denounced the open sale of indulgences by " the
profligate monk Tetzel," and affixed his celebrated
ninety-five Theses to the outer pillars of the cathedral

---

[1] *Œuvres Complétes de Bernard
Palissy*, édition conforme aux
textes originaux imprimés du
vivant de l'auteur ; avec des
notes et une Notice Historique,
Par PAUL-ANTOINE CAP, Paris,
1844.

of Wittemberg.[1] The propositions were at once printed
in thousands, read, devoured, and spread abroad in
every direction. In 1518, Luther appeared, under the
safe-conduct of the Elector of Saxony, before the Pope's
legate at Augsburg ; and in 1520 he publicly burnt the
Pope's bull at Wittemberg, amidst the acclamations
of the people. All Germany was now in a blaze,
and Luther's books and pamphlets were everywhere
in demand. It was shortly after this, that Palissy
travelled through the excited provinces. Wherever he
went he heard of " Luther," " the Bible," and the New
Revelation which the latter volume had brought to
light. The men of his own class, with whom he most
freely mixed in the course of his travels—artists,
mechanics, and artizans [2]—were full of the new ideas
which were stirring the heart of Germany. These
were embraced with especial fervour by the young
and the energetic. Minds formed and grown old in
the established modes of thought, were unwilling to be
disturbed, and satisfied to rest as they were. " Too old
for change " was their maxim. But it was different
with the young, the ardent, and the inquiring—who
looked before rather than behind, to the future rather
than the past. These were, for the most part, vehement
in support of the doctrines of the Reformation.

---

[1] A copy of the Indulgence
issued by Pope Leo X. for the
rebuilding of St. Peter's, is now
to be seen in the King's Library,
British Museum. It is well
worthy of general perusal.
The Indulgence was printed
in the year 1517, under the
direction of Albert, Archbishop
of Mentz and Magdeburg; and
it was sold by John Tetzel and
Bernardinus Samson as sub-
commissaries. The manner in
which Tetzel carried on the
traffic led, everybody knows, to
the remonstrance of Luther, and
the Reformation. It is placed
close to the original printed copy

of the ninety-five Theses against
Indulgences and other Papal
practices, posted by Luther on
the doors of the church of Wittemberg, on the 31st of October,
1517. It is also close to Luther's
appeal to a General Council, dated
November, 1518.

[2] An old Roman Catholic historian says : "Above all, painters,
watchmakers, sculptors, goldsmiths, booksellers, printers, and
others, who from their callings
have some nobility of mind, were
among the first easily surprised."
—REMOND—*Histoire de l'Here-
sie de ce Siécle*, book vii., 931.

Palissy was then of an age at which the mind is most open to receive new impressions. He was, moreover, by nature a shrewd observer and an independent thinker; and he could not fail to be influenced by the agitation which stirred society to its depths. Among the many things which Palissy learned in the course of his travels, was the art of reading printed books; and one of the books which he learned to read, and most prized, was the printed Bible, the greatest marvel of his time. It was necessarily read in secret, for the ban of the Church was still upon it; but the prohibition was disregarded, and probably gave an additional zest to the study of the forbidden book. Men recognised each other's love for it as by a secret sympathy; and they gathered together in workshops and dwellings to read and meditate over it, and exhort one another from its pages. Among these was Palissy, who, by the time he was thirty years old, had become a follower of the Gospel, and a believer in the religion of the Open Bible.[1]

Palissy returned to France in 1539, at a time when persecution was at the hottest; when printing had been suppressed by royal edict; when the reading of the Bible was prohibited on pain of death; and when many were being burnt alive for reading and believing it. The persecution especially raged in Paris and the neighbourhood,—which may account for Palissy's avoidance of the city. An artist so skilled as he was, would naturally have desired to settle there; but he passed it, and went on to settle at Saintonge, in the south-

---

[1] We cannot learn from Palissy's writings what his creed was. He never once mentions the names of either Luther or Calvin; but he often refers to the "teachings of the Bible," and "the statutes and ordinances of God as revealed in His Word." Here, for example, is a characteristic passage:— "Je n'ay trouvé rien meilleur que suivre le conseil de Dieu, ses esdits, statuts et ordonnances: et en regardant quel estoit son vouloir, j'ay trouvé que, par testament dernier, il a commandé à ses héritiers qu'ils eussent à manger le pain au labeur de leurs corps, et qu'ils eussent à multiplier les talens qu'ils leur avoit laissez par son testament."— *Recepte Véritable*, 1563.

western corner of France. There he married, and began
to pursue his manifold callings,—more particularly
glass-painting, portrait-painting, and land-measuring.
He had a long and hard fight for life. His employment
was fitful, and he was often reduced to great straits.
Some years after his settlement at Saintes, while still
struggling with poverty, chance threw in his way an
enamelled cup of Italian manufacture, of great beauty,
which he had no sooner seen, than he desired to imitate
it; and from that time, the determination to discover
the art by which it was enamelled possessed him like a
passion.

The story of Palissy's heroic ardour in prosecuting
his researches in connection with this subject, is well
known: how he built furnace after furnace, and made
experiments with them again and again, only to end in
failure; how he was all the while studying the nature
of earths and clays, and learning chemistry, as he described it, " with his teeth "; how he reduced himself
to a state of the most distressing poverty, which he
endured amidst the expostulations of his friends, the
bitter sarcasms of his neighbours, and, what was still
worse to bear, the reproaches of his wife and children.
But he was borne up throughout by his indomitable
determination, his indefatigable industry, and his irrepressible genius.

On one occasion he sat by his furnace for six successive days and nights without changing his clothes.
He made experiment after experiment, and still the
enamel did not melt. At his last and most desperate
experiment, when the fuel began to run short, he rushed
into his house, seized and broke up sundry articles
of furniture, and hurled them into the furnace to keep
up the heat. No wonder that his wife and children,
as well as his neighbours, thought the man had gone
mad. But he himself was in a measure compensated
by the fact that the last great burst of heat had melted
the enamel; for when the common clay jars, which
had been put in brown, were taken out after the

furnace had cooled, they were found covered with the white glaze of which he had been so long and so furiously in search. By this time, however, he had become reduced to a state of the greatest poverty. He had stripped his dwelling, he had beggared himself, and his children wanted food. " I was in debt," said he, " at many places, and when two children were at nurse, I was unable to pay the nurse's wages. No one helped me. On the contrary, people mocked me, saying, ' He will rather let his children die of hunger than mind his own business.'" Others said of him that he was "seeking to make false money." These jeerings of the townsfolk reached his ears as he passed along the streets of Saintes, and cut him to the heart.

Like Brindley the engineer, Palissy betook himself to bed to meditate upon his troubles and study how to find a way out of them. "When I had lain for some time in bed," says he, "and considered that if a man has fallen into a ditch his first duty is to try and raise himself out of it, I, being in like case, rose and set to work to paint some pictures, and by this and other means I endeavoured to earn a little money. Then I said to myself that all my losses and risks were over, and there was nothing now to hinder me from making good pieces of ware; and so I began again, as before, to work at my old art." [1] But he was still very far from success, and continued to labour on for years amidst misfortune, privation, and poverty. "All these failures," he continues, "occasioned me such labour and sadness of spirit, that before I could render my various enamels fusible at the same degree of heat, I was obliged, as it were, to roast myself to death at the door of the sepulchre; moreover, in labouring at such work, I found myself, in the space of about ten years, so worn out that I was shrunk almost to a skeleton; there was no appearance of muscle on my

---

[1] PALISSY—*De l' Art de Terre:* Œuvres Complètes, p. 318.

arms or legs, so that my stockings fell about my feet
when I walked abroad."

His neighbours would no longer have patience with
him ; he was despised and mocked by them all. Yet
he persevered with his art, and proceeded to make
vessels of divers colours, which he at length began to
be able to sell, and thus earned a slender maintenance
for his family. "The hope which inspired me," says
he, " enabled me to proceed with my work, and when
people came to see me I sometimes contrived to entertain them with pleasantry, while I was really sad at
heart. . . . Worst of all the sufferings I had to endure
were the mockeries and persecutions of those of my
household, who were so unreasonable as to expect
me to execute work without the means of doing so.
For years my furnaces were without any covering or
protection ; and while attending to them I have been
exposed for nights, at the mercy of the wind and the
rain, without any help or consolation, save it might be
the meauling of cats on the one side, or the howling
of dogs on the other. Sometimes the tempest would
beat so furiously against the furnaces that I was compelled to leave them, and seek shelter within doors.
Drenched by rain, and in no better plight than if I
had been dragged through mire, I have gone to lie
down at midnight, or at daybreak, stumbling into the
house without a light, and reeling from one side to
another, as if I had been drunken, my heart filled
with sorrow at the loss of my labour after such long
toiling. But, alas ! my home proved no refuge for
me ; for, drenched and besmeared as I was, I found in
my chamber a second persecution worse than the first,
which makes me even now marvel that I was not
utterly consumed by my many sorrows." [1]

In the midst of his great distress, religion came to
Palissy as a consoler. He found comfort in recalling
to mind such passages of the Bible as he carried in

---

[1] PALISSY—*De l'Art de Terre:* Œuvres Complètes, p. 321.

his memory, and which from time to time gave him fresh hope. "You will thus observe," he afterwards wrote, "the goodness of God to me : when I was in the depth of suffering because of my art, He consoled me with His Gospel; and when I have been exposed to trials because of the Gospel, then it has been with my art that He has consoled me." When wandering abroad in the fields about Saintes, at the time of his greatest troubles, Palissy's attention was wont to be diverted from his own sorrows by the wonderful beauty and infinite variety of nature, of which he was a close and accurate observer. What were his petty cares and trials in sight of the marvellous works of God, which spoke in every leaf, and flower, and plant, of His infinite power, and goodness, and wisdom? "When I contemplated these things," says Palissy, "I have fallen upon my face, and, adoring God, cried to Him in spirit, ' What is man that Thou art mindful of him? Not to us, Lord, not to us, but to Thy name be the honour and the glory!'"[1]

There were already many followers of The Religion in Saintes and the adjoining districts. It so happened that Calvin had, at an early period in his life, visited Saintonge, and sowed the seeds of the Gospel there. Calvin was a native of Noyon, in Picardy, and had from his childhood been destined for the priesthood. When only twelv years old, he was provided with a benefice; but by the time he grew to man's estate, a relative presented him with a copy of the Bible, and he became a religious reformer. He began, almost involuntarily, to exhort others from its pages, and proceeded to preach to the people at Bourges, at Paris, and in the adjoining districts. From thence he went into Poitou and Saintonge on the same errand, holding his meetings late at night or early in the morning, in retired places—in a cellar or a garret—in a wood or in the opening of a rock in a mountain-side; a hollow

---

[1] PALISSY—*Recepte Véritable* : Œuvres Complètes, pp. 116-17.

place of this sort, near Poitiers, in which Calvin and his friends secretly celebrated the Lord's Supper, being still known as " Calvin's Cave."

We are not informed by Palissy whether he ever met Calvin in the course of his mission in Saintonge, which occurred shortly after the latter had settled at Saintes; but certain it is, that he was one of the first followers and teachers of the new views in that neighbourhood. Though too poor himself to possess a copy of the Bible, Palissy had often heard it read by others as well as read it himself while on his travels; and his retentive memory enabled him to carry many of its most striking passages in his mind,[1] which he was accustomed to reproduce in his ordinary speech. Hence the style of his early writings, which is strongly marked by Biblical terms and similitudes. He also contrived to obtain many written extracts from the Old and New Testament, for the purpose of reading them to others; and these formed the texts from which he exhorted his fellow Gospellers. For Palissy was one of the earliest preachers of the Reformed Church in the town of Saintes, if he was not indeed its founder.

The meetings of the little congregation soon became popular in Saintes. The people of the town went at first out of curiosity to observe their proceedings, and they were gradually attracted by the earnestness of the worshippers. The members of "The Religion" were known throughout the town to be persons of blameless lives, peaceable, well-disposed, and industrious, who commanded the respect even of their enemies. At length the Roman Catholics of Saintes began to say to

---

[1] The Vaudois peasantry knew the Bible almost by heart. Raids were from time to time made into their district by the agents of the Romish Church for the purpose of seizing and burning all such copies of the Bible as they could lay hands on. Knowing this, the peasants formed societies of young persons, each of whom was appointed to preserve in his memory a certain number of chapters; and thus, though their Bibles were seized and burnt, the Vaudois were still enabled to refer to their Bibles through the memories of the young minds in which the chapters were preserved.

their monks and priests—"See these ministers of the new religion: they make prayers; they lead a holy life: why cannot you do the like?" The monks and priests, not to be outdone by the men of The Religion, then began to pray and to preach like the ministers; "so that in those days," to use the words of Palissy, "there were prayers daily in this town, both on one side and the other."

So kindly a spirit began to spring up under the operation of these influences, that the religious exercises of both parties—of the old and the new religion—were for a short time celebrated in several of the churches by turns; one portion of the people attending the prayers of the old Church, and another portion the preachings of the new; so that the Catholics, returning from celebrating the mass, were accustomed to meet the Huguenots on their way to hear the exhortation, as is usual in Holland at this day. The effects of this joint religious action on the morals of the people, are best described in Palissy's own words :—

"The progress made by us was such, that in the course of a few years, by the time that our enemies rose up to pillage and persecute us, lewd plays, dances, ballads, gormandizings, and superfluities of dress and head-gear, had almost entirely ceased. Scarcely was any bad language to be heard on any side ; nor were there any more crimes and scandals. Lawsuits greatly diminished ; for no sooner had any two persons of The Religion fallen out, than means were found to bring them to an agreement ; moreover, very often before beginning any lawsuit, the one would not begin it before first exhorting the other. When the time for celebrating Easter drew near, many differences, dissensions, and quarrels, were thus stayed and settled. There were then no questions amongst them, but only psalms, prayers, and spiritual canticles ; [1] nor was there any more desire for lewd

---

[1] The Reformers early enlisted music in their service, and it exercised a powerful influence in extending the new movement amongst the people. "Music," said Luther, "is the art of the prophets. It is one of the most magnificent and delightful presents that God has given us. Satan cannot make head against music." Luther was a poet as well as a musician ; his "Ein' feste Burg ist unser Gott" (one of the themes of Meyerbeer's *Huguenots*), which rang through all Germany, was the "Marseillaise"

and dissolute songs. Indeed, The Religion made such progress,
that even the magistrates began to prohibit things that had
grown up under their authority. Thus, they forbade innkeepers
to permit gambling or dissipation to be carried on within their
premises, to the enticement of men away from their own homes
and families.

"In those days might be seen, on Sundays, bands of workpeople walking abroad in the meadows, the groves, and the
fields, singing psalms and spiritual songs, or reading to and
instructing one another. There might also be seen girls and
maidens seated in groups in the gardens and pleasant places,
singing songs on sacred themes ; or boys accompanied by their
teachers, the effects of whose instruction had already been so
salutary, that those young persons not only exhibited a manly
bearing, but a manful steadfastness of conduct. Indeed, these
various influences, working one with another, had already
effected so much good, that not only had the habits and modes
of life of the people been reformed, but their very countenances
themselves seemed to be changed and improved."

But this happy state of affairs did not last long.
While the ministers of the new religion and the priests
of the old (with a few exceptions) were thus working
harmoniously together at Saintes, events were rapidly
drawing to a crisis in other parts of France. The
heads of the Roman Catholic Church saw with alarm

---

of the Reformation. Luther had
improvised both the words and
the music two days before his
appearance at the Diet of Worms.
As he was journeying towards
that city, he caught sight of its
bell-towers in the distance, on
which he rose up in his chariot
and sang the noble song.

The French Reformers also enlisted music in their service at an
early period. The psalms were
translated by Clement Marot and
Theodore de Beza, set to attractive
music, and sung in harmony in
family worship, in the streets and
the fields, and in congregational
meetings. During a lull in the
persecution at Paris in 1558,
thousands of persons assembled
at the Pré-aux-Clercs to listen to
the psalms sung by the men of

"The Religion " as they marched
along. But when the persecution
revived, the singing of psalms
was one of the things most strictly
interdicted, even on pain of
death.

Calvin also, at Geneva, took
great care to have the psalms set
to good music. He employed,
with that object, the best com-
posers, and distributed printed
copies of the music throughout all
the churches. Thus psalmody, in
which the whole people could join,
everywhere became an essential
part of the service of the Reformed Church ; the chaunts of
the Roman Catholics having, until then, been sung only by the
priests or by hired performers.

¹ PALISSY—Œuvres Complètes:
Recepte Véritable, p. 108.

the rapid strides which the new religion was making, and that a large proportion of the population were day by day escaping from their control. Pope Pius IV., through his agents, urged the decisive interference of the secular authority to stay the progress of heresy; and Philip II. of Spain supported him with all his influence.

The Huguenots had now, by virtue of their increasing numbers, become a political power. Many of the leading politicians of France embraced the Reformed cause, not so much because they were impressed by the truth of the new views, as because they were capable of being used as an instrument for party warfare. Ambitious men, opposed to the court party, arrayed themselves on the side of the Huguenots, caring perhaps little for their principles, but mainly actuated by the desire of promoting their own personal ends. Thus political and religious dissension combined together to fan the fury of the contending parties into a flame. The councils of state became divided and distracted. There was no controlling mediating power. The extreme partizans were alike uncompromising; and a social outbreak, long imminent, at length took place.

The head of the Church in France alarmed the King with fears for his throne and his life. " If the secular arm," said the Cardinal de Lorraine to Henry II., " fails in its duty, all the malcontents will throw themselves into this detestable sect. They will first destroy the ecclesiastical power, after which it will be the turn of the royal power." The secular arm was not slow to strike. In 1559, a royal edict was published declaring the crime of heresy punishable by death, and forbidding the judges to remit or mitigate the penalty. The fires of persecution, which had long been smouldering, again burst forth all over France. The provincial Parliaments instituted *Chambres ardentes*, so called because they condemned to the fire all who were accused and convicted of the crime of heresy. Palissy himself has vividly narrated the

3

effect of these relentless measures in his own district
of Saintes:

"The very thought of the evil deeds of those days," says he,
"when wicked men were let loose upon us to scatter, overwhelm, ruin, and destroy the followers of the Reformed faith,
fills my mind with horror. That I might be out of the way of
their frightful and execrable tyrannies, and in order not to be a
witness of the cruelties, robberies, and murders perpetrated in
this rural neighbourhood, I concealed myself at home, remaining there for the space of two months. It seemed to me as if
during that time hell itself had broken loose, and that raging
devils had entered into and taken possession of the town of
Saintes. For in the place where I had shortly before heard only
psalms and spiritual songs, and exhortations to pure and honest
living, I now heard nothing but blasphemies, assaults, threaten-
ings, tumults, abominable language, dissoluteness, and lewd and
disgusting songs, of such sort that it seemed to me as if all
purity and godliness had become completely stifled and extinguished. Among other horrors of the time, there issued forth
from the Castle of Taillebourg a band of wicked imps who
worked more mischief even than any of the devils of the old
school. On their entering the town, accompanied by certain
priests, with drawn swords in their hands, they shouted—
'Where are they? let us cut their throats instantly!' though
they knew well enough that there was no resistance to them,
those of the Reformed Church having all taken to flight. To
make matters worse, they met an innocent Parisian in the
street, reported to have money about him, and him they set
upon and killed without resistance, first stripping him to his
shirt before putting him to death. Afterwards they went from
house to house, stealing, plundering, robbing, gormandising,
mocking, swearing, and uttering foul blasphemies both against
God and man." [1]

During the two months that Palissy remained
secluded at home, he occupied himself busily in per-
fecting the secret of the enamel, which he had so
long been in search of. Notwithstanding his devotion to the exercises of his religion, he continued to
devote himself with no less zeal to the practice of
his art; and his fame as a potter already extended
far beyond the bounds of his district. He had indeed been so fortunate as by this time to have

---

[1] PALISSY —Œuvres Complètes: *Recepte Véritable*, p. 111.

attracted the notice of a powerful noble, the Duke of Montmorency, Constable of France, then engaged in building the magnificent château of Ecouen, at St. Denis, near Paris. Specimens of Palissy's enamelled tiles had been brought under the duke's notice, who admired them so much, that he at once gave Palissy an order to execute the pavement for his new residence. He even advanced a sum of money to the potter, to enable him to enlarge his works, so as to complete the order with despatch.

Palissy's opinions were of course well known in his district, where he had been the founder, and was in a measure the leader, of the Reformed sect. The duke was doubtless informed of the danger which his potter ran, at the outbreak of the persecution; and he accordingly used his influence to obtain a safeguard for him from the Duke of Montpensier, who then commanded the royal army in Saintonge. But even this protection was insufficient; for, as the persecution waxed hotter, and the search for heretics became keener, Palissy found his workshop no longer safe. At length he was seized, dragged from his home, and hurried off by night to Bordeaux, to be put upon his trial for the crime of heresy. And this first great potter of France —this true man of genius, religion, and virtue—would certainly have been tried and burnt, as hundreds more were, but for the accidental circumstance that the Duke of Montmorency was in urgent want of enamelled tiles for his castle-floor, and that Palissy was the only man in France capable of executing them.

It is not improbable that the sending of Palissy to Bordeaux, to be tried there instead of at Saintes, was a ruse on the part of the Duke of Montpensier, to gain time until the Constable could be informed of the danger which threatened the life of his potter; for Palissy says,—"It is a certain truth, that had I been tried by the judges of Saintes, they would have caused me to die before I could have obtained from you any help."

But no sooner did Montmorency hear of the peril
into which his potter had fallen, and find that unless
he bestirred himself, Palissy would be burnt and his
tiles for Ecouen remain unfinished, than he at once
used his influence with Catharine de Medicis, the
Queen-mother, with whom he was then all-powerful,
and had him forthwith appointed "Inventor of Rustic
Figulines to the King." This appointment had the
effect of withdrawing Palissy from the jurisdiction
of the Parliament of Bordeaux, and transferring him
to that of the Grand Council of Paris, which was
tantamount to an indefinite adjournment of his case.
The now royal potter was accordingly released from
prison, and returned to Saintes to find his workshop
roofless and devastated. He at once made arrangements for leaving the place; and, shaking the dust
of Saintes from his feet, he shortly after removed to
the Tuileries[1] at Paris, where he long continued to
carry on the manufacture of his famous pottery.

It is not necessary to pursue the career of Palissy
further than to add, that the circumstance of his
being employed by Catherine de Medicis had not the
slightest effect in inducing him to change his religion.
He remained a Huguenot, and stoutly maintained his
opinions to the last—so stoutly, indeed, that towards
the close of his life, when an old man of seventy-
eight, he was again arrested as a heretic and imprisoned
in the Bastile. He was threatened with death unless
he recanted. But though he was feeble, and trembling on the verge of the grave, his spirit was as brave
as ever. He was as obstinate now in holding to his

---

[1] *Tuileries*—so called from the
tile-works originally established
there by Francis I. in 1518. A
remarkable and unexpected discovery was recently made in the
Place du Carrousel, while dig-
ging out the foundations for part
of the new buildings of the
Louvre — recently completed—
neither more nor less than one
of the ovens in which Palissy
baked his *chefs-d'œuvre.* Several
moulds of faces, plants, animals,
etc., were dug up in an excellent
state of preservation, and also
some fragments of plates, etc.,
bearing the potter's well-known
stamp.

religion, as he had been more than thirty years before in hunting out the secret of the enamel. Mathieu de Launay, minister of state, one of the sixteen members of council, insisted that Palissy should be publicly burnt; but the Duc de Mayenne, who protected him, contrived to protract the proceedings and delay the sentence.

The French historian D'Aubigné describes Henry III. as visiting Palissy in prison with the object of inducing him to abjure his faith. "My good man," said the King, "you have now served my mother and myself for forty-five years. We have put up with your adhering to your religion amid fires and massacres. But now I am so pressed by the Guise party, as well as by my own people, that I am constrained to leave you in the hands of your enemies; and to-morrow you will be burnt, unless you become converted." "Sire," answered the unconquerable old man, "I am ready to give my life for the glory of God. You have said many times that you have pity on me: now I have pity on you, who have pronounced the words 'I am constrained.' It is not spoken like a king, sire; it is what you, and those who constrain you, the Guisards and all your people, can never effect upon me, for I know how to die."

Palissy was not burnt, but died in the Bastile, after about a year's imprisonment, courageously persevering to the end, and glorying in being able to lay down his life for his faith. Thus died a man of truly great and noble character, of irrepressible genius, indefatigable industry, heroic endurance, and inflexible rectitude— one of France's greatest and noblest sons.

CHAPTER III.

PERSECUTIONS OF THE REFORMED.

PALISSY was not the only man of genius in France who embraced the Reformed faith. The tendency of books and the Bible was to stimulate inquiry on the part of all who studied them; to extend the reign of thought, and emancipate the mind from the dominion of human authority. Hence we find among the men of "The Religion," Peter Ramus and Joseph Justus Scaliger, the philosophers; Charles Dumoulin, the jurist; Ambrose Paré, the surgeon; Henry Stephens (or Estienne), the printer and scholar;[1] Jean Cousin, founder of the French school of painting; Barthélemy Prieur and Jean Goujon, sculptors; Jean Bullant, Debrosses, and Du Cerceau, architects; Charles Goudimel, the musical composer; and Oliver de Serre, the agriculturist. These were among the first men of their time in France.

Persecution did not check the spread of the new views: on the contrary, it extended them. The spectacle of men and women publicly suffering death for their faith,—expiring under the most cruel tortures rather than deny their convictions,—arrested the attention even of the most incredulous. Their curiosity was roused; they desired to learn what there was in

---

[1] The Stephenses or Estiennes, being threatened with persecution by the Sorbonne, because of the editions of the Bible and New Testament printed by them, were under the necessity of leaving Paris for Geneva, where they settled, and a long succession of illustrious scholars and printers handed down the reputation of the family.

the forbidden Bible to inspire such constancy and endurance; and they too read the book, and in many cases became followers of The Religion.

Thus the new views spread rapidly all over France. They not only became established in all the large towns, but penetrated the rural districts, more especially in the south and south-east of France. The social misery which pervaded these districts doubtless helped the spread of the new doctrines among the lower classes; for " there was even more discontent abroad," said Brantome, " than Huguenotism." But they also extended amongst the learned and the wealthy. The heads of the house of Bourbon, Antoine duke of Vendôme and Louis prince of Condé, declared themselves in favour of the new views. The former became the husband of the celebrated Jeanne D'Albret, Queen of Navarre, daughter of the Protestant Margaret of Valois; and the last became the recognised leader of the Huguenots. The head of the Coligny family took the same side. The Montmorencies were divided : the Constable halting between the two opinions, waiting to see which should prove the stronger; while others of the family openly sided with the Reformed. Indeed, it seemed at one time as if France were on the brink of becoming Protestant. In 1561 the alarmed Cardinal de Sainte-Croix wrote to the Pope, " The kingdom is already half Huguenot."

Unhappily for France, the country fell into the hands of the Queen and the Guises. Henry II. had married an Italian wife, Catherine de Medicis, niece of the Pope. Great magnificence was displayed at the Queen's coronation. Voluptuousness and cruelty are usually combined. The pomp of the tournaments was combined with the burning of four Lutherans. Persecution prevailed; and many persons of influence left the country. The King confiscated to himself the property of those who took refuge abroad. Pope Paul IV., the Cardinal de Lorraine, the Sorbonne, and the priests demanded that the Inquisition should be established in France. A bull to this effect was issued, and the King confirmed it by an edict; but Parliament would not enforce it, and France was spared the disgrace.

The Doctors of the Sorbonne did their utmost to inflame the minds of the people against the heretics. They influenced the power of the State, which went on persecuting and burning. Henry II. concluded a peace with Spain, and entered into a treaty to exterminate heresy; and, in pledge of this treaty, his daughter Elizabeth was to espouse Philip II. The Cardinal de Lorraine proposed, as the most agreeable exhibition to the Spanish ambassadors, who had arrived in Paris to take away the betrothed princess, to burn before them half a dozen Lutheran counsellors. "We must," to use his own expression, "give this junket to these grandees of Spain."

The King died by the splinter of a lance received in a tournament; and Francis II. reigned in his stead. He was only sixteen years old, and was feeble in body and mind; so that his mother, Catherine de Medicis, became the real governor of France. She was surrounded by the Guises, Châtillons, Saint Andrés, the Constable de Montmorency, and others, who worked for their own advantage the fictitious royalty of Francis II. Catherine de Medicis was artful and vindictive, ambitious of power, devoid of moral feelings, though of considerable intellectual capacity. De Félice says that "no wife and mother of our kings has done so much injury to France as this Italian woman." He adds: "We are speaking of the Italians of the sixteenth century—nobles and priests—who, eternally witnessing at Rome, Florence, Naples, scenes of assassination, poisoning, and the utmost turpitude, had sunk into the very lowest state of depravity. It is they—history attests it—who planned, devised, and finally executed in France the most monstrous crimes of the epoch."

The Guises were the true leaders of the Roman Catholic party. They formed a younger branch of the family of the Dukes of Lorraine. Although foreigners (for Lorraine formed then no part of France), they soon acquired a considerable influence. Claude de Lorraine had by Antoinette de Bourbon six sons and four daughters, all of whom rose to offices of distinction. One of his daughters, Mary of Lorraine, married James V. of Scotland, whose sole surviving issue was Mary, afterwards Queen of Scots. At six years old Mary was sent to France, where she was educated with the King's daughters. At the age of sixteen she was married to the Dauphin. When the Dauphin became king, the Guises became all-powerful. Francis II. entrusted the government of France to Francis duke of Guise and to his brother the Cardinal of Lorraine, both uncles of Mary Stuart. The Duke obtained command of the army; the Cardinal became Archbishop of Rheims, and the possessor of the enormous income of three hundred thousand crowns annually.

These two foreigners, together with the Italian Queen-mother, having virtually taken possession of France, excited the envy of the French aristocracy. The persecutions and burnings with which the Guises treated the Huguenots, could not fail to excite their hostility. Anthony of Bourbon, King of Navarre, and Louis his brother, Prince of Condé, with the other princes of the blood, and the great officers of State, being indignant at seeing the supreme powers of France in such hands, entered into a conspiracy against the Guises,—proposing to expel the Lorraines and place the government of France in the hands of French princes.

Louis de Condé was the invisible chief of the conspiracy, and he induced many of his Huguenot followers to join it. But Coligny and many other Huguenot chiefs knew nothing about it, and many of those of The Religion were strongly opposed to it. La Renaudie represented the political malcontents, and was the visible chief of the conspiracy.

The advocate, Des Avenelles, informed the Guises of the plot, and they immediately took steps to prevent its success. The Court was then at Blois,—in olden times the residence of the kings and princes of France. The château is seated on the side of a picturesque hill, overlooking the Loire. Being incapable of defence, the Guises removed the Court to the magnificent castle of Amboise, situated a little lower down the Loire, on the left bank of that beautiful river.

Before the conspiracy had come to a head, the Guises arrested those who had proposed to take part in it. Twelve hundred prisoners were then brought to Amboise to be executed.

To please the royal personages at the castle, they were brought out to a balcony, that still exists, in order to witness the butchery. There were then present, in Court costumes, Francis II., King of France, and Mary Stuart his wife, afterwards Queen of Scots; Catherine de Medicis; Charles and Henry, afterwards Charles IX. and Henry III., Kings of France. The Cardinal of Lorraine was also present, as well as the Ladies in waiting.

La Renaudie, the chief of the conspiracy, was first hung on a gibbet in the centre of the bridge over the Loire. The remainder of the twelve hundred were hung and beheaded within sight of the ladies. No inquiry, no trial, was permitted. They were merely executed and strung up as fast as possible. The castle walls were decorated with their hanging bodies. The wearied headsman below resigned his axe, and consigned the remainder to other executioners, who, tying their feet and hands together, threw them into the Loire, where they were drowned. The butchery did not end so pleasantly after all. The stench arising from the dead bodies was such, that the Court was driven from the castle in the course of a few days.

Francis II. and Queen Mary did not enjoy their honours long. The King died in his seventeenth year,

after a reign of seventeen months. As he had shown
some symptoms of rebelling against the constraints
to which he was subject, it was supposed that he had
died from poison. At all events, his funeral was disregarded. He was borne to his grave by an old blind
bishop and two servitors. His queen, Mary, returned
to Scotland, to attempt to exercise upon a rougher,
but more sturdy people, the methods of government
which she had learnt from Catherine de Medicis and
her uncles the Guises.

When Francis II. was laid in his grave, Charles IX.,
eleven years old, was proclaimed king, Catherine de
Medicis regent, and Anthony de Bourbon lieutenant-
governor of the kingdom.

The Prince of Condé, who had been imprisoned,
was set free. The Constable, Anne de Montmorency,
resumed his office of Grand Master near the new
King. The Guises suffered a fall; but they bided
their time, and before long, they were once more to the
front again.

When Charles IX. succeeded to the throne, it was
found that the finances of the kingdom were in a
deplorable state. Society was distracted by the feuds
of the nobles—over whom, as in Scotland about the
same period, the monarch exercised no effective control.

France had, however, her Parliament or States-
General, which in a measure placed the King's government *en rapport* with the nation. On its assembling
in December 1560, the Chancellor de L'Hôpital exhorted men of all parties to rally round the young
King; and, while condemning the odious punishments
which had recently been inflicted upon persons of the
Reformed faith, he announced the intended holding of
a national council, and expressed the desire that
thenceforward France should recognise neither Huguenots nor Papists, but only Frenchmen.

A Roman Catholic himself, he advised his co-
religionists to adorn themselves with virtues and a

good life, and to attack their adversaries with the arms of charity, of prayer, and of persuasion. "The knife," he said, "avails but little against the mind. Gentleness will do more than severity. Give up those fiendish names,—Lutherans, Huguenots, Papists; change them to the name of Christian."

This was the first utterance of the voice of conciliation. The Protestants heard it with joy, their enemies with rage. Jean Quintin, the representative of the clergy, demanded that measures should be taken to deliver France from heresy, and that Charles IX. should vindicate his claim to the title of "Most Christian King." Lange, the spokesman of the Tiers Etat, on the other hand, declared against "the three principal vices of the ecclesiastics—pride, avarice, and ignorance"; and urged that they should return to the simplicity of the primitive Church. The nobles, divided amongst themselves, demanded, some that the preaching of the Gospel should be forbidden, and others that there should be general freedom of worship; but all who spoke were unanimous in acknowledging the necessity for a reform in the discipline of the Church.

While the state of religion thus occupied the Deputies, an equally grave question occupied the Court. There was no money in the exchequer; the rate of interest was twelve per cent.; and forty-three millions of francs were required to be raised from an impoverished nation. The Deputies were alarmed at the appalling figure which the chancellor specified; and, declaring that they had not the requisite power to vote the required sum, they broke up amidst agitation, leaving De l'Hôpital at variance with the Parliament, which refused to register the edict of amnesty to the Protestants which the King had proclaimed.

The King's minister, being most anxious to bring all parties to an agreement if possible, and to allay the civil discord which seemed to be fast precipitating France into civil war, arranged, with the sanction of

CHARLES IX.

[To face p. 44.

the Queen-mother, for a conference between the heads of the religious parties; and it took place at Vassy in the presence of the King and his court, in August 1561. Pope Pius IV. was greatly exasperated when informed of the intended conference, and declared himself to have been betrayed by Catherine de Medicis. It appeared to him that the granting of such a conference was a recognition of the growing power of Heresy in France,—the same heresy which had already deprived Rome of her spiritual dominion over England and Germany. The Pope's fears were, doubtless, not without foundation; and had France at that juncture possessed a Knox or a Luther —a Regent Murray or a Lord Burleigh—the results would have been widely different. But as it was, the Reformed party had no better leader than the scholarly and pious Theodore de Beza; and the conference had no other result than to drive the contending parties more widely asunder than before.

Although a royal edict was published in January 1562, guaranteeing to the Protestants liberty of worship, the concession was set at defiance by the Papal party, whose leaders urged on the people in many districts to molest and attack the followers of the new faith. The Papists denounced the heretics, and called upon the Government to extirpate them; the Huguenots, on their part, denounced the corruptions of the Church, and demanded their reform. There was no dominant or controlling power in the State, which drifted steadily in the direction of civil war. Both parties began to arm; and in such a state of things a spark may kindle a conflagration.

The Queen-mother, being a profound dissimulator. appeared still disposed to bargain with the Reformed, She sounded Coligny as to the number of followers that he could, in event of need, place at the service of the King. His answer was, " We have two thousand and fifty churches, and four hundred thousand men able to bear arms, without taking into account our

secret adherents." [1] Such was the critical state of
affairs when matters were precipitated to an issue by
the action of the Duke of Guise, the leader of the
Catholic party.

On Christmas Day 1562, the Protestants of Vassy,
in Champagne, met to the number of about three
thousand, to listen to the preaching of the Word, and
to celebrate the Sacrament according to the practice
of their Church. Vassy was one of the possessions of
the Guises, the mother of whom, Antoinette de Bourbon, an ardent Roman Catholic, could not brook the
idea of the vassals of the family daring to profess a
faith different from that of their feudal superior.
Complaint had been made to her Grace, by the Bishop
of Châlons, of the offence done to religion by the proceedings of the people of Vassy; and she threatened
them, if they persisted in their proceedings, with the
the vengeance of her son the Duke of Guise.

Undismayed by this threat, the Protestants of
Vassy continued to meet publicly, and listen to their
preachers, believing themselves to be under the protection of the law, according to the terms of the royal
edict. On the 1st of March 1563, they held one of
their meetings, at which about twelve hundred persons were present, in a large barn which served for a
church. The day before, the Duke of Guise, accompanied by the duchess his wife, the Cardinal of Lorraine, and about two hundred men armed with arquebusses and poniards, set out for Vassy. They rested
during the night at Dampmarten, and next morning
marched direct upon the congregation assembled in
the barn. The minister, Morel, had only begun his
opening prayer, when two shots were fired at the persons on the platform. The congregation tried in vain
to shut the doors; the followers of the Duke of Guise
burst in, and precipitated themselves on the unarmed

---

[1] *Mémoires de Condé,* ii. 587.

men, women, and children. For an hour they fired,
hacked, and stabbed amongst them, the duke coolly
watching the carnage. Sixty persons of both sexes
were left dead on the spot; more than two hundred
were severely wounded; the rest contrived to escape.
After the massacre, the duke sent for the local judge,
and severely reprimanded him for having permitted
the Huguenots of Vassy thus to meet. The judge
intrenched himself behind the edict of the King. The
duke's eyes flashed with rage, and striking the hilt of
his sword with his hand, he said, "The sharp edge of
this will soon cut your edict to pieces."[1]

The massacre of Vassy was the match applied to
the charge which was now ready to explode. It was
the signal to Catholic France to rise in mass against
the Huguenots. The clergy glorified the deed from
the pulpit, and compared the duke to Moses, when he
ordered the extermination of all who had bowed the
knee to the golden calf. A fortnight later, the duke
entered Paris in triumph, followed by about twelve
hundred noblemen and gentlemen, mounted on horses
richly caparisoned. The provost of merchants went
out to meet and welcome him at the Porte Saint-
Denis; and the people received him with immense
acclamations as the defender of the faith and the
saviour of the country.

Theodore de Beza, overwhelmed with grief, waited
on his Majesty, to complain of the gross violation of
the terms of the royal edict, of which the Guise party
had been guilty. But the King and the Queen-mother
were powerless amidst the whirlwind of excitement
which prevailed throughout Paris. They felt that
their own lives were not safe ; and they at once secretly departed for Fontainebleau. The Duke of Guise
followed them, accompanied by a strong escort. Arrived there, and admitted to an interview, the duke

---

[1] DAVILA—*Histoire des Guerres Civiles de France.* liv. ii. p. 379.

represented to Catherine that, in order to prevent the
Huguenots obtaining possession of the King's person,
it was necessary that he should accompany them to
Melun; but the Queen-mother might remain if she
chose. She determined to accompany her son. After
a brief stay, the Court was again installed in the
Louvre on the 6th of April. The Queen-mother was
thus for a time vanquished by the Guises.

The court waverers and the waiters on fortune at
once arrayed themselves on the side of the strong.
The old Constable de Montmorency, who had been
halting between two opinions, signalised his re-ad-
herence to the Church of Rome by a characteristic act.
Placing himself at the head of the mob, whose idol he
was desirous of being, he led them to the storming of
the Protestant church outside the Porte Saint-Jacques,
called the "Temple of Jerusalem." Bursting in the
doors of the empty place, they tore up the seats, and
placing them and the Bibles in a pile upon the floor,
they set the whole on fire, amidst great acclamations.
After this exploit, the Constable made a sort of trium-
phal entry into Paris, as if he had won some great
battle. Not content, he set out on the same day to
gather more laurels at the village of Popincourt, where
he had the Protestant church there set on fire ; but the
conflagration extending to the adjoining houses, many
of them were also burnt down. For these two great
exploits the Constable received the nickname of "Captain Burnbenches ! "

More appalling, however, than the burning of
churches, were the massacres which followed that of
Vassy all over France—at Paris, at Senlis, at Amiens,
at Meaux, at Châlons, at Troyes, at Bar-sur-Seine, at
Epernay, at Nevers, at Mans, at Angers, at Blois, and
many other places. At Tours the number of the slain
was so great, that the banks of the Loire were almost
covered with the corpses of men, women, and children.
The persecution especially raged in Provence, where
the Protestants were put to death after being sub-

jected to a variety of tortures.[1]   Any detail of these
events would present only a hideous monotony of massacre. We therefore pass them by.

Measures were also taken by the Guise party to put
down the pestilent nuisance of printing; and printers
were forbidden to print or publish anything without permission, on pain of death. The decree to this
effect, relating to Lyons, bearing the signature of
Charles IX., and dated the 10th September 1563, is
still preserved at the Bibliothèque Impériale, Paris,
and runs as follows :—" It is forbidden to publish or
print any work or writing, in rhyme or in prose, without the previous authorisation of our lord the King,
under pain of being hanged or strangled." Another
clause says :—" Three times every year a visit shall be
made in the shops and printing-houses of the printers
and booksellers of Lyons by two trustworthy persons
belonging to the Church, one representing the Archbishop and the other the Chapter of the said city, and
they shall be accompanied by the seneschal of Lyons."

When the Roman Catholics fell upon the Huguenots
with such fury, the latter gave way in all directions.
The Prince of Condé, however, having raised the standard of resistance, numbers of followers gathered round
his banner. Admiral Coligny at first refused to join
him, but, yielding to the entreaties of his wife, he at
length placed himself by the side of Condé. A period
of fierce civil war ensued, in which the worst passions
were evoked on both sides, and frightful cruelties were
perpetrated, to the shame of religion, in whose name
these things were done. The whole of France became
a battle-field. The Huguenots revenged themselves
on the assassins of their co-religionists, by defacing
and destroying the churches and monasteries. In their

---

[1] PUAUX, ii. p. 152. This writer
says that, although the massacre
of Saint Bartholomew is usually
cited as the culminating horror
of the time, the real Saint Bartholomew was not that of 1572,
but of 1562—which year contained
by far the most dolorous chapter
in the history of French Protestantism.

4

iconoclastic rage they hewed and broke the images, the
carvings, and the richly-decorated work of the cathedrals at Bourges, at Lyons, at Orleans, at Rouen, at
Caen, at Tours, and many other places. They tore
down the crucifixes, and dragged them through the
streets; they violated the tombs of saints and sovereigns, and profaned the sacred shrines of the Roman
Catholics. "It was," says Henri Martin, "as if a blast
of the infernal trumpet had everywhere awakened the
spirit of destruction, and the delirious fury grew and
became drunk with its own excess." All this rage,
however, was but the inevitable reaction against the
hideous cruelties of which the Huguenots had so long
been the passive victims. They decapitated beautiful
statues of stone, it is true; but the Guises had decapitated the living men.

The year after the massacre of Vassy, the Duke of
Guise, during the siege of Orleans, was assassinated by
a Calvinist named Poltrot de Mené. Several of Poltrot's relations had been murdered by Roman Catholics.
Coligny was accused of complicity in the assassination,
but he himself denied all knowledge of it. Every
party was alike enraged. Many pacifications were
arrived at, but they brought no peace.

It is not necessary, in our rapid sketch, to follow
the course of the civil war. The Huguenots were
everywhere outnumbered. They fought bravely, but
they fought as rebels,—the King and the Queen-mother
being now at the head of the Guise party. In nearly
all the great battles fought by them, they were defeated,—at Dreux,[1] at Saint Denis, at Jarnac, and at

---

[1] This was nearly a drawn
battle; and that it was decided
in favour of the Guise party, was
almost entirely due to the Swiss
infantry, who alone resisted the
shock of Condé's cavalry. When
Condé and Coligny withdrew
their forces in good order, 8,000
men lay dead on the field. Mont-
luc, one of the Guise generals,
says in his Commentaries :—" If
this battle had been lost, what
would have become of France?
Its government would have been
changed as well as its religion;
for with a young king parties
can do what they will."

Montcontour. But they rallied again, sometimes in greater numbers than before; and at length Coligny was enabled to collect such reinforcements as seriously to threaten Paris.

France had now been devastated throughout by the contending armies, and many of the provinces were reduced almost to a state of desert. The combatants on both sides were exhausted, though their rancour remained unabated. Peace, however, had at last become a necessity; and a treaty was signed at Saint Germains, in 1570, by which the Protestants were guaranteed liberty of worship, equality before the law, and admission to the universities : while the four principal towns of La Rochelle, Montauban, Cognac, and La Charité, were committed to them as pledges of safety.

Under the terms of this treaty, France enjoyed a state of peace for about two years; but it was only the quiet that preceded the outbreak of another storm.

CHAPTER IV.

THE DUKE OF ALVA IN FLANDERS—MASSACRE OF SAINT BARTHOLOMEW.

WHILE these events were proceeding in France, a furious civil war was raging in Flanders, which then formed part of the extensive dominions of Spain. This war arose out of the same desire on the part of the Roman Church to crush the Reform movement, which had been making considerable progress in the Low Countries.

The Provinces of the Netherlands had reached the summit of commercial and manufacturing prosperity. They were inhabited by a hard-working, intelligent, and enterprising people—great as artists and merchants, painters and printers, architects and iron-workers,—as the decayed glories of Antwerp, Bruges, and Ghent, testify to this day. Although the two latter cities never completely recovered from the injuries inflicted on them by the tyranny of the trades' unions, there were numerous other towns, where industry had been left comparatively free, in which the arts of peace were cultivated in security. Under the mild sway of the Burgundian dukes, Antwerp became the centre of the commerce of northern Europe; and more business is said to have been done there in a month, than at Venice in two years when at the summit of its grandeur. About the year 1550, it was no uncommon sight to see as many as 2500 ships in the Scheldt, laden with merchandise for all parts of the world.

Such was the prosperity of Flanders, when Philip II.

of Spain succeeded to the rich inheritance of Burgundy, on the resignation of Charles V. in the year
1566. Philip inherited from his father two passions
—hatred of the Reformed Church, and hatred of
France. To destroy the one and humiliate the other
constituted the ambition of his life; and to accomplish both objects, he spared neither the gold which
Pizarro and his followers had brought from the New
World, nor the blood of his own subjects.

Had his subjects been of the same mind with himself in religious matters, Philip might have escaped
the infamy which attaches to his name. But a large
proportion of the most skilled and industrious people
of the Netherlands, had imbibed the new ideas as to
reform in religion, which had swept over northern
Europe. They had read the newly-translated Bible
with avidity. They had formed themselves into religious communities, and appointed preachers and
teachers of their own. In a word, they were Protestants; and the King determined that they should
forthwith be reconverted to Roman Catholicism.

Shortly before this time, there had risen up in the
bosom of the Roman Catholic Church a man in all
respects as remarkable as Luther, who exercised as
extraordinary an influence, though in precisely the
opposite direction, upon the religious history of Europe.
This was Ignatius Loyola, the founder of the Jesuits,
who infused into his followers a degree of zeal, energy,
devotion, and it must be added, unscrupulousness—
never stopping to consider the means, provided only
the ends could be accomplished—which told most
powerfully in the struggle of Protestantism for life or
death throughout northern Europe.

Loyola was born in 1491. He was wounded at the
siege of Pampeluna in 1520. After a period of medi-
tation and mortification, he devoted himself, in 1522, to
the service of the Church; and in 1540, the Order of
the Jesuits was recognised at Rome and established
by papal bull. The Society early took root in France,

where it was introduced by the Cardinal de Lorraine ; and it shortly after acquired almost supreme influence in the State. Under the Jesuits, the Romish Church, reorganised and redisciplined, became one of the most complete of spiritual machines. The Jesuits enjoined implicit submission and obedience. Against liberty they set up authority. To them the Individual was nothing, the Order everything. They were vigilant sentinels, watching night and day over the interests of Rome. One of the first works to which they applied themselves, was the extirpation of the heretics who had strayed from the fold. The principal instrument which they employed with this object, was the Inquisition ; and wherever they succeeded in establishing themselves, that institution was set up or was armed with fresh powers. They tolerated no half-measures. They were unsparing and unpitying; and wherever a heretic was brought before them, and they had the power to deal with him, he must either recant or die.

Accordingly, Philip had no sooner succeeded to the Spanish throne, than he ordered a branch of the Inquisition to be set up in Flanders, with the Cardinal Granvelle as Inquisitor-General. The institution excited great opposition amongst all classes, Catholic as well as Protestant. It very soon evoked much hostility and resistance, which eventually culminated in civil war. Sir Thomas Gresham, writing to Cecil from Antwerp in 1566, said, "There are above 40,000 Protestants in this toune, which will die rather than the word of God should be put to silence."

The struggle which now began was alike fierce and determined on both sides. It extended over many years. The powerful armies which the King directed against his revolted subjects, were led by able generals —by the Duke of Alva, and Alexander Farnese, Prince of Parma. In course of time, they succeeded in exterminating or banishing the greater number of Pro-

testants south of the Scheldt; at the same time that
they ruined the industry of Flanders, destroyed its
trade, and reduced the Catholics themselves to beggary.
Bruges and Ghent became crowded with thieves and
paupers. The busy quays of Antwerp were deserted,
and its industrious artizans, tradesmen, and merchants
fled from the place, leaving their property behind them,
a prey to the spoiler.[1]

The Duchess of Parma, writing to Philip in 1567,
said that "in a few days 100,000 men had already
left the country with their money and goods, and
that more were following every day." Clough, writing to Gresham from Antwerp in the same year,
said—"It is marveylus to see how the pepell packe
away from hense; some for one place, and some for
another; as well the Papysts as the Protestants; for
it is thought that howsomever it goeth, it cannot go
well here; for that presently all the welthy and rich
men of both sydes, who should be the stay of matters,
make themselves away." [2]

The Duke of Alva carried on this frightful war of
extermination and persecution for six years, during
which he boasted that he had sent 18,000 persons to
the stake and the scaffold, besides the immense numbers destroyed in battles and sieges, and in the unrecorded acts of cruelty perpetrated on the peasantry
by the Spanish soldiery. The sullen bigot, Philip II.,
heard of the depopulation and ruin of his provinces
without regret; and though Alva was recalled, the
war was carried on with increased fury by the generals
who succeeded him. What mainly comforted Philip
was, that the people who remained were at length
terrified into orthodoxy. The ecclesiastics assured
the Duke of Parma, the governor, that, notwithstanding the depopulation of the provinces, more

---

[1] It is said that for some years
the plunder of the murdered and
proscribed Protestants of the
Low Countries brought into the
royal treasury of Philip twenty
millions of dollars annually.

[2] *Flanders Correspondence* —
State-Paper Office.

people were coming to them for confession and absolution at the last Easter, than had ever come since the beginning of the revolt. Parma immediately communicated the consoling intelligence to Philip, who replied, " You cannot imagine my satisfaction at the news you give me concerning last Easter."

The flight of the Protestants from the Low Countries continued for many years. All who were strong enough to fly, fled; only the weak, the helpless, and the hopeless, remained. The fugitives turned their backs on Flanders, and their faces towards Holland, Germany, and England. They fled thither with their wives and children, and the goods that they could carry with them, to seek new homes. Several hundred thousands of her best artizans—clothiers, dyers, weavers, tanners, cutlers, and iron-workers of all kinds—left Flanders, carrying with them into the countries of their adoption, their skill, their intelligence, and their spirit of liberty. The greater number of them went directly into Holland, then gallantly struggling with Spain for independent existence. There they founded new branches of industry, which eventually proved a source of wealth and strength to the United Provinces. Many others passed over into England, hailing it as " Asylum Christi," and formed the settlements of which an account will be given in succeeding chapters.

Having thus led the reader up to the period at which the Exodus of Protestants from the Low Countries took place, we return to France, where Catherine de Medicis was stealthily maturing her plans for the extirpation of heresy in the dominions of her son. The treaty of 1570 was still observed. The Huguenots were allowed to worship God after their own forms ; and France was slowly recovering from the fratricidal wounds which she had received during the recent civil wars. We must, however, revert to an interview which took place at Bayonne between Catherine de Medicis and her daughter the Queen of Spain, who was accompanied by the Duke of Alva, in the month of

June 1564. The Queen-mother had travelled south to the Spanish frontier, to hold this interview,—of sinister augury for the Huguenots.

The Queen-mother had by this time gone entirely round to the Guise party, and carried her son, Charles IX., with her. She was equally desirous, with the Duke of Alva, to extirpate heresy. But while the duke urged their immediate extermination, in accomplishing which he offered the help of a Spanish army, Catherine, on the contrary, was in favour of temporising with them. It might be easy for Philip to extirpate heresy by force in Spain or Italy, where the Protestants were few in number ; but the case was different in France, where the Huguenots had shown themselves able to bring large armies into the field, led by veteran generals ; and where they actually held in their possession many of the strongest places in France.

Alva urged that the Queen-mother should strike at the leaders of the party, and cut them off at once. He would rather catch the large fish and let the small fry alone. " One salmon," said he, " is worth a thousand frogs."[1]

The Queen-mother assured the duke of her ardent desire to extirpate the Reformed religion ; her only difficulty consisted in the means by which it was to be accomplished. She had been brought up in the school of Machiavelli, and could bide her time.

In the meanwhile, she determined to retain the governing power as much as possible in her own hands. One method by which she effected this, was by the corruption of her son. "Will there be no pity," asked M. de Chateaubriand,[2] " for this monarch of twenty-three years of age, born with good talents, with a taste for literature and the arts, a character naturally generous, whom a detestable mother had

---

[1] Davila, the Italian historian, a confidant of Catherine de Medicis, mentions this famous expression. Mathieu does the same.

[2] *Etudes Historiques.*

delighted to deprave by all the abuses of debauchery and power ? "

The means which she employed are horrible to contemplate. She surrounded him with the worst specimens of both sexes; and the young king was brought up amidst gambling, drunkenness, and debauchery of the worst description. The Queen never lost sight of the promise she had made to the Duke of Alva. The Protestants were to be extirpated, and murder was to be the instrument employed.

The young chief of the Huguenots, Henry of Navarre, afterwards Henry IV., was invited, with the other nobles and princes of the Reformers, to attend Court at the nuptials of the King with Elizabeth of Austria, in 1570. But the rejoicings at Paris had no temptations for the cautious chiefs. They preferred to remain in security at their strong fortress of Rochelle.

Another plan remained to be adopted. Catherine de Medicis arranged a match between her daughter Margaret and Henry of Navarre; and she desired the King to offer his sister's hand in marriage to the chief of the Huguenots. The King wrote to Admiral Coligny in terms of praise and admiration, and offered to send an army into Flanders under his command, to co-operate with the Prince of Orange against the King of Spain.

Henry of Navarre accepted the proposal of marriage with the King's sister. Admiral Coligny himself was won over by the King's offered terms of reconciliation. Jeanne D'Albret, Henry's mother, concurred in the union; and the Huguenot chiefs generally believed that the marriage might put an end to the feuds and civil wars that had so long prevailed between the rival religious communities of France.

Pope Pius V., however, refused to grant the necessary dispensation to enable the marriage to be celebrated according to the rites of the Roman Catholic Church; but the Queen-mother got over this little difficulty by causing a dispensation to be forged in the Pope's name.[1]

As Catherine de Medicis had anticipated, the heads of the Reformed party, regarding the marriage as an important step towards national reconciliation, resorted to Paris in large numbers, to celebrate the event and grace the royal nuptials. Amongst those present were Admiral Coligny and his family. Some of the Huguenot chiefs were not without apprehensions for their personal safety, and even urged the admiral to quit Paris. But he believed in the pretended friendship of the Queen-mother and her son, and insisted on staying until the ceremony was over. The marriage was celebrated with great splendour in the cathedral church of Notre Dame on the 18th of August 1572,—the principal members of the nobility, Protestant as well as Roman Catholic, being present on the occasion. It was followed by a succession of feasts and gaieties, in which the leaders of both parties participated ; and the fears of the Huguenots were thus completely disarmed.

On the day after the marriage, a secret council was held in Catherine de Medicis' private chamber, at which it was determined to proclaim a general massacre of the Huguenots.

There were present at this meeting, Catherine, her son Henry duke of Anjou, Henry of Guise, an Italian bishop, and other favourites. There is no doubt about the premeditation of the massacre. The French Roman Catholic historians admit it,—De Thou, Mézeray, Péréfixe, and Mainbourg. The Italian historians go further : Davila, Capilupi, Adriani, and Catena, admire the premeditation, and see in the massacre the wonderful effect of the blessings of Heaven !

The rejoicings on the occasion of the marriage lasted for four days. On the fourth day, the 22nd of August,

---

[1] VAUVILLIERS—*Histoire de Jeanne d'Albret.*

Coligny attended a council at the Louvre, and went afterwards with the King to the tennis court, where Charles and the Duke of Guise played a game against two Huguenot gentlemen. In the meantime, Maurevel, the king's assassin (*le tueur du roi*) had been sent for, and invited to murder the Huguenot leader. The assassin lay in wait for the Admiral in a house situated near the church of Saint Germain l'Auxerrois, between the Louvre and the Rue Béthisy. As Coligny was walking home from his interview with the King, and reading a paper, Maurevel fired at him, and wounded him in the hand and arm.[1] Coligny succeeded in reaching his hotel, where he was attended by Ambrose Paré, who performed upon him a painful operation. The King visited the wounded man at his hotel, professed the greatest horror at the dastardly act which had been attempted, and vowed vengeance against the assassin.

The conspirators met again on the following day, the 23rd of August, at the Louvre. After dinner, the Queen-mother entered the King's chamber; and, shortly after, his brother, the Duke of Anjou, and several lords of the Roman Catholic party. Charles was then informed that the admiral (who was at that moment lying helplessly wounded) and his friends, were at that moment plotting his destruction, and that if he did not anticipate them, he and his family would be sacrificed. Maddened by the malicious representations of his mother, he cried out, "Kill all! Kill all! Let not one escape to reproach me with the deed!"

The plan of the massacre had already been arranged. Its execution was entrusted to the Dukes of Guise, Anjou, Aumale, Montpensier, and Marshal Favannes. Midnight approached, and the day of St. Bartholomew arrived. It wanted two hours of the appointed time. All was still at the Louvre. The

---

[1] Maurevel, though his shot failed, was rewarded. He received from the King 2,000 crowns and the Collar of the Order.

ADMIRAL COLIGNY.

[*To face p.* 60

Queen-mother, and her two sons, Charles IX. and the Duke of Anjou, went to an open balcony and awaited the result in breathless silence. Two o'clock struck. The die was cast. The great bell of the church of St. Auxerrois rang to early prayer. It was the arranged signal for the massacre to begin. Almost immediately after, the first pistol-shot was heard. Three hundred of the royal guard, who had been held in readiness during the night, rushed out into the streets, shouting "For God and the King!" To distinguish themselves in the darkness, they wore a white sash on the left arm, and a white cross in their hats.

Before leaving the palace, a party of the guard murdered the retinue of the young King of Navarre, then the guests of Charles IX. in the Louvre. On the evening of St. Bartholomew, and after he had given his orders for the massacre, Charles redoubled his kindness to the King of Navarre, and desired him to introduce some of his best officers into the Louvre, that they might be at hand in case of any disturbances from the Guises. One by one these officers were called by name from their rooms, and marched down unarmed into the quadrangle, where they were hewed down before the very eyes of their royal host. A more perfidious butchery is probably not recorded in history.

At the same time, mischief was afoot throughout Paris. Le Charron, provost of the merchants, and Marcel, his ancient colleague, had mustered a large number of desperadoes, to whom respective quarters had been previously assigned, and they now hastened to enter upon their frightful morning's work.

The Duke of Guise determined to anticipate all others in the murder of Coligny. Hastening to his hotel, the Duke's party burst in the outer door. The admiral was roused from his slumber by the shots fired at his followers in the courtyard below. He rose from his couch, and, though scarcely able to stand, he fled to an upper chamber. Thither he was tracked by his

assassins, who stabbed him to death as he stood lean-
ing against the wall. His body was flung out of the
window into the courtyard.

The Duke of Guise, who had been waiting impa-
tiently below, hurried up to the corpse, and wiping
the blood from the admiral's face, said, "I know him
—it is he!" then, kicking the body with his foot, he
called out to his followers—"Courage, comrades, we
have begun well. Now for the rest! The King
commands it." They then rushed out into the street.

The fury of the Court was seconded by the long-
pent-up hatred of the Parisians. The massacre of St.
Bartholomew was infinitely more ferocious than the
butcheries of the Revolutionists of 1792, or of the Com-
munists of 1871. The Huguenots were slaughtered in
their beds, or while endeavouring to escape unarmed,
without any regard to age or sex or condition. The
Court leaders galloped through the streets, cheering the
armed citizens to the slaughter. "Death to the Huguenots!" "Kill—kill : bleeding is as wholesome in
August as in May!" shouted the Marshal Favannes;
"Kill all! Kill all! God will know His own!" Nor
were the populace slow to imitate the bloodthirsti-
ness of their superiors. The slaughter, however, was
not wholly confined to the Huguenots. Secret revenge and personal hatred embraced this glorious
opportunity; and many Roman Catholics fell by the
hands of these Roman Catholic assassins.

Firing was heard in every quarter throughout Paris.
The houses of the Huguenots, which had been
marked, were broken into; and men, women, and
children, were sabred or shot down. It was of no
use trying to fly. The fugitives were slaughtered in
the streets. The King himself seized his arquebus,
and securely fired upon his subjects from a window in
the Louvre.

Corpses blocked the doorways; mutilated bodies lay
in every lane and passage; and thousands were cast
into the Seine, then swollen by a flood.

Jean Goujon, the famous sculptor, sometimes styled the French Phidias, was shot from below, whilst employed on a scaffold in executing the decorative work of the old Louvre. Goudimal, the musical composer, and Ramus, the philosopher, were slain during the massacre. Before this time, Ramus's house had been pillaged and his library destroyed. Dumoulin, the great jurisconsult, had previously escaped by death. " The execrable day of St. Bartholomew," said the Catholic Chateaubriand, " only made martyrs : it gave to philosophical ideas an advantage over religious ideas which has never since been lost."

At the same time, there were many who escaped the swords of the assassins. Some of the Huguenots on the southern side of the Seine had time to comprehend their position, and escaped. But what of Henry of Navarre and Henry of Condé ? The King sent for them during the massacre, and said to them in a ferocious tone, " The mass, death, or the Bastille !" After some resistance, the princes consented to make profession of the Romish faith.

Palissy, of whom we have already spoken, was now an old man, and he owed his escape to the circumstance that he was then in the employment of Catherine de Medicis. Ambrose Paré, the surgeon, also escaped. He had won the confidence of the King, by saving him from the effects of a wound inflicted on him by a clumsy surgeon, when performing the operation of venesection. Paré, though a Huguenot, held the important office of Surgeon-in-ordinary to the King, and was constantly about his person. To this circumstance he owed his escape from the massacre,—the King having concealed him during the first night in a private room adjoining his own chamber.

The massacre lasted for three days. At length, on the fourth day, when the fury of the assassins had become satiated, and the Huguenots had for the most part been slain, a dead silence fell upon the streets of Paris. Perhaps the people began to reflect that it was their own countrymen whom they had slain.

These dreadful deeds at the capital were almost immediately followed by similar massacres all over France. From fifteen to eighteen hundred persons were killed at Lyons; and the dwellers on the Rhone, below that city, were horrified by the sight of the dead bodies floating down the river. Six hundred were killed at Rouen; and many more at Dieppe and Havre. The massacre in the provinces lasted more than six weeks! The numbers killed throughout France have been variously estimated. Sully says 70,000 were slain; the Roman Catholic Bishop Péréfixe has said that 100,000 were destroyed.

While the streets of Paris were still besmeared with blood, the clergy celebrated an extraordinary jubilee. They appeared in a general procession. They determined to consecrate an annual feast to a triumph so glorious. A medal was struck in commemoration of the event, bearing the legend," Piety has awakened justice"!

Catherine de Medicis wrote in triumph to the Duke of Alva, to Philip II., and to the Pope, describing the results of the three days' dreadful work in Paris. When Philip heard of the massacre, he is said to have laughed for the first and only time in his life. Rome was thrown into a delirium of joy at the news. The cannon were fired at St. Angelo; Gregory XIII. and his cardinals went in procession from sanctuary to sanctuary to give God thanks for the massacre. The subject was ordered to be painted, and a medal was struck to celebrate the event, with the Pope's head on one side, and on the other an angel, with a cross in one hand and a sword in the other, pursuing and slaying a band of flying heretics—strange work for an angel! The legend it bears—UGONOTTORUM STRAGES, 1572 (Massacre of the Huguenots, 1572)—briefly epitomises the horrible story.[1]

---

[1] An authentic copy of this medal is to be seen at the British Museum.

The Cardinal of Lorraine, the head of the Guises, was at Rome at the time of the massacre, and he celebrated the affair by a procession to the French church of St. Louis. He had an inscription written upon the gates in letters of gold, saying that " the Lord had granted the prayers which he had offered to Him for twelve years."

Cardinal Orsini was despatched on a special mission to Paris to congratulate the King ; and on his passage through Lyons, the assassins of the Huguenots, with the blood on their hands scarcely dry, knelt before the holy man in the cathedral, and received his blessing.

As for the wretched young King of France, the terrible crime, to which he had been a party, weighed upon his mind to the last moment of his life. He survived the massacre for about two years ; but the recollection of the scenes of which he had been a witness, constantly haunted him. He became restless, haggard, and miserable. He saw his murdered guests sitting by his side, at bed and at board. " Ambrose," said he to his confidential physician, " I know not what has happened to me these two or three days past, but I feel my mind and body as much at enmity with each other as if I was seized with a fever. Sleeping or waking, the murdered Huguenots seem ever present to my eyes, with ghastly faces, and weltering in blood. I wish the innocent and helpless had been spared." He died in tortures of mind impossible to be described,—attended in his last moments, strange to say, by a Huguenot physician and a Huguenot nurse : one of the worst horrors that haunted him being that his own mother was causing his death by slow poisoning,—an art in which he knew that great bad woman to be fearfully accomplished.

To return to the surviving Huguenots, and the measures adopted by them for self-preservation. Though they were at first stunned by the massacre, they were not slow to associate themselves together, in those districts in which they were sufficiently strong, for purposes of self-defence. Along the western sea-board, at points where they felt themselves unable to make head against their persecutors, they put to sea in ships and boats, and made for England, where they landed in great numbers—at Rye, at Hastings, at Southampton, and the numerous other ports on the south coast. This was particularly the case with the artizans and skilled labour class, whose means of living are always imperilled by civil war. These fled into England, to endeavour, if possible, to pursue their respective callings in peace, and to worship God according to conscience.

But the Huguenot nobles and gentry would not and could not abandon their followers to destruction. They gathered together in their strong places, and prepared to defend themselves, by force against force. In the Cevennes, Dauphiny, and other quarters, they betook themselves to the mountains for refuge. In the plains of the south, fifty towns closed their gates against the royal troops. Wherever resistance was possible, it showed itself. The little town of Sancerre held out successfully for ten months, during which the inhabitants, without arms, heroically defended themselves with slings called "the arquebusses of Sancerre"; enduring meanwhile the most horrible privations; and reduced to eat moles, snails, bread made of straw mixed with scraps of horse-harness, and even the parchment of old title-deeds.

A violent attack was made upon the Huguenot fortress of La Rochelle by the Duke of Anjou, the King's brother,—one of the principal authors of the massacre of St. Bartholemew. While the assassins were at work throughout the country, the Huguenots resorted to their towns of refuge. La Rochelle was one of these. Fugitives fled thither from all quarters. Sixteen hundred citizens and 1500 strangers occupied the place.

The King despatched General Biron with a strong force to garrison the town. It was too late: the citizens refused to admit him. Hence it was determined to attack La Rochelle, and reduce it to submission. Towards the end of 1572, the place was accordingly invested by the royal army, which continued to receive reinforcements during the winter; and in spring the Duke of Anjou arrived and assumed the chief command. He was accompanied by the Duke of Alençon, the Guises, and other royalist chiefs, as well as by Henry of Navarre and Henry Prince of Condé; and the Duke of Anjou now desired to show them, how speedily and thoroughly he could root out this nest of piracy and sedition.

La Rochelle was well provisioned and garrisoned. The citizens had made good use of the winter months to strengthen the ramparts, and improve the defences of the place. The besiegers erected forts on either side of the entrance to the port, and stationed a large vessel, heavily armed with artillery, in the centre of the bay, thus entirely cutting off all communication with the place by sea.

La Noue, the commander of the garrison, was disposed to negotiate, but the people would not hear of capitulation on any terms. They knew that their admiral, Jean Sore, and the Count of Montgomery, were organizing in England an army of refugee Huguenots, and they daily expected to see the sails of their squadron in the offing. After five weeks' battering of the walls, attended with many skirmishes, the besiegers determined upon a general assault. The first proved a total failure. Three other furious assaults followed, which were repulsed with great loss. Four times the Huguenot hymn,

" Que Dieu se montre seulement !"[1]

sounded as a chant of triumph from the towers of La Rochelle ; and the besiegers were driven back again and again. The fourth and most desperate assault was made on the Bastion de l'Evangile, now occupied as a cemetery, at the north-west corner of the town. The

---

[1] Psalm lxviii.—The Huguenot war-song.

Duke of Anjou had just been elected King of Poland, and he determined to celebrate the event by the capture of the place. After a *feu de joie* from all the guns, which were heavily shotted and pointed at the bastion, a breach was made, and the troops rushed forward to the assault. The defenders crowded the breach, desperately contesting every inch of ground. The townspeople and the women cheered them on. The women even mounted the bastions and poured boiling tar down on the assailants, as well as stink-pots, hot iron, and showers of stones. The loss of life in the assault was dreadful. The Bastion de l'Evangile proved the cemetery of the royal army. The Duke of Nevers, the Marquis of Mayenne, Count Retz, Du Guast (the Duke of Anjou's favourite), and many other distinguished officers, were more or less severely wounded. Cosseins, the captain of the guard who superintended the assassination of Admiral Coligny, was one of the numerous heap of dead that filled the breach.

By the month of June, 20,000 royalist troops had perished, and the place was not yet taken. The provisions of the besieged began to run short, but not their courage. An unusual supply of shell-fish in 'he bay and the harbour, seemed to them a supply of food from heaven. Their admiral, Jean Sore, appeared with a small squadron off the bay, but he could not force the entrance to the harbour. The royal army, however, did not renew the attack. The Duke of Anjou, desirous of entering into possession of his kingdom, negotiated for peace ; and a peace was arranged on the 24th of June, 1573, by which the Protestants of La Rochelle, Nismes, and Montauban were guaranteed the free exercise of their religion. The siege was raised three days later, after having lasted six months and a half.

The Duke of Anjou then proceeded to Poland to assume the rule of his kingdom. That country was then in a wretched state. The people were discontented; the aristocracy were venal : all were corrupt. Their

new king very soon detested the country as well as
the people. At length, when Charles IX., tortured
in mind and body, died in May 1574, less than two
years after the massacre of Saint Bartholomew, the
Duke of Anjou suddenly returned to Paris to assume
the title of king, under the name of Henry III.

This was the third son of Catherine de Medicis'
who ruled France; but his reign was not more
successful than those of his elder brothers. He was
more bigoted than either of them; and though he
flogged himself in the public street, and went in
procession from shrine to shrine, yet he jeered at the
saints he pretended to reverence. He turned religion
into ridicule. He was surrounded by minions and
favourites, male and female, and made his court a
scene of debauchery.

The feeling of loyalty was rudely shaken, amongst
Roman Catholics as well as Huguenots. Disgust
took possession of the hearts of all honourable and
religious men. They saw knighthood covered with
disgrace, and religion degraded into ridicule. Henry of
Navarre, who had been detained at court, virtually a
prisoner, since the events of St. Bartholomew's Day,
made his escape, accompanied by the Prince of Condé.
They abjured the Roman Catholic religion, which had
been imposed upon them by Charles IX. under fear of
assassination. They set up the old standard of freedom
of religion, and levies flocked to their support. The
Queen-mother granted another peace. The worship
of the Huguenots was permitted in all parts of France,
except in Paris; the massacre of Saint Bartholomew
was disavowed; and several additional towns were
surrendered to the Protestants as pledges for their
security.

All this, however, was most galling to the Roman
Catholics. They were still determined to put down
the Reformed religion. Accordingly, in 1576, a Holy
League was formed, the object of which was to extirpate heresy, and to spare neither friend nor foe until

the pestilence was banished. The leader of this
League was Henry of Guise, son of that old Francis
of Guise who had led the Royal assassins at the
massacre of Saint Bartholomew. Henry's whole heart
was devoted to Rome. He was the most popular
man in Paris. The Parisians even hailed him as
the future king of France. "No Protestant king of
Navarre," they cried: "we will have Catholic Henry
of Guise ! "

The States-General met at Blois, when the members,
being bribed or bullied by the Guises, passed an edict
interdicting the Huguenot faith, and withdrawing all
the guarantee towns from their hands. This amounted
to a declaration of war. The King himself joined the
League, and instead of being the King of the nation,
degraded himself into being the King of a party.
But the policy of the Medicis and the Guises was of
a piece throughout.

The Holy League was followed by a dreary and
wasteful succession of civil wars. The country was
overrun by lawless troops, who robbed, burned, and
murdered everywhere. There were seven civil wars in
all. One was called the " War of the Lovers," having
originated in an intrigue of the court. Another was
called the "War of the three Henrys," the King having
separated himself from Henry of Guise, but refused to
unite with Henry of Navarre. Another was called the
" War of the Barricades," the troops of Henry of Guise
having attacked the Royal troops (chiefly Swiss) in
the streets of Paris. Henry III. then fled to Chartres,
leaving Paris in the possession of Henry of Guise.

The States were summoned to meet at Blois in
December 1588. Henry of Guise went, at the earnest
invitation of the King, to meet him and the Queen-
mother. As he crossed the hall that led to the great
staircase, the King's attendants locked and barred
the gates. Guise entered the council-chamber, and
was warming himself at the fire, when he was sent for
by the King. Turning aside the tapestry hung over

the door, he was set upon by forty-five gentlemen-in-waiting armed with daggers, and fell pierced with more than forty wounds. The royal murderer, issuing from the oratory of Catherine de Medicis, came to look at the corpse of the once mighty Henry of Guise, kicked it in the face (as Henry's father had before kicked the face of Admiral Coligny), and saying, "Je ne le croyais pas aussi grand," he ordered the corpse to be burnt and the ashes thrown into the Loire.

On the following day, the Cardinal de Lorraine, brother of the Duke, was murdered in another part of the castle. Catherine de Medicis had now finished the atrocities of her life. She died twelve days after the murder of Henry of Guise; and eight months later, her son Henry III. was assassinated by Jacques Clement, the Dominican monk, in the camp before Paris, in August 1589.[1]

Such was the end of the Guises, and such was the end of Catherine de Medicis and her sons. They all carried on their foreheads the ineffaceable brand of the massacre of Saint Bartholomew.

Henry III. was the last of the House of Valois. At his death, Henry of Navarre, by virtue of his right as next heir to the crown, succeeded to the throne of France, as Henry the Fourth.

---

[1] The murder of the Duke of Guise roused the hostility of the Papal party. Henry III. had joined Henry of Navarre in endeavouring to restore peace to France. The compromise proved fatal to him. The regicide, Jacques Clement, was canonized from all the pulpits as "the most blessed child of Dominique, the Holy Martyr of Jesus Christ." His portrait was placed on the altars with these words: "Saint Jacques, pray for us!" Pope Sixtus V. declared, in full consistory, that the action of the martyr Jacques Clement might be compared, as regarded the safety of the world, to the incarnation and resurrection of Jesus Christ. "It was the policy of this Pope," says Chateaubriand, the Catholic historian, "to encourage fanatics who were ready to kill kings in the name of the Papal power." (*Etudes Historiques*, iv. 371.)

CHAPTER V.

WHILE the rulers of France and Spain were making these determined efforts to crush the principles of the Reformation in their dominions, the Protestants of England regarded their proceedings with no small degree of apprehension and alarm. They had themselves suffered from sanguinary persecutions, during the reign of Queen Mary, commonly known as "the bloody." Mary had married Philip, Prince of Spain, afterwards Philip II., one of the cruelest and most bigoted of kings. Protestant writers affirm that about two hundred and eighty victims perished at the stake, from the 4th of February 1555, when John Rogers was burnt at Smithfield,—to the 10th of November 1558, when three men and two women were burnt at Colchester. Dr. Lingard, after making every allowance, admits that "in the space of four years almost two hundred persons perished in the flames for religious opinion."[1]

The bond which, for a time, united England to Spain, had enabled Mary to engage in a war with France, during which the English and Spanish troops fought together. The only result, so far as England was concerned, was that the town and territory of Calais, which up to that time had been possessed by England, were taken by the French under the Duke of Guise in

---

[1] Among the most distinguished sufferers were Hooper, bishop of Gloucester, Ferrar of St. David's, Latimer of Worcester, Ridley of London, and Cranmer, archbishop of Canterbury.

CATHERINE DE MÉDICIS.

To face p. 72.

1558, after a siege of a few days. This event, which was regarded as a national disgrace, excited the bitterest feelings of dissatisfaction throughout the country. But towards the end of the year Mary died; and the burnings of heretics and the defeats of English soldiers came to an end. She was succeeded by her half-sister Elizabeth, who completely reversed the policy which Mary and her husband had adopted in England.

Though the Reformed faith had made considerable progress in the English towns at the period of Elizabeth's accession to the throne in 1558, it was still in a considerable minority throughout the country.[1] The great body of the nobility, the landed gentry, and the rural population, adhered to the old religion; while there was a considerable middle class of Gallios, who were content to wait the issue of events before declaring themselves for either side.

During the reigns which had preceded that of Elizabeth, the country had been ill-governed and the public interests neglected. The nation was in debt and unarmed, with war raging abroad. But Elizabeth's greatest difficulty consisted in the fact of her being a Protestant, and the successor of a Roman Catholic queen who had reigned with undisputed power during the five years which preceded her accession to the

---

[1] Soames, in his *Elizabethan Religious History*, says that at the accession of Elizabeth two-thirds of the people were Catholics. Butler, in his *Memoirs of the Catholics*, holds the same view. On the other hand, Mr. Hallam, in his *Constitutional History*, estimates that in 1559 the Protestants were two-thirds of the population. Mr. Buckle inclines to the view that the Protestants were still in the minority. "Of the two great parties," he says, "one occupied the north and the other the south, and a line drawn from the Humber (to the mouth of the Severn) formed the boundary of their respective dominions. The Catholics of the north were headed by the great families (of the Percys and Nevilles), and had on their side all those advantages which the prescription of ages alone can give. To the south were the Protestants, who, though they could boast of none of those great historical names which reflected a lustre on their opponents, were supported by the authority of the government, and felt that enthusiastic confidence which only belongs to a young religion."

throne. No sooner had she become queen than the embarrassment of her position was at once felt. The Pope denied her legitimacy, and refused to recognise her authority. The bishops refused to crown her. The two universities united with Convocation in presenting to the House of Lords a declaration in favour of the papal supremacy. The King of France openly supported the claim of Mary Queen of Scots to the English throne, and a large and influential body of the nobility and gentry were her secret if not her avowed partisans.

From the day of her ascending the throne, Elizabeth was the almost constant object of plots formed to destroy her, and thus to pave the way for the re-establishment of the old religion. Elizabeth might possibly have escaped from her difficulties by accepting the hand of Philip II. of Spain, which was offered her. She refused, and determined to trust to her people. But her enemies were numerous, powerful, and active, in conspiring against her authority. They had their emissaries at the French and Spanish courts, and at the camp of Alva in the Netherlands, urging the invasion of England and the overthrow of the English queen.

One of the circumstances which gave the most grievous offence to the French and Spanish monarchs, was the free asylum which Elizabeth offered in England to the Protestants flying from persecution abroad. Though these rulers would not permit their subjects to worship according to conscience in their own country, neither would they tolerate their leaving it to worship in freedom elsewhere. Conformity, not depopulation, was their object: conformity by force, if not by suasion. All attempts made by the persecuted to leave France or Flanders were accordingly interdicted. They were threatened with confiscation of their property and goods if they fled, and with death if they remained. The hearts of the kings were hardened: they "would not let the people go!" But the ocean was a broad

and free road that could not be closed; and the persecuted escaped by sea. Tidings reached the kings of
the escape of their subjects, whom they had failed
either to convert or to kill. They could only gnash
their teeth and utter threats against the queen and
the nation that had given their persecuted people
asylum.

The French king formally demanded that Elizabeth
should banish his fugitive subjects from her realm as
rebels and heretics; but he was unable to enforce his
demands, and the fugitives remained. The Spanish
monarch called upon the Pope to interfere; and he in
his turn tried to close the ports of England against
foreign heretics. In a communication addressed by
him to Elizabeth, the Pope proclaimed the fugitives to
be "drunkards and sectaries"—*ebriosi et sectarii*,—
and declared "that all such as were the worst of the
people resorted to England, and were by the Queen
received into safe protection"—*ad quam velut ad
asylum omnium impestissimi perfugium invenerunt.*

The Pope's denunciations of the refugees were
answered by Bishop Jewell, who vindicated their character, and held them up as examples of industry and
orderly living. "Is it not lawful," he asked, "for the
Queen to receive strangers without the Pope's war-
rant?" Quoting the above-cited Latin passages, he
proceeded: "Thus he speaketh of the poor exiles of
Flanders, France, and other countries, who either lost or
left behind them all that they had—goods, lands, and
houses—not for adultery, or theft, or treason, but for
the profession of the Gospel. It pleased God here to
cast them on land; the Queen, of her gracious pity
hath granted them harbour. Is it so heinous a thing
to show mercy?" The bishop proceeded to retort
upon the Pope for harbouring 6000 usurers and 20,000
courtezans in his own city of Rome; and he desired
to know whether, if the Pope was to be allowed to
entertain such "servants of the devil," the Queen of
England was to be denied the liberty of receiving "a

few servants of God"? "They are," he continued, "our brethren: they live not idly. If they have houses of us, they pay rent for them. They hold not our grounds but by making due recompense. They beg not in our streets, nor crave anything at our hands, but to breathe our air and to see our sun. They labour truefully, they live sparingly. They are good examples of virtue, travail, faith, and patience. The towns in which they abide are happy; for God doth follow them with His blessings."[1]

When the French and Spanish monarchs found that Elizabeth continued to give an asylum to their Protestant subjects, they proceeded to compass her death.

Assassination was in those days regarded as the readiest method of getting rid of an adversary; and in the case of an excommunicated person, it was regarded almost in the light of a religious duty. When the Regent Murray (of Scotland) was assassinated by Bothwellhaugh, in 1570, Mary Queen of Scotland gave the assassin a pension. Attempts were made about the same time on the life of William of Orange, surnamed "The Silent." One made at Mechlin, in 1572, proved a failure; but William was eventually assassinated at Delft, in 1585, by Balthazar Gerard, an avowed agent of Philip II. and the Jesuits; and Philip afterwards ennobled the family of the assassin.

In the meantime Mary, Queen of Scotland, after her return from France, had assumed the government of her northern subjects. Mary never forgot the school of the Guises, in which she had been trained. She desired to enforce Popery upon Scotland as the Guises had enforced it upon France. But under the spiritual direction of Knox, the principles of the Reformation had already taken strong hold of the minds of her Scotch subjects. Her reign was a reign of bitterness and defeat. Her marriage with Bothwell, the murderer of her second husband, was the consummation of her

---

[1] *Bishop Jewell's Works* (Parker Society), pp. 1148-9.

government of Scotland. After the rout of her troops
at Longside, she fled across the Border and took
refuge in England.

Mary gave herself up a prisoner into the hands of
the English government. She was confined in various
castles. When the French and Spanish ambassadors,
who were then at the English court, were privily engaged in stirring up discontent against Elizabeth, and
organizing plots against her, they found a ready instrument in the Queen of Scots, then confined in Tut-
bury Castle. Mary was not held so strict a prisoner
as to be precluded from carrying on an active correspondence with her partizans in England and Scotland,
with the Duke of Guise and others in France, and with
the Duke of Alva and Philip II. in Flanders and Spain.
Guilty though the Queen of Scots had been of the
death of her husband, the Roman Catholics of England
regarded her as their rightful head, and were ready to
rise in arms in her cause.

Mary was an inveterate intriguer. We find her entreating the Courts of France and Spain to send her
soldiers, artillerymen, and arms; and pressing the king
of Spain to set on foot the invasion of England, with
the object of dethroning Elizabeth and restoring the
Roman Catholic faith. Her importunities, as well as
the fascinations of her person, were not without their
effect upon those under her immediate influence; and
she succeeded in inducing the Duke of Norfolk, who
cherished the hope of becoming her fourth husband,
to undertake a scheme for her liberation. A conspiracy of the leading nobles was formed, at the head
of which were the Earls of Northumberland and Westmoreland; and in the autumn of 1568 they raised the
standard of revolt in the northern counties, where the
power of the Roman Catholic party was the strongest.[1]

---

[1] "After having written to Pope
Pius V., the Spanish ambassador,
and the Duke of Alva, to request
their assistance, and to advise
that a port should be seized on
the eastern coast of England,
where it would be easy to
disembark troops, ... they

But the rising was speedily suppressed; some of its leaders fled into Scotland, and others into foreign countries ; the Duke of Norfolk was sent to the Tower ; and the Queen's authority was for the time upheld.

The Pope next launched against Elizabeth the most formidable missile of the Church—a bull of excommunication—in which he declared her to be cut off, as the minister of iniquity, from the community of the faithful, and forbade her subjects to recognise her as their sovereign. This document was found nailed up on the Bishop of London's door on the morning of the 15th of May, 1570. The French and Spanish Courts now considered themselves at liberty to compass the life of Elizabeth by assassination. The Cardinal de Lorraine, head of the Church in France, and the confidential adviser of the Queen-mother, hired a party of assassins in the course of the same year, for the purpose of destroying Elizabeth, because of the encouragement she had given to Coligny and the French Huguenots. Again, the Duke of Alva, in his correspondence with Mary Queen of Scots and the leaders of the Roman Catholic party in England, insisted throughout that the first condition of sending a Spanish army to their assistance, was the death of Elizabeth.

Such was the state of affairs when the Bishop of Ross, one of Mary's most zealous partizans, set on foot a conspiracy for the destruction of the Queen. The principal agent employed in communicating with foreign powers on the subject was one Ridolfi, a rich Florentine banker in London, director of the company

---

left Brancepath on the 14th of November, at the head of 500 horsemen, and marched towards Durham. The insurrection was entirely Catholic. They had painted Jesus Christ on the cross, with His five bleeding wounds, upon a banner borne by old Norton, who was inspired by the most religious enthusiasm. The people of Durham opened their gates and joined the rebels. Thus made masters of the town, the insurgents proceeded to the cathedral, burned the Bible, destroyed the Book of Common Prayer, broke in pieces the Protestant communion-table, and restored the old form of worship."— MIGNET—*History of Mary Queen of Scots.*

of Italian merchants, and an ardent Papist. Minute
instructions were drawn up and intrusted to Ridolfi,
to be laid by him before Pope Pius V. and Philip II.
of Spain.   On his way to Rome through the Low
Countries, he waited on the Duke of Alva, and presented to him a letter from Mary Queen of Scots,
beseeching him to furnish her with prompt assistance,
with the object of "laying all this island" under
perpetual obligations to his master the King of Spain
as well as to herself, as the faithful executor of his
commands.[1]

At Rome Ridolfi was welcomed by the Pope, who
eagerly adopted his plans, and furnished him with a
letter to Philip II., conjuring that monarch by his
fervent piety towards God to furnish all the means
he might judge most suitable for carrying them into
effect.   Ridolfi next proceeded to Madrid to hold an
interview with the Spanish Court, and arrange for the
murder of the English Queen.   He was received to a
Conference with the Council of State, at which were
present the Pope's nuncio, the Cardinal Archbishop
of Seville (Inquisitor-General); the Grand Prior of
Castille, the Duke of Feria, the Prince of Eboli, and
other high ministers of Spain.

Ridolfi proceeded to lay his plan for assassinating
Elizabeth before the Council.[2]   He said "the blow
would not be struck in London, because that city was
the stronghold of heresy; but while she was travelling."
On the Council proceeding to discuss the expediency of
the proposed murder, the Pope's nuncio at once undertook to answer all objections.   The one sufficient pretext, he said, was the bull of excommunication.   The
vicar of God had deprived Elizabeth of her throne, and
the soldiers of the Church were the instruments of his
decree to execute the sentence of Heaven against the

Prince Labanoff's Collection,
iii. 216-20.

[2] The minutes of this remarkable meeting of Council were

fully written out by Zayas, Secretary of State, and are preserved
in the archives of Simancas (In-
glaterra, fol. 823).

heretical tyrant. On this, one Chapin Vitelli, who had come from Flanders to attend the Council, offered himself as the assassin. He said, if the matter was intrusted to him, he would take or kill the Queen. The councillors of state present then severally stated their views, which were placed on record, and are still to be seen in the archives at Simancas.

Philip II. concurred in the plot, and professed himself ready to undertake the conquest of England by force if it failed; but he suggested that the Pope should supply the necessary money. Philip, however, was a man of hesitating purpose; and, foreseeing the dangers of the enterprise, he delayed embarking in it, and eventually resolved to leave the matter to the decision of the Duke of Alva.

While these measures against the life of Elizabeth were being devised abroad, Mary Queen of Scots was diligently occupied at Chatsworth in encouraging a like plot at home with the same object. Lord Burleigh, however, succeeded in gaining a clue to the conspiracy, on which the principal agents in England were apprehended, and the Queen was put upon her guard. The Spanish ambassador, Don Gerau, being found in secret correspondence with Mary, was warned to depart the realm; his last characteristic act being to hire two bravoes to assassinate Burleigh. He lingered on the road to Dover, hoping to hear that the deed had been done. But the assassins were detected in time, and instead of taking Burleigh's life, they only lost their own.

The Protestant party were from time to time thrown into agonies of alarm by the rumour of these plots against the life of their Queen, and by the reported apprehension of agents of foreign powers arriving in England for the purpose of stirring up rebellion and preparing the way for the landing of the Duke of Alva and his army. The intelligence brought by the poor hunted Flemings, who had by this time landed in England in large numbers, and settled in London and the principal towns of the south, and the accounts which they spread abroad of the terrors of Philip's rule in the Low Countries, told plainly enough what the English Protestants had to expect if the threatened Spanish invasion succeeded.

The effect of these proceedings was to rouse a general feeling of indignation against the foreign plotters and persecutors, and to evoke an active and energetic public opinion in support of the Queen and her government. Though a large proportion of the English people were in a great measure undecided as to their faith, their feeling of nationality was intense. The conduct of Elizabeth herself was doubtless influenced quite as much by political as religious considerations ; and in the midst of the difficulties by which she was surrounded, her policy often seemed tortuous and inconsistent. The nation was, indeed, in one of the greatest crises of its fate. The Queen, her ministers, and the nation at large, every day more clearly recognised in the great questions at stake, not merely the cause of Protestantism against Popery, but of English nationality against foreign ascendency, and of resistance to the threatened yoke of Rome, France, and Spain.

The massacre of Saint Bartholomew, which shortly followed, exercised a powerful influence in determining the sympathies of the English people. The news of its occurrence called forth a general shout of execration. The Huguenot fugitives, who crowded for refuge into the southern ports, brought with them accounts of the barbarities practised on their fellow-countrymen, which filled the national mind with horror. The people would have willingly rushed into a war, to punish the perfidy and cruelty of the French Roman Catholics, but Elizabeth forbade her subjects to take up arms except on their own account as private volunteers.

What the Queen's private feelings were, may be inferred from the reception which she gave to La Mothe

6

Fénélon, the French ambassador, on his first appearance at Court after the massacre. For several days she refused to see him, but at length she admitted him to an audience. The lords and ladies in waiting received him in profound silence. They were dressed in deep mourning, and grief seemed to sit on every countenance. They did not deign to salute, or even to look at the ambassador, as he advanced towards the Queen, who received him with a severe and mournful countenance; and, stammering out his odious apology, he hastened from her presence. Rarely, if ever, had a French ambassador appeared at a foreign court, ashamed of the country he represented; but on this occasion, La Mothe Fénélon declared, in the bitterness of his heart, that he blushed to bear the name of Frenchman.

The perfidious butchery of the Huguenots excited the profoundest indignation throughout Scotland. John Knox denounced it from the pulpit of St. Giles's. "The sentence is gone forth," he said, "against this murderer, the King of France; and the vengeance of God will not be withdrawn from his house. His name shall be held in execration by posterity; and no one who shall spring from his loins shall possess the kingdom in peace, unless repentance come to prevent the judgment of God."

The massacre of Saint Bartholomew most probably sealed the fate of Mary Stuart. She herself rejoiced in it as a bold stroke for the Faith, and, it might be, as the signal for a like enterprise on her own behalf. Accordingly, she went on plotting as before; and in 1581 she was found engaged in a conspiracy with the Duke of Lennox for the re-establishment of Popery in Scotland, under the auspices of the Jesuits. These intrigues of the Queen of Scots at length became intolerable. Her repeated and urgent solicitations to the King of Spain to invade England with a view to the re-establishment of the old religion—the conspiracies against the life of Elizabeth in which she was

from time to time detected [1]—excited the vehement
indignation of the English nation, and eventually led
to her trial and execution ; for it was felt that so long
as Mary Stuart lived, the life of the English Queen, as
well as the liberties of the English people, were in
constant jeopardy.

It is doubtless easy to condemn the policy of Elizabeth in this matter, now that we are living in the light
of the nineteenth century, and peacefully enjoying the
freedom won for us through the sufferings and agony of
our forefathers. But, in judging of the transactions of
those times, it is right that allowance should be made
for the different moral sense which then prevailed,
as well as for the circumstances amidst which the
nation carried on its life-and-death struggle for independent existence. Right is still right, it is true ;
but the times have become completely changed, and
public opinion has changed with them.

In the meanwhile, religious persecutions continued
to rage abroad with as much fury as before ; and

---

[1] One of such conspiracies
against the life of Elizabeth was
that conducted by John Ballard,
a Roman Catholic priest, in 1586.
The principal instrument in the
affair was one Anthony Babington, who had been for two years
the intermediary correspondent
between Mary Stuart, the Archbishop of Glasgow, and Paget
and Morgan, his co-conspirators.
Ballard, Babington, and the rest
of the gang, were detected,
watched, and eventually captured and condemned, through
the vigilance of Elizabeth's ever-
watchful minister Walsingham.
Mary had been kept fully advised
of all their proceedings. Babington wrote to her in June 1587,
explaining the intention of the
conspirators, and enumerating
all the means for getting rid of
Elizabeth. " Myself in person,"
he said, " with ten gentlemen and
a hundred others of our company and suite, will undertake
the deliverance of your royal
person from the hands of your
enemies. As regards getting
rid of the usurper, from subjec-
tion to whom we are absolved
by the act of excommunication
issued against her, there are six
gentlemen of quality, all of them
my intimate friends, who, for the
love they bear to the Catholic
cause and to your Majesty's
service, will undertake the tragic
execution." In the same letter
Babington requested Mary Stuart
to appoint persons to act as her
lieutenants, and to raise the populace in Wales, and in the counties
of Lancashire, Derby, and Staf-
ford. This letter, with others to
a like effect, duly came into the
possession of Walsingham.

fugitives from Flanders and France continued to take
refuge in England, where they received protection and
asylum. Few of the refugees brought any property
with them : the greater number were entirely destitute.
But many brought with them that kind of wealth
which money cannot buy—intelligence, skill, virtue,
and the spirit of independence,—those very qualities,
which made them hateful to their persecutors, rendering them all the more valuable to the countries of
their adoption.

A large part of Flanders, before so rich and so prosperous, had by this time become reduced almost to a
state of desert. The country was eaten bare by the
Spanish armies. Wild beasts infested the abandoned
dwellings of the peasantry, and wolves littered their
young in the deserted farmhouses. Bruges and Ghent
became the resort of thieves and paupers. The sack
of Antwerp in 1585 gave the last blow to the staggering industry of that great city ; and though many of
its best citizens had already fled from it into Holland
and England, one-third of the remaining merchants
and workers in silks, damasks, and other stuffs, shook
the dust of the Low Countries from their feet, and left
the country for ever.

Philip of Spain at length determined to take
summary vengeance upon England. He was master
of the most powerful army and navy in the world, and
he believed that he could effect by force what he had
been unable to compass by intrigue. The most stern
and bigoted of kings, the great colossus of the Papacy,
the duly-appointed Defender of the Faith, he resolved,
at the same time that he pursued and punished his
recreant subjects who had taken refuge in England, to
degrade and expel the sacrilegious occupant of the
English throne. Accordingly, in 1588, he prepared
and launched his Sacred Armada, one of the most
powerful armaments that ever put to sea. It consisted of 130 ships, besides transports, carrying 2650
great guns and 33,000 soldiers and sailors, besides 180

priests and monks under a Vicar-General of the Holy Inquisition. It was also furnished with chains and instruments of torture, and with smiths and mechanics to set them to work,—destined for the punishment of the audacious and pestilent heretics who had so long defied the triumphant power of Spain.

This armament was to be joined in its progress by another equally powerful fleet off the coast of Flanders, consisting of an immense number of flat-bottomed boats, carrying an army of 100,000 men, equipped with the best weapons and materials of war, who were to be conveyed to the mouth of the Thames under the escort of the great Spanish fleet.

The expedition was ably planned. The Pope blessed it, and promised to co-operate with his money ; pledging himself to advance a million of ducats so soon as the expedition reached the British shores. At the same time, the bull issued by Pope Pius V., excommunicating Elizabeth and dispossessing her of her throne, was confirmed by Sextus V., and re-issued with additional anathemas. Setting forth under such auspices, it is not surprising to find that Catholic Europe entertained the conviction that the expedition must necessarily prove successful, and that Elizabeth and Protestantism in England were doomed to inevitable destruction.

No measure could, however, have been better calculated than this to weld the English people of all ranks and classes, Catholics as well as Protestants, into one united nation. The threatened invasion of England by a foreign power—above all by a power so hated as Spain—roused the patriotic feeling of all classes. There was a general rising and arming, by land and by sea. Along the south coast the whole maritime population arrayed themselves in arms ; and every available ship, sloop, and wherry, was manned and sent forth to meet and fight the Spaniards.

The result is matter of history. The Sacred and

Invincible Armada was shattered by the ships of
Drake, Hawkins, and Howard, and finally scattered
by the tempests of the Almighty. The free asylum
of England was maintained. The hunted exiles were
thenceforward free to worship and to labour in peace;
and the beneficent effects of the addition of so many
skilled, industrious, and free-minded men to our population, are felt in England to this day.

Philip II. of Spain died in 1598, the same year in
which Henry IV. of France promulgated the Édict of
Nantes. At his accession to the Spanish throne in
1556, Philip was the most powerful monarch in
Europe, served by the ablest generals and admirals,
with an immense army and navy at his command.
At his death, Spain was distracted and defeated, with
a bankrupt exchequer; Holland was free, and Flanders
in ruins. The intellect and energies of Spain were
prostrate; but the priests were paramount. The only
institution that flourished throughout the dominions
of Philip, at his death, was the Inquisition.

Elizabeth of England, on the other hand, succeeded,
in 1558, to an impoverished kingdom, an empty exchequer, and the government of a distracted people,
one-half of whom denied, and were even ready to
resist, her authority. England was then without any
weight in the affairs of Europe. She had no army,
and her navy was contemptible. After a reign of
forty-five years, the aspect of affairs had become completely changed. The nation was found firmly united,
content, free, and prosperous. An immense impulse
had been given to industry. The intellect of the
people had become awakened, and a literature sprang
up which is the wonder even of modern times. The
power of England abroad was everywhere recognised.
The sceptre of the seas was wrested from Spain, and
England thenceforward commanded the high-road to
America and the Indies.

The Queen was supported by able ministers, though
not more able than those who surrounded the King

of Spain.   But the spirit that moved them was wholly
different—the English monarch encouraging freedom,
the Spanish repressing it.   As the one was the
founder of modern England, so the other was of
modern Spain.

It is true, Elizabeth did not rise to the high idea
of complete religious liberty.   But no one then did—
not even the most advanced thinker.   Still, the foundations of such liberty were laid, while industry was
fostered and protected.   It was accomplishing a great
deal, to have accomplished this much.   The rest was the
work of time and experience, and the action of free
and energetic men living in an atmosphere of freedom.

MEDAL STRUCK AT ROME

In Commemoration of the Massacre of St. Bartholomew.

CHAPTER VI.

SETTLEMENTS AND INDUSTRIES OF THE PROTESTANT REFUGEES IN ENGLAND.

In early times, the English were for the most part a pastoral and agricultural, and not a manufacturing people. In the thirteenth and fourteenth centuries, most articles of clothing, excepting such as were produced by ordinary domestic industry, were imported from Flanders, France, and Germany.[1] The great staple of England was Wool, which was sent abroad in large quantities. "The ribs of all people throughout the world," wrote Matthew Paris, "are kept warm by the fleeces of English wool."

The wool and its growers were on one side of the English Channel, and the skilled workmen who dyed and wove it into cloth were on the other. When war broke out, and communication between the two shores

---

[1] Besides the cloth of Flanders, England was also supplied with most of its finer fabrics from abroad—the names of the articles to this day indicating the places where they were manufactured. Thus, there was the *mechlin* lace of Mechlin, the *duffle* of Duffel, the *diaper* of Ypres (d'Ypres), the *cambric* of Cambray, the *arras* of Arras, the *tulle* of Tulle, the *damask* of Damascus, and the *dimity* of Damietta. Besides these, we imported *delph* ware from Delft, *venetian glass* from Venice, *cordovan leather* from Cordova, and *milanery* from Milan. The Milaners of London were a special class of general dealers. They sold not only French and Flemish cloths, but Spanish gloves and girdles, Milan caps and cutlery, silk, lace, needles, pins for ladies' dresses (before which skewers were used), swords, knives, daggers, brooches, glass, porcelain, and various articles of foreign manufacture. The name of "milliner" (from Milaner) is now applied only to dealers in ladies' caps and bonnets.

was interrupted, great distress was occasioned in Flanders by the stoppage of the supply of English wool. On one occasion, when the export of wool from England was prohibited, the effect was to reduce the manufacturing population throughout the Low Countries to destitution and despair. " Then might be seen throughout Flanders," says the local historian, " weavers, fullers, and others living by the woollen manufacture, either begging, or, driven by debt, tilling the soil."[1]

At the same time, the English wool-growers lost the usual market for their produce. It naturally occurred to the English kings that it would be of great advantage to this country to have the wool made into cloth by the hands of their own people, instead of sending it abroad for the purpose. They accordingly held out invitations to the distressed Flemish artizans to come over and settle in England, where they would find abundant employment at remunerative wages ; and as early as the reign of Edward III. a large number of Flemings came over and settled in London, Kent, Norfolk, Devon, Somerset, Yorkshire, Lancashire, and Westmoreland.

The same policy was pursued by successive English kings, down to the reign of Henry VIII., who encouraged skilled artizans of all kinds to settle in England—as armourers, cutlers, miners, brewers, and shipbuilders ; the principal craftsmen employed by the court being Flemings and Germans.

The immigration of foreign Protestants began in the reign of his successor Edward VI.

The disturbed state of the Continent at that time had the effect of seriously interfering with the pursuits of industry; and in many of the German and Low Country towns, the working-classes were beginning to suffer from want of employment.

The unemployed sought to remove to some foreign

---

[1] Meyer—*Annales Flandriæ,* p. 137.

country less disturbed by party strife, in which they might find remunerative employment for their industry; while the men of The Religion longed for some secure asylum in which they might worship God according to conscience. John Bradford, the Englishman, writing to his friend Erkenwalde Rawlins, the Fleming, in 1554, advised him thus:—" Go to, therefore, dispose your goods, prepare yourselves to trial, that either you may stand to it like God's champions, or else, if you feel such infirmity in yourselves that you are not able, give place to violence, and go where you may with free and safe conscience serve the Lord."

There were indeed many who felt themselves wanting in the requisite strength to bear persecution, and who, accordingly, prepared to depart. Besides, the world was wide, and England was near at hand, ready to give them asylum. At first, the emigration was comparatively small; for it was a sore trial to many to break up old connections, to leave home, country, and relatives behind, and begin the world anew in a foreign land. Nevertheless, small bodies of emigrating Protestants at length began to move, dropping down the Rhine in boats, and passing over from the Dutch and Flemish ports into England. Others came from Flanders itself; though at first the immigration from that quarter, as well as from France, was of a very limited character.

The foreigners were welcomed on their arrival in England, being generally regarded as a valuable addition to the skilled working classes of the country. Thus Latimer, when preaching before Edward VI. shrewdly observed of the foreigners persecuted for conscience' sake :—" I wish that we could collect together such valuable persons in this kingdom, as it would be the means of insuring its prosperity." Very few years passed before Latimer's wish was fully realised ; and there was scarcely a town of any importance in England in which foreign artizans were not found settled and diligently pursuing their respective callings.

The immigration of the Protestant Flemings in Edward VI.'s reign was already so considerable, that the King gave them the church in Austin Friars, Broad Street, "to have their service in, and for avoiding all sects of anabaptists and the like." The influx continued at such a rate as to interfere with the employment of the native population, who occasionally showed a disposition to riot, and even to expel the foreigners by violence. In a letter written by Francis Peyto to the Earl of Warwick, then at Rome, the following passage occurs:—"Five or six hundred men waited upon the mayor and aldermen, complaining of the late influx of strangers, and that, by reason of the great dearth, they cannot live for these strangers, whom they were determined to kill up through the realm if they found no remedy. To pacify them, the mayor and aldermen caused an esteame to be made of all strangers in London, which showed an amount of forty thousand, besides women and children, for the most part heretics fled out of other countries."[1] Although this estimate was probably a gross exaggeration, there can be no doubt that by this time a large number of the exiles had arrived and settled in London and other English towns.

The influx of the persecuted Protestants, however, did not fully set in until about ten years later, about the beginning of the reign of Elizabeth. The fugitives, in the extremities to which they were reduced, naturally made for that part of the English coast which lay the nearest to Flanders and France. In 1561, a considerable body of Flemings landed near Deal, and subsequently settled at the then decayed town of Sandwich. The Queen was no sooner informed of their landing, than she wrote to the mayor, jurats, and commonalty of the burgh, enjoining them to give liberty to the

---

[1] *Calendar of State Papers*, Foreign Series. 1547-53.

foreigners to settle there and carry on their respective trades. She recommended the measure as calculated to greatly benefit the town by "plantynge in the same men of knowledge in sundry handycrafts," in which they "were very skilful"; and her Majesty more particularly enjoined that the trades the foreign artizans were to carry on were "the makinge of says, bays, and other cloth, which hath not been used to be made in this our realme of Englonde."

Other landings of Flemings took place about the same time, at Harwich, at Yarmouth, at Dover, and other towns on the south-east coast. Some settled at the places where they had landed, and began to pursue their several branches of industry; whilst others proceeded to London, Norwich, Maidstone, Canterbury, and other inland towns, where the local authorities gave them protection and succour.

The year after the arrival of the Flemings at Sandwich, the inhabitants of the little seaport of Rye, on the coast of Sussex, were thrown into a state of commotion by the sudden arrival of a number of destitute French people from the opposite coast. Some came in open boats, others in sailing-vessels. They were of all classes and conditions, and amongst them were many women and children. They had fled from their own country in great haste, and were nearly all alike destitute. Some crossed the Channel in midwinter, braving the stormiest weather; and when they reached the English shore they would often fall upon their knees and thank God for their deliverance.

In May 1562, we find John Young, mayor of Rye, writing to Sir William Cecil, the Queen's chief secretary, as follows:—" May it please your honour, there is daily great resort of Frenchmen here, insomuch as already there is esteemed to be 500 persons; and we be in great want of corn for their and our sustentation, by reason the country adjoining is barren. . . . Also may it please your honour, after night and this day is

come two shippis of Dieppe into this haven, full of
many people." [1]

It will be remembered that Rye is situated at the
south-western extremity of the great Romney Marsh ;
and as no corn is grown in that neighbourhood, the
wheat consumed in the place was all brought thither
by sea, or from a distance inland, over the then almost
impassable roads of Sussex. The townspeople of Rye
nevertheless bestirred themselves in aid of the poor
refugees. They took them into their houses, fed them,
and supplied their wants as well as they could; but
the fugitives continued to arrive in such numbers that
the provisions of the place soon began to run short.

These landings continued during the summer of
1562 ; and even as late as November the mayor again
wrote to Cecil: " May it please your honour to be
advertised that the third day of the present month, at
twelve of the clocke, there arrived a bote from Dieppe,
with Frenchmen, women, and children, to the number
of a hundred and fiftye, there being a great number
also which were here before." And as late as the 10th
of December, the French people still flying for refuge,
though winter had already set in severely, the mayor
again wrote that another boat had arrived with " many
poor people, as well men and women as children, which
were of Rouen and Dieppe."

Six years passed, and again, in 1568, we find another
boat-load of fugitives from France landing at Rye :
" Monsieur Gamayes, with his wife and children and
ten strangers ; and Captain Sowes, with his wife and
two servants, who had all come out of France, as they
said, for the safeguard of their lives." Four years later,
in 1572, there was a further influx of refugees at Rye,
—the mayor again writing to Lord Burleigh, informing
him that between the 27th of August and the 4th of
November no fewer than 641 had landed. The records
have been preserved of the names and callings of most

---

[1] *Domestic State Papers*—Elizabeth, 1562. No. 35.

of the immigrants; from which it appears that they were of all ranks and conditions, including gentlemen, merchants, doctors of physic, ministers of religion, students, schoolmasters, tradesmen, mechanics, artizans, shipwrights, mariners, and labourers. Among the fugitives were also several widows, who had fled with their children across the sixty miles of sea which there divide France from England, sometimes by night in open boats, braving the fury of the winds and waves in their eagerness to escape.[1]

The mayor of Rye made appeals to the Queen for help, and especially for provisions, which from time to time ran short; and the help was at once given. Collections were made for the relief of the destitute refugees in many of the churches in England, as well as in Scotland;[2] and, among others, we find the refugee Flemings at Sandwich giving out of their slender means "a benefaction to the poor Frenchmen who have left their country for conscience' sake."[3]

The landings continued for many years. The people came flying from various parts of France and Flanders —cloth-makers from Antwerp and Bruges, lace-makers from Valenciennes, cambric-makers from Cambray, glass-makers from Paris, stuff-weavers from Meaux, merchants and tradesmen from Rouen, and shipwrights and mariners from Dieppe and Havre. As the fugitives continued to land, they were sent inland as speedily as possible, to make room for new-comers,—the household accommodation of the little towns along the English coast being but limited. From Rye, many proceeded to London to join their countrymen who had settled there; others went forward to Canterbury, to Southampton, to Norwich, and the other towns

---

[1] W. DURRANT COOPER — *Sussex Archæological Collections,* vol. xiii. p. 179: "The Protestant Refugees in Sussex."

[2] James Melville, in his diary, mentions that subscriptions were raised in Scotland for French Protestants in indigent circumstances, in 1575; and Calderwood has a similar notice in 1622.

Borough Records of Sandwich, 1572.

where Walloon congregations had already been established. A body of them settled at Winchelsea, an ancient town, formerly of much importance on the south coast, though now left high and dry inland.[1]

Many fugitives also landed at Dover, which was a convenient point for both France and Flanders. Some of the immigrants passed through to Canterbury and London, while others settled permanently in the place. Early in the seventeenth century, a census was taken of the foreigners residing in Dover, when it was found that there were seventy-eight persons "which of late came out of France by reason of the troubles there." The description of them is interesting, as showing the classes to which the exiles principally belonged. There were two "preachers of God's Word"; three physicians and surgeons; two advocates; two esquires; three merchants; two schoolmasters; thirteen drapers, grocers, brewers, butchers, and other trades; twelve mariners; eight weavers and wool-combers; twenty-five widows, "makers of bone-lace and spinners"; two maidens; one woman, designated as the wife of a shepherd; one button-maker; one gardener; and one undescribed male.[2] There were at the same time settled in Dover thirteen Walloon exiles, of whom five were merchants, three mariners, and the others of different trades.

In the meantime, the body of Flemings who had first settled at Sandwich began to show signs of considerable prosperity. The local authorities had readily responded to the wishes of Queen Elizabeth, and did what she required. They appointed two markets to be held weekly for the sale of their cloths, in the making

---

[1] Winchelsea, now a village almost in ruins, was once a flourishing seaport. The remains of the vaults and warehouses where the merchants' goods were stored are still pointed out, and the wharves may still be seen where ships discharged their cargoes, lying with their broadsides to the shore. The place is now some miles from the sea, and sheep and cattle graze over a wide extent of marsh-land, over which the tide formerly flowed.

[2] *Dom. Col.*—James I., 1622.

of which we very shortly find them busily occupied.
When Archbishop Parker visited Sandwich, in 1563,
he took notice of " the French and Dutche, or both,"
who had settled in the town, and wrote to a friend at
court that the refugees were as godly on the Sabbath-
days as they were industrious on week-days ; observing that such " profitable and gentle strangers ought
to be welcome, and not to be grudged at."[1]

Before the arrival of the Flemings, Sandwich had
been a poor and decayed place.   It was originally a
town of considerable importance, and one of the Cinque
Ports.   But when the river Stour became choked with
silt, the navigation, on which it had before depended,
was so seriously impeded, that its trade soon fell into
decay, and the inhabitants were reduced to great
poverty.   No sooner, however, had the first colony of
Flemings, above four hundred in number, settled there
under the Queen's protection, than the empty houses
were occupied, the town became instinct with new life,
and was more than restored to its former importance.
The artizans set up their looms, and began to work at
the manufacture of sayes, bayes, and other kinds of
cloth, which met with a ready sale; the London
merchants resorting to the bi-weekly markets, and
buying up the goods at remunerative prices.

The native population also shared in the general
prosperity—learning from the strangers the art of
cloth-making, and becoming competitors with them for
the trade.   Indeed, before many years had passed, the
townspeople, forgetful of the benefits they owed to the
foreign artizans, became jealous, and sought to impose
upon them special local taxes.   On this the Flemings
memorialised the Queen,[2] who again stood their friend ;

---

[1] Strype's *Parker*, p. 139.

[2] The memorial, which is still
preserved amongst the town records, concludes with the following prayer :—" Which condition
(viz. the local imposition on the
foreign settlers) is suche, that by
means of their chardges they
should finally be secluded and
syndered from the hability of
those manifolde and necessary
contributions which yet in this

and, on her intercession, the corporation were at length
induced to relieve them of the unjust burden.   At that
time they constituted about one-third of the entire
population of the town ; and when Elizabeth visited
Sandwich in 1573, it is recorded that "against the
school-house, upon the new turfed wall, and upon a
scaffold made upon the wall of the school-house yard,
were divers children, to the number of a hundred or
six score, all spinning of fine bag yarn, a thing well
liked both of Her Majesty and of the Nobility and
Ladies." [1]

The Protestant exiles at Sandwich did not, however, confine themselves to cloth-making,[2] but engaged
in various other branches of industry.   Some of them
were millers, who erected the first windmills near the
town, in which they plied their trade.   Two potters
from Delft began the pottery manufacture.   Others
were smiths, brewers, hat-makers, carpenters, or shipwrights.   Thus trade and population increased ; new
buildings arose on all sides, until Sandwich became
almost transformed into a Flemish town ; and to this
day, though fallen again into comparative decay, the
quaint, foreign-looking aspect of the place never fails to
strike the visitor with surprise.

Among other branches of industry introduced by the
Flemings at Sandwich, that of gardening is worthy

---

our exile are practised amongst
us, as well towards the maintenance of the ministry of God's
word as lykewise in the sustentation of our poore, besydes the
chardges first above rehearsed :
performyng therefore our fore-
sayde humble petition, we shall
be the more moved to directe our
warmest prayers to our mercyfull
God, that of his heavenly grace
he will beatify your common
weall more and more, grauntynge
to ytt his spiritual and temporal
blessyngs, which he gracefully
powreth uppon them that showe

favour and consolation to the
poore afflicted straungers. " —
BOYS' *History of Sandwich*, p.
744.

[1] *Antiquarian Repertory*, iv.
65.

[2] The principal trades which
they followed were connected
with the manufacture of cloths
of different kinds.   Thus, of 351
Flemish householders resident in
Sandwich in 1582, 86 were bay-
makers, 74 bay-weavers, 17 fullers,
24 linsey-wolsey weavers, and 24
wool-combers.

of notice. The people of Flanders had long been famous for their horticulture; and one of the first things which the foreign settlers did, on arriving in the place, was to turn to account the excellent qualities of the soil in the neighbourhood. Though long before practised by the monks, Gardening had become almost a lost art in England. It is said that Katherine, Queen of Henry VIII., unable to obtain a salad for her dinner in England, had her table supplied from the Low Countries.[1] The first Flemish gardens proved highly successful. The cabbage, carrots, and celery produced by the foreigners met with so ready a sale, and were so much in demand in London itself, that a body of gardeners shortly after removed from Sandwich and settled at Wandsworth, Battersea, and Bermondsey, where many of the rich garden-grounds first planted by the Flemings, still continue to be the most productive in the neighbourhood of the metropolis.

It is also supposed, though it cannot be exactly ascertained, that the Protestant Walloons introduced the cultivation of the hop in Kent, bringing slips of the plant with them from Artois. The old distich—

> " Hops, Reformation, Bays, and Beer,
> Came into England all in one year "—

marks the period (about 1524) when the first English hops were planted. There is a plot of land at Bourne, near Canterbury, where there is known to have been

---

[1] Vegetables were formerly so scarce that they were salted down. Even in the sixteenth century, a cabbage from Holland was deemed an acceptable present (Fox's *Life of James II.*, 205). Hull then carried on a thriving import-trade in cabbages and onions. The rarity of vegetables in the country may be inferred from the fact, that in 1595 a sum equal to twenty shillings was paid at that port for six cabbages and a few carrots by the purveyor for the Clifford family (WHITAKER—*History of Craven*, 321). Hartlib, writing in 1650, says that an old man then living remembered " the first gardener who came into Surrey to plant cabbages and cauliflowers, and to sow turnips, carrots, and parsnips, and to sow early pease—all of which at that time were great wonders, we having few or none in England but what came from Holland or Flanders."

a hop-plantation in the reign of Elizabeth.[1]   Another
kind of crop introduced by the Flemings at Sandwich
was canary-grass, which still continues to be grown on
the neighbouring farms, and is indeed almost peculiar
to the district.

As might naturally be expected, by far the largest
proportion of the Protestant exiles — Flemish and
French—settled in London :—London, the world's
asylum—the refuge of the persecuted of all lands,
whether for race, or politics, or religion—a city of
Celts, Danes, and Saxons—of Jews, Germans, French,
and Flemings, as well as of English—an aggregate of
men of all European countries, and probably one of
the most composite populations to be found in the
world.   Large numbers of French, Germans, and
Flemings, of the industrious classes, had already
taken refuge in London from the political troubles
which had prevailed abroad.   About the beginning of
the reign of Henry VIII. so many foreigners had
settled in the western parts of the metropolis, that
"Tottenham is turned French" passed into a proverb;
and now the religious persecutions which raged abroad,
compelled foreigners of various nations to take refuge
in London, in still greater numbers than they had done
at any former period.

Fortunately for London, as for England, the men
who fled thither for refuge were not idle, dissolute,
and ignorant; but peaceable, gentle, and laborious.
Though they were poor, they were not pauperised,
but thrifty and self-helping, and above all things
eager in their desire to earn an honest living.   They
were among the most skilled and intelligent inhabitants of the countries which had driven them forth.
Had they been weak men, they would have gone with

---

[1] Reginald Scot, the author of
*The Perfite Platforme of a
Hoppe Garden*, speaks of "the
trade of the Flemminge" (*i.e.*
his method of culture), and his
"ostes at Poppering" as "a
profytable patterne and a neces-
sarie instruction for as manie as
shall have to doe therein."

the stream as others did, and conformed ; but they
were men with convictions, earnest for the truth,
and ready to sacrifice their worldly goods and everything else to follow it.

Of the Flemings and French who settled in London,
the greater number congregated in special districts, for
the convenience of carrying on their trades together.
Thus a large number of the Flemings settled in Southwark and Bermondsey,[1] where they began many branches
of industry which continue to this day—Southwark
being still the principal manufacturing district of
London. There was a quarter in Bermondsey, known
as " The Borgeney," or " Petty Burgundy," because
of the foreigners who inhabited it. Joiners' Street,
which still exists in name, lay in the district, and was
so called because of its being almost wholly occupied
by Flemish joiners, who were skilled in all kinds of
carpentry. Another branch of trade begun by the
Flemings in Bermondsey, was the manufacture of felts
or hats. Tanneries and breweries were also started
by them, and carried on with great success. Henry
Leek, originally Hoek or Hook,[2] from Wesel, was one
of the principal brewers of his time, to whose philan-
thropic bequest Southwark owes the foundation of the
excellent free school of St. Olave's—one of the best of
its class.

Another important settlement of the Flemings was
at Bow, where they established dye-works on a
large scale. Before their time, white cloth of English
manufacture was usually sent abroad to be dyed, after

---

[1] The *Flemish burying-ground*,
appropriated to the foreigners as
a place of sepulture, was situated
near the south end of London
Bridge. It is now covered by
the approaches to the London
Bridge Railway Station.

[2] Many of the foreigners adopted names of English sound, so
that it is now difficult to trace

them amidst the population in
which they have become merged.
Thus, in the parish church of
Allhallows, Barking, we find the
monument of a distinguished
Fleming, one Roger Hæstrecht,
who changed his name to James.
He was the founder of the family
of James, of Ightham Court, in
Kent.

which it was reimported and sold as Flemish cloth. The best known among the early dyers, were Peter de Croix and Dr. Kepler, the latter of whom established the first dye-work in England; and cloth of "Bow dye" soon became famous.

Another body of the refugees settled at Wandsworth, and began several branches of industry—such as the manufacture of felts, and the making of brass plates for culinary utensils—which, Aubrey says, they "kept a mystery." One Fromantel introduced the manufacture of pendulum or Dutch clocks, which shortly came into use. At Mortlake, the French exiles began the manufacture of arras, and at Fulham of tapestry. The art of printing paperhangings was introduced by some artizans from Rouen, where it had been originally practised; and many other skilled workers in metal settled in different parts of the metropolis—such as cutlers, jewellers, and makers of mathematical instruments, in which the French and Flemish workmen then greatly excelled.[1]

The employment given to the foreign artizans seems to have excited considerable discontent amongst the London tradesmen, who, from time to time, beseeched the interference of the corporations and of Parliament. Thus, in 1576, we find the London shoemakers petitioning for a commission of inquiry as to the alien shoemakers who were carrying on their trade in the metropolis. In 1586, the London apprentices raised a riot in the city against the foreigners; and several youths of the Plaisterers' Company were apprehended and committed to Newgate by order of the Queen and council. A few years later, in 1592, the London freemen and shopkeepers complained to Parliament that

---

[1] A French refugee, named Briot, was the first to introduce the coining-press, which was a French invention, into England. He was appointed chief engraver to the Mint: and forty years after his time, in the reign of Charles II., another Frenchman, named Blondeau, was selected to superintend the stamping of our English money.

the strangers were spoiling their trades; and a bill
was brought in for the purpose of restraining them.
The bill was strongly supported by Sir Walter Raleigh,
who complained bitterly of the strangers; but it was
opposed by Cecil and the Queen's ministers; and
though it passed the Commons, it failed through the
dissolution of Parliament—so that the refugees were
left to the enjoyment of their former protection and
hospitality.

Many of the foreigners established themselves as
merchants in the city, and soon became known as
leading men in commercial affairs. Several of them
had already been distinguished as merchants in their
own country; and they brought with them a spirit
and enterprise which infused quite a new life into
London business. Among the leading foreign merchants of Elizabeth's time we recognise the names
of Houblon, Palavicino, De Malines, Corsellis, Van
Peine, Tryan, Buskell, Corsini, De Best, and Cotett.
That they prospered by the exercise of their respective callings, may be inferred from the fact that when,
in 1588, Queen Elizabeth proceeded to raise a loan in
the city by voluntary subscriptions, thirty-eight of the
foreign merchants subscribed £5000, in sums of £100
and upwards.

The accounts given of the numbers of the exiles
from Flanders and France who settled in London, are
very imperfect; yet they enable us to form some idea
of the extensive character of the immigration. Thus,
a return of the population, made in 1571, the year
before the massacre of St. Bartholomew, shows that
in the city of London alone (exclusive of the large
number of strangers settled in Southwark, at Bow, and
outside the liberties) there were, of foreigners belonging to the English church, 889; to the Dutch, French,
and Italian churches, 1763; certified by their elders,
but not presented by the wards, 1828; not yet joined
to any particular church, 2663; "strangers that do
confesse themselves that their comyng hether was

onlie to seek worck for their lyvinge," 2561; or a total of 9704 persons.[1] From another return of about the same date, in which the numbers are differently given, we obtain some idea of the respective nationalities of the refugees. Out of the 4594 strangers then returned as resident in the city of London, 3643 are described as Dutch (*i.e.* Flemings); 657 French; 233 Italians; and 53 Spaniards and Portuguese.[2]

That the foreign artizans continued to resort to England in increasing numbers is apparent from a further census taken in 1621, from which it appears that there were then 10,000 strangers in the city of London alone (besides still larger numbers in the suburbs), carrying on 121 different trades. Of 1343 persons whose occupations are specified, there were found to be 11 preachers, 16 schoolmasters, 349 weavers, 183 merchants, 148 tailors, 64 sleeve-makers, 43 shoemakers, 39 dyers, 37 brewers, 35 jewellers, 25 diamond-cutters, 22 cutlers, 20 goldsmiths, 20 joiners, 15 clockmakers, 12 silk-throwsters, 10 glass-makers, besides hemp-dressers, thread-makers, button-makers, coopers, engravers, gunmakers, painters, smiths, watchmakers, and other skilled craftsmen.[3]

Numerous other settlements of the refugees took place throughout England, more particularly in the southern counties. "The foreign manufacturers," says Hasted, "chose their situations with great judgment, distributing themselves with the Queen's licence throughout England, so as not to interfere too much

---

[1] *State Papers, Dom.*—Elizabeth, vol. 84, anno 1571. It appears from the Bishop of London's certificate of 1567 (four years before), that the number of persons of foreign birth then settled in London was 4581, and 512 French. There were at the same time in London 36 Scots, 128 Italians, 23 Portuguese, 54 Spaniards, 10 Venetians, 2 Blackamoors, and two Greeks.

[2] *State Papers, Dom.*—Elizabeth, vol. 82, anno 1571.

[3] *Lists of Foreign Protestants and Aliens resident in England* 1618-88. Edited by William Durrant Cooper, F.S.A. Camden Society's Papers, 1862.

with each other."[1]   One of the most important of such
settlements was that formed at Norwich, where the
Refugees founded and carried on many important
branches of trade.

Although Norwich had been originally indebted
mainly to foreign artizans for its commercial and
manufacturing importance, the natives of the city
were among the first to turn apon their benefactors.
The local guilds, in their usual narrow spirit, passed
stringent regulations directed against the foreign
artizans who had originally taught them their trade.
The jealousy of the native workmen was also roused,
and riots were stirred up against the Flemings, many
of whom left Norwich for Leeds and Wakefield in
Yorkshire, where they prosecuted the woollen manufacture free from the restrictions of the trades-unions,
whilst others left the country for Holland, to carry on
their trades in the free towns of that country.[2]

The consequence was that Norwich, left to its native
enterprise and industry, gradually fell into a state of
stagnation and decay.   Its population rapidly diminished ; a large proportion of the houses stood empty ;
riots among the distressed workpeople were of frequent
occurrence ; and it was even mooted in Parliament
whether the place should not be razed.   Under such
circumstances, the corporation determined to call to
their aid the skill and industry of the exiled Protestant artizans now flocking into the country: In the
year 1564, a deputation of the citizens, headed by the
mayor, waited on the Duke of Norfolk at his palace in
the city, and asked his assistance in obtaining a settle-

---

[1] HASTED—*History of Kent*,
x. p. 160.
[2] In the reign of Henry VII. an
attempt was made by a body of
Flemings to establish the manufacture of felt hats at Norwich.
To evade the fiscal regulations
of the guilds, they settled outside
the boundaries of the city.   But
an act having been passed enjoining that hats were only to
be manufactured in some city,
borough, or market-town, the
Flemings were thereby brought
under the bondage of the guilds.
The making of hats by them was
suppressed ; and the Flemish hat-
makers left the neighbourhood,

ment in the place of a body of Flemish workmen.
The Duke used his influence with this object, and
he shortly succeeded in inducing some 300 Dutch and
Walloon families to settle in Norwich at his charge,
and to carry on their trades under a licence granted
by the Queen.

The exiles were very shortly enabled, not only to
maintain themselves by their industry, but to restore
the city to more than its former prosperity. The
houses which had been standing empty were again
tenanted, the native population again became fully
employed, and the adjoining districts shared in the
general prosperity. In the course of a few years, 3000
foreign workmen were found settled in the city,
and many entirely new branches of trade were introduced and successfully carried on by them. Besides
the manufacture of sayes, bayes, serges, arras, mou-
chade, and bombazines, they introduced the striping
and flowering of silks and damasks, which shortly
became one of the principal branches of trade in the
place.

The manufacture of beaver and felt hats, before imported from abroad, was also successfully established
in Norwich. One Anthony Solen introduced the art
of printing, for which he was awarded the freedom of
the city. Two potters from Antwerp, Jasper Andries
and Jacob Janson, started a pottery, though in a very
humble way.[1] Other Flemings introduced the art of

---

[1] Stowe makes the following
reference to these men in his
Survey of London :—" About the
year 1567 Jasper Andries and
Jacob Janson, potters, came away
from Antwerp to avoid the persecution there, and settled themselves in Norwich, where they
followed their trade, making galley paving-tiles and apothecaries'
vessels, and others, very arti-
ficially. Anno 1570 they removed
to London. They set forth, in a
petition to Queen Elizabeth, that
they were the first that brought
in and exercised the said science
in this realm, and were at great
charges before they could find
the materials in this realm. They
beseeched her, in recompense of
their great cost and charges, that
she would grant them house-
room in or without the liberties
of London by the water-side."
The brothers Elers afterwards, in
1688, began the manufacture of a

gardening in the neighbourhood, and culinary stuffs
became more plentiful in Norwich than in any other
town or city in England. The general result was—
abundant employment, remunerative trade, cheap food,
and great prosperity; Bishop Parkhurst declaring his
persuasion that "these blessings from God have happened by reason of the godly exiles who were so kindly
harboured there."

But not so very kindly after all. As before, the
sour native heart grew jealous; and notwithstanding
the admitted prosperity of the place, the local population began to mutter discontent against the foreigners,
who had been mainly its cause. Like Jeshurun, the
natives waxed fat and kicked. It is true, the numbers
of Dutch, French, and Walloons in Norwich had become very considerable, by reason of the continuance
of the persecutions abroad, which drove them across
the Channel in increasing numbers. But who so likely
to give them succour and shelter as their own countrymen, maintaining themselves by the exercise of their
skill and industry in the towns of England?

The hostile movement against the foreign artizans
is even said to have been encouraged by some of the
gentlemen of the neighbourhood, who in 1570 set on
foot a conspiracy, with the object of expelling them by
force from the city and realm. But the conspiracy
was discovered in time. Its leader and instigator,
John Throgmorton, was seized and executed, with two
others; and the strangers were thenceforward permitted
to pursue their respective callings in peace.

Whatever may have been the shortcomings of
Elizabeth in other respects, she certainly proved herself the steadfast friend and protector of the Protestant
exiles. Her conduct with reference to the Norwich
conspiracy clearly shows the spirit which influenced

---

better sort of pottery in Staffordshire. They were natives of
Nuremberg in Germany. In 1710

they removed from Staffordshire,
and settled in Lambeth or Chelsea.

her. In a letter written by her from the palace at Greenwich, dated the 19th March 1570, she strongly expostulated with the citizens of Norwich respecting the jealousy entertained by them against the authors of their prosperity. She reminded them of the advantages they had derived from the settlement amongst them of so many skilled artizans, who inhabited the houses which had before stood desolate, and were furnishing employment to large numbers of persons who must otherwise have remained unemployed. She therefore entreated and enjoined them to continue their favours " to the poor men of the Dutch nation, who, seeing the persecution lately begun in their country for the trewe religion, hath fledd into this realm for succour, and be now placed in the city of Norwich, and hath hitherto been favourablye and jintely ordered, which the Queen's Majestie, as a mercifull and religious Prince, doth take in very good part, praeing you to continue your favour unto them so long as they shall lyve emongste you quyetlye and obedyently to God's trewe religion, and to Her Majesty's lawes, for so one chrystian man (in charitie) is bound to help another, especially them who do suffre afflixion for the gospelle's sake." [1]

---

[1] The following is a copy of a document in the State Paper Office (Dom. Eliz. 1561), giving an account of " the benefite receyved by the strangers in Norwich for the space of tenne yeres." Several passages of the paper have been obliterated by age :—

" *In primis*, They brought a grete comoditie thether—viz. the making of bayes, moucades, grograynes, all sorts of tufts, etc. —wch were not made there before, whereby they do not onely set on worke their owne people, but [do also] set on worke o^r owne people wthin the cittie, as

alsoe a grete nomber of people nere xx^{ti} myles aboute the cittie, to the grete relief of the [poorer] sorte there.

" *Item*, By their means o^r cittie [is well inhabited, o^r] decayed houses re-edified & repaired that [were in rewyn and more wolde be]. And now good rents [are] paide for the same.

" *Item*, The marchants by their comoditi[es have] and maye have grete trade as well wthin the realme as wthoute the [realme], being in good estimacon in all places.

" *Item*, It cannot be, but whereas a nomber of people be but the

A census was shortly after taken of the foreigners settled in Norwich, when it was ascertained that they amounted to about 4000, including women and children; and that they were effectually protected in the exercise of their respective callings, and continued to prosper, may be inferred from the circumstance that, when the numbers were again taken, about ten years later, it was found that the foreign community had increased to 4679 persons.

It would occupy too much space to enter into a detailed account of the settlement of the industrious strangers throughout the country, and to describe the various branches of manufacture which they introduced, in addition to those already described. "The persecution for religion in Brabant and Flanders," says Hasted, "communicated to all the Protestant parts of Europe the paper, woollen, and other valuable manufactures of Flanders and France, almost peculiar at that time to these countries, and till then in vain practised elsewhere." [1]

Although the manufacture of cloth had already made some progress in England, only the coarser sorts were produced, the best being imported from abroad; and

---

one receyve comodite of the other as well of the cittie as men of the countrie.

" *Item,* They be contributors to all paym^{ts}, as subsidies, taskes, watches, contribusions, mynisters' wagis, etc.

" *Item,* O^r owne people do practice & make suche comodities as the strangers do make, whereby the youthe is set on worke and kept from idlenes.

" *Item,* They digge & delve a nomber of acres of grounde, & do sowe flaxe & do make it out in lynnen cloth, wch set many on worke.

" *Item,* They digge and delve a grete quantitie of grounde for rootes, [w^{ch}] is a grete succour &

sustenance for the [pore], both for themselves as for all others of cittie and countrie.

" *Item,* They live holy of themselves wthout [o^r chardge], and do begge of no man, & do sustayne [all their owne] poore people.

" And to conclude, they for the [moste p^{te} feare] God & diligently & laboriously attende upon their several occupations, they obay all maiestratis & all good lawes & ordynances, they live peaceblie amonge themselves & towards all men, & we thinke o^r cittie happy to enioye them."

[1] HASTED—*History of Kent,* x. p. 160.

it was not until the settlement among us of the Flemish weavers that this branch of industry became one of national importance. They spread themselves through the towns and villages in the west of England, as well as throughout the north, and wherever the woollen weavers set up their looms they carried on a prosperous trade.[1] Among other places in the west they settled at Worcester, Evesham, Droitwich, Kidderminster, Stroud, and Glastonbury.[2] In the east they settled at Colchester, Hertford, Stamford, and other places. Colchester became exceedingly prosperous in consequence of the settlement of the Flemish artizans there. In 1609 it contained as many as 1300 Walloons and other persons of foreign parentage; and every house was occupied. In the north we find them establishing themselves at Manchester, Bolton, and Halifax, where they made "coatings";[3] and at Kendal, where

---

[1] Fuller specifies the following textile manufactures as having been established by the immigrants :—In Norwich, cloths, fustians, etc.; Sudbury, baizes; Colchester, sayes and serges; Kent, Kentish broad-cloths; Devonshire, kerseys; Gloucestershire and Worcestershire, cloths; Wales, Welsh friezes; Westmoreland, Kendal cloth; Lancashire, coatings or cottons; Yorkshire, Halifax cloths; Somerset, Taunton serges; Hants, Berks, and Sussex, cloth.

[2] A settlement of Flemish woollen-weavers took place at Glastonbury as early as 1549, through the influence of the Duke of Somerset, who advanced them money to buy wool, at the same time providing them with houses and small allotments of land from the domain of the Abbey, which the king had granted him. After the fall of the Duke, the weavers were protected by the Privy Council, and many documents

relating to them are to be found in the State Paper Office.—(Edwd. VI., Dom. xiii. 71-77, and xiv. 2-14 and 55).

[3] The "coatings" or "cottons" of Lancashire were in the first instance but imitations in woollen of the goods known on the Continent by that name; the importation of cotton wool from the Levant having only begun, and that in small quantities, about the middle of the seventeenth century. "There is one fact," says the editor of the *Shuttleworth Papers*, "which seems to show that the Flemings, after their immigration, had much to do with the fulling-mill at Manchester; for its ordinary name was the 'walken-milne' — *walche* being the Flemish name for a fulling-mill. So persistent do we find this name, that a plot of land occupied by a mill on the banks of the Irk still retains its old name of the Walker's Croft (*i.e.* the fuller's field or ground), and

they made cloth caps and woollen stockings. The native population gradually learned to practise the same branches of manufacture; new sources of employment were opened up to them; and in the course of a few years, England, instead of depending upon foreigners for its supply of cloth, was not only able to produce sufficient for its own use, but to export the article in considerable quantities abroad.

Other Flemings introduced the art of thread and lace making. A body of them who settled at Maidstone, in 1567, carried on the thread manufacture— flax spun for the threadman, being still known there as "Dutch work." Some lace-makers from Alençon and Valenciennes settled at Cranfield, in Bedfordshire, in 1568; after which others settled at Buckingham, Stoney-Stratford, and Newport-Pagnel, from whence the manufacture gradually extended over the shires of Oxford, Northampton, and Cambridge. About the same time the manufacture of bone-lace, with thread obtained from Antwerp, was introduced into Devonshire by the Flemish exiles, who settled in considerable numbers at Honiton, Colyton, and other places, where the trade continued to be carried on by their descendants almost to our own time—the Flemish and French names of Stocker, Murch, Spiller, Genest, Maynard, Gerard, Raymunds, Rochett, Kettel, etc., being still common in the lace-towns of the west.

Besides these various branches of textile manufacture, the immigrants applied themselves to mining, working in metals, salt-making, fish-curing, and other arts, in which they were much better skilled than the English then were. Thus, we find a body of them

---

in the earlier Manchester directories, the fullers were styled 'walkers.' "—*House and Home Accounts of the Shuttleworth Family* (Chetham Society Papers, 1856-8), pp. 637-8. The name of Walker, so common in Yorkshire, Lancashire, and the clothing districts of the west of England, doubtless originated in this calling, which was followed by so considerable a proportion of the population.

from the neighbourhood of Liege establishing themselves at Shotley Bridge, in the neighbourhood of
Newcastle-on-Tyne, where they introduced the making
of steel, and became celebrated for the swords and
edge-tools which they manufactured. The names of
the settlers, some of which have been preserved—Ole,
Mohl, Vooz, etc.—indicate their origin; and some of
their descendants are still to be found residing in the
village, under the names of Oley, Mole, and such
like.[1]

Another body of Flemings established a glasswork
at Newcastle-on-Tyne, where the manufacture still
continues to flourish. Two Flemings, Anthony Been
and John Care, erected premises for making window-
glass in London in 1567, and the manufacture was
continued by their two fellow-countrymen, Brut and
Appell. At that tin e, glass was so precious that when
the Duke of Northumberland left Alnwick Castle, the
steward was accustomed to take out the glazed windows, and stow them away until his Grace's return ;
and even in the middle of the following century glass
had not been generally introduced, the royal palaces

---

[1] Mr. Spencer read a paper on
the " Manufacture of Steel" at
the meeting of the British Asso-
ciation at Newcastle in 1863, in
which he thus referred to these
early iron-workers:—"In the wall
of an old two-storey dwelling-
house, the original materials of
which are hidden under a coat of
rough-cast, there still exists a
stone above the doorway with an
inscription in bad German, to
the following effect :—DES. HER-
REN. SECEN. MACHET. REICH.
OHN. ALLF. SORC. WAN. DVZV-
GLEICH. IN. DEINEM. STAND.
TREVW. VND-LLEISIC. BIST. VND.
DVEST. WAS. DIR. BELOHLEN.
IST. 1691, of which the following
is a free translation, showing that
the original importers of the stee¹

manufacture to the district were
probably good Lutherans, who
had suffered persecution for conscience' sake :—" The blessing of
the Lord makes rich without care,
so long as you are industrious in
your vocation, and do what is
ordered you." There is, however, a much earlier reference to
the immigrants in the parish
register of Ebchester Church,
which contains the entry of a
baptism in 1628 of the daughter
of one Mathias Wrightson Ole
or Oley—the name indicating a
probable marriage of the grandfather of the child into a native
family of the name of Wrightson,
and thereby marking the third
generation in the neighbourhood.

of Scotland being glazed only in their upper windows, the lower ones being provided with wooden shutters.

Manufactories for the better kinds of glass were in like manner established in London by Venetians, assisted by Flemish and French refugee workmen. One of them was carried on at Greenwich, and another at Pinner's Hall in Austin Friars. The Flemings especially excelled in glass-painting,—one of them, Bernard van Linge, who was established in London in 1614, being the first to practise the art in England. It was this artist who supplied the windows for Wadham College, the fine window of Lincoln's Inn Chapel, and several subjects for Lincoln College Chapel.

Flemish workers in iron and steel settled at Sheffield under the protection of the Earl of Shrewsbury, on condition that they should take English apprentices and instruct them in their trade. What the skill of the Low Country iron-workers then was, may be understood by any one who has seen the beautiful specimens of ancient iron-work to be met with in Belgium—as, for instance, the exquisite iron canopy over the draw-well in front of the cathedral at Antwerp, or the still more elaborate iron gates enclosing the little chapels behind the high altar of the cathedral of St. Bavon, at Ghent. Only the Nurembergers, in all Germany, could vie with the Flemings in such kind of work. The effects of the instruction given by the Flemish artizans to their Sheffield apprentices were soon felt in the impulse which the improvement of their manufactures gave to the trade of the town; and Sheffield acquired a reputation for its productions in steel and iron which it retains to this day.

A body of refugees of the seafaring class established themselves, with the Queen's licence, at Yarmouth in 1568, and there carried on the business of fishing with great success. Before then, the fish along the English coasts were mostly caught by the Dutch, who cured them in Holland, and brought them back for sale in the English markets. But shortly after the establishment of the fishery at Yarmouth by the Flemings, the home demand was almost entirely supplied by their industry.   They also introduced the arts of salt-making and herring-curing, originally a Flemish invention ; and the trade gradually extended to other places, and furnished employment to a large number of persons.

By the enterprise chiefly of the Flemish merchants settled in London, a scheme was set on foot for the reclamation of the drowned lands in Hatfield Chase and the great level of the Fens ;[1] when a large number of labourers assembled under Cornelius Vermuyden to execute the necessary works.   They were, however, a very different class of men from the modern "navvies"; for, wherever they went, they formed themselves into congregations, erected churches, and appointed ministers to conduct their worship.   Upwards of two hundred Flemish families settled on the land reclaimed by them in the Isle of Axholm ; the ships which brought the immigrants up the Humber to their new homes being facetiously hailed as " the navy of Tarshish." The reclaimers afterwards prosecuted their labours, under Vermuyden, in the great level of the Fens, where they were instrumental in recovering a large extent of drowned land, before then a mere watery waste, but now among the richest and most fertile soil in England.

A few of the exiles found an asylum in Scotland ; though that country was then too poor to hold out much encouragement to the banished artizans.   Of those who arrived in Edinburgh, due care was taken for their maintenance and support.   Collections were made in the churches, and a place was provided for their worship.   It appears from the City records that, in May 1586, the magistrates granted the use of the University Hall for that purpose ; and that at the

---

[1] *Lives of the Engineers,* i. 15-65.

same time they agreed to pay a stipend to Pierre du Moulin, the pastor of the refugees.

Several years later, an attempt was made to introduce into Scotland the manufacture of cloth. In 1601, seven Flemings were engaged to settle in the country, and set the work a-going,—six of them for serges, and one for broadcloth. But disputes arose amongst the boroughs as to the towns in which the settlers were to be located, during which the strangers were "entertained in meat and drink."[1] At length, in 1609, a body of Flemings became settled in the Canongate of Edinburgh, under one Joan Van Hedan, where they were engaged in "making, dressing, and litting of stuffis, giving great licht and knowledge of their calling to the country people."[2]

An attempt was also made to introduce the manufacture of paper into Scotland about the middle of the seventeenth century,when French workmen were introduced for the instruction of the natives. The first mill was erected at Dalry, on the Water of Leith; but though the manufacturers succeeded in making grey and blue paper, the speculation does not seem to have answered,—as we find Alexander Daes, one of the principal proprietors, shortly after occupied in showing an elephant about the country!—the first animal of the kind that had been seen north of the Tweed.[3]

Besides the settlements of the foreigners in England, others passed into Ireland, and settled in Dublin, Waterford, Limerick, Belfast, and other towns. Sir

---

[1] CHAMBERS—*Domestic Annals of Scotland*, i. p. 351.

[2] *Ibid.* i. p. 421.

[3] *Ibid.* ii. pp. 390-410.—The art of paper-making was not successfully established in Scotland until the middle of the following century. Literature must then have been at a low ebb north of the Tweed. In 1683 there was only *one* printing-press in Scotland; and when it was proposed to license a second printer, the widow of Andrew Anderson, who held the only licence, endeavoured to keep the new printer (one David Lindsay) out of the trade, alleging that she had been previously invested with the sole privilege, and that "*one press is sufficiently abʓ to supply all Scotland*"*!*

Henry Sidney, in the "Memoir of his Government in Ireland," written in 1590, thus speaks of the little colony of refugees settled at Swords, near Dublin :— "I caused to plant and inhabit there about fourtie families of the Reformed Churches of the Low Countries, flying thence for religion's sake, in one ruinous town called Swords ; and truly, sir, it would have done any man good to have seen how diligently they wrought, how they re-edified the quite spoiled ould castell of the same town, and repayred almost all the same, and how godlie and cleanly they, their wifes, and children lived.   They made diaper and tickes for beddes, and other good stuffes for man's use ; and as excellent leather of deer skynnes, goat and sheep fells, as is made in Southwarke."

In short, wherever the refugees took up their abode, they acted as so many missionaries of skilled work,— exhibiting the best practical examples of diligence, industry, and thrift,—and teaching the people amongst whom they settled, in the most effective manner, the begnnings of those various industrial arts by which they have since acquired so much distinction and wealth.

"I am persuaded," said the Rev. Elnathan Parr, in his Expositions on the Epistle to the Romans, published in 1632, "that England fares the better for kindness showed, in dangerous times, to French and Dutch strangers.   Long may England be a sanctuary, and refuge, and harbour for the persecuted saints! For 'he that receiveth a righteous man in the name of a righteous man, shall have a righteous man's reward.'"

CHAPTER VII.

THE chief object which the foreign Protestants had in
view in flying for refuge into England, was not, however, so much to follow industry as to be free to worship God according to conscience. For that they had
sacrificed all,—possessions, home, and country. Accordingly, no sooner did they settle in any place, than they
formed themselves into congregations for the purpose
of worshipping together. While their numbers were
small, they were content to meet in each other's houses,
or in workshops or other roomy places; but, as the
influx of refugees increased with the increase of persecution abroad, and as many pastors of eminence came
with them, the strangers besought the government
to grant them places for holding their worship in
public. This was willingly conceded; and as early
as the reign of Edward VI. churches were set apart
for their use in London, Norwich, Southampton, and
Canterbury.

The first Walloon and French churches in London
owed their origin to the young King Edward VI., and
to the protection of the Duke of Somerset and Archbishop Cranmer. On the 24th of July 1550, the King
issued royal letters patent, appointing John A'Lasco,
a learned Polish gentleman,[1] superintendent of the

---

[1] In 1544, John A'Lasco gave
up the office of provost of the
church of Gnezne, in Posen, of
which his uncle was archbishop,
to go and found a Protestant
church at Embden, in East Fries-

refugee Protestant churches in England ; and at the same time he assigned to such of the strangers as had settled in London the church in Austin Friars called the Temple of Jesus, wherein to hold their assemblies and celebrate their worship according to the custom of their country. Of this church Walter Deloen and Martin Flanders, François de la Riviere, and Richard François, were appointed the first ministers ; the two former, of the Dutch or Flemish part of the congregation, and the two latter, of the French. The King further constituted the superintendent and the ministers into a body politic, and placed them under the safeguard of the civil and ecclesiastical authorities of the kingdom.

But the number of refugees settled in London shortly became so great, that one church was found insufficient for their accommodation, although the Dutch and French met at alternate times during the day. In the course of a few months, therefore, a second place of worship was granted to the French-speaking section of the refugees ; and the church of St. Anthony's Hospital, in Threadneedle Street, was set apart for their use.[1]

---

land. An order of Charles V. obliged him to leave that town four years later; when he came over to England, in the year 1548, and placed himself in communication with Cecil, who recommended him to the Duke of Somerset and Archbishop Cranmer. During his residence in England, A'Lasco was actively engaged in propagating the new views. He established the first French printing-house in London for the publication of religious books, of which he produced many; and he also published others, written in French by Edward VI. himself. During the reign of Mary, when Protestantism in all its forms was temporarily suppressed, A'Lasco

fled for his life, and took refuge in Switzerland, where he died. The foreign churches in Austin Friars and Threadneedle Street were reopened on the accession of Elizabeth.

[1] Both these churches were subsequently destroyed by fire. The church in Austin Friars was burnt down quite recently, and has since been restored. The church in Threadneedle Street was burnt down during the great fire of London, and was afterwards rebuilt; but it has since been demolished to make way for the approaches to the new Royal Exchange, when it was removed to the new French church in St. Martin's-le-Grand. There were other foreign Pro-

Walloon and French congregations were also formed in various country places. The first of the Walloon churches out of London was that of Glastonbury, where a body of Flemish Protestants settled as early as the year 1550, under the protection of Archbishop Cranmer, the Duke of Somerset, and Sir William Cecil. They brought with them a well-known preacher, Valaren Pullen, and at once constituted themselves as a church. The Duke of Somerset advanced them money to buy wool, at the same time granting them small allotments of land from the Abbey domain. After the fall of the Duke, the weavers were taken under the protection of the Privy Council, and many papers relating to them are to be found in the State Paper Office; but when Mary succeeded to the throne, the little colony was broken up, and, accompanied by their pastor Pullen, they returned to the Continent, and eventually settled at Frankfort-on-the-Maine.

Another of the early Walloon churches was that of Winchelsea, formed in 1560; but it was of comparatively less importance than the others, inasmuch as, —the town being poor and decaying,—most of the refugees, shortly after landing there, proceeded inland to London, Canterbury, or the other places where settlements had already been formed. The Dutch church at Dover long continued to thrive, being fed by increasing immigrants from the opposite coast, until at length it became known as the French Church.

At Sandwich the old church of St. Peter's was set apart for the special use of the refugees; but, at the same time, they were enjoined not to dispute openly concerning their religion.[1] At Rye they were allowed

---

testant churches in London besides those of the Walloons and French,—such as the Spanish Protestants, who, though few in number, had a church of their own as early as 1559; and the Italian Protestants, who formed a congregation in the reign of

Edward VI., and continued to worship together during that of Elizabeth, after which they seem to have become merged in the French congregations.

[1] This church long continued to flourish. The Rev. Gerard de Gols, rector of St. Peter's, and

the use of the parish church during one part of the day, until a special place of worship could be provided for their accommodation. The Walloon church at Yarmouth was founded in 1568, and its members were mostly fishermen. Queen Elizabeth granted them a license to carry on their trade and to form a congregation; and they held their public worship in the building which had originally been the mansion of Thomas de Drayton, representative of the town in the time of Edward III. At Norwich, where the number of the settlers was greater in proportion to the population than in most other towns, the choir of Friars Preachers Church, on the east side of St. Andrew's Hall, was assigned for the use of the Dutch, and the Bishop's Chapel, afterwards the church of St. Mary's Tombland, was appropriated for the use of the French and Walloons.

Two of the most ancient and interesting of the churches founded by the refugees, are those of Southampton and Canterbury, both of which survive to this day. Southampton was resorted to at an early period by fugitives from religious persecution in Flanders and France. Many came from the Channel Islands, where they had first fled for refuge, on account of the proximity of these places to the French coast. This appears from the register of the Southampton church,— —a document of great interest, preserved amongst the records of the Registrar-General at Somerset House.

It is stated in Fallé's *History of Jersey,* that forty-two Protestant ministers of religion, besides a large number of lay families, passed over from France into Jersey in the reign of Elizabeth,—many of them before the massacre of Saint Bartholomew. And although the refugees for the most part regarded the Channel Islands as merely temporary places of refuge,—or as a sort

minister of the Dutch congregation in Sandwich between 1713 and 1737, was highly esteemed in his day as an author, and was so much respected by his fellow-townsmen that he was one of the persons selected by the corporation to support the canopies at the coronation of George II. and Queen Caroline,

of stepping-stone to England,—a sufficient number
remained to determine the Protestant character of
the community, and to completely transform the
islands by their industry; since which time, Jersey and
Guernsey, from being among the most backward and
miserable places on the face of the earth, have come to
be recognised as among the most happy and prosperous.

The first French church at Southampton, which was
so largely fed by arrivals from the Channel Islands,
was, like the two earliest foreign Protestant churches
in London, established in the reign of Edward VI.   An
old chapel in Winkle Street, near the harbour, called
Domus Dei, or "God's House," forming part of an
ancient hospital founded by two merchants in the time
of Henry III., was set apart for the accommodation
of the refugees.   The hospital and chapel had originally
been dedicated to St. Julian, the patron of travellers,
and was probably used in ancient times by pilgrims
passing through Southampton to and from the adjoining monastic establishments of Netley and Beaulieu,
and the famous shrines of Winchester, Wells, and
Salisbury.

There are no records of this early French church
beyond what can be gathered from their Register,[1]—
which, however, is remarkably complete and well preserved, and presents many points of curious interest.
The first entries are dated 1567, when the register
began to be kept.   From the first list of communicants
entered in that year, it appears that their number was
then only fifty-eight, of whom eight were distinguished
as "Anglois."   The callings of the members were
various, medical men being comparatively numerous;
whilst others are described as weavers, bakers, cutlers,
and brewers.   The places from which the refugees had

---

[1] "Register of the Church of St.
Julian, or God's House, of South-
ampton," in the Archives of the
Registrar-General at Somerset
House.

come are also given—those most frequently occurring being Valenciennes, Lisle, Dieppe, Gernése (Guernsey), and Jersé.

It further appears from the entries, that satisfactory evidence was required of the character and religious standing of the new refugees, who from time to time arrived from abroad, before they were admitted to the privileges of membership; the words "avec attestation," "témoinage par écrit," or simply "témoinage," being attached to a large number of names. Many of the fugitives, before they succeeded in making their escape, appear to have been forced to attend Mass; and their first care on landing seems to have been, to seek out the nearest pastor, confess their sin, and take the sacrament according to the rights of their Church. On the 3rd of July 1574 (more than a year after the massacre of St. Bartholomew) occurs this entry— "Tiebaut de Béfroi, his wife, his son, and his daughter, after having made their public acknowledgment of having been at the mass, were all received to the sacrament."

One of the most interesting portions of the register is the record of fasts and thanksgivings held at "God's House"; in the course of which we see the poor refugees anxiously watching the current of events abroad, deploring the increasing ferocity of their persecutors, praying God to bridle the strong and wicked men who sought to destroy His Church, and to give the help of His outstretched arm to its true followers and defenders. The first of such fasts (Jeûsnes) relates to the persecutions in the Netherlands by the Duke of Alva. It runs as follows :—"The year 1568, the 3rd day of September, was celebrated a public fast; the occasion was that Monseignor the Prince of Orange had descended from Germany into the Low Countries, to try with God's help to deliver the poor churches there from affliction; and now to beseech the Lord most fervently for the deliverance of His people, this fast was celebrated."

Another fast was held in 1570, on the occasion of the defeat of the Prince of Condé at the battle of Jarnac, when the little church of Southampton again beseeched help for their brethren against the calamities which threatened to overwhelm them. Two years later, on the 25th of September 1572, we find them again entreating help for the Prince of Orange, who had entered the Low Countries from Germany with a new army, to deliver the poor churches there from the hands of the Duke of Alva, " that cruel tyrant ; and also, principally, for that the churches of France have suffered a marvellous and extremely horrible calamity —a horrible massacre having been perpetrated at Paris on the 24th day of August last, in which a great number of nobles and of the faithful were killed in one night, about twelve or thirteen thousand ; preaching forbidden ; and all the property of the faithful given up to pillage throughout the kingdom. Now for the consolation of them and of the Low Countries, and to pray the Lord for their deliverance, was celebrated this solemn fast."

Other fasts were held, to pray God to maintain her Majesty the Queen in good friendship and accord with the Prince of Orange,[1] to uphold the Protestant churches in France, to stay the ravages of the plague, to comfort and succour the poor people of Antwerp, driven out of that city on its destruction by the Spaniards,[2] and to help and strengthen the churches of the refuge established in England. Several of these fasts were appointed to be held by the conference (colloque) of the churches, the meetings of which were held annually in London, Canterbury, Norwich, Southampton, and other places ; so that at the same time the same fast was being held in all the foreign churches throughout the kingdom.

In one case the shock of an earthquake is recorded. The entry runs as follows :—" The 28th of April, 1580,

---

[1] Fast, 29th August, 1576.   [2] Fast, 22nd November, 1576.

a fast was celebrated to pray God to preserve us
against His anger, since on the 6th of this month we
have been appalled by a great trembling of the earth,
which has not only been felt throughout all this kingdom, but also in Picardy and the Low Countries of
Flanders; as well as to preserve us against war and
plague, and to protect the poor churches of Flanders
and France against the assaults of their enemies,
who have joined their forces to the great army of
Spain for the purpose of working their destruction."
Another fast commemorates the appearance of a comet,
which was first seen on the 8th of October, and continued in sight until the 12th of December in the
year 1581.

A subsequent entry relates to the defeat of the great
Spanish Armada. On this occasion the little church
united in a public thanksgiving. The record is as
follows :—" The 29th of November, 1588, thanks were
publicly rendered to God for the wonderful dispersion
of the Spanish fleet, which had descended upon the
coast of England with the object of conquering the
kingdom and bringing it under the tyranny of the
Pope." And, on the 5th of December following,
another public fast was held, for the purpose of praying the Lord that He would be pleased to grant to
the churches of France and of Flanders a like happy
deliverance as had been vouchsafed to England. A
blessing was also sought upon the English navy,
which had put to flight the Armada of Spain.

In the midst of these events, Queen Elizabeth visited
Southampton with her court; on which occasion the
refugees sought to obtain access to her Majesty, to
thank her for the favour and protection which they
had enjoyed at her hands. They were unable to obtain
an interview with the Queen, until she had set out on
her way homeward, when a deputation of the refugees
waited for her outside the town and craved a brief
interview. This she graciously accorded, when their
spokesman thanked her for the tranquillity and rest

which they had enjoyed during the twenty-four years
that they had lived in the town; to which the Queen
replied very kindly, giving praise to God who had
given her the opportunity and the power of welcoming
and encouraging the poor foreigners.

A considerable proportion of the fasts relate to the
plague, which was a frequent and unwelcome visitor—
on one occasion sweeping away almost the entire settlement. In 1583, the communicants were reduced to
a very small number; but those who remained met
daily at " God's House" to pray for the abatement of
the pestilence. It returned again in 1604, and again
swept away a large proportion of the congregation,
which had considerably increased in the interval.
One hundred and sixty-one persons are set down as
having died of plague in that year, the number of
deaths amounting to four and five a-day.

The greater number of the inhabitants of Southampton abandoned their dwellings, and the clergy
seem to have accompanied them; for on the 23rd
of July, 1665, an English child was brought to the
French church to be baptized, by authority of the
mayor, and the ceremony was performed by M.
Courand, the pastor. Shortly after, M. Courand died
at his post, after registering with his own hand the
deaths of the greater part of his flock. On the 21st
of September, 1665, the familiar handwriting of the
pastor ceases, and the entry is made by another hand,
" *Monsieur Courand, notre pasteur—peste.*"

While death was thus busy, marrying and giving
in marriage went on. Some couples were so im-
patient to be united that they could not wait for the
return of the English clergy, who had left the town,
but hastened to be married by the French pastor at
" God's House," as we find from the register.

Another highly-interesting memorial of the asylum
given to the persecuted Protestants of Flanders and
France so many centuries ago, is presented by the
Walloon or French church which exists to this day

in Canterbury Cathedral. It was formed at a very early period—some suppose as early as the reign of Edward VI., like those of London and Southampton; though the first record preserved of its existence is early in the reign of Elizabeth. Shortly after the landings of the foreign Protestants at Sandwich and Rye, a body of them proceeded to Canterbury, and sought permission of the mayor and aldermen to settle in the place. They came principally from Lisle, Nuelle, Turcoing, Waterloo, Darmentières, and other places situated along the present French frontier.

The first arrivals of the fugitives consisted of eighteen families, led by their pastor, Hector Hamon, "minister verbi Dei." They are described as having landed at Rye, and temporarily settled at Winchelsea, from which place they had come across the country to Canterbury. Persecution had made these poor exiles very humble. All that they sought was freedom to worship and to labour. They had no thought but to pursue their several callings in peace and quiet—to bring up their children virtuously—and to lead a diligent, sober, and religious life, according to the dictates of their conscience. Men such as these are the salt of the earth at all times; yet they had been forced by a ruthless persecution from their homes, and driven forth as wanderers on the face of the earth.

In their memorial to the mayor and aldermen, in 1564, they set forth that they had, for the love of religion (which they earnestly desired to hold fast with a free conscience), relinquished their country and their worldly goods; and they humbly prayed that they might be permitted the free exercise of their religion within the city, and allowed the privilege of a temple to hold their worship in, together with a place of sepulture for their dead. They further requested that lest, under the guise of religion, profane and evil-minded men should seek to share in the privileges which they sought to obtain, none should be permitted to join them without giving satisfactory evidences of their probity of character. And, in order that the young persons belonging to their body might not remain untaught, they also asked permission to maintain a teacher, for the purpose of instructing them in the French tongue. Finally, they declared their intention of being industrious citizens, and of proceeding, under the favour and protection of the magistrates, to make Florence serges, bombazine, Orleans silk, bayes, mouquade, and other stuffs.[1]

Canterbury was fortunate in being appealed to by these fugitives for an asylum—bringing with them, as they did, skill, industry, and character. The authorities at once cheerfully granted all that they asked, in the terms of their own memorial. The mayor and aldermen gave them permission to carry on their trades within the precincts of the city. At the same time, the liberal-minded Matthew Parker, then Archbishop of Canterbury, with the sanction of the Queen, granted to the exiles the free use of the Under Croft of the cathedral, where "the gentle and profitable strangers," as the Archbishop styled them, not only celebrated their worship and taught their children, but set up their looms and carried on their industry.

The Under Croft, or Crypt, extends under the choir and high altar of Canterbury Cathedral, and is of considerable extent. The body of Thomas à Becket was buried first in the Under Croft, and lay there for fifty years, until it was translated with great ceremony to the sumptuous shrine prepared by Stephen Langton, his successor, at the east end of the cathedral. Part of the Under Croft, immediately under the cross aisle of the choir, was dedicated and endowed as a chapel by Edward the Black Prince; and another part of the area was enclosed by rich Gothic stone-work, and dedicated to the Virgin.[2]

---

[1] The memorial is given in the appendix to SOMNER'S *Antiquities of Canterbury.*

[2] Canterbury Cathedral contains an interesting Huguenot memorial of about the same date as the settlement of the Walloons in the Under Croft. The visitor

The Lady Undercroft Chapel was one of the most gorgeous shrines of its time. It was so rich and of such high esteem, that Somner says, " The sight of it was debarred to the vulgar, and reserved only for persons of great quality." Erasmus, who by special favour (Archbishop Warham recommending him) was brought to the sight of it, describes it thus :—" There," said he, " the Virgin-mother hath a habitation, but somewhat dark, inclosed with a double sept or rail of iron, for fear of thieves. For indeed I never saw a thing more laden with riches. Lights being brought, we saw a more than royal spectacle. In beauty it far surpasseth that of Walsingham. This chapel is not showed but to noblemen and especial friends." [1] Over the statue of the Virgin, which was in pure gold, there was a royal purple canopy, starred with jewels and precious stones ; and a row of silver lamps was suspended from the roof in front of the shrine.

All these decorations were, however, removed by Henry VIII., who took possession of the greater part of the gold and silver jewels of the cathedral, and had them converted into money. The Under Croft became

---

to the cathedral observes behind the high altar, near the tomb of the Black Prince, a coffin of brick plastered over, in the form of a sarcophagus. It contains the ashes of Cardinal Odo Coligny, brother of the celebrated Admiral Coligny, who was one of the first victims to the massacre of St. Bartholomew. In 1568, the cardinal visited Queen Elizabeth, who received him with marked respect, and lodged him sumptuously at Sheen. Three years later he died at Canterbury after a brief illness. Strype, and nearly all subsequent writers, allege that he died of poison, administered by one of his attendants because of his supposed conversion to Protestantism. From a full report of his death made to Burghley and Leicester, preserved in the State Paper Office, there does not, however, appear sufficient ground for the popular belief. His body was not interred, but was placed in the brick coffin behind the high altar, in order that it might be the more readily removed for interment in the family vault in France, when the religious troubles which then prevailed had come to an end. But the massacre of St. Bartholomew shortly followed ; the Coligny family were then almost destroyed ; and hence the body of Odo Coligny has not been buried to this day.

[1] SOMNER. — *Antiquities of Canterbury,* 1703. p 97.

deserted; the chapels it contained were disused; and it remained merely a large, vaulted, ill-lighted area, until permission was granted to the Walloons to use it by turns as a weaving-shed, a school, and a church. Over the capitals of the columns on the north side of the crypt are several texts of Scripture taken from the Psalms, the Proverbs, and the New Testament, —still to be seen in old French, written up for the benefit of the scholars, and doubtless taught to them by heart.

Desolate, gloomy, and sepulchral though the place might seem—with the ashes of former archbishops and dignitaries of the cathedral mouldering under their feet,—the exiles were thankful for the refuge it afforded them in their time of need, and they daily made the vaults resound with their prayer and praise. Morning and night they " sang the Lord's song in a strange land, and wept when they remembered Zion."

The refugees worked, worshipped, and prospered. They succeeded in maintaining themselves; they supported their own poor; and they were able, out of their small means, to extend a helping hand to the fugitives who continued to arrive in England, still fleeing from the persecutions in Flanders and France. Every corner of the Under Croft was occupied; and so many fresh immigrants continued to join them, that the place was soon found too small for their accommodation.

Somner, writing in 1639, thus refers to the exiles:—
" Let me now lead you to the Under Croft—a place fit, and haply (as one cause) fitted to keep in memory the subterraneous temples of the primitives, in the times of persecution. The west part whereof, being spacious and lightsome, for many years hath been the strangers' church : a congregation for the most part of distressed exiles, grown so great, and yet daily multiplying, that the place in short time is likely to prove a hive too little to contain such a swarm."

The Huguenot exiles remained unmolested in the exercise of their worship until the advent of Charles I.

as King of England, and of Laud as Archbishop of Canterbury. An attempt was then made to compel the refugees, who were for the most part Calvinists, to conform to the Anglican ritual. The foreign congregations appealed to the King, pleading the hospitality extended to them by the nation when they had fled from Papal persecution abroad, and the privileges and exemptions granted to them by Edward VI., which had been confirmed by Elizabeth and James, and even by Charles I. himself. The utmost concession that the King would grant was, that those who were born aliens might still enjoy the use of their own church service; but that all their children born in England should regularly attend the parish churches. Even this small concession was limited only to the congregation at Canterbury, and measures were taken to enforce conformity in the other dioceses.

The refugees thus found themselves exposed to an Anglican persecution, instead of a Papal one. Rather than endure it, several thousands of them left the country, abandoning their new homes, and again risking the loss of everything, in preference to giving up their views as to religion. About a hundred and forty families emigrated from Norwich into Holland, where the Dutch received them hospitably, and gave them house-accommodation free, with exemption from taxes for seven years, during which they instructed the natives in the woollen manufacture, of which they had before been ignorant. But the greater number of the exiles emigrated with their families to North America, and swelled the numbers of the little colony already formed in Massachusetts Bay, which eventually laid the foundation of the New England States.

After the lapse of a few years, the reactionary course upon which Charles I. and Archbishop Laud had entered, was summarily checked. The foreign refugees were again permitted to worship God according to conscience, and the right of free asylum in England was again recognised and established.

9

CHAPTER VIII.

THE immigrations of foreign Protestants into England in a great measure ceased towards the end of the sixteenth century. In Flanders, the Protestants had for the most part been killed or expatriated, and their persecutors were left to enjoy their triumph amidst ruins. France also experienced a period of temporary repose. The ferocious wars of the League had been terminated by the accession of Henry of Navarre, the Huguenot leader, to the French crown,—on which both parties laid down their arms for a time. Nothing seemed to be wanting to secure the permanent unity and peace of the kingdom but the acceptance by the King of the religion of the majority; and to accomplish this great object, Henry conformed, or pretended to conform,—making his public abjuration of the Protestant faith in the church of St. Denis, on the 25th of July 1593.

In that age of assassination, Henry was probably influenced by the consideration that, unless he made his peace with the Romish Church, his life was in daily peril. Besides, religion formed no part of his genuine character. Although, as a king, he was magnanimous, large-hearted, and brave; in his private life, he was profligate and sensual. He had been a Huguenot for political, rather than religious reasons; and for political reasons he ceased to be a Huguenot, and became a Roman Catholic. But it was a mistake on his part to suppose that his life was safer after his recantation than before. On the contrary, it was placed in still greater peril; and his speedy assassination was predicted on the very day of his pretended conversion, A member of the Grand Council, himself a zealous Roman Catholic, immediately on Henry's abjuration, whispered to a friend,—" The King is lost! He is killable from this hour; before he was not."[1]

One of Henry's justest and greatest acts was the promulgation by him, in 1598, of the celebrated Edict of Nantes. By that edict the Huguenots, after sixty years of persecution, were allowed at last comparative liberty of conscience and freedom of worship. What the Roman Catholics thought of it, may be inferred from the protest of Pope Clement VIII., who wrote to Henry to say, that "a decree which gave liberty of conscience to all was *the most accursed that had ever been made."*

From the date of that edict, persons of the Reformed Faith were admitted to public employment; their children were allowed access to the schools and universities; they were provided with equal representation in some of the provincial parliaments, and permitted to hold a certain number of places of surety in the kingdom. And thus was a treaty of peace established for a time between the people of the contending faiths throughout France.

But though Henry IV. governed France ably and justly for a period of sixteen years, his enemies, the Jesuits, never forgave him, nor did his apostasy avert their vengeance. After repeated attempts made upon his life by their emissaries, he was eventually assassinated by Francis Ravaillac, a lay brother of the monastery of St. Bernard, on the 14th of May 1610.

Although the edicts of toleration were formally proclaimed by Henry's successor, they were practically disregarded and violated. Marie de Medicis, the queen-regent, was, like all of her race, the bitter

---

[1] *Memoires de L'Estoile,*

enemy of Protestantism. She was governed by Italian
favourites, who inspired her policy. They distributed
amongst themselves the public treasures with so lavish
a hand, that the Parisians rose in insurrection against
them, murdered Concini, whom the queen had created
Marshal d'Ancre, and afterwards burned his wife as a
sorceress; the young king, Louis XIII., then only about
sixteen years old, joining in the atrocities.

Civil war shortly broke out between the court and
the country factions, which soon became embittered
by the old religious animosities. There was a great
massacre of the Huguenots in Bearn, where their
worship was suppressed, and the Roman Catholic
priests were installed in their places. Other massacres
followed, and occasioned general alarm among the
Protestants. In those towns where they were the
strongest, they shut their gates against the King's
forces, and determined to resist force by force. In
1621 the young King set out with his army to reduce
the revolted towns, and first attacked St. Jean d'Angely,
which he captured after a siege of twenty-six days.
He next assailed Montauban, but, after a siege of two
months, he retired from the place defeated, with tears
in his eyes.

In 1622, the King called to his councils Armand
Duplessis de Richelieu, the Queen's favourite adviser,
whom the Pope had recently presented with a cardinal's hat. His force of character was soon felt, and
in all affairs of government the influence of Richelieu
became supreme. One of the first objects to which he
applied himself, was the suppression of the anarchy
which prevailed throughout France, occasioned in a
great measure by the abuse of the feudal powers still
exercised by the ancient noblesse. Another object
which he considered essential to the unity and power
of France, was the annihilation of the Protestants as
a *political* party. Accordingly, shortly after his accession to office, he advised the attack of Rochelle, the
head-quarters of the Huguenots—then regarded as

the citadel of Protestantism in France. His advice was followed, and a powerful army was assembled and marched on the doomed place—Richelieu combining in himself the functions of bishop, prime-minister, and commander-in-chief. The Huguenots of Rochelle defended themselves with great bravery for more than a year, during which they endured the greatest privations. But their resistance was in vain. On the 28th of October, 1628, Richelieu rode into Rochelle by the King's side, in velvet and cuirass, at the head of the royal army; after which he proceeded to perform high mass in the church of St. Margaret, in celebration of his victory.

The siege of Rochelle, while in progress, excited much interest among the Protestants throughout England; and anxious appeals were made to Charles I. to send help to the besieged. This he faithfully promised to do; and he despatched a fleet and army to their assistance, commanded by his favourite the Duke of Buckingham. The fleet duly arrived off Rochelle; and the army landed on the Isle of Rhé, but were driven back to their ships with great slaughter. Buckingham attempted nothing further on behalf of the Rochellese. He returned to England with a disgraced flag and a murmuring fleet, amidst the general discontent of the people. A second expedition sailed for the relief of the place, under the command of the Earl of Lindsay; but though the fleet arrived in sight of Rochelle, it sailed back to England without making any attempt on its behalf. The popular indignation rose to a greater height even than before. It was bruited abroad, and generally believed, that both expeditions had been a mere blind on the part of Charles I., and that, acting under the influence of his queen, Henrietta Maria, sister of the French king, he had never really intended that Rochelle should be relieved. However this might be, the failure was disgraceful; and when, in later years, the unfortunate Charles was brought to trial by his subjects, the abor-

tive Rochelle expeditions were bitterly remembered
against him.

Meanwhile Cardinal Richelieu was vigorously prosecuting the war against the Huguenots, wherever
they stood in arms against the King. His operations
were uniformly successful. The Huguenots were
everywhere overthrown, and in the course of a few
years they had ceased to exist as an armed power in
France. Acting in a wise and tolerant spirit, Richelieu
refrained from pushing his advantage to an extremity;
and when all resistance was over, he advised the King
to issue an edict, granting them freedom of worship
and other privileges. The astute statesman was doubtless induced to adopt this course by considerations of
state policy, for he had by this time entered into a league
with the Swedish and German Protestant powers, for
the humiliation of the house of Austria; and with that
object he sought to enlist the co-operation of the King's
Protestant as well as Roman Catholic subjects. The
result was, that, in 1629, "the Edict of Pardon" was
issued by Louis XIII., granting to the Protestants
various rights and privileges, together with liberty of
worship and equality before the law.

From this time forward, the Huguenots ceased to
exist as a political party, and were distinguished from
the rest of the people by their religion only. Being
no longer available for purposes of faction, many
of the nobles, who had been their leaders, fell away
from them and rejoined the Roman Catholic Church;
though a large number of the smaller gentry, the merchants, manufacturers, and skilled workmen, remained
Protestants. Their loyal conduct fully justified the
indulgences granted to them by Richelieu; and these
were confirmed by his successor Mazarin. Repeated
attempts were made to involve them in the civil broils
of the time, but they sternly kept aloof, and if they
took up arms, it was on the side of the government.
When, in 1632, the Duke of Montmorency sought,
for factious purposes, to re-awaken religious passion

in Languedoc, of which he was governor, the Huguenots refused to join him.   The Protestant inhabitants
of Montauban even offered to march against him.
During the wars of the Fronde, they sided with the
King against the factions.   Even the inhabitants of
Rochelle supported the regent against their own governor.   Cardinal Mazarin, then prime-minister, frankly
acknowledged the loyalty of the Huguenots.   " I have
no cause," he said, " to complain of the little flock; if
they browse on bad herbage, at least they do not stray
away."   Louis XIV. himself, at the commencement of
his reign, formally thanked them for the consistent
manner in which they had withstood the invitations
of powerful chiefs to resist the royal authority; while,
at the same time, he professed to confirm them in the
enjoyment of their rights and privileges.

The Protestants, however, continued to labour under
many disabilities.   They were in a great measure excluded from civil office and from political employment.
They accordingly devoted themselves for the most
part to industrial pursuits.   They were acknowledged
to be the best agriculturists, wine-growers, merchants,
and manufacturers in France.   " At all events," said
Ambrose Paré, one of the most industrious men of his
time, " posterity will not be able to charge us with
idleness."   No heavier crops were grown in France
than on the farms in Bearn and the south-western
provinces.   In Languedoc, the cantons inhabited by
the Protestants were the best cultivated and the most
productive.   The slopes of the Aigoul and the Eperon
were covered with their flocks and herds.   The valley
of Vaunage, in the diocese of Nismes, where they had
more than sixty temples, was celebrated for the rich-
ness of its vegetation, and was called by its inhabitants
" the Little Canaan."   The vinedressers of Berri and
the Pays Messin, on the Moselle, restored these districts to more than their former prosperity; and the
diligence, skill, and labour with which they subdued
the stubborn soil and made it yield its increase of

flowers and fruits and corn and wine, bore witness in all quarters to the toil and energy of the men of The Religion.

The Huguenots of the towns were similarly industrious and enterprising. At Tours and Lyons they prosecuted the silk manufacture with great success. They made taffetas, velvets, brocades, ribbons, and cloth of gold and silver, of finer qualities than were produced in any other country in Europe. They also carried on the manufacture of fine cloth in various parts of France, and exported their articles in large quantities to Germany, Spain, and England. They established linen manufactories at Vire, Falaise, and Argentine, in Normandy; manufactories of bleached cloth at Morlaix, Landerman, and Brest, and of sail-cloth at Rennes, Nantes, and Vitré, in Brittany;—the greater part of their productions being exported to Holland and England.

The Huguenots also carried on large manufactories of paper in Auvergne and the Angoumois. In the latter province they had no fewer than six hundred paper-mills; the article they produced being considered the best in Europe. The mills at Ambert supplied the paper on which the choicest books, emanating from the presses of Paris, as well as of Amsterdam and London, were printed. The celebrated leather of Touraine, and the hats of Caudebec, were almost exclusively produced by Protestant manufacturers; who also successfully carried on, at Sedan, the fabrication of articles of iron and steel, which were exported abroad in large quantities.

Perhaps one reason why the Huguenots were so successful in conducting these great branches of industry, consisted in the fact that their time was so much less broken in upon by saints' days and festival-days, and that their labour was thus much more continuous, and consequently more effective, than in the case of the Roman Catholic portion of the population. Besides this, however, the Protestants were almost of necessity

men of stronger character; for they had to swim
against the stream and hold to their convictions in
the face of obloquy, opposition, and often of active persecution. The sufferings they had endured for religion
in the past, and perhaps the presentiment of heavier
trials in the future, made them habitually grave and
solemn in their demeanour. Their morals were severe,
and their piety was considered rigid. Their enemies
called them sour and fanatical, but no one called in
question their honesty and their integrity.[1]

"If the Nismes merchants," wrote Baville, Intendant
of that province, one of the bitterest persecutors of the
Protestants, "are bad Catholics, at any rate they have
not ceased to be very good traders." The Huguenot's
word was as good as his bond, and to be "honest as
a Huguenot" passed into a proverb. This quality of
integrity—which is so essential to the merchant, who
deals with foreigners whom he never sees—so characterised the business transactions of the Huguenots,
that the foreign trade of the country fell almost entirely into their hands. The English and Dutch were
always found more ready to open a correspondence
with them than with the Roman Catholic merchants;
although religious affinity may possibly have had some
influence in determining the preference. And thus at
Bordeaux, at Rouen, at Caen, at Metz, at Nismes, and
the other great centres of commerce, the foreign business of France came to be almost entirely conducted
by Huguenot merchants.

The enlightened minister Colbert gave every encouragement to these valuable subjects. Entertaining
the conviction that the strength of states consisted in
the number, the intelligence, and the industry of their

---

[1] It is worthy of note, that
while the Huguenots were stig-
matised in contemporary Roman
Catholic writings as "heretics,"
"atheists," "blasphemers," "mon-
sters vomited forth of hell," and
the like ; not a word is to be
found in them as to their morality
and integrity of character. The
silence of their enemies on this
head is perhaps the most eloquent
testimony in their favour.

citizens, he laboured in all ways to give effect to this idea.[1] He encouraged the French to extend their manufactures; and at the same time he held out inducements to skilled foreign artizans to settle in the kingdom and establish new branches of industry. His invitation was accepted, and considerable numbers of Dutch and Walloon Protestants came across the frontier, and settled as cloth manufacturers in the northern provinces.

Colbert was the friend, so far as he dared to be, of the Huguenots, whose industry he encouraged as the most effective means of enriching France, and enabling the nation to recover from the injuries inflicted upon it by the devastations and persecutions of the preceding century. With that object he granted privileges, patents, monopolies, bounties, and honours, after the old-fashioned method of protecting industry. Some of these expedients were more harassing than prudent. One merchant, when consulted by Colbert as to the best means of encouraging commerce, answered curtly —" *Laissez faire et laissez passer :* " " Let us alone,

---

[1] Some of the measures adopted by Colbert to increase the population, and to supply the loss of life occasioned by war, were of a remarkable character. Thus, in 1666, a decree was issued for the purpose of encouraging early marriages and the rearing of large families. The preamble of this decree set forth that matrimony being " the fertile source of the power and greatness of states," it was desirable that certain privileges should be granted for its encouragement. Accordingly, it was decreed that all young married men were to be wholly exempted from taxation until their twenty-fifth year, as well as all fathers of families of ten children and upwards. A further premium on the rearing of large families was offered in the form of an actual pension to the fathers, of 1000 livres for ten children, and 2000 livres for twelve. At first such pensions were only offered to the nobles, but two years later they were extended to plebeians of every degree. This law continued in force until 1683, when it was abolished by another royal decree, in which it was stated that the privileges and pensions granted for the encouragement of matrimony and of large families had to be repealed " on account of the frauds and abuses which they had occasioned.'' All that remained of Colbert's scheme, was the famous Hôpital des Enfants-trouvés, which continues to the present day.

and let our goods pass,"—a piece of advice which was
not at that time either understood or followed.

Colbert also applied himself to the improvement of
the internal communications of the country. With
his active assistance and co-operation, Riquet de Bon-
repos was enabled to construct the magnificent canal
of Languedoc, which connected the Bay of Biscay
with the Mediterranean. He restored the old roads
of the country, and constructed new ones. He established free ports, sent consuls to the Levant, and
secured a large trade with the Mediterranean. He
bought Dunkirk and Mardyke from Charles II. of
England, to the disgust of the English people. He
founded dockyards at Brest, Toulon, and Rochefort.
He created the French navy ; and instead of possessing only a few old ships lying rotting in the harbours,
in the course of thirty years France came to possess
190 vessels, of which 120 were ships of the line.

Colbert was withal an honest man. His predecessor
Mazarin had amassed enormous wealth, whilst Colbert
died possessed of a modest fortune, the fruits of long
labour and rigid economy. His administration of the
finances was admirable. When he assumed office, the
state was over-burdened by debt, and all but bankrupt.
The public books were in a state of inextricable con-
fusion. His first object was to get rid of the debt by
an arbitrary composition, which was tantamount to an
act of bankruptcy. He simplified the public accounts,
economised the collection of taxes, cut off unnecessary
expenditure, and reduced the direct taxation—placing
his chief dependence upon indirect taxes on articles of
consumption. After thirty years' labour, he succeeded
in raising the revenue from thirty-two millions of livres
to ninety-two millions net,—one-half only of the increase being due to additional taxation, the other half
to better order and economy in the collection.

At the same time, Colbert was public-spirited and
generous. He encouraged literature and the arts, as
well as agriculture and commerce. He granted

£160,000 in pensions to men of letters and science, amongst whom we meet with the names of the two Corneilles, Molière, Racine, Perrault, and Mezerai. Nor did he confine his liberality to the distinguished men of France, for he was equally liberal to foreigners who had settled in the country. Thus Huyghens, the distinguished Dutch natural philosopher, and Vossius, the geographer, were among his list of pensioners. He granted £208,000 to the Gobelins and other manufactures in Paris, besides other donations to those in the provinces. He munificently supported the Paris Observatories, and contributed to found the Academy of Inscriptions, the Academy of Sciences, and the Academy of Painting and Sculpture. In short, Colbert was one of the most enlightened, sagacious, liberal, and honourable ministers who ever served a monarch or a nation.

But behind the splendid *ordonnances* of Colbert, there stood a superior power—the master of France himself, Louis XIV.—"the Most Christian King." Richelieu and Mazarin had, by crushing all other powers in the state—nobles, parliament, and people —prepared the way for the reign of this most absolute and uncontrolled of French monarchs.[1] He was proud, ambitious, fond of power, and believed himself to be the greatest of men. He would have everything to centre in the king's majesty. At the death of Mazarin in 1661, when his ministers asked to whom they were thenceforward to address themselves, his reply was —"A moi." The well-known saying—"L'état, c'est moi," belongs to him. His people took him at his word. Rank, talent, and beauty bowed down before

---

[1] The engrained absolutism and egotism of Louis XIV., M. Feuillet contends, were at their acme from his earliest years. In the public library at St. Petersburg, under a glass case, may be seen one of the copybooks in which he practised writing when a child. Instead of such maxims as "Evil communications corrupt good manners," or "Virtue is its own reward," the copy set for him was this : "Les rois font tout ce qu'ils veulent."—*Edin. Review.*

him : they even vied with each other who should bow
the lowest.

While Colbert was striving to restore the finances
of France by the peaceful development of its industry,
this magnificent king, with a mind far above mercantile considerations, was bent on achieving glory by the
conquest of adjoining territories. Thus, while his
minister was, in 1668, engaged in organising a commercial system, Louis wrote to Charles II. with the
air of an Alexander the Great :—" If the English are
satisfied to be the merchants of the world, and leave
me to conquer it, the matter can easily be arranged ;
of the commerce of the globe, three parts to England,
and one part to France."[1] Nor was this a mere whim
of the King ; it was the fixed idea of his life.

Louis went to war with Spain. He overran Flanders, won victories, and France paid for the glory
in augmented taxation. He next made war with
Holland. There were more battles, less glory, but the
same inevitable increase of taxes. War in Germany
followed, during which there were the great sieges of
Besançon, Salin, and Dôle ; though this time there was
no glory. Again Colbert was appealed to for money ;
but France had already been taxed almost to the utmost.
The King told the minister, in 1673, that he must find
sixty millions of livres more ; "if he did not, *another
would.*" Thus the war had become a question mainly
of money, and the money Colbert *must* find. Forced
loans were then had recourse to, the taxes were increased, honours and places were sold, and the money
was eventually raised.

The extravagance of Louis knew no bounds. Versailles was pulled down, and rebuilt at enormous cost.
Immense sums were lavished in carrying out the designs of Vauban. France became surrounded with a
belt of three hundred fortresses. Various other spend-
thrift schemes were set on foot, until Louis had accu-

---

[1] MIGNET—*Negoc. de la Succcss. d'Esp.* iii. 63.

mulated a debt equal to £100,000,000 sterling. Colbert at last succumbed, crushed in body and mind. He died in 1683, worn out with toil, mortified and heartbroken at the failure of all his plans. The people, enraged at the taxes which oppressed them, laid the blame at the door of the minister ; and his corpse was buried at night, attended by a military escort to protect it from the fury of the mob.

Colbert did not live to witness the more disgraceful events which characterised the latter part of the reign of Louis XIV. The wars which that monarch waged with Spain, Germany, and Holland, for conquest and glory, were carried on against men with arms in their hands, capable of defending themselves. But the wars which he waged against his own subjects—the dragonnades and persecutions which preceded and followed the revocation of the edict of Nantes, of which the victims were defenceless men, women, and children—were simply ferocious and barbarous, and cannot fail in the long run to attach the reputation of *Infamous* to the name of Louis XIV., in history miscalled " The Great."

CHAPTER IX.

ONE of the first acts of Louis XIV. on assuming the supreme control of affairs at the death of Mazarin, was significant of his future policy with regard to the Huguenots. Among the representatives of the various public bodies who came to tender him their congratulations, there appeared a deputation of Protestant ministers, headed by their president Vignole. The King refused to receive them, and directed that they should leave Paris forthwith. Louis was not slow to follow up this intimation with measures of a more positive kind. He had been carefully taught to hate Protestantism ; and now that he possessed unrestrained power, he entertained the notion of compelling the Huguenots to abandon their religious convictions, and adopt his own. His minister Louvois wrote to the governors throughout the provinces—"His Majesty will not suffer any person in his kingdom but those who are of *his* religion ;" and orders were shortly after issued that Protestantism must cease to exist, and that the Huguenots must everywhere conform to the Royal Will.

A series of edicts was accordingly published with the object of carrying the King's purpose into effect. The conferences of the Protestants were declared to be suppressed. Though worship was still permitted in their churches, the singing of psalms in private dwellings was ordered to be forbidden. Spies were sent amongst them to report the terms on which the Huguenot pastors spoke of the Roman Catholic religion, and if any fault could be found with them they were cited before the tribunals for blasphemy. The priests were authorised to enter the chambers of sick Protestants, and entreat them whether they would be converted or die in heresy. Protestant children were invited to declare themselves against the religion of their parents. Boys of fourteen and girls of twelve years old might, on embracing Roman Catholicism, become enfranchised and entirely free from parental control. In such cases, the parents were further required to place and maintain their children in any Roman Catholic school into which they might desire to enter.

The Huguenots were again debarred from holding public offices; though a few, such as Marshal Turenne and Admiral Duquesne, who were Protestants, broke through this barrier by the splendour of their services to the state. In some provinces, the exclusion was so severe that a profession of the Roman Catholic faith was required from simple artizans—shoemakers, carpenters, and the like—before they were permitted to labour at their callings.[1]

Colbert, while he lived, endeavoured to restrain the King, and to abate the intolerable persecutions which dogged the Huguenots at every step. He continued to employ them in the departments of finance, finding no honester nor abler servants. He also encouraged the merchants and manufacturers to persevere in their industrial operations, which he regarded as essential to the prosperity and well-being of the kingdom. He took the opportunity of cautioning the King lest the

---

[1] A ludicrous instance of this occurred at Paris, where the corporation of laundresses laid a remonstrance before the council that their community, having been instituted by St. Louis, could not admit heretics, and this reclamation was gravely confirmed by a decree of the 21st August, 1665. The corporation nevertheless notoriously contained many abandoned women, but the orthodox laundresses were more distressed by heresy than by profligacy.—DE FELICE, *History of the Protestants of France.*

measures he was enforcing might tend, if carried out,
to the impoverishment of France and the aggrandise-
ment of her rivals. " I am sorry to say it," said he to
Louis, " that too many of your Majesty's subjects are
already amongst your neighbours as footmen and valets
for their daily bread ; many of the artizans, too, are
fled from the severity of your collectors; they are at
this time improving the manufactures of your enemies." But all Colbert's expostulations were in vain.
The Jesuits were stronger than he was, and the King
was in their hands. Besides, Colbert's power was on
the decline; he too had to succumb to the will of his
royal master, who would not relieve even the highest
genius from that absolute submission which he required
from his courtiers.

In 1666, the Queen-mother died, leaving to her son,
as her last bequest, that he should suppress and
exterminate Heresy within his dominions. The King
knew that he had often grieved his royal mother by
his notorious licentiousness, and he was now ready to
atone for the wickedness of his past life, by obeying
her wishes. The Bishop of Meaux exhorted him to
press on in the path his sainted mother had pointed
out to him. " O kings !" said he, " exercise your power
boldly, for it is divine—ye are gods ! " Louis was not
slack to obey the injunction, which so completely fell
in with his own ideas of royal omnipotence.

The Huguenots had already taken alarm at the
renewal of the persecution, and such of them as could
readily dispose of their property and goods, were
beginning to leave the kingdom for the purpose of
establishing themselves in other countries. To prevent
this, the King issued an edict forbidding French subjects to proceed abroad without express permission,
under the penalty of confiscation of their goods and
property. This was followed by a succession of severe
measures for the conversion or extirpation of such of
the Protestants—in number about a million and a
half—as had not by this time contrived to make their

10

escape from the kingdom. The kidnapping of Protestant children was actively set on foot by the agents of Roman Catholic priests; and the parents were subjected to heavy penalties if they ventured to complain. Orders were issued to pull down certain Protestant places of worship, and as many as eighty were destroyed in one diocese.

The Huguenots offered no resistance. All that they did was to meet together, and pray that the King's heart might yet be softened towards them. Blow upon blow followed. Protestants were forbidden to print books without the authority of magistrates of the Romish Communion. Protestant teachers were interdicted from teaching children anything but reading, writing, and arithmetic. Such pastors as held meetings amid the ruins of the churches which had been pulled down, were condemned to do penance with a rope round their neck, after which they were banished from the kingdom. Protestants were only allowed to bury their dead at daybreak or at nightfall. They were prohibited from singing psalms on land or on water, in workshops or in dwellings. If a priestly procession passed one of their churches while psalms were being sung, they must stop instantly, on pain of fine of the congregation, and imprisonment of the officiating minister.

In short, from the pettiest annoyance to the most exasperating cruelty, nothing was wanting on the part of the Most Christian King and his abettors. Their intention probably was to exasperate the Huguenots into open resistance, with the object of finding a pretext for a second massacre of St. Bartholemew. But the Huguenots would not be exasperated. They bore their trials bravely and patiently, hoping and praying that the King's heart would relent, and that they might yet be permitted to worship God according to conscience.

All their patience and resignation were in vain. From day to day the persecution became more oppressive and intolerable. In the intervals of his scandalous

amours, the King held conferences with his spiritual
directors, to whom he was from time to time driven
by bilious disease and the fear of death. He forsook
Madame de La Vallière for Madame de Montespan,
and Madame de Montespan for Madame de Maintenon,
ever and anon taking counsel with his Jesuit confessor
Père La Chaise. Madame de Maintenon was the instrument of the latter, and between the two the "conversion" of the King was believed to be imminent.
In his recurring attacks of illness, his conscience
became increasingly uneasy. Confessor and mistress
co-operated in turning his moroseness to account, and
it was observed that every royal attack of bile was
followed by some new edict of persecution against the
Huguenots.

Madame de Maintenon, the last favourite, was the
widow of Scarron, the deformed wit and scoffer. She
belonged to the celebrated Huguenot family of
D'Aubigny, her grandfather having been one of the
most devoted followers of Henry IV. Her father led
a profligate life, but she herself was brought up in the
family faith. A Roman Catholic relative, however,
acting on the authority conferred by the royal edict,
of abducting Protestant children, had the girl forcibly
conveyed to the convent of Ursulines at Niort, from
which she was transferred to the Ursulines at Paris,
where, after some resistance, she abjured her faith and
became a Roman Catholic. She left the convent to
enter the world through Scarron's door. When the
witty cripple married her, he said, "his bride had
brought with her an annual income of four louis, two
large and very mischievous eyes, a fine bust, an exquisite pair of hands, and a large amount of wit."

Scarron's house was the resort of the gayest and
loosest, as well as the most accomplished persons of the
time. There his young wife acquired that knowledge
of the world, conversational accomplishment, and probably social ambition, which she afterwards turned so
artfully and unscrupulously to account. One of her

intimate friends was the notorious Ninon de l'Enclos; and it is not improbable that the appearance of that woman, courted by the fashionable world after thirty years of polished profligacy, exercised a powerful influence on the subsequent career of Madame Scarron.

At Scarron's death, his young widow succeeded in obtaining the post of governess to the children of Madame de Montespan, the King's then mistress, whom she speedily superseded. She secured a footing in the King's chamber, to the exclusion of the Queen, who was dying by inches,[1] and by her adroitness, tact, and pretended devotion, she contrived to exercise an extraordinary influence over Louis,—so much so, that at length even the priests could only obtain access to him through her. She undertook to assist them in effecting his "conversion," and laboured at the work four hours a day, reporting progress from time to time to Père la Chaise, his confessor. She early discovered the King's rooted hatred towards the Huguenots, and conformed herself to it accordingly, increasing her influence over him by artfully fanning the flames of his fury against her quondam co-religionists; and fiercer and fiercer edicts were issued against them in quick succession.

Before the extremest measures were resorted to, however, an attempt was made to buy over the Protestants wholesale. The King consecrated to this traffic one-third of the revenue of the benefices which fell to the Crown during the period of their vacancy; and the fund became very large through the benefices having been purposely left vacant. A "converted" Huguenot named Pelisson was employed to administer the fund. He published long lists of "conversions" in the *Gazette*; but he concealed the fact that the takers of

---

[1] Le roi tua la reine, comme Colbert, sans s'en apercevoir. . . . . Elle mourut (30 juillet 1683). Madame de Maintenon la quittait expirée et sortait de la chambre, lorsque M. de la Rochefoucauld la prit par les bras, lui dit: "Le roi a besoin de vous." Et il la poussa chez le roi. A l'instant tous les deux partirent pour Saint-Cloud.—MICHELET, *Louis XIV.*, 273-4.

his bribes belonged to the dregs of the people. At length many were detected undergoing " conversion " several times over; upon which a proclamation was published, that persons found guilty of this offence would have their goods and property forfeited, and be sentenced to perpetual banishment.

The great body of the Huguenots remaining immovable and refusing to be converted, it was found necessary to resort to more violent measures. They were attacked through their affections. Children of seven years old were empowered to leave their parents and become converted; and many were forcibly abducted from their homes, and immured in convent-prisons, for education in the Romish faith at the expense of their parents. Another exquisite stroke of cruelty followed. While such Huguenots as conformed were declared to be exempt from supplying quarters for the soldiery, the obstinate and unconverted were ordered to have an extra number quartered on them.

Louvois, the King's minister, wrote to Marillac, Intendant of Poitou, in March 1681, that he was about to send a regiment of horse into that province. " His Majesty," he said, " has heard with much joy of the great number of persons who continue to be converted in your department. He wishes you to persist in your endeavours, and desires that the greater number of horsemen and officers should be billeted upon the Protestants. If, according to a just distribution, ten would be quartered upon the members of the Reformed religion, you may order them to accommodate twenty." This was the first attempt at the Dragonnades.

Two years later, in 1683, the military executions began. Pity, terror, and anguish had by turns agitated the minds of the Protestants, until at length they were reduced to a state of despair. Their life was made intolerable. Every career was closed against them. Protestants of the working class were under the necessity of abjuring or starving. The mob, observing that the Protestants were no longer within the pale of the

law, took the opportunity of wreaking all manner of
outrages on them. They broke into their churches, tore
up the benches, and, placing the Bibles and hymnbooks
in a pile, set the whole on fire; the authorities usually
setting their sanction on the proceedings of the rioters
by banishing the burned-out ministers, and interdicting
the further celebration of worship in their destroyed
churches.

The Huguenots of Dauphiny were at last stung
into a show of resistance, and furnished the King with
the pretext which he wanted for ordering a general
slaughter of those of his subjects who would not be
"converted" to his religion. A large congregation of
Huguenots assembled one day amidst the ruins of a
wrecked church, to celebrate worship and pray for
the King. The Roman Catholics thereupon raised the
alarm that this meeting was held for the purpose of
organising a rebellion. The spark thus kindled in
Dauphiny burst into flame in the Viverais, and even
in Languedoc; and troops were brought from all
quarters to crush the apprehended outbreak. Meanwhile the Huguenots continued to hold their religious
meetings; and numbers of them were found one day
assembled outside Bordeaux, where they had met to
pray. There the dragoons fell upon them, cutting
down hundreds, and dispersing the rest. "It was a
mere butchery," says Rulhières, "without the show of
a combat." Several were apprehended and offered
pardon if they would abjure; but they refused, and
were hanged.

Noailles, then governor, seized the opportunity of
advancing himself in the royal favour by ordering a
general massacre. He obeyed to the letter the cruel
orders of Louvois, the King's minister, who prescribed
desolation. Cruelty raged for a time uncontrolled from
Grenoble to Bordeaux. There were massacres in the
Viverais and massacres in the Cevennes. An entire
army had converged on Nismes, and there was so
horrible a dragonnade that the city was "converted"

in twenty-four hours. Noailles wrote to the King that there had indeed been some slight disorder, but that everything had been conducted with great judgment and discipline; and he promised with his head that before the next 25th of November (1683) there would be no more Huguenots in Languedoc.

Similar cruelties occurred all over France. More Protestant churches were pulled down, and the property that belonged to them was confiscated for the benefit of the Roman Catholic hospitals.   Many of the Huguenot landowners had already left the kingdom, and others were preparing to follow them.   But this did not suit the views of the monarch and his advisers; and the Ordinances were ordered to be put in force, which interdicted emigration, with the addition of condemnation to the galleys for life, of heads of families found attempting to escape, and a fine of three thousand livres against any person found encouraging or assisting them.   By the same Ordinance, all contracts for the sale of property made by the Reformed within one year before the date of their emigration, were declared nullified.   The consequence was that many landed estates were seized and sold, of which Madame de Maintenon, the King's mistress, artfully improved the opportunity.   Writing to her brother, for whom she had obtained from the King a gratuity of 800,000 francs, she said: "I beg of you carefully to use the money you are about to receive. Estates in Poitou may be got for nothing; the desolation of the Huguenots will drive them to sell more. You may easily acquire extensive possessions in Poitou."

Thus were the poor Huguenots trodden under foot —persecuted, maltreated, fined, flogged, hanged, or sabred; nevertheless, many of those who survived remained faithful.   Towards the end of 1684, a painful incident occurred at Marennes in Saintonge, where the Reformed religion extensively prevailed, notwithstanding the ferocity of the persecution. The church there comprised from 13,000 to 14,000 persons; but

on the pretence that some children of the new converts to Romanism had been permitted to enter
the building (a crime in the eye of the law), the
congregation was ordered, late one Saturday evening,
to be suppressed. On the Sunday morning a large
number of worshippers appeared at the church-doors,
some of whom had come from a great distance—their
own churches being already closed or pulled down,—
and amongst them were twenty-three infants brought
for baptism. It was winter. The cold was intense.
No shelter was permitted within the closed church; so
that the poor things were, for the most part, frozen to
death on their mother's bosoms. Loud sobbing and
wailing rose from the crowd. All wept—even the men.
They could only find consolation in prayer; but they
resolved, in this their darkest hour, to be faithful to the
end, even unto death.

A large body of troops lay encamped in Bearn in
the early part of 1685, to watch the movements of the
Spanish army; but a truce having been agreed upon, the
Marquis de Louvois resolved to employ the regiments
in converting the Huguenots of the surrounding districts after the methods adopted by Noailles at Nismes.
Some hundreds of Bearnese Protestants having been
driven by force into a church where the Bishop of Lescar
officiated, the doors were closed, and the poor people
were forced to kneel down and receive the bishop's
absolution at the point of the sword. To escape their
tormentors, the Reformed fled into the woods, the
wildernesses, and the caverns of the Pyrenees. They
were pursued like wild beasts, brought back to their
dwellings by force, and compelled to board and lodge
their persecutors. The dragoons entered the houses
with drawn swords, shouting, " Kill, kill, or become
Catholics." The scenes of brutal outrage which occurred
during these dragonnades cannot be described. The
soldiers were among the roughest, loosest, cruellest of
men. They suspended their victims with ropes, blow-
ing tobacco-smoke into their nostrils and mouths, and

practising upon them a hundred other nameless cruelties; until the sufferers promised everything, to rid themselves of their persecutors. No wonder that the constancy of the Bearnese at length yielded to the cruelty of their persecutors, and that they hastened to the priests in crowds to abjure their religion.

The success of the dragonnades in enforcing conversion in Bearn, encouraged the King to employ the same means elsewhere; and in the course of four months, Languedoc, Guienne, Saintonge, Poitou, Viverais, Dauphiny, Cevennes, Provence, and Gex were scoured by these missionaries of the Church. Neither age nor sex was spared. The men who refused to be converted were thrown into dungeons, and the women were immured in prison-convents. Louvois thus reported the result of his operations, in September 1685 :—"Sixty thousand conversions have been made in the district of Bordeaux, and twenty thousand in that of Montauban. So rapid is the progress, that before the end of the month ten thousand Protestants will not be left in the district of Bordeaux, where there were one hundred and fifty thousand on the 15th of last month." Noailles wrote to a similar effect from Nismes :—"The most influential people," said he, "abjured in the church the day following my arrival. There was a slackening afterwards, but matters soon assumed a proper shape with the help of some billetings on the dwellings of the most obstinate." The King jocularly called the dragoons, who effected these conversions,—"*ses missionnaires bottés!*"

In the meantime, while these forced conversions of the Huguenots were being made by the dragoons of De Louvois and De Noailles, Madame de Maintenon continued to labour at the conversion of the King himself. She was materially assisted by her royal paramour's bad digestion, and by the qualms of conscience which from time to time beset him at the dissoluteness of his past life. Every twinge of pain, every fit of colic, every prick of conscience was succeeded by new resolutions to extirpate heresy. Penance must be done for his incontinence; but not by himself. It was the virtuous Huguenots that must suffer vicariously for him; and, by punishing them, he flattered himself that he was expiating his own sins. " It was not only his amours which deserve censure," says Sismondi, "although the scandal of their publicity, the dignities to which he raised the children of his adultery, and the constant humiliation to which he subjected his wife, add greatly to his offence against public morality. . . . He acknowledged in his judgments, and in his rigour towards his people, no rule but his own will. At the very moment that his subjects were dying of famine, he retrenched nothing from his prodigalities. Those who boasted of having converted him, had never represented to him more than two duties—that of renouncing his incontinence, and that of extirpating heresy in his dominions."[1]

The farce of Louis' "conversion" went on. In August, 1684, Madame de Maintenon wrote thus:— "The King is prepared to do everything that shall be judged useful for the welfare of religion; this undertaking will cover him with glory before God and man!" The dragonnades were then in full career throughout the southern provinces, and a long wail of anguish was rising from the persecuted all over France. In 1685 the King's sufferings increased, and his conversion became imminent. His miserable body was already beginning to decay; but he was willing to make a sacrifice to God of what the devil had left of it. Not only did he lose his teeth, but caries in the jaw-bone developed itself; and when he drank, the liquid passed through his nostrils.[2] In this shocking state, Madame de Maintenon became his nurse.

The Jesuits now obtained all that they wanted. They made a compact with Madame, by which she

---

De Sismondi—*Histoire de France.* xxv. 481.
[2] *Journal MS. des Medecins,* 1685.

was to advise the King to revoke the Edict of Nantes, while they were to consent to her marriage with him. Père la Chaise, the Royal confessor, advised a private marriage. The ceremony was performed at Versailles by the Archbishop of Paris, in the presence of the confessor and two more witnesses. The precise date of the transaction is not known; but it is surmised that the Edict was revoked one day, and that the marriage took place the next.[1]

The Act of Revocation was published on the 22nd of October, 1685. It was the death-knell of the Huguenots.

---

[1] Madame dit (*Memoires*, ii. 108) que le mariage eut lieu *deux ans après la mort de la reine*, donc dans les derniers mois de 1685. M. de Noailles (ii. 121) établit la même date. Pour le jour précis, on l'ignore. On doit conjecturer qu'il eut lieu après le jour de la Revocation, déclarée à la fin d'octobre, ce jour où le roi tint parole, accorda l'acte qu'elle avait consenti, et où elle fut ainsi engagée sans retour. —MICHELET—*Louis XIV. et la Revocation*, 300.

CHAPTER X

GREAT was the rejoicing of the Jesuits on the Revocation of the Edict of Nantes. Rome sprang up with a shout of joy to celebrate the event. Te Deums were sung, processions went from shrine to shrine, and the Pope sent a brief to Louis conveying to him the congratulations and praises of the Romish Church. Public thanksgivings were held at Paris, in which the people eagerly took part,—thus making themselves accomplices in the proscription by the King of their fellow-subjects. The provost and sheriffs had a statue of Louis erected at the Hotel de Ville, the bas-reliefs displaying a frightful bat, whose wings enveloped the books of Calvin and Huss, and bearing the inscription, *Luduvico Magno, victori perpetuo, ecclesiæ ac regum, dignitatis assertori.*[1] Lesueur was employed to paint the subject for the gallery at Versailles, and medals were struck to commemorate the extinction of Protestantism in France.

The Roman Catholic clergy were almost beside themselves with joy. The eloquent Bossuet was especially fervent in his praises of the monarch:— "Touched by so many marvels," said he (15th January, 1686), "let us expand our hearts in praise of the piety of the Great Louis. Let our acclamations ascend to heaven, and let us say to this new Constantine, this new Theodosius, what the six hundred and thirty

---

[1] The statue was pulled down in 1792, and cast into cannon which thundered at Valmy

THE CATHEDRAL AT NANTES.

[*To face p.* 156.

fathers said in the Council of Chalcédon, 'You have strengthened the faith, you have exterminated the heretics : King of Heaven, preserve the king of earth.'" Massillon indulged in a like strain of exultation : " The profane temples," said he, " are destroyed, the pulpits of seduction are cast down, the prophets of falsehood are torn from their flocks. At the first blow dealt to it by Louis, heresy falls, disappears, and is reduced either to hide itself in the obscurity whence it issued, or to cross the seas, and to bear with it into foreign lands its false gods, its bitterness, and its rage."

Let us now see what the Revocation of the Edict of Nantes involved :—The demolition of all the remaining Protestant temples throughout France, and the entire proscription of the Protestant religion; the prohibition of even private worship, under penalty of confiscation of body and property ; the banishment of all Protestant pastors from France within fifteen days; the closing of all Protestant schools ; the prohibition of parents to instruct their children in the Protestant faith ; the injunction, under a penalty of five hundred livres in each case, to have their children baptized by the parish priest, and brought up in the Roman Catholic religion ; the confiscation of the property and goods of all Protestant refugees who failed to return to France within four months ; the penalty of the *galleys for life* to all men, and of *imprisonment for life* to all women, detected in the act of attempting to escape from France !

Such were a few of the dastardly and inhuman provisions of the Edict of Revocation. It was a proclamation of war by the armed against the unarmed— a war against peaceable men, women and children—a war against property, against family, against society, against public morality, and, more than all, against religion and the rights of conscience.

The military jacquerie at once began. The very day on which the Edict of Revocation was registered, steps were taken to destroy the great Protestant church at

Charenton, near Paris. It had been the work of the celebrated architect Debrosses, and was capable of containing 14,000 persons. In five days it was levelled with the ground. The great temple of Quevilly, near Rouen, of nearly equal size, in which the celebrated minister Jacques Basnage preached, was in like manner demolished. At Tours, at Nismes, at Montauban, and all over France, the same scenes were enacted,—the mob eagerly joining in the work of demolition with levers and pickaxes. Eight hundred Protestant temples were thrown down in a few weeks.

The provisions of the Edict of Revocation were rigorously put in force. They were also followed by other edicts still more severe. The Protestants were commanded to employ only Roman Catholic servants under penalty of a fine of 1000 livres, while Protestant servants were forbidden to serve either Protestant or Roman Catholic employers. If any men-servants were detected violating this law, they were liable to be sent to the galleys; whereas women-servants were to be flogged and branded with a *fleur-de-lis*—the emblazonment of the "Most Christian King." Protestant pastors found lurking in France after the expiry of fifteen days, were to be *condemned to death;* and any of the King's subjects found giving harbour to the pastors were to be condemned—the men to be galley-slaves, the women to imprisonment for life! The reward of 5500 livres was offered for the apprehension of any Protestant pastor.

The Huguenots were not even permitted to die in peace. They were pursued to death's door, and into the grave itself. They were forbidden to solicit the offices of those of their own faith, and were required to confess and receive unction from the priests, on penalty of having their bodies, when dead, removed from their dwelling by the common hangman, and flung into the public sewer. In the event of the sick Protestant recovering, after having rejected the viaticum, he was to be condemned to perpetual confinement at the galleys, or imprisonment for life, with confiscation of all his property.

Crushed, tormented, and persecuted by these terrible enactments, the Huguenots felt that life in France had become intolerable. It is true, there was an alternative—conversion. But Louis XIV., with all his power, could not prevail against the impenetrable rampart of conscience, and a large proportion of the Huguenots persistently refused to be converted. They would not act the terrible lie to God, and seek their personal safety at the price of hypocrisy. They would not become Roman Catholics ; they would rather die.

There was only one other means of relief—flight from France. Yet it was a frightful alternative,—to tear themselves from the country they loved, from their friends and relatives, from the homes of their youth and the graves of their kindred, and fly—they knew not whither. The thought of self-banishment was so agonising that many hesitated long and prepared to endure much before taking the irrevocable step ; and many more prepared to suffer death rather than leave their country and their homes.

Indeed, to fly in any direction became increasingly difficult from day to day. The frontiers were strongly patrolled by troops and gensdarmes; the coast was closely watched by an armed coast-guard, while ships of war cruised at sea to intercept and search outward-bound vessels. The law was strictly enforced against all persons taken in the act of flight. Under the original edict, detected fugitives were to be condemned to the galleys for life, while their denouncers were to be rewarded with half their goods. But this punishment was not considered sufficiently severe ; and on the 7th of May, 1686, the King issued another edict, proclaiming that any captured fugitives, as well as any person found acting as their guide, would be *condemned to death.*

Amidst the general proscription, a few distinguished exceptions were made by the King, who granted per-

mission to several laymen, in return for past public
services, to leave the kingdom and settle abroad.
Amongst these were Marshal Schomberg, one of the
first soldiers of France, who had been commander-in-
chief of its armies, and the Marquis de Ruvigny, one of
its ablest ambassadors,—whose only crime consisted in
being Protestants. The gallant Admiral Duquesne
also, the first sailor of France, was a Huguenot. The
King sent for him, and urged him to abjure his religion. But the old hero, pointing to his gray hairs,
replied, " For sixty years, sire, have I rendered unto
Cæsar the things which are Cæsar's ; suffer me still
to render unto God the things which are God's."
Duquesne was permitted to end his few remaining
days in France, for he was then in his eightieth year ;
but his two sons were allowed to emigrate, and they
shortly after departed into Holland.

The banished pastors were treated with especial
severity. Fifteen days only had been allowed them
to fly beyond the frontier ; and if they tarried longer
in their agonising leave-taking of their flocks, they
were liable to be sent to the galleys for life. Yet
with that exquisite malignity which characterised
the acts of the monarch and his abettors, they were in
some cases refused the necessary permits to pass the
frontier, in order that they might thereby be brought
within the range of the dreadful penalties proclaimed
by the Act of Revocation. The pastor Claude, one of
the most eloquent preachers of his day, who had been
one of the ministers of the great church at Charenton,
was ordered to quit France within twenty-four hours ;
and he set out forthwith, accompanied by one of the
King's footmen, who saw him as far as Brussels.

The other pastors of Paris were allowed two days
to make their preparations for leaving. More time
was allowed to those in the provinces ; but they were
prevented carrying anything with them,—even their
children,—all under seven years of age being taken
from them, to be brought up in the religion of their

persecutors. Even infants at the breast were to be given up; and many a mother's heart was torn by conflicting feelings,—the duty of following a husband on the road to banishment, or remaining behind to suckle her helpless infant.

When all the banished pastors had fled, those of their flocks who still remained steadfast prepared to follow them into exile; for many felt it easier to be martyrs than apostates. Those who possessed goods and movables, made haste to convert them into money in such a way as to excite the least possible suspicion; for spies were constantly on the watch, ready to inform against them. Such as were engaged in trade, commerce, and manufactures, were surrounded by difficulties; yet they were prepared to dare and risk all rather than abjure their religion. They prepared to close their workships, their tanneries, their paper-mills, their silk-manufactories, and the various branches of industry which they had built up, and to fly with the merest wreck of their fortunes into other countries. The owners of land had still greater difficulties to encounter. They were in a measure rooted to the soil; and according to the royal edict, if they emigrated without special permission, their property was liable to immediate confiscation by the state. Nevertheless, many of these, too, resolved to brave all risks and fly from France.

When the full tide of the emigration set in, it was found difficult to guard the extensive French frontier, so as effectually to prevent the escape of the fugitives. The high-roads as well as the by-ways were regularly patrolled day and night, and all the bridges leading out of France were strongly guarded. But the fugitives avoided the frequented routes, and crossed the frontier through forests, over trackless wastes, or by mountain-paths, where no patrols were on the watch; and they thus contrived to escape in large numbers into Switzerland, Germany, and Holland. They mostly travelled by night, not in bands but in small parties,

11

and often singly. When the members of a family prepared to fly, they fixed a rendezvous in some town across the nearest frontier; then, after prayer and taking a tender leave of each other, they set out separately, and made for the agreed point of meeting, usually travelling by different routes.

Many of the fugitives were of course captured by the King's agents. Along so extensive a frontier, it was impossible to elude their vigilance. To strike terror into such of the remaining Huguenots as might be contemplating their escape; the prisoners who were caught were led as a Show through the principal towns, with heavy chains round their necks, in some cases weighing over fifty pounds. Sometimes they were placed in carts, with irons on their feet,— the chains being made fast to the cart. They were forced to make long marches; and, when they sank under fatigue, blows compelled them to rise. After they had been thus driven through the chief towns by way of example, the prisoners were sent to the galleys,—where there were already more than a thousand by the end of 1686. The galley-slaves included men of all conditions: pastors and peasants; old men with white hairs and boys of tender years; magistrates, officers, and men of gentle blood, mixed with thieves and murderers; and no discrimination whatever was made in their classification, or in the barbarity of their treatment.

These cruelties were, however, of no avail in checking the emigration. The Huguenots continued to flee out of France in all directions. The Great Louis, still bent on their "conversion," increased his guards along the frontiers. The soldiers were rewarded in proportion to the captures they effected. The aid of the frontier peasantry was also invited, and thousands of them joined the troops in guarding the highways, the bridges, the ferries, and all the avenues leading out of France. False statements were published by authority, to the effect that such of the emigrants as

had reached foreign countries were destitute and
starving. It was alleged that ten thousand of them
had died of misery in England, and that most of
those who survived were imploring permission to
return to France and abjure!

In vain!—the emigration continued. Some bought
their way across the frontier; others fought their way.
They went in all sorts of disguises; some as pedlars,
others as soldiers, huntsmen, valets and beggars. Some,
to disarm suspicion, even pretended to sell chaplets
and rosaries. The Huguenots conducted the emigration on a regular system. They had Itineraries prepared and secretly distributed, in which the safest
routes and hiding-places were described in detail,—a
sort of "underground railroad," such as existed in
the United States before the abolition of slavery
Many escaped through the great forest of Ardennes
into Luxembourg; others through the Vosges mountains into Germany; and others through the passes of
the Jura into Switzerland. Some were shot by the
soldiers and peasantry; a still greater number were
sent to the galleys; yet many thousands of them
nevertheless continued to make their escape.

Many a tradition is still preserved in Huguenot
families of the hairbreadth escapes of their ancestors
in those terrible times. Thus De la Rive (afterwards
an officer under William III.) and his wife escaped
across the frontier into Holland in the guise of orange-
sellers, leading a donkey and panniers. The young
D'Albiacs, whose blood now intermingles with the
ducal family of Roxburgh, were smuggled out of the
country in hampers. The sisters De la Cherois, whose
descendants still exist in Ireland, fled in disguise
on horseback, travelling only after dark, and conceal-
ing themselves in the woods in the daytime. The
two La Condamine children, whose descendants still
flourish in England and Scotland, were carried off in
baskets slung across a mule, travelling only at night.
The ancestor of the Courtaulds, now settled in Essex,

was carried off, when quite a boy, in a donkey's pannier from Saintonge to the northern frontier, accompanied by a faithful servant, who, upon approaching any town where their progress was likely to be opposed, covered up the child with greens and garden stuffs.

The flight of men was accompanied by that of women, old and young ; often by mothers with infants in their arms. The hearts of the women were especially lacerated by the cruelties inflicted on them through their affections ; by the tearing of their children from them for the purpose of being educated in convents; by the quartering of dragoons in their dwellings; and by the various social atrocities which preceded as well as followed the Edict of Revocation.[1] While many Protestant heads of families were ready to conform, in order to save their families from insult and outrage by a lawless and dissolute soldiery, the women often refused to follow their example, and entreated their husbands to fly from the land where such barbarities had become legalised, and where a daily war was being carried on against womanhood and childhood—against innocence, morality, religion, and virtue. To women of pure feelings, life under such circumstances was more intolerable even than death.

---

[1] The frightful cruelty of these measures shocked the Roman Catholic clergy themselves, and, to their honour be it said, in many districts they refrained from putting them in force. On discovering this, Louis XIV., furiously zealous for the extirpation of heresy, ordered his minister De Portchartrain to address a circular to the bishops of France, charging them with want of zeal in carrying his edicts into effect, and calling upon them to require the curates of their respective dioceses to enforce them without fail.—COQUEREL, *Histoire des Eglises du Desert.* i. p. 68. The priests who visited the slaves at the galleys were horribly shocked at the cruelties practised on them. The Abbé Jean Bion shed tears at the sight of the captives covered with bleeding wounds inflicted by the whip, and he could not resist the impression : " Their blood preached to me," says he in his *Relation,* " and I felt myself a Protestant."

Everywhere, therefore, were the Huguenot women, as well as the Huguenot men, found fleeing into exile. They mostly fled in disguise, often alone, to join their husbands or fathers at the appointed rendezvous. Benoit says that they cut off their hair, disfigured their faces with dyes, assumed the dress of pedlars or lacqueys, and condescended to the meanest employ-ments, for the purpose of disarming suspicion and en-suring their escape.[1] Young women, in many cases of gentle birth, who under ordinary circumstances would have shrunk from the idea of walking a few miles from home, prepared to set out upon a journey on foot of hundreds of miles, passing through woods, along un-frequented paths, across mountain-ranges, and braving all dangers, so that they might but escape, though it were with their bare lives, from the soil of France.

The adventures of some of the women who suc-ceeded in making their escape are full of romance, and cannot be read without painful interest. Thus, Lord du Bourdieu's widow, the daughter of Count de la Valade, escaped disguised as a peasant, with her infant son slung in a shawl at her back, passing through the frontier guards into German Switzerland, from whence

---

[1] Women of quality, even sixty and seventy years of age, who had, so to speak, never placed a foot upon the ground except to cross their apartments or to stroll in an avenue, travelled a hundred leagues, to some village which had been indicated by a guide. Girls of fifteen, of every rank, exposed themselves to the same hazard. They drew wheelbar-rows, they bore manure, panniers, and other burdens. They dis-figured their faces with dyes to embrown their complexion, with ointments or juices that blistered their skins, and gave them a wrinkled aspect. Women and girls were seen to counterfeit sickness, dumbness, and even in-sanity. Some went disguised as men; and some, too delicate and small to pass as grown men, donned the dress of lacqueys, and followed on foot, through the mud, a guide on horseback, who assumed the character of a man of importance. Many of these females reached Rotterdam in their borrowed garments, and hastening to the foot of the pulpit, before they had time to assume a more decent garb, pub-lished their repentance of their compulsory signature. — ELIE BENOIT—*Histoire de l'Edit de Nantes*, v. 554. 953.

she found her way to London and rejoined her relatives.[1] Another young married woman, equally noble,
though untitled—Judith Mariengault, from whom some
of the best blood in America has come—has herself told
the story of her flight. She says : " We quitted our
home in the night, leaving the soldiers in their beds,
and abandoning to them our home and all that it contained. Well knowing that we should be sought for
in every direction, we remained ten days concealed in
Dauphiny, at the house of a good woman, who had
no thought of betraying us." Making a long circuit
through Germany and Holland, and suffering many
misfortunes, the family at last reached London, from
whence they took ship to Carolina. But their sufferings were not ended. "The red fever," Judith continues, " broke out on board the ship : many of us died
of it, and among them our aged mother. We touched
at the island of Bermuda, where the vessel which
carried us was seized. We spent all our money there,
and it was with great difficulty that we procured a
passage on board of another ship. New misfortunes
awaited us in Carolina. At the end of eighteen months
we lost our eldest brother, who succumbed to such
unusual fatigues ; so that after our departure from
France we endured all that it was possible to suffer. I
was six months without tasting bread, besides working
like a slave ; and during three or four years I never
had the wherewithal completely to satisfy the hunger
which devoured me." " Yet," adds this admirable
woman, " God accomplished great things in our favour
by giving us the strength necessary to support these
trials."

At a village in Champagne, during a dreadful day of
persecution, when blood was streaming in the streets,
two soldiers entered the house of a Protestant, and
after killing some of the inmates, one of them, seeing

---

[1] The child she carried across
the frontier on her back, grew up
to manhood, and became minister of the Savoy church, London.

an infant in a cradle, rushed at it with his drawn
sword and stabbed it, but not fatally. The child was
snatched up by a bystander, who exclaimed, " At least
the babe is not a Protestant," and saved it.[1] The child
proved to be a boy, and was given to a Protestant
woman to nurse, who had a male child of her own at
the breast. The boys grew up together. When old
enough, they emigrated into Holland together ; entered
the army of the Prince of Orange, accompanied him to
England, and fought in Ireland together. There they
settled and married ; and the son of the one emigré
married the daughter of the other. Such were the
ancestors of the Morell family, which has produced so
many distinguished ministers of religion and men of
science in England.

Many fled with nothing but their clothes and their
Bibles. Such was the case of Henri de Dibon, whose
short story is contained in a leaf written inside the
Bible [2] carried with him in his flight, as thus related
to the late Rev. George Stanley Faber, D.D., by his
maternal grandmother, Margaret de Dibon, the granddaughter of the refugee :—

" This Bible once belonged to M. de Dibon, a Huguenot gentleman, whose family estate and residence were
situated in the Isle of France.

" At the Revocation of the Edict of Nantes, in the
year 1685, M. de Dibon was arrested by order of Louis
XIV. ; and on his firm refusal to abandon the religion
of his ancestors, his whole property was confiscated,
and he himself was thrown into prison.

" Before the arrival of the dragoons at his residence,
he had time sufficient to bury this, his family Bible,
within a chest in his garden. There he left it, in
hopes of some day recovering what he esteemed his
best treasure.

---

[1] *A Sketch of the Life and
Character of the Rev. J. Morell,
LL.D.*, by the Rev. J. R. Wreford.
F.S.A.

[2] This French Bible is still in
the possession of the Faber family,
and is greatly prized by them.

" While in confinement he was frequently tortured by the application of fire to wreaths of straw, which were fastened round his legs ; but through the grace of God, he was enabled to persevere in making a good confession. This particular torture was especially resorted to, in consequence of his being a victim to the gout.

" He at length effected his escape; but ere he quitted his native land for ever, he had the resolution to visit the estate of his forefathers, now no longer his, for the purpose of recovering his Bible. This he accomplished; and with the word of God in his hand, he finally reached England in the reign of William III. of glorious memory."

Jean Marteilhe of Bergerac, in his highly interesting autobiography,[1] has described the remarkable difficulties which Huguenot young ladies occasionally encountered in their efforts to escape. He had himself been taken prisoner in his attempt to escape across the French frontier near Marienbourg, and was lodged in the gaol at Tournay to wait his trial. While lying there, five Huguenot fugitives, who had been captured by the dragoons, were ushered into his cell. Three of these he at once recognised, through their disguises, as gentlemen of Bergerac; but the other two he failed to recognise. They eventually proved to be two young ladies, Mademoiselle Madras and Conceil of Bergerac, disguised as boys, who had set out, though it was winter, to make their escape from France through the forest of Ardennes. They had travelled thirty leagues on foot, under dripping trees, along broken roads, and by almost trackless paths, enduring cold, hunger, and

---

[1] The narrative of Jean Marteilhe, entitled *Mémoires d'un Protestant condamné aux Galéres de France pour cause de Religion, écrits par lui-même,* originally appeared at Rotterdam in 1755, and was translated into English by Oliver Goldsmith, under the fictitious name of "J. Willington," in the following year. It has since been republished by the Religious Tract Society, under the title of *Autobiography of a French Protestant condemned to the Galleys for the sake of his Religion.*

privations, "with a firmness and constancy," says Marteilhe, "extraordinary for persons brought up in refinement, and who previous to this expedition would not have been able to walk a league." They were, however, captured and put in gaol; and when they recognised in their fellow-prisoners other Huguenot fugitives from Bergerac, they were so happy that they wept for joy. Marteilhe strongly urged that the gaoler should be informed of their sex, to which the young ladies assented, when they were removed to a separate cell. They were afterwards tried, and condemned to be immured in the Convent of the Repentants at Paris, where they wept out the rest of their lives and died.

Marteilhe himself refused all the tempting offers, as well as the dreadful threats, which were made to induce him to abjure his religion; and at seventeen years of age he was condemned to be sent to the galleys. Marched from gaol to gaol, and from town to town, loaded with chains like his fellow-prisoners, he was first placed in the galleys at Dunkirk, where he endured the most horrible hardships [1] during twelve years; after which, on the surrender of Dunkirk to the English, he was marched, with twenty-two other Protestant galley-slaves, still loaded with chains, through Paris and the other principal towns, to Marseilles, to serve out the remainder of his sentence.

There were other galley-slaves of even more tender years than Marteilhe. Andrew Bosquet was only sixteen, and he remained at the galleys twenty-six years. Francis Bourry and Matthew Morel were but fifteen; and only a few years since, Admiral Boudin, maritime prefect at Toulon, in turning over the ancient records of his department, discovered the register of a child

---

[1] What life at the galleys was, may be learned from Marteilhe's own narrative above cited, as well as from a highly interesting account of the Protestants sent to the galleys, by Athanase Cocquerel fils, entitled *Les Forçats pour la Foi* (Galley-Slaves for the Faith), published at Paris by Lévy Brothers.

who had been sent to the galleys at twelve years of age " for having accompanied his father and mother to the preaching " !

On the other hand, age did not protect those found guilty of adhering to their faith. David de Caumont, baron of Montbelon, was seventy years old when he was sent to the galleys. Antoine Astruc was of the same age ; and Antoine Morlier seventy-one. Nor did distinction in learning protect the hapless Protestants ; for the celebrated counsellor of the King, Louis de Marolles, was sent to the galleys with the rest. At first, out of regard for his eminence, the gaoler chained him by only one foot ; but next day, by the express orders of Louis the Great, a heavy chain was fixed round his neck. It was while chained with all sorts of malefactors that Marolles compiled his *Discourse on Providence,* which was afterwards published and translated into English. Marolles was a profound mathematician—the author of one of the best treatises on algebra ; and, while chained in his dungeon, he proposed a problem to the mathematicians of Paris which was afterwards inserted in the works of Ozanam.

Another distinguished galley-slave was John Huber, father of three illustrious sons—Huber of the Birds, Huber of the Ants, and Huber of the Bees. The following touching incident is from the elder Huber's journal :—" We arrived one night at a little town, chained, my wife and my children, with fourteen galley-slaves. The priests came to us, offering freedom on condition that we abjured. We had agreed to preserve a profound silence. After them came the women and children of the place, who covered us with mud. I made my little party fall on their knees, and we put up this prayer, in which all the fugitives joined : ' Gracious God, who seest the wrongs to which we are hourly exposed, give us strength to support them, and to forgive in charity those who wrong us. Strengthen us from good even unto better.' The people about us expected to hear complaints and outcries : our words astonished them.   We finished our little act of worship by singing the hundred and sixteenth psalm.   At this the women began to weep.   They washed off the mud with which our children's faces had been covered, and they sought permission to have us lodged in a barn separate from the other galley-slaves, which was done at their request."

To return to the fugitives who evaded the dragoons, police, and coast-guard, and succeeded in making their escape from France.   Many of them fled by sea, for it was difficult to close that great highway, or to guard the coast so strictly as to preclude the escape of those who dared to trust themselves upon it.   Some of the fugitives from inland places, who had never seen the sea in their lives, were so appalled at the sight of the wide and stormy waste of waters, and so agonised by the thought of tearing themselves from their native land for ever, that their hearts sank within them, and they died in sheer despair, without being able to accomplish their purpose.   Others, stronger and more courageous, prepared to brave all risks ; and on the first opportunity that offered, they put out to sea, from all parts of the coast, in open boats, in shallops, in fishing-smacks, and in trading-ships, eager to escape from France in anything that would float.

"The Protestants of the seaboard," says Weiss, "got away in French, English, and Dutch merchant-vessels, whose masters hid them under bales of goods and heaps of coals, and in empty casks, where they had only the bunghole to breathe through.   There they remained, crowded one upon another, until the ship sailed.   Fear of discovery and of the galleys gave them courage to suffer.   Persons brought up in every luxury, pregnant women, old men, invalids, and children vied with each other in constancy to escape from their persecutors,—often risking themselves in mere boats upon voyages the thought of which would in ordinary times have made them shudder. A Norman gentleman, Count de Marancé, passed the Channel, in the depth of winter, with forty persons, amongst whom were several pregnant women, in a vessel of seven tons burthen. Overtaken by a storm, they remained long at sea, without provisions or hope of succour, dying of hunger; he, the countess, and all the passengers, reduced, for sole sustenance, to a little melted snow, with which they appeased their burning thirst, and moistened the parched lips of their weeping children, until they landed, half-dead, upon England's shores."

The Lord of Castlefranc, near Rochelle, was even less fortunate than the Count de Marancé. He was captured at sea, in an open boat, while attempting to escape to England with his wife and family. Three of his sons and three of his daughters thus taken, were sent to the Caribbee Islands as slaves. His three other daughters were detained in France in strict confinement; and after much suffering, during which they continued steadfast to their faith, they were at length permitted to depart for Geneva. The father contrived in some way to escape from France and to reach London, where he lived for many years in Bunhill Fields. The six slaves in the Caribbee Islands were eventually liberated by the crew of an English vessel, and brought to London. The three young men entered the English army, under William III. Two of them were killed in battle in Flanders, and the third retired on half-pay, settling at Portarlington in Ireland, where he died.

Among the many who escaped in empty casks may be mentioned the Misses Raboteau, of Pont-Gibaud, near Rochelle. Their relatives had become "new Catholics," by which name the converts from Protestantism, often pretended, were called; but the two young ladies refused to be converted, and they waited an opportunity for making their escape from France. The means were at length provided by an exiled relative, John Charles Raboteau, who had emigrated long before, and settled as a wine-merchant in Dublin. He carried on a brisk trade with the French wine-growers, and occasionally sailed in his own ship to Rochelle, where he became the temporary guest of his relatives. At one of his visits, the two young ladies confided to him that they had been sentenced to adopt the alternative of either marrying two Roman Catholic gentlemen selected for their husbands, or being shut up in a convent for life. There was one other alternative—flight,—upon which they had resolved, if their uncle would assist them. He at once assented, and made arrangements for their escape. Two horses were obtained, on which they rode by night to Rochelle, where lodgings had been taken for them at the house of a widow. There was still, however, the greater difficulty to be overcome of getting the delicate freight put on board. Raboteau had been accustomed to take to Ireland, as part of his cargo, several large casks of French apples; and in two of such casks the young ladies were carried on board ship. They reached Dublin in safety, where they settled and married, and their descendants still survive.[1]

The Rev. Philip Skelton mentions the case of a French gentlewoman brought from Bordeaux to Portsmouth by a sea-captain of his acquaintance, which shows the agonies of mind which must have been endured by these noble women before they could bring themselves to fly alone across the sea to England for refuge. This lady had sold all the property she could convert into money, with which she purchased jewels, as being the easiest to carry. She contrived to

---

[1] One of them married Alderman Peter Barré, whose son was the famous Isaac Barré, M.P., and Privy Councillor ; the other married Mr. Stephen Chaigneau, descended from an ancient family in the Charente, where their estate of Labellonière was confis-cated and sold as belonging to "Religionaires fugitifs du royaume pour cause de la religion." Several of their descendants have filled important offices in the State, Army, and Church of England and Ireland.

get on board the Englishman's ship by night, bringing
with her the little casket of jewels—her sole fortune.
She remained in a state of the greatest fear and
anxiety till the ship was under sail. But no sooner
did she find herself fairly out at sea and the land
disappearing in the distance, than she breathed freely,
and began to give way to her feelings of joy and
gratitude. This increased in proportion as she neared
England, though about to land there an exile, a solitary
woman, and a foreigner ; and no sooner did she reach
the shore than she threw herself down and passion-
ately kissed the ground, exclaiming, "Have I at last
attained my wishes ? Yes, gracious God ! I thank
Thee for this deliverance from a tyranny exercised
over my conscience, and for placing me where Thou
alone art to reign over it by Thy word, till I shall
finally lay down my head upon this beloved earth ! " [1]

Another notable escape by sea was that of David
Garric, or Garigue, the grandfather of Garrick, the
celebrated actor. He first escaped himself, next his
wife escaped, and finally, more than two years later,
their only child escaped, whom they had left an infant
at nurse. The story is best told in the touching little
narrative of the refugee himself :—

"The 5th October, 1685.—I, David Garric, arrived at
London, having come from Bourdeaux the 31st August,
running away from the persecution of our Holy Religion. I passed through Saintonge, Poitou, and Brittany. I embarked at St. Malo for Guernsey, where I
remained for the space of a month, leaving everything,
even my wife and a little boy four months old, called
Peter Garric, who was then out at nurse at the Bastide,
near Bourdeaux.

"The 5th December, 1685, English style.—God gave
me my wife at London. She embarked from Bourdeaux the 19th November, from whence she saved

---

[1] PHILIP SKELTON [Rector of
Fintona, county Tyrone]—*Com-* *passion for the French Protest
ant Refugees recommended,* 1751

herself, and in a bark of 14 ton, being hid in a hole, and was a month upon sea with strong tempests, and at great peril of being lost and taken by our persecutors, who are very inveterate. Pray God convert them.   *   *   *

"The 22d May, 1687.—Little Peter arrived at London, by the grace of God, in the ship of John White, with a servant, Mary Mongorier, and I paid for their passage 22 guineas."[1]

The measures adopted by the French king to prevent the escape of fugitives by sea, proved as futile as those employed to prevent their escape by land. The coast-guard was increased, and more tempting rewards were offered for the capture of the flying Protestants. The royal cruisers were set to watch every harbour and inlet, to prevent any vessel setting sail without a most rigid search of the cargo for concealed Huguenots.

When it became known that many had escaped in empty casks, provision was made to meet the case, and the royal order was issued that, before any ship was allowed to set sail for a foreign port, the hold should be fumigated with deadly gas, so that any hidden Huguenot who could not be detected might thus be suffocated.[2]   This expedient was only of a piece with the refined and malignant cruelty of the Great Louis. But it failed like the other measures; for the Huguenots still continued to make their escape.

It can never be known, with anything approaching accuracy, how many persons fled from France during this Great Exodus. Vauban, the military engineer, writing only a few years after the Revocation, said

---

[1] Our acknowledgments are due to Sir Bernard Burke, Ulster king-at-arms, for the copy of the document (*Heard Collection,* College of Arms, London) from which we make the above extracts.

[2] " On se servait d'une composition qui, lorsq'on y mettait le feu développait une odeur mortelle dans tous les recoins du navire, de sorte que, en la respirant, ceux qui s'étaient cachés trouvaient une mort certaine!"
—ROYER—*Histoire de la Colonie Française en Prusse,* p. 153.

that "France had lost a hundred thousand inhabitants, sixty millions of money, nine thousand sailors, twelve thousand tried soldiers, six hundred officers, and its most flourishing manufactures." But the emigration was not then by any means at its height; and for many years after, the Huguenots continued to swarm out of France and join their exiled compatriots in other lands. Sismondi computed the total number of emigrants at from three to four hundred thousand; and he was further of opinion that an equal number perished in prison, on the scaffold, at the galleys, and in their attempts to escape.[1]

The emigration gave the death-blow to several great branches of industry. Hundreds of manufactories were closed, whole villages were depopulated, many large towns became half deserted, and a large extent of land went entirely out of cultivation.[2] The skilled Dutch cloth-workers, whom Colbert had induced to settle at Abbeville, emigrated in a body, and their manufacture was extinguished. At Tours, where some 40,000 persons had been employed in the silk manufactures, the number fell to little more than 4000; and instead of 8000 looms at work there remained only about 100; while of 800 mills, 730 were closed. Of the 400 tanneries which had before enriched Lorraine, Weiss says there remained but 54 in 1698. The population of Nantes, one of the most prosperous cities of France, was reduced from 80,000 to less than one-half; and a blow was struck at its prosperity from which it has never recovered.

---

[1] Boulainvilliers states that under the intendancy of Lamoignon de Baville, a hundred thousand persons were destroyed by premature death in the single province of Languedoc, and that one-tenth of them perished by fire, strangulation, or the wheel. — DE FELICK. p. 340.

[2] Fénelon thus describes France in the later years of Louis XIV.'s reign:—" The cultivation of the soil is almost abandoned; the towns and the country are becoming depopulated. All industries languish, and fail to support the labourers. France has become as but a huge hospital without provisions."

The Revocation proved almost as fatal to the prosperity of Lyons as it did to that of Tours and Nantes. That city had originally been indebted for its silk manufactures to the civil and religious wars of Sicily, Italy, and Spain, which occasioned numerous refugees from those countries to settle in Lyons and carry on their trade. And now the same religious persecutions which had made the prosperity of Lyons, threatened to prove its ruin. Of about 12,000 artizans employed in the silk manufacture, some 9000 fled into Switzerland and other countries. The industry of the place was for a time completely prostrated. More than a hundred years passed before it was restored to its former prosperity ; and then only to suffer another equally staggering blow from the violence and outrages which accompanied the outbreak of the French Revolution.

Although Protestantism seemed to be utterly stamped out in France during the century which followed the Revocation of the Edict of Nantes—although its ministers were banished, its churches and schools suppressed, and it was placed entirely beyond the pale of the law,—it nevertheless continued to have an active existence. Banished ministers from time to time returned secretly, to minister to their flocks; but they were liable to be seized and suffer death in consequence,—as many as twenty-nine Protestant pastors having been hanged between 1684 and 1762. During the same period thousands of their followers were sent to the galleys, and died there. The names of 1546 of these illustrious galley-slaves are given in *Les Forçats pour la Foi*, but the greater number have long since been forgotten on earth. The principal offence for which they were sent to the galleys was, for attending the Protestant meetings, which still continued to be held ; for the Protestants, after the Revocation, constituted a sort of underground church, regularly organised, though its meetings were held by night, in forests, in caves among the hills, or in unsuspected places, and even

12

in the heart of large towns and cities, in all parts of France.[1]

Without pursuing the subject of the sufferings of the Huguenots who remained in France,—of whom there were more than a million, notwithstanding the frightful persecutions to which they continued to be subjected,—let us now follow the fugitives into the countries in which they found a refuge, and observe the important influence which they exercised, not only on their industrial prosperity, but also on their political history.

---

[1] The Churches of the Desert, as they were called, continued to exist down to the period of the French Revolution, when Protestantism in France was again allowed openly to show itself. An interesting account of the Protestant church in France during this " underground " period is to be found in Charles Coquerel's *Histoire des Eglises du Désert*, in 2 vols., Paris, 1841. The present author has also endeavoured to describe the same subject in a separate book, entitled *The Huguenots in France, after the Revocation of the Edict of Nantes.*

CHAPTER XI.

THE HUGUENOTS AND THE ENGLISH REVOLUTION
OF 1688.

THE Exodus of the French Protestants exercised a highly important influence on European politics. Among its other effects, it contributed to establish religious and political freedom in Switzerland, and to render it, in a measure, the Patmos of Europe. It strengthened the foundations of liberty in the then comparatively insignificant electorate of Brandenburg,—which has since become developed into the great German Empire. It fostered the strength and increased the political power and commercial wealth of the States of Holland. And, lastly, it contributed to the success of the English Revolution of 1688, and to the establishment of the British Constitution on its present basis.

Long before the Revocation of the Edict of Nantes, the persecutions of the French Protestants had excited the pity and indignation of Europe; and Switzerland and the northern nations vied with each other in extending to them their sympathy and their help. The principal seats of Protestantism being in Languedoc, Dauphiny, and the south western provinces of France, the first emigrants readily passed across the frontier, through Jura and Savoy into Switzerland, where they made for the asylum of Geneva. That city had in a measure been created by the genius of Calvin, who strove to make it a sort of Christian Sparta. Under his regime the place became entirely changed.

It had already emancipated itself from the authority
of the Duke of Savoy, and established alliances with
adjoining cantons for the purpose of ensuring its
independence, when Calvin undertook the administration of its ecclesiastical policy. There can be no doubt
as to the rigour as well as the severity of Calvin's rule;
but Geneva was surrounded by ferocious enemies, and
had to struggle for its very life. Mignet has in a few
words described the rapid progress made by that city :
"In less than half a century the face of Geneva
had become entirely changed. It passed through
three consecutive revolutions. The first delivered
it from the Duke of Savoy, who lost his delegated
authority in the attempt to convert it into an absolute sovereignty. The second introduced into Geneva
the Reformed worship, by which the sovereignty
of the bishop was destroyed. The third constituted
the Protestant administration of Geneva, and the
subordination to it of the civil power. The first of
these revolutions gave Geneva its independence of the
ducal power; the second, its moral regeneration and
political sovereignty ; the third its greatness. These
three revolutions not only followed each other ; they
were linked together. Switzerland was bent on liberty,
the human mind on emancipation. The liberty of
Switzerland made the independence of Geneva, the
emancipation of the human mind effected its reformation. These changes were not accomplished without
difficulties, nor without wars. But if they troubled
the peace of the city, if they agitated the people's
hearts, if they divided families, if they occasioned im-
prisonments, if they caused blood to be shed in the
streets, they tempered characters, they awoke minds,
they purified morals, they formed citizens and men,
and Geneva issued transformed from the trials through
which it passed. It had been subject, and it had
grown independent; it had been ignorant, and it had
become one of the lights of Europe; it had been a little
town, and it was now the Capital of a great Cause.

Its science, its constitution, its greatness, were the
work of France, through its exiles of the sixteenth
century, who, unable to realise their ideas in their own
country, had carried them into Switzerland, whose
hospitality they repaid by giving them a new worship,
and the spiritual government of many peoples." [1]

Geneva having thus been established as a great
Protestant asylum and stronghold, mainly through
the labours of Frenchmen—Calvin, Farel, De Beze,
D'Aubigné, and many more—the fugitive Protestants
naturally directed their steps thither in the first place.
In 1685, hundreds of them arrived in Geneva daily ;
but, as the place was already crowded, and the accommodation it provided was but limited, the greater
number of the new arrivals travelled onward, into the
interior cantons.   Two years later, the refugees were
arriving in thousands, mostly from Dauphiny and
Lyons ; the greater number of them being artizans.
While the persecution raged in Gex, close to the Swiss
frontier, it seemed as if the whole population were
flying.   Geneva became so crowded with fugitives that
they had to camp out at night in the public squares.

The stream of emigrants was not less considerable
at Basle, Zurich, Berne, and Lausanne.   The ambassador of Louis XIV. wrote to his royal master : " The
fugitives continue to crowd to Zurich ; I met a number
of them on the road from Basle to Soleure."   A month
later he informed his court that all the roads were full
of French subjects making for Berne and Zurich ; and
a third despatch informed Louis that carts laden with
fugitives were daily passing through the streets of
Basle.   As the fugitives were mostly destitute, the
Protestant cantons provided a fund [2] to facilitate the

---

[1] MIGNET — *Memoires Historiques*, Paris, 1854, pp. 385-7.
[2] The city of Geneva was su-
perbly bountiful.   In 1685, the
citizens contributed 88,161 florins
to the Protestant refugee fund.

As the emigration increased, so
did their bounty, until, in 1707,
they contributed as much as
234,672 florins towards the expenses of the emigration. "Within a period of forty years," says

transit of those whom the country was unable to maintain. Thus 15,591 persons were forwarded to Germany at the expense of the League.

Louis XIV. beheld with vexation the departure of so large a portion of his subjects, who preferred emigration and destitution, to French citizenship and forcible "conversion"; and he determined to interpose with a strong hand, so as, if possible, to prevent their further flight. Accordingly, when the people of Gex went flying into Geneva in crowds, Louis called upon the magistrates to expel them at once. The republican city was comparatively small and unarmed, and unable to resist the will of a monarch so powerful as Louis the Great then was. The magistrates, therefore, made a show of compliance with his orders, and directed the expulsion of the fugitives by sound of trumpet. The exiles left the city by the French gate in a long and sad procession; but at midnight the citizens went forth and led them round the walls, bringing them into Geneva again by the Swiss gate, on the opposite side of the city.

On this proceeding being reported to Louis, he vowed vengeance upon Geneva for thus trifling with his express orders, and giving refuge to his contumacious subjects. But Berne and Zurich having hastened to proffer their support to Geneva, the French king's threats remained unexecuted. The refugees, accordingly, remained in Switzerland, and settled in the various Protestant cantons, where they founded many important branches of industry, which continue to flourish to this day.

The Protestant refugees received a like cordial wel-

Graverol, in his *History of the City of Nismes* (London 1703), "Geneva furnished official contributions towards the assistance of the refugees of the Edict of Nantes, amounting to not less than 5,143,266 florins." The sums expended by the cantons of Berne and Vaud during the same period exceeded 4,000,000 florins. This expenditure was altogether exclusive of the individual contributions and private hospitality of the Swiss people, which were alike liberal and bountiful.

come in the provinces of North Germany, where they succeeded in establishing many important and highly flourishing colonies. The province of Brandenburg,— the nucleus of modern Prussia,—had been devastated and almost ruined by the Thirty Years' War. Its trade and manufactures were destroyed, and a large proportion of its soil lay uncultivated. The Elector Frederick William was desirous of replenishing the population; and, with that view, he sought to attract to it men of skill and industry from all quarters. The Protestants whom the king of France was driving out of his kingdom, were precisely the sort of men whom the Elector desired for subjects; and he sent repeated invitations to them to come and settle in Brandenburg, with the promise of liberty of worship, protection, and hospitality. As early as 1661, numerous refugees embraced his offer, and settled in Berlin, where they prospered, increased, and eventually founded a flourishing French Protestant colony.

The Revocation of the Edict of Nantes furnished the Elector with an opportunity for renewing his invitation with greater effect than before. The promulgation of the Edict of Paris was almost immediately followed by the promulgation of the Edict of Potsdam. By the latter edict, men of the Reformed religion, driven out of France for conscience' sake, were offered a free and safe retreat through all the dominions of the Elector. They were promised rights, franchises, and other advantages, on their settlement in Brandenburg, " in order to relieve them, and in some sort to make amends for the calamities with which Providence had thought fit to visit so considerable a part of His Church." Facilities were provided to enable the emigrants from France to reach the Prussian States. Those from the southern and eastern provinces of France were directed to make for the Rhine, and from thence to find their way by boats to Frankfort-on-the-Maine, or to Cleves, where the Prussian authorities awaited them with subsidies, and the means for travelling eastward.

Free shipping was also provided for them at Amsterdam, from whence they were to proceed to Hamburg, where the Prussian resident was directed to assist them in reaching their intended destination.

These measures shortly had the effect of attracting large numbers of Huguenots into the northern provinces of Germany. The city of Frankfort became crowded with exiles arriving from the eastern provinces of France. The fugitives were everywhere made welcome, and succoured and helped. The Elector assisted them with money out of his own private means. " I will sell my plate," he said, " rather than they should lack assistance."

On arriving in Brandenburg, the emigrants proceeded to establish their colonies throughout the electorate. Nearly every large town in Prussia had its French church, and one or more French pastors. The celebrated Ancillon was pastor of the church at Berlin ; and many of the Protestant gentry resorted thither, attracted by his reputation. The Huguenot immigration into Prussia consisted of soldiers, gentlemen, men of letters and artists, traders, manufacturers, and labourers.[1]

Numerous other bodies of the refugees settled in the smaller states of Germany, in Denmark, in Sweden, and even in Russia. Others crossed the ocean and founded settlements abroad ; in Dutch Surinam, at the Cape, and in the United States of America. The settlement formed at the Cape of Good Hope was of considerable importance. It was led by a nephew of Admiral Duquesne, and included members of some of the most distinguished families of France—Du Plessis de Mornay, Roubaix de la Fontaine, De Chavannes, De Villiers, Du Pré, Le Roux, Rous-

---

[1] The personal history and particulars of the refugees who settled in Prussia are given at full length in a work published at Berlin, in 9 vols. 8vo, by Messrs. Erman and Réclam, entitled *Memoires pour servir à l'Histoire des Refugiés François dans les Etats du Roi.*

seau, D'Abling, De Cilliers, Le Sueur, Maudé, and many more. The names of some of these are to be found among the roll of governors of the colony under the Dutch. The refugees mostly settled in the Berg Valley, afterwards known as French Valley, and now as De Fransche Hoek. Weiss says their descendants number as many as 4000 persons; and that they are still Huguenots in religion, and proud of their descent. The old families treasure their original French Bibles, and Clement Marot's hymn books, brought from France by their ancestors. A simple-minded farmer of Stellenbosch, near Cape Town, now represents the ancient ducal house of Du Plessis. It is said that when Napoleon I., in the early part of his reign, wished to rally round his throne all the old French families he could induce to acknowledge his pretensions, he offered to the Du Plessis at the Cape the restoral of his family title and estates; but the offer was declined. The Cape boer, in whose mind all recollection of his family traditions had died away, preferred his quiet vineyard on the Berg River to the brilliant saloons of the Tuileries.[1] The news of the outer world took a long time to reach the secluded descendants of the exiles. Weiss says that in 1828, when the evangelical missionaries told them that religious toleration had existed in France for forty years, the old men shed tears, and could with difficulty believe that their brethren could be so favourably treated in a country from which their ancestors had been so cruelly expelled.

The emigration to the United States of America was also of considerable importance. The first settlement of Walloons was on Staten Island, where they built a little church near Richmond, afterwards removed to Wahle Bocht, or the "Bay of Foreigners," since corrupted into Wallabout. The Staten Island refugees are still represented by the Disosways and Grisons, who occupy the same farms which their an-

---

[1] HENRY HALL, in *Notes and Queries*, April 24 1869.

cestors held a century and a half ago. Other settlements were established in the State of New York,—at
Albany, under their patron Van Ransselaer, and at
Manhattan, where they were joined by a body of persecuted Vaudois from the south of France. At New
Rochelle also, in Westchester County, another settlement was formed, which long continued to flourish.
Among the descendants of these emigrants, were the
celebrated families of Jay and De Lancey, well known
in the political history of the United States. In Mas-
sachussets they formed several settlements ; and the
celebrated Faneuil Hall, at Boston,—where the plea for
national independence was so early heard,—was the
gift of the son of a refugee. Worcester, in the same
state, was originally a Huguenot colony.

In Maryland, and in Virginia, other settlements were
formed; and from the Maurys and Fontaines of the
latter state, some of the best blood of America has
come. South Carolina was even styled " The Home
of the Huguenots,"—nearly a thousand fugitives having
reached it from the ports of Holland alone. There
they formed three colonies, at Charlestown, at Santee,
and Orange Quarter on the Cooper River. The first
pastor of the Huguenot church at Charlestown was
Elias Prioleau, a descendant of Antoine Prioli, Doge of
Venice in 1618. From the French settlers in Carolina
have come the Ravenels, Fravezants, Pèronneaus,
Laurens, Neuvilles, Boudinots, Manigaults, Marions,
Legares, Hugers, Gaillards, Benorts, Bayards, Duprés,
Chevaliers, and many illustrious Americans.

But Holland and England constituted the principal
asylums of the exiled Huguenots—Holland in the
first instance, and England in the next; many of the
refugees passing from the one country into the other,
in the course of the great political movements which
followed close upon the Revocation of the Edict of
Nantes.

Holland had long been a refuge for the persecuted
Protestants of Europe. During the religious troubles

of the sixteenth century, exiles fled to it from all
quarters—from Germany, Flanders, France, and England. During the reign of Queen Mary, thirty thousand
English Protestants fled thither, who for the most part
returned to England on the accession of Elizabeth.
There were colonies of foreign exiles settled in nearly
all the United Provinces—of Germans in Friesland
and Guelderland, and of Walloons in Amsterdam,
Haarlem, Leyden, Delft, and other towns in North
and South Holland. And now these refugees were
joined by a still greater influx of persecuted Protestants from all parts of France. Bayle designated
Holland "the great ark of the fugitives." It became
the chief European centre of free thought, free religion, and free industry. A healthy spirit of liberty
pervaded it, which awakened and cultivated the best
activities and energies of its people.

The ablest minds of France, proscribed by Louis
XIV., took refuge in the Low Countries, where they
taught from professors' chairs, preached from pulpits,
and spoke to all Europe through the medium of the
printing-press. Descartes, driven from France, betook
himself to Holland, where he spent twenty years, and
published his principal philosophical works. It was
the retreat of Bayle, Huyghens,[1] Jurieu, and many
more of the best men of France, who there uttered
and printed freely what they could do nowhere else.
Among the most stirring books which emanated from
the French press in Holland, were those of Jurieu—
formerly professor of theology and Hebrew in the
university of Sedan—who now sought to rouse the
indignation of Europe against the tyranny of Louis
XIV. His writings were not permitted to circulate
in France, where all works hostile to the King and
the Jesuits were seized and burnt; but they spread

---

[1] Though Huyghens was a
native of Holland, he had long
lived in Paris, having been induced to settle there by the
invitation of Colbert.

over northern Europe, and fanned the general indignation against Louis XIV. into a still fiercer flame.

Among the celebrated French Protestant divines
who took refuge in Holland were Claude, Basnage,
Martin, Benoit, and Saurin. Academies were expressly
established at Leyden, Rotterdam, and Utrecht, in
which the more distinguished of the banished ministers were appointed to professors' chairs, whilst others
were distributed throughout the principal towns, and
placed in charge of Protestant churches. A fund was
raised by voluntary subscription for the relief of the
fugitives, to which all parties cheerfully and liberally
contributed,—not only Lutherans and Calvinists, but
Jews and even Roman Catholics.

The public as well as the private hospitality of
Holland towards the fugitives was indeed splendid.
The magistrates of Amsterdam not only freely conferred on them the rights of citizenship, with liberty
to exercise their respective callings, but granted them
exemption from local taxes for three years. The
States of Holland and the province of Friesland
granted them similar privileges, with an exemption
from all imposts for a period of twelve years. Every
encouragement was given to the immigration. There
was not a town but was ready to welcome and help
the destitute foreigners. The people received them
into their houses as guests; and when the private
dwellings were filled, public establishments were
opened for their accommodation. Yet this was not
enough. The Dutch, hearing of the sufferings of the
poor exiles in Switzerland, sent invitations to them
to come into Holland, where they held out that there
was room enough for all.

The result was an immense increase of the emigration from France into Holland, of men of all ranks
—artizans, cloth-makers, silk-weavers, glass-makers,
printers, and manufacturers. They were distributed,
on their arrival, throughout the various towns and
cities, where they settled down to pursue their re-

spective callings ; and in the course of a short time they more than repaid, by the exercise of their industry and their skill, the hospitality of their benefactors.

Another important feature of the immigration into Holland remains to be mentioned. This was the influx of a large number of the best sailors of France, from the coasts of Guienne, Saintonge, La Rochelle, Poitou, and Normandy, together with a still larger number of veteran officers and soldiers of the French army. This accession of refugees had the effect of greatly adding to the strength both of the Dutch navy and army; and, as we shall hereafter find, it exercised an important influence on the political history both of Holland and England.

Louis XIV. endeavoured to check the emigration of his subjects into Holland, as he had tried to stop their flight into Switzerland and England, but in vain. His envoy expostulated against their reception by the States; and the States reiterated their proclamations of privileges to the refugees. The people began to fear that Louis would declare war against Holland ; though the Prince of Orange did not shrink from an encounter with the French king.

William, Prince of Orange and Stadtholder of Holland, hated France as his forefathers had hated Spain. Under an appearance of physical weakness and phlegmatic indifference he concealed an ardent mind and an indomitable will. He was cool and taciturn, yet full of courage and even daring. He was one of those rare men who never knew despair. When the great French army of 100,000 men, under Condé and Turenne, swept over Flanders in 1672, capturing city after city, and approached Amsterdam, the inhabitants became filled with dread. De Witt proposed submission; but William, then only twenty-two years of age, urged resistance, and his view was supported by the people. He declared that he would die in the last ditch rather than see the ruin of his country ; and, true to his word, he ordered the dykes to be cut and the country laid under water. The independence of Holland was saved, but at a frightful cost; and William never forgot, perhaps never forgave, the injury which Louis XIV. had thus caused him to inflict upon Holland.

William had another and more personal cause of quarrel with Louis. The Prince took his title from the small but independent principality of Orange, situated in the south-east of France, a little to the north of Avignon. Though Orange was a fief of the Imperial and not of the French crown, Louis, disregarding public law, overran it, dismantled the fortifications of the principal town, and subjected the Protestants of the district to the same cruelties which he had practised upon his own subjects of the same faith. On being informed of these outrages, William declared aloud at his table that the Most Christian King "should be made to know one day what it was to offend a Prince of Orange." Louis' ambassador at the Hague having questioned the Prince as to the meaning of the words, the latter positively refused either to retract or explain them.

It may not be unimportant to remark that William was, like the other princes of his race, an enthusiastic Protestant. The history of his family was identified with the rise and progress of the new views, as well as with the emancipation of the United Provinces from the yoke of Spain and the Inquisition. His great-grandsire had fallen a victim to the dagger of Gérard, the agent of the Jesuits, and expired in the arms of his wife, the daughter of Admiral Coligny. Thus, the best Huguenot blood flowed in the veins of the young Prince of Orange; and his sympathies were wholly on the side of the fugitives who sought the asylum of Holland against the cruelty of their persecutors.

At the same time, William was doubly related to the English royal family. His mother was the daughter of Charles I., and his wife was the daughter of James II., reigning king of England. James being then without male issue, the Princess of Orange was the heiress-presumptive to the British throne. Though William may have been ambitious, he was cautious and sagacious, and probably had not the remotest idea of anticipating the succession of his wife by the overthrow of the government of his father-in-law, but for the circumstances about to be summarily described, and which issued in the Revolution of 1688.

Although the later Stuart kings, who were Roman Catholics at heart, hated Protestantism, they nevertheless felt themselves under the necessity of continuing the policy initiated by Queen Elizabeth, of giving a free asylum in England to the persecuted Huguenots. In 1681, Charles II. was constrained by public opinion to sanction a bill granting large privileges to such of the refugees as should land on our shores. They were to have free letters-patent granted them ; and on their arrival at any of the out-ports, their baggage and stock-in-trade—when they had any—were to be landed duty free. But the greater number arrived destitute. For example, a newspaper of the day thus announced the landing of a body of the refugees at Plymouth : "Plymouth, 6th September, 1681.—An open boat arrived here yesterday, in which were forty or fifty Protestants who resided outside La Rochelle. Four other boats left with this, one of which is said to have put into Dartmouth, but it is not yet known what became of the other three."

Large numbers of the fugitives continued to land at all the southern ports — at Dover, at Rye, at Southampton, at Dartmouth, and at Plymouth ; and, wherever they landed, they received a cordial welcome. Many were pastors, who came ashore hungering and in rags, lamenting the flocks, and some the wives and children, which they had left behind them in France. The people crowded round the venerable sufferers with indignant and pitying hearts. They

received them into their dwellings, and hospitably
relieved their wants. Very soon the flocks followed
in the wake of their pastors. These landings continued for many years, during which the refugees
crowded all the southern ports. The local clergy
led and directed the hospitality of the inhabitants,
usually placing the parish church at the disposal of
the exiles during a part of each Sunday, until they
could be provided with accommodation of their own.[1]

The sight of so much distress borne so patiently
and uncomplainingly, deeply stirred the heart of the
nation ; and every effort was made to succour and
help the poor refugees for conscience' sake. Public
collections were made in the churches. A fund was
raised for the relief of the most necessitous, and for
enabling the foreigners to proceed inland to places
where they could pursue their industry. Many
were thus forwarded from the sea-coast to London,
Canterbury, Norwich, and other places, where they
eventually formed prosperous settlements, and laid
the foundations of important branches of industry.

James II. succeeded to the British throne at the
death of his brother Charles II. on the 6th of January,
1685,—the year in which the Edict of Nantes was re-

---

[1] At Rye, the refugees were
granted the use of the parish
church from eight to ten in the
morning, and from twelve to two
in the afternoon, the appropriation being duly confirmed by the
Council of State. Reports having
been spread abroad, that the fugitives were persons of bad character, disaffected, and Papists in
disguise, the vicar and principal
inhabitants of Rye drew up and
published the following testi-
monial in their behalf :—

"These are to certifie to all
whom it may concern, that the
French Protestants that are
settled inhabitants of this town
of Rye, are a sober, harmless,
innocent people, such as serve
God constantly and uniformly,
according to the usage and
custom of the Church of England. And further, that we believe them to be falsely aspersed
for Papists and disaffected persons, no such thing appearing
unto us by the conversations of
any of them. This we do freely
and truly certifie, for and of
them. In witness whereof, we
have hereunto set our hands,
the 18th day of April, 1682.
Wm. Williams, vicar ; Thos.
Tournay," etc. etc.—*State Papers, Domestic Calendar*, 1682,
No. 65.

voked. Charles and James were both Roman Catholics,—Charles when he was not a scoffer, James always. The latter had long been a friend of the Jesuits, in disguise; but no sooner did he become king, than he threw off the mask, and exhibited himself in his true character. James was not a man to gather wisdom from experience. During the exile of his family, he had learnt nothing and forgotten nothing; and it shortly became clear to the English nation that he was bent on pursuing almost the identical course which had cost his father his crown and his head.

If there was one feeling that characterised the English people about this time, more than another, it was their aversion to Popery,—not merely Popery as a religion, but as a policy. It was felt to be contrary to the whole spirit, character, and tendency of the nation. Popery had so repeatedly exhibited itself as a persecuting policy, that not only the religious but the non-religious,—not only the intelligent few, but the illiterate many,—regarded it with feelings of deep aversion. Great, therefore, was the public indignation when it became known that one of the first acts of James, on his accession to the throne, was to order the public celebration of the Mass at Westminster, after an interval of more than a century. The King dismissed from about his person clergymen of the English Church, and introduced well-known Jesuits in their stead. He degraded several of the bishops, though he did not yet venture openly to persecute them. But he showed his temper and his tendency, by actively reviving the persecutions of the Scotch Presbyterians, whom he pursued with a cruelty only equalled by Louis XIV. in his dealings with the Huguenots.[1]

James II. was but the too ready learner of the lessons

---

[1] In Scotland, whoever was detected preaching in a conventicle or attending one, was *punishable with death and the confiscation of all his property.* Macaulay says that the Scotch Act of Parliament (James VII., 8th May, 1685) enacting these penalties was passed at the special instance of the King.

of despotism taught him by Louis XIV., whose pensioner he was, and whose ultimate victim he proved to be. The two men indeed resembled each other in many respects, and their actions ran in almost parallel lines; though those who concede to Louis the title of " Great," will probably object that the English king was merely the ape of the French one. They were both dissolute, and both bigots, vibrating alternately between their mistresses and their confessors. What La Valliere, Montespan, and Maintenon were to Louis XIV., Arabella Churchill and Catherine Sedley were to James II. The principal difference between them in this respect was, that Louis sinned with comely mistresses, and James with ugly ones. Louis sought absolution from Père la Chaise, and James from Father Petre; and when penance had to be done, both laid it alike upon their Protestant subjects,—Louis increasing the pressure of persecution on the Huguenots, and James upon the Puritans and Covenanters. Both employed military missionaries in carrying out their designs of conversion; the agents of Louis being the " dragons " of Noailles, those of James being the dragoons of Claverhouse. Both were despisers of constitutional power, and sought to centre the government in themselves. But while Louis succeeded in crushing the Huguenots, James ignominiously failed in crushing the Puritans. Louis, it is true, brought France to the verge of ruin, and paved the way for the French Revolution of 1792; whilst, happily for England, the designs of James were summarily thwarted by the English Revolution of 1688, and the ruin of his kingdom was thus averted.

The designs of James upon the consciences of his people, were not long in developing themselves. The persecution of the Scotch Covenanters was carried on with increased virulence, until resistance almost disappeared; and then he turned his attention to the English Puritans. Baxter, Howe, Bunyan, and hundreds of nonconformist ministers, were thrown into gaol; but there were as yet no hangings nor shootings

of them, as there had been in Scotland. To strengthen
his power, and enable him to adopt more decisive
measures, James next took steps to augment the standing army,—a measure which exposed him to increased
public odium. Though contrary to law, he in many
cases dismissed the Protestant officers of regiments,
and appointed Roman Catholics in their stead. To
render their appointments legal, he proposed to repeal
the Test Act, as well as the Habeas Corpus Act; but
his minister Halifax refusing to concur in this course,
he was dismissed, and Parliament was adjourned.
Immediately before its re-assembling, the news arrived
from France of the Revocation of the Edict of Nantes,
and of the horrible cruelties perpetrated on the Huguenots. The intelligence caused a thrill of indignation
to run throughout England; and very shortly, crowds
of the destitute fugitives landed on the southern coast,
spreading abroad the tale of horror.

Shortly after, there came from France the report of
a speech addressed by the Bishop of Valance to Louis
XIV. in the name of the French clergy. " The pious
sovereign of England," said the orator, " looked to the
Most Christian King, the eldest son of the Church,
for support against a heretical nation." The natural
inference drawn was, that what Louis had done in
France, James was about to imitate in England by
means of his new standing army, commanded by
Roman Catholic officers.

To allay the general alarm which began to prevail,
James pretended to disapprove of the cruelties to
which the Huguenots had been subjected; and, in
deference to public opinion, he granted some relief to
the exiles from his privy purse, inviting his subjects
to imitate his liberality, by making a public collection
for them in the churches throughout the kingdom.
His acts, however, belied his words. At the instiga-
tion of Barillon, he had the book published in Holland
by the banished Huguenot pastor Claude, describing
the sufferings of his brethren, burnt by the hangman

before the Royal Exchange; and when the public collection was made in the churches, and £40,000 was paid into the chamber of London, James gave orders that none should receive a farthing of relief unless they first took the sacrament according to the Anglican ritual. Many of the exiles who came for help, when they heard of the terms on which alone it was to be granted, went away unrelieved, with sad and sorrowful hearts.

James proceeded steadily in his reactionary course. He ordered warrants to be drawn in defiance of the law, authorising priests of the Church of Rome to hold benefices in the Church of England. A Jesuit was quartered as chaplain in University College, Oxford; and the Roman Catholic rites were there publicly celebrated. The deanery of Christ Church was conferred upon a minister of the Church of Rome, and mass was duly celebrated there. Roman Catholic chapels and convents rose all over the country; and Franciscan, Carmelite, and Benedictine monks, appeared openly, in their cowls, beads, and conventual garbs. The King made little secret of his intention to destroy the Protestant Church; and he lost no time in carrying out his measures, even in the face of popular tumult and occasional rioting,—placing his reliance mainly upon his standing army, which was encamped on Hounslow Heath. At the same time, Tyrconnel was sent over to Ireland to root out the Protestant colonies there. One of his first acts was to cast adrift about 4000 Protestant officers and soldiers, supplanting them with as many staunch Papists. Those in his confidence boasted that within a few months there would not be a man of English race left in the Irish army. The Irish Protestants, indeed, began to fear another massacre; and a number of families, principally gentlemen, artificers, and tradesmen, left Dublin for England in the course of a few days.

At length resistance began to show itself. The Parliaments both of England and Scotland pronounced

against the King's policy, and he was unable to carry
his measures by constitutional methods. He accordingly resolved, like Louis XIV., to rule by the strong
hand, and to govern by royal edict. Such was the
state of affairs, rapidly verging on anarchy and civil
war, when the English nation, sick of the rule of
James II., after a reign of only three years, and
eager for relief, looked abroad for succour; and, with
almost general consent, they fixed their eyes upon
William, Prince of Orange, as the one man capable of
helping them in their time of need.

The Prince of Orange had meanwhile been diligently
occupied, amongst other things, with the reorganisation
of his army ; and the influx of veteran officers and
soldiers of the French king, banished from France
because of their religion, furnished him with every
facility for the purpose. He proposed to the States
of Holland that they should raise two new regiments,
to be composed entirely of Huguenots ; but the States
were at first unwilling to make such an addition to
their army. They feared the warlike designs of their
young prince, and were mainly intent upon reducing
the heavy imposts that weighed upon the country, occasioned by the recent invasion of Louis XIV., from the
effects of which they were still suffering.

William, fearing lest the veterans whom he so
anxiously desired to retain in his service should depart into other lands, then publicly proclaimed that he
would himself pay the expenses of all the Military
Refugees, rather than that they should leave Holland.
On this the States hesitated no longer, but agreed to
pension the French officers until they could be incorporated in the Dutch army; and 180,000 florins a year
were voted for the purpose. Companies of French
cadets were also formed and maintained at the expense
of the state. The Huguenot officers and men were
drafted as rapidly as possible into the Dutch army;
and before long William saw his ranks swelled by
a formidable body of veteran troops, together with a

large number of officers of fusiliers from Strasburg,
Metz, and Verdun,   Whole companies of Huguenot
troops were drafted into each regiment under their
own officers, while the principal fortresses at Breda,
Maestricht, Bergen-op-Zoom, Bois-le-Duc, Zutphen,
Nimuegen, Arnheim, and Utrecht, were used as so
many depôts for such officers and soldiers as continued
to take refuge in Holland.

William's plans were so carefully prepared, and he
conducted his proceedings with so much secrecy, that
both James II. and Louis XIV. were kept entirely in
the dark as to his plans and intentions.   At length the
Prince was ready to embark his army, and England
was ready to receive him.   It forms no part of our
purpose to relate the circumstances connected with the
embarkation of William, his landing in England, and
the revolution which followed, further than to illustrate the part which the banished Huguenots played
in that great political transaction.   The narrative will
be found in the pages of Macaulay, though that historian passes over with too slight notice the services of
the Huguenots.

Michelet observes with justice: — " The army of
William was strong precisely in that Calvinistic element which James repudiated in England—I mean in
our Huguenot soldiers, the brothers of the Puritans. I
am astonished that Macaulay has thought fit to leave
this circumstance in the background. I cannot believe
that great England, with all her glories and her inheritance of liberty, is unwilling nobly to avow the part
which we Frenchmen had in her deliverance.   In the
Homeric enumeration which the historian gives of the
followers of William, he reckons up English, Germans,
Dutch, Swedes, Swiss, with the picturesque detail of
their arms, uniforms, and all, down even to the two
hundred negroes with their black faces set off by em-
broidered turbans and white feathers, who followed the
body of English gentry led by the Earl of Macclesfield.
But he did not see our Frenchmen.   Apparently the

proscribed Huguenot soldiers who followed William
did not do honour to the Prince by their clothes!
Doubtless many of them wore the dress in which they
had fled from France—and it had become dusty, worn,
and tattered." [1]

There is indeed little reason to doubt that the
flower of the little army with which William landed at
Torbay, on the 15th of November, 1688, consisted of
Huguenot soldiers, trained under Schomberg, Turenne,
and Condé. The expedition included three entire
regiments of French infantry, numbering 2250 men,
and a complete squadron of French cavalry. These
were nearly all veteran troops, whose valour had been
proved on many a hard-fought field. Many of them
were gentlemen born, who, unable to obtain commissions as officers, were content to serve in the ranks.
The number of French officers was very large in
proportion to the whole force,—736, besides those in
command of the French regiments, being distributed
through all the battalions. It is, moreover, worthy of
note that William's ablest and most trusted officers
were Huguenots. Schomberg, the refugee marshal of
France, was next in command to the Prince himself;
and such was the confidence which that skilful general
inspired, that the Princess of Orange gave him secret
instructions to assert her rights, and carry out the
enterprise, should her husband fall. William's three
aides-de-camp, De l'Etang, De la Melonière, and the
Marquis d'Arzilliers, were French officers, as were also
the chiefs of the engineers and the artillery, Gambon
and Goulon, the latter being one of Vauban's most distinguished pupils. Fifty-four French gentlemen served
in William's regiment of horse-guards, and thirty-four
in his body-guard. Among the officers of the army of
liberation, distinguished alike by their birth and their
military skill, were the cavalry officers Didier de
Boncourt and Chalant de Remeugnac, colonels; Danser-

---

[1] MICHELET—*Louis XIV. et la Revocation*, pp. 418-19.

ville, lieutenant-colonel ; and Petit and Picard, majors; whilst others of equal birth and distinction as soldiers served in the infantry.[1]

Marshal Schomberg was descended from the Dukes of Cleves, whose arms he bore. Several of his ancestors had held high rank in the French service. One of them was killed at the battle of Ivry on the side of Henry IV., and another commanded under Richelieu at the siege of Rochelle. The marshal, whose mother was an Englishwoman of the noble house of Dudley, began his career in the Swedish army in the Thirty Years' War, after which he entered the service of the Netherlands, and subsequently that of France. There he led an active and distinguished career, and rose by successive steps to the rank of marshal. The great Condé had the highest opinion of his military capacity, and compared him to Turenne. He commanded armies successfully in Flanders, Portugal, and Holland; but on the Revocation of the Edict, being unable to conform to popery, he felt compelled to resign his military honours and emoluments, and leave France for ever.

Schomberg first went to Portugal, which was assigned to him as his place of exile ; but he shortly after left that country to take service, with numerous other French officers, under Frederick William of Brandenburg. His stay at Berlin was, however, of short duration ; for, when he heard of the intentions of William of Orange with respect to England, he at once determined to join him. Offers of the most tempting kind were held out by Frederick William to induce him to remain in Prussia. The Elector proposed to appoint him governor-general, minister of state, and member

---

[1] Among the captains of horse were Massole de Montant, Petit, De Maricourt, De Boncourt, De Fabricè, De Lauray, Baron d'Entragues, Le Coq de St. Leger, De Saumaise, De Lacroix, De Dampierre; while among the captains of infantry we find De Saint Sauveur, Rapin (afterwards the historian), De Cosne-Chavernay, Danserville, Massole de Montant, Jacques de Baune, Baron de Avejan, Nolibois, Belcastel, Jaucourt de Villarnouc, Lislemaretz, De Montazier, and the three brothers De Batz.

of the privy council; but in vain. Schomberg felt that the interests of Protestantism, of which William of Orange was the recognised leader, required him to forego his own personal interests ; and though nearly seventy years of age, he quitted the service of Prussia to enter that of Holland. He was accompanied by a large number of veteran Huguenot officers, full of bitter resentment against the monarch who had driven them forth from France, and who burned to meet their persecutors in the field and avenge themselves of the cruel wrongs which they had suffered at their hands.

What the embittered feelings of the French Protestant gentry were, and what was the nature of the injuries they had suffered because of their religion, may, however, best be explained by the following narrative of the sufferings and adventures of a Norman gentleman who succeeded in making his escape from France,—who joined the liberating army of William of Orange as captain of dragoons, took part in the expedition to England, served with the English army in the Irish campaigns, and afterwards settled at Portarlington in Ireland, where he died in 1709.

CHAPTER XII.

ISAAC DUMONT DE BOSTAQUET was a Protestant gentleman possessing considerable landed property near
Yerville in Normandy, about eight leagues from
Dieppe. He had been well educated in his youth,
and served with distinction in the French army as
an officer of Norman horse. After leaving the army,
he married, and settled on his paternal estates, where
he lived the life of a retired country gentleman.[1]

It was about the year 1661, that the first muttering
of the coming storm reached De Bostaquet in his
ancient château of La Fontelaye. The Roman Catholics, supported by the King, had begun to pull down
Protestant churches in many districts; and now it
began to be rumoured abroad that several in Normandy were to be demolished; amongst others the
church of Lindebœuf, in which De Bostaquet and his
family worshipped. He at once set out for Paris, to
endeavour, if possible, to prevent the outrage. He saw
his old commander Turenne, and had interviews with
the King's ministers, but without any satisfactory
result; for on his return to Normandy he found that
the temple at Lindebœuf had been demolished during
his absence.

---

[1] The account given in this
chapter is mainly drawn from
the *Mémoires Inédits de Dumont
de Bostaquet, Gentilhomme, Nor-
mand*, edited by MM. Read and
Waddington, and published at
Paris in 1864. The MS. was
in the possession of Dr. Vignoles, Dean of Ossory, a lineal
descendant of De Bostaquet.

When De Bostaquet complained to the local authorities of the outrage, he was told that the King was resolved to render the exercise of the Protestant worship so difficult that it would be necessary for all Protestants throughout France to conform themselves to the King's religion. This, however, De Bostaquet was not prepared to do; and a temporary place of worship was fitted up in the château at La Fontelaye, where the scattered flock of Lindebœuf reassembled, and the seigneur himself on an emergency preached, baptized, and performed the other offices of religion. And thus he led an active and useful life in the neighbourhood for many years.

But the persecution of the Protestants became increasingly hard to bear. More of their churches were pulled down, and their worship was becoming all but proscribed. De Bostaquet began to meditate emigration into Holland; but he was bound to France by many ties—of family as well as property. By his first wife he had a family of six daughters and one son. Shortly after her death he married a second time, and a second family of six children was added to the first. But his second wife also died, leaving him with a large family to rear and educate; and, as intelligent female help was essential for this purpose, he was thus induced to marry a third time; and a third family, of two sons and three daughters, was added to the original number.

At last the Edict was revoked, and the dragoons were let loose on the provinces to compel the conversion of the Protestants. A body of cuirassiers was sent into Normandy, which had hitherto been exempt from their visitations. On the intelligence of their advance reaching De Bostaquet, he summoned a meeting of the neighbouring Protestant gentry at his house at La Fontelaye, to consider what was best to be done. He then declared to them his intention of leaving France should the King persist in his tyrannical course. Although all who were present praised his

resolution, none offered to accompany him,—not even
his eldest son, who had been married only a few
months before. When the ladies of the household
were apprised of the resolution he had expressed,
they implored him, with tears in their eyes, not to
leave them; if he did, they felt themselves lost. His
wife, on the eve of another confinement, joined her
entreaties to those of his children; and he felt that
under such circumstances, the idea of flight must be
given up.

The intelligence shortly reached La Fontelaye that
the cuirassiers had entered Rouen sword in hand,
under the Marquis de Beaupré Choiseul; that the
quartering of the troops on the inhabitants was producing "conversions" by wholesale; and that crowds
were running to M. de Marillac, the Intendant, to sign
their abjuration, and thus get rid of the soldiers. De
Bostaquet then resolved to go over to Rouen himself,
and see with his own eyes what was going on there.
He was greatly shocked both by what he saw and
by what he heard. Sorrow sat on all countenances
except those of the dragoons, who paraded the streets
with a truculent air. There was the constant moving
of them from house to house. Wherever they were
quartered, they swore, drank, and hectored, until the
inmates signed their abjuration, when they were withdrawn for the purpose of being quartered elsewhere.
De Bostaquet was ineffably pained to find that these
measures were generally successful; that all classes
were making haste to conform; and that even his
brother-in-law, M. de Lamberville, who had been so
staunch but a few days before, had been carried
along by the stream and abjured.

De Bostaquet hastened from the place, and returned
to La Fontelaye sad at heart. The intelligence which
he brought with him, of the dragonnades at Rouen, occasioned deep concern in the minds of his household;
but only one feeling pervaded them,—resignation and
steadfastness. De Bostaquet took refuge in the hope

that, belonging as he did to the noblesse, he would be spared the quartering of troops in his family. But he was mistaken. At Rouen, the commandant quartered thirty horsemen upon Sieur Chauvel, until he and his lady, to get rid of them, signed their abjuration; and an intimation was shortly after made to De Bostaquet, that unless he and his family abjured, a detachment of twenty-five dragoons would be quartered in his château. Fearing the effects on his wife, in her then delicate state of health, as well as desirous of saving his children from the horrors of such a visitation, he at once proceeded to Dieppe with his eldest son, and promised to sign his abjuration after placing himself for a time under the instruction of the reverend penitentiary of Notre Dame de Rouen.

No sooner had he put his name to the paper, than he felt degraded in his own eyes. He felt that he had attached his signature to a falsehood, for he had no intention of attending mass or abjuring his religion. But his neighbours were now abjuring all round. His intimate friend, the Sieur de Boissé, had a company of musketeers quartered on him until he signed. Another neighbour, the Sieur de Montigny, was in like manner compelled to abjure,—his mother and four daughters, to avoid the written lie, having previously escaped into Holland. None were allowed to go free. Old M. de Grosménil, De Bostaquet's father-in-law, though laid up by gout and scarce able to hold a pen, was compelled to sign. In anticipation of the quartering of the dragoons on the family, his wife had gone into concealment, the children had left the house, and even the domestics could with difficulty be induced to remain. The eldest daughter fled through Picardy into Holland; the younger daughters took refuge with their relatives in Rouen; the son also fled, none knew whither. Madame de Grosménil issued from her concealment to take her place by her suffering husband's bed, and she too was compelled to sign her abjuration; but she was so shocked

and grieved by the sin she had committed, that she
shortly after fell ill and died. "All our families,"
says De Bostaquet, "succumbed by turns." A body
of troops next made their appearance at La Fontelaye, and required all the members of the household
to sign their abjuration. De Bostaquet's wife, his
mother—whose grey hairs did not protect her—his
sons, daughters, and domestics, were all required to
sign.

The whole family now began seriously to meditate
flight from France,—De Bostaquet's mother, notwithstanding her burden of eighty years, being one of the
most eager to escape. Attempts were first made to
send away the girls singly, and several journeys were
made to the nearest port with that object; but no
ship could be met with, and the sea-coast was found
strictly guarded. De Bostaquet's design having become
known to the commandant at Dieppe, he was privately
warned of the risk he ran of being informed against,
and of having his property confiscated and himself
sent to the galleys. But the ladies of the family
became every day more urgent to flee, declaring that
their consciences would not allow them any longer
hypocritically to conform to a Church which they
detested, and that they were resolved to escape from
their present degradation at all risks.

At length it was arranged that an opportunity
should be taken of escaping during the fêtes of Pentecost, when there was to be a grand review of the
peasantry appointed to guard the coast, during which
they would necessarily be withdrawn from their posts
as watchers of the Huguenot fugitives. The family
plans were thus somewhat precipitated, before De
Bostaquet had been enabled to convert his property
into money, and thereby provide himself with the
means of conducting the emigration of so large a
family. It was at first intended that the young
ladies should endeavour to make their escape, their
father accompanying them to the coast to see them

safe on board ship, and then returning to watch over
his wife, who was approaching the time of her confinement.

On the morning of Pentecost Sunday, the whole
family assembled at worship, and besought the blessing
of God on their projected enterprise.   After dinner
the party set out.   It consisted of De Bostaquet, his
aged mother, several grown daughters, and many
children.   The father had intended that his youngest
son should stay behind ; but with tears in his eyes he
implored leave to accompany them.   The cavalcade
first proceeded to the village of La Halière, where
arrangements had been made for their spending the
night, while De Bostaquet proceeded to Saint Aubin
to engage an English vessel lying there to take them
off the coast.

The following night, about ten o'clock, the party
set out from Luneray, accompanied by many friends,
and a large number of fugitives like themselves,
making for the sea-coast.   De Bostaquet rode first,
with his sister behind him on a pillion.   His son-
in-law, De Renfreville, and his wife, rode another
horse in like manner.   De Bostaquet's mother, the
old lady of eighty, was mounted on a quiet pony,
and attended by two peasants.   His son and daughter
were also mounted, the latter on a peasant's horse,
which carried the valises.   De Renfreville's valet rode
another nag, and was armed with a musketoon.   Thus
mounted, and after many adieux, the party set out for
Saint Aubin.   On their way thither they were joined
by other relatives—M. de Montcornet, an old officer
in the French army, De Bostaquet's brother-in-law,
and M. de Béquigny, who was accompanied by a
German valet, with another young lady behind him
on a pillion.

" We found before us in the plain," says De Bostaquet, " more than three hundred persons — men,
women, and children—all making for the sea-coast,
some for Saint Aubin, and others for Quiberville.

Nearly the whole of these people were peasants, there being very few of the better class among them; and none bore arms but ourselves and the two valets of De Béquigny and De Renfreville, who carried musketoons. The facility with which fugitives had heretofore been enabled to escape, and the belief that there was no danger connected with our undertaking, made us travel without much precaution. The night was charming, and the moon shone out brightly. The delicious coolness which succeeded the heat of the preceding day enabled the poor peasants on foot to march forward with a lighter step; and the prospect of a speedy deliverance from their captivity made them almost run towards the shore with as much joy as if they had been bound for a wedding-party. * * *

"Those who intended to embark at Quiberville now left us, while those who were bound for Saint Aubin proceeded in that direction. As yet we had encountered no obstacle. We passed through Flainville without any one speaking to us; and, flattering ourselves that everything was propitious, we at length reached the shore. We found the coast-guard station empty; no one appeared; and without fear we alighted to rest our horses. We seated the ladies on the shingle by the side of my mother, a tall girl from Caen keeping them company.

" I was disappointed at seeing no signs of the vessel in which we were to embark. I did not know that they were waiting for some signal to approach the land. While I was in this state of anxiety, my son came to inform me that his aunt had arrived. Her carriage had not been able to reach the shore, and she waited for me about a gun-shot off. I went on foot, accompanied by my son, to find her. She and her children were bathed in tears at the thought of their separation. She embraced me tenderly, and the sight of herself and little ones afflicted me exceedingly. My daughter from Ribœuf alighted from the carriage to salute me, as well as Mademoiselle Duval.

"I had been with them for a very little while, when I perceived that there was a general movement down by the margin of the sea, where I had left my party. I asked what it was, and fearing lest the vessel might appear too far off, I proposed to have the carriage brought nearer to the shore; but I was not left long in uncertainty, A peasant called out to me, that there was a great disturbance going forward; and soon after, I heard the sound of drums beating, followed by a discharge of musketry. It immediately occurred to me that it must be the coast-guard returned to occupy their post, who had fallen on our party; and I began to fear that we were irretrievably lost. I was on foot alone, with my little son, near the carriage. I did not see two horsemen, who were coming down upon us at full speed, but I heard voices crying with all their might, 'Help! help!' I found myself in a strange state of embarrassment, without means of defence, when my lacquey, who was holding my horses on the beach, ran towards me with my arms.

"I had only time to throw myself on my horse and call out to my sister-in-law in the carriage, to turn back quickly, when I hastened, pistol in hand, to the place whence the screams proceeded. Scarcely was I clear of the carriage, when a horseman shouted, 'Kill! kill!' I answered, 'Fire, rascal!' At the same moment he fired his pistol full at me, so near that the discharge flashed along my left cheek and set fire to my peruke, but without wounding me. I was still so near the carriage, that both the coachmen and lacquey saw my hair in a blaze. I took aim with my pistol at the stomach of the scoundrel, but, happily for him, it missed fire, although I had primed it afresh on leaving Luneray. The horseman at once turned tail, accompanied by his comrade. I then took my other pistol, and followed the two at the trot, when one called out to the other, 'Fire! fire!' The one that had a musket proceeded to take aim at me, and as it was nearly as light as day, and I was only two or three horselengths

14

from him, he fired and hit me in the left arm, with
which I was holding my bridle. I moved my arm
quickly, to ascertain whether it was broken, and putting spurs to my horse, I gained the crupper of the
man who had first fired at me, who was now on my
left, and as he bent over his horse's neck, I discharged
my pistol full into his haunch. The two horsemen at
once disappeared and fled.

"I now heard the voice of De Béquigny, who, embar-
rassed by his assailants on foot, was furiously defending
himself; and, without losing time in pursuing my
fugitives, I ran up to him sword in hand, encountering
on the way my son-in-law, who was coming towards
me. I asked him whither he was going; and he said that
he was running in search of the horses which his valet
had taken away. I told him it was in vain, and that
he was flying as fast as his legs could carry him, for I
had caught sight of him passing as I mounted my horse.
But I had no time to reason with him. In a moment
I had joined De Béquigny, who had with him only
old Montcornet, my wife's uncle; but before a few
minutes had passep, we had scattered the canaille, and
found ourselves masters of the field. De Béquigny
informed me that his horse was wounded, and that he
could do no more; and I told him that I was wounded
in the arm, but that it was necessary, without loss of
time, to ascertain what had become of the poor women.

"We found them at the place where we had left
them, but abandoned by everybody; the attendants
and the rest of the troop having run away along the
coast, under the cliffs. My mother, who was extremely
deaf through age, had not heard the firing, and did not
know what to make of the disturbance, thinking only
of the vessel, which had not yet made its appearance.
My sister, greatly alarmed, on my reproaching her
with not having quietly followed the others, answered
that my mother was unable to walk, being too much
burdened by her dress ; for, fearing the coldness of the
night, she had clothed herself heavily. M. de Béquigny

then suggested that it might yet be possible to rally
some of the men of our troop, and thereby rescue the
ladies from their peril. Without loss of time I ran
along the beach for some distance, supposing that some
of the men might have hidden under the cliffs through
fear. But my labour was useless: I saw only some
girls, who fled away weeping. Considering that my
presence would be more useful to our poor women, I
rejoined them at the gallop. M. de Béquigny, on his
part, had returned from the direction of the coast-
guard station, to ascertain whether there were any
persons lurking there, for we entertained no doubt
that it was the coast-guard that had attacked us; and
the two horsemen with whom I had the affair confirmed me in this impression, for I knew that such
men were appointed to patrol the coasts, and visit the
posts all the night through. On coming up to me,
Béquigny said he feared we were lost; that the rascals
had rallied to the number of about forty, and were
preparing for another attack.

"We had no balls remaining with which to reload
our pistols. Loss of blood already made me feel very
faint. De Béquigny's horse had been wounded in the
shoulder by a musket-shot, and had now only three
legs to stand upon. In this extremity, and not knowing
what to do to save the women and children, I begged
him to set my mother behind me on horseback. He
tried, but she was too heavy, and he set her down
again. M. de Montcornet was the only other man we
had with us, but he was useless. He was seventy-
two, and the little nag he rode could not be of much
service. De Béquigny's valet had run away, after
having in the skirmish fired his musketoon and
wounded a coast-guardsman in the shoulder, of which
the man died. The tide, which began to rise, deterred
me from leading the women and children under the
cliffs; besides, I was uncertain of the route in that
direction. My mother and sister conjured me to fly
instantly, because, if I was captured, my ruin was

certain, whilst the worst that could happen to them would be, confinement in a convent.

"In this dire extremity, my heart was torn by a thousand conflicting emotions, and I was overwhelmed with despair at being unable to rescue those so dear to me from the perils which beset them. I knew not what course to take. While in this state of irresolution, I felt myself becoming faint through loss of blood. Taking out my handkerchief, I asked my sister to tie it round my arm, which was still bleeding; but wanting the nerve to do so, as well as not being sufficiently tall to reach me on horseback, I addressed myself to the young lady from Caen, who was with them, and whom they called La Rosière. She was tall, and by the light of the moon she looked a handsome girl. She had great reluctance to approach me in the state in which I was; but at last, after entreating her earnestly, she did me the service which I required, and the further flow of blood was stopped.

"After resisting for some time the entreaties of my mother and sister to leave them and fly for my life— but seeing that my staying longer with them was useless, and that De Montcornet and De Béquigny also urged me to fly—I felt that at length I must yield to my fate, and leave them in the hands of Providence. My sister, who feared being robbed by the coast-guard on their return, gave me her twenty louis d'or to keep, and praying Heaven to preserve me, they forced me to leave them and take to flight, which I did with the greatest grief that I had ever experienced in the whole course of my life."[1]

De Bostaquet and his friend De Béquigny first fled along the shore, but the shingle greatly hindered them. On their way they fell in first with De Béquigny's valet, who had fled with the horses, and shortly after with Judith-Julie, Dumont's little daughter, accompanied by a peasant and his wife. She was lifted up

---

[1] *Mémoires Inédits*, pp. 121-5.

and placed in front of the valet, and they rode on. Leaving the sea-shore by a road which led from the beach inland, Dumont preceded them, his drawn sword in his hand. They had not gone far when they were met by six horsemen, who halted and seemed uncertain whether to attack or not; but observing Dumont in an attitude of defence, they retired, and the fugitives fled, as fast as Béquigny's wounded horse would allow them, to Luneray, to the house from which they had set out on the previous night. There Dumont left his daughter, and again De Béquigny and he rode out into the night. As day broke, they reached St. Laurent. They went direct to the house of a Huguenot surgeon, who removed Dumont's bloody shirt, probed the wound to his extreme agony, but could not find the ball,—the surgeon concluding that it was firmly lodged between the two bones of the fore-arm. The place was too unsafe for Dumont to remain; and though suffering much and greatly needing rest, he set out again, and made for his family mansion at La Fontelaye. But he did not dare to enter the house. Alighting at the door of one of his tenants named Malherbe, devoted to his interest, he despatched him with a message to Madame de Bostaquet, who at once hastened to her husband's side. Her agony of grief may be imagined on seeing him, pale and suffering, his clothes covered with blood, and his bandaged arm in a sling. Giving her hasty instructions as to what she was to do in his absence—amongst other things with respect to the sale of his property and everything that could be converted into money—and after much weeping and taking many tender embraces of his wife and daughters, committing them to the care of God, he mounted again and fled northwards for liberty and life.

De Bostaquet proceeds in his narrative to give a graphic account of his flight across Normandy, Picardy, Artois, and Flanders, into Holland, in the course of which he traversed woods, swam rivers, and had many hairbreadth escapes. Knowing the country thoroughly, and having many friends and relatives in Normandy and Picardy, Roman Catholics as well as Protestants, he often contrived to obtain a night's shelter, a change of linen, and sometimes a change of horses, for himself and his friend Saint-Foy, who accompanied him. They lodged the first night at Varvannes with a kinsman on whom he could rely; for M. de Verdun, says De Bostaquet, "was a good man, though a papist and even a bigot." A surgeon was sent for to dress the fugitive's arm, which had become increasingly painful. The surgeon probed the wound, but still no ball could be found. Mounting again, the two rode all day, and by nightfall reached Grosmésnil. Sending for a skilled army surgeon, the wound was probed again, but with no better result. Here the rumour of the affair at Saint Aubin, greatly magnified, reached De Bostaquet, and finding that his only safety lay in flight, he started again with his friend and took the route for Holland through Picardy. They rode onwards to Belozane, then to Neufchâtel, where Saint-Foy parted, returning home.

The fugitive reached Foucarmont alone by moonlight in great pain, his arm being exceedingly swollen and much inflamed. He at once sent for a surgeon, who dressed the wound, but feared gangrene. Next morning the inflammation had subsided, and he set out again, reaching the outskirts of Abbeville, which he passed on the left, and arriving at Pont-de-Remy, he there crossed the Somme. He was now in Picardy. Pressing onward, he reached Proville, where he was kindly entertained for the night by a Protestant friend, M. de Monthuc. The pain and inflammation in his arm still increasing, the family surgeon was sent for. The wound, when exposed, was found black, swollen, and angry-looking. The surgeon sounded again, found no ball, and concluded by recommending perfect rest and low diet. The patient remained with his friend for two days, during which M. Montcornet arrived, for the purpose of accompanying him in his flight into Holland.

Next day, to De Bostaquet's great surprise, the ball, for which the surgeons had so often been searching in vain, was found in the finger of one of his gloves, into which it had dropped. He was now comparatively relieved; and, unwilling to trespass longer on the kindness of his friends, after a few more days' rest he again took the road with his aged relative. They travelled by Le Quesnel and Doullens, then along the great high road of Hesdin and through the woods of the Abbey of Sercan; next striking the Arras road (where they were threatened with an attack by foot-pads), they arrived at La Guorgues; and crossing the frontier, they at last, after many adventures and perils, arrived in safety at Courtrai, where they began to breathe freely. But Dumont did not consider himself safe until he had reached Ghent; for Courtrai was still under the dominion of Spain. So again pushing on the fugitives rested not until they arrived at Ghent, late at night, where the two way-worn travellers at length slept soundly. Next day, Montcornet, who though seventy-two years old, had stood the fatigues of the journey surprisingly well, proceeded to join his son, then lying with many other refugee officers in garrison at Maestricht; while De Bostaquet went forward into Holland to join the fugitives who were now flocking thither in great numbers from all parts of France.

Such is a rapid outline of the escape of Dumont de Bostaquet into the great Protestant asylum of the north. His joy, however, was mingled with grief, for he had left his wife and family behind him in France, under the heel of the persecutor. After many painful rumours of the severe punishments to which his children had been subjected, he was at length joined by his wife, his son, and one of his daughters, who succeeded in escaping by sea. The ladies taken prisoners by the coast-guard at St. Aubin, besides being heavily fined, were condemned to be confined in convents' some for several years each, and others for life. The gentlemen and men-servants who accompanied them, were condemned to the galleys for life, and their property and goods were declared forfeited to the King. This completed the ruin of Dumont de Bostaquet, so far as worldly wealth was concerned; for by the law of Louis XIV., the property not only of all fugitives, but of all who abetted fugitives in their attempt to escape, was declared confiscated,—while they were themselves liable, if caught, to suffer the penalty of death.

De Bostaquet was hospitably received by the Prince of Orange, and, on his application for employment, he was appointed to the same rank in the Dutch army that he had before held in that of Louis XIV. When the expedition to England was decided upon, such of the refugee officers as were disposed to join William were invited to send in their names; and De Bostaquet at once volunteered, with numbers more. Fifty of the French officers were selected for the purpose of being incorporated in the two dragoon regiments, red and blue; and De Bostaquet was appointed to a captaincy in the former regiment, of which De Louvigny was the colonel.

The fleet of William had already been assembled at Maasluis, and with the troops on board, shortly spread its sails for England. But the expedition, consisting of about five hundred sail, had scarcely left the Dutch shores before it was dispersed by a storm, which raged for three days. One ship, containing two companies of French infantry, commanded by Captains de Chauvernay and Rapin-Thoras (afterwards the historian), was driven towards the coast of Norway. Those on board gave themselves up for lost; but the storm abating, the course of the vessel was altered, and she afterwards reached the Maas in safety. Very few ships were missing when the expedition re-assembled; but among the lost was one containing four companies of a

Holstein regiment and some sixty French officers and volunteers. When De Bostaquet's ship arrived in the Maas, it was found that many of the troop horses had been killed in the storm, or were so maimed as to be rendered unfit for service. After a few days' indefatigable labour, however, all damages were made good, the fleet was refitted anew, and again put to sea,—this time with better prospects of success.

"Next day," says De Bostaquet, in his Memoirs, " we saw the coasts of France and England stretching before us on either side. I confess that I did not look upon my ungrateful country without deep emotion, as I thought of the many ties of affection which still bound me to it,—of my children, and the dear relatives I had left behind : but as our fleet might even now be working out their deliverance, and as England was drawing nearer, I felt that one must cast such thoughts aside, and trust that God would yet put it into the heart of our Hero to help our poor country under the oppressions beneath which she was groaning. The fleet was regarded by the people on the opposite shores of the Channel with very different emotions. France trembled; while England, seeing her deliverer approaching, leapt with joy. It seemed as if the Prince took a pleasure in alarming France, whose coast he long kept in sight. But at length, leaving it behind, we made for the opposite shore, and all day long we held along the English coast, sailing towards the west. Night hid the land from further view, and next morning not a trace of it was to be seen. As the wind held good, we thought that by this time we must have passed out of the English Channel, though we knew not whither we were bound. Many of our soldiers from Poitou hoped that we might effect a landing there. But at three in the afternoon we again caught sight of the English land on our right, and found that we were still holding the same course. M. de Bethencour, who knew the coast, assured us that we were bound for Plymouth; and it seemed to me that such

was the Prince's design. But the wind having shifted,
we were astonished to see our vanguard put about,
and sail as if right down upon us. Nothing could be
more beautiful than the evolution of the immense
flotilla which now took place under a glorious sky.
The main body of the fleet and the rear-guard lay to,
in order to allow the Prince's division to pass through
them, on which every ship in its turn prepared to
tack. There were no longer any doubts as to where we
were to land. We distinctly saw the people along the
heights watching, and doubtless admiring, the magnificent spectacle; but there appeared to be no signs of
alarm at sight of the multitude of ships about to enter
their beautiful bay."

De Bostaquet proceeds to describe the landing at
Torbay, and the march of the little army inland, through
mud and mire, under heavy rain and along villainous
roads, until they entered Exeter amidst the acclamations of the people. De Bostaquet found that many of
his exiled countrymen had already settled at Exeter,
where they had a church and minister of their own.
Among others, he met with a French tailor from Lintot
in Normandy, who had become established in business,
besides other refugees from Dieppe and the adjoining
country, who were settled and doing well. De Bostaquet expressed himself much gratified with his short
stay in Exeter, which he praised for its wealth, its
commerce, its manufactures, and the hospitality of its
inhabitants.

After resting six or seven days at Exeter, William
and his army marched upon London through Salisbury,
being daily joined by fresh adherents,—gentry, officers,
and soldiers. The army of James made no effort at
resistance, but steadily retired; the only show of a
stand being made at Reading, where five hundred of
the King's horse, doubtless fighting without heart, were
put to flight by a hundred and fifty of William's
dragoons, led by the Huguenot Colonel Marouit. Not
another shot was fired before William arrived in

London, where he was welcomed as the nation's deliverer. By this time James was making arrangements for flight, together with his Jesuits. He might easily have been captured and made a martyr of; but the mistake made with Charles I. was not repeated in his case, and James, having got on board a smack in the Thames, was allowed to slink ignominiously out of the kingdom.

The Huguenot officers and soldiers of William's army found many of their exiled countrymen already settled in London. Soho in the west, and Spitalfields in the east, were almost entirely French quarters. Numbers of new churches were about this time opened for the accommodation of the immigrants, in which the service was conducted in French by their own ministers, some of the most eminent of whom had taken refuge in England. The exiles formed communities by themselves ; they were for the most part organised in congregations ; and a common cause and common sufferings usually made them soon acquainted with each other. De Bostaquet and his compatriots, therefore, did not find themselves so much strangers in London as they expected to be; for they were daily encountering friends and brothers in misfortune.

A distinguished little circle of exiles had by this time been formed at Greenwich, of which the aged Marquis de Ruvigny formed the centre. That nobleman had for many years been one of the most trusted servants of the French Government. He held various high offices in his own country,—being a general in the French army and a councillor of state ; and he had on more than one occasion represented France as envoy at the English court. But he was a Protestant, and was therefore precluded from holding public office subsequent to the Revocation of the Edict of Nantes. "Had the Marquis," says Macaulay, " chosen to remain in his native country, he and his household would have been permitted to worship God privately according to their own forms. But Ruvigny rejected all offers, cast in

his lot with his brethren, and, at upwards of eighty
years of age, quitted Versailles, where he might still
have been a favourite, for a modest dwelling at Greenwich.   That dwelling was, during the last months of
his life, the resort of all that was most distinguished
among his fellow-exiles.   His abilities, his experience,
and his munificent kindness, made him the undisputed
chief of the refugees.   He was at the same time half
an Englishman; for his sister had been Countess of
Southampton, and he was uncle of Lady Russell.   He
was long past the time of action.   But his two sons,
both men of eminent courage, devoted their swords to
the service of William." [1]

A French church had been founded by the Marquis
of Ruvigny at Greenwich, in 1686,[2] of which M. Severin,
an old and valued friend of De Bostaquet and his wife,
was appointed pastor; so that our Huguenot officer at
once found himself at home.   He was cordially received
by the aged Marquis, who encouraged him to bring
over his family from Holland and settle them in the
place.   This De Bostaquet did accordingly, and during
his brief residence at Greenwich, his wife presented
him with another son, his nineteenth child, to which
the Marquis de Ruvigny stood godfather, and after
whom he was named.   Only a month later, the good
old Marquis died, and De Bostaquet, with many of the
more illustrious exiles, followed his remains to his
tomb in the church of the Savoy, in the Strand, where
he was buried.

Meanwhile, William had been occupied in consoli-
dating his government, and reducing the disaffected
parts of the kingdom to obedience.   With Scotland
this was comparatively easy; but with Ireland the

---

[1] MACAULAY—*History of England,* vol. iii. ch. 14.

[2] The French chapel at Greenwich was recently in existence,
and used as a Baptist chapel.   It
was situated in London Street,
behind the shop of Mr. Harding,
oilman. The Commandments were
written up in French on each side
of the pulpit, until the year 1814,
when they were effaced.

case was very different.   The Irish Roman Catholics
remained loyal to James, because of his religion ; and
when he landed at Kinsale, in March 1689, he saw
nearly the whole country at his feet.   Only the little
Presbyterian colony established in Ulster made any
show of resistance.   James had arrived in Ireland
with substantial help in arms and money obtained
from the French king ; and before many weeks had
elapsed, 40,000 Irish stood in arms to support his
authority.   The forces of William in Ireland were few
in number and bad in quality, consisting for the most
part of raw levies of young men taken suddenly from
the plough.   They were therefore altogether unequal
to cope with the forces of James, Tyrconnel, and the
French Marshal de Rosen ; and but for vigorous measures on the part of William and his government, it was
clear that Ireland would be lost to the English crown.

The best troops of William had by this time been
either sent abroad or disbanded.   The English and
Dutch veteran regiments had for the most part been
despatched to Flanders to resist the French armies of
Louis, who threatened a diversion in favour of James
in that quarter ; while, in deference to the jealousy
which the English people naturally entertained against
the maintenance amongst them of a standing army
—especially an army of foreigners—the Huguenot
regiments had been disbanded, almost immediately
after the abdication of James and his flight into
France.   So soon, however, as the news of James's
landing in Ireland reached London, measures were
taken for their re-embodiment ; and four excellent
regiments were at once raised—one of cavalry and
three of infantry.   The cavalry regiment was raised
by Schomberg, who was its colonel ; and it was entirely composed of French gentlemen—officers and
privates.   The infantry regiments were raised with
the help of the aged Marquis de Ruvigny ; and at his
death, in July 1689, the enterprise was zealously prosecuted by his two sons—Henry, the second Marquis,

and Pierre de Ruvigny, afterwards better known as La Caillemotte. These regiments were respectively commanded by La Caillemotte, Cambon, and La Melonière.

The French regiments were hastily depatched to join the little army of about 10,000 men sent into the north of Ireland, to assist the Protestants in arms there, during the same month in which they were raised. Their first operation was conducted against the town of Carrickfergus, which fell after a siege of a week, but not without loss,—for the Huguenot regiments who led the assault suffered heavily, the Marquis de Venours and numerous other officers being amongst the killed.

Shortly after, the Huguenot regiment of cavalry arrived from England; and, joined by three regiments of Enniskilleners, the army marched southward. De Bostaquet held his former rank of captain in Schomberg's horse; and he has recorded in his memoirs the incidents of the campaign with his usual spirit. The march lay through burnt villages and a country desolated by the retiring army of James. They passed through Newry and Carlingford, both of which towns were found in ashes. They at length arrived in the neighbourhood of Dundalk, where they encamped. James lay at Drogheda with an army of 20,000 men, or double their number. But the generals of neither force wished for battle;—Schomberg, because he could not rely upon his troops, who were ill-fed and (excepting the Huguenot veterans) ill-disciplined;[1] and Count Rosen, James's French general, because he did not wish to incur the risk of a defeat. The raw young English soldiers in the camp at Dundalk, unused to campaigning, died in

---

[1] Schomberg found that the greater number of them had never before fired a gun. " Others can inform your Majesty," he wrote to William (12th Oct., 1689) that the three regiments of French infantry and their regiment of cavalry do their duty better than the others." And a few months later he added— " From these three regiments, and from that of cavalry, your Majesty has more service than from double the number of the others."

great numbers. The English foot were mostly without
shoes and very badly fed; yet they were eager to fight,
thinking it better to die in the field than in the camp.
When they clamoured to be led into action, Schomberg
good-humouredly said, " We English have stomach
enough for fighting: it is a pity that we are not equally
fond of some other parts of a soldier's business."

At length, after enduring great privations, and
leaving many of his men under the sod at Dundalk, Schomberg decided to follow the example of
the Jacobite army, and go into winter quarters. His
conduct of the campaign occasioned much dissatisfaction in England, where it was expected that he
should meet and fight James with a famished army
of less than half the number, and under every disad-
vantage. It had now, however, become necessary to
act with vigour if the policy initiated by the Revolution of 1688 was to be upheld; for a well-appointed
army of 7300 excellent French infantry, commanded
by the Count of Lauzun, with immense quantities of
arms and ammunition, were on their way from France,
with the object of expelling the Protestants from Ireland and replacing James upon the British throne.

William now felt that the great crisis of the struggle
had arrived. Determining to take the field in person,
he made his arrangements accordingly. He ordered
back from Flanders his best English and Dutch regiments. He also endeavoured, so far as he could, to
fight Frenchmen with Frenchmen; and he despatched
agents abroad, into all the countries where the banished
Huguenot soldiers had settled, inviting them to take
arms with him against the enemies of their faith. His
invitation was responded to with alacrity. Many of
Schomberg's old soldiers, who had settled in Brandenburg, Switzerland, and the provinces of the Lower
Rhine, left their new homes and flocked to the standard of William. The Baron d'Avejan, lieutenant-
colonel of an English regiment, wrote to a friend in
Switzerland, urging the immediate enlistment of expa-

triated Protestants for his regiment. "I feel assured," said he, "that you will not fail to have published in all the French churches in Switzerland the obligations under which the refugees lie to come and aid us in this expedition, which is directed to the glory of God, and ultimately to the re-establishment of His Church in our country."

These stirring appeals had the effect of attracting a large number of veteran Protestant soldiers to the army of William. Sometimes four and five hundred men left Geneva in a week for the purpose of enlisting in England. Others were despatched from Lausanne, where they were provided by the Marquis d'Arzilliers with the means of reaching their destination. Many more, scattered along the shores of Lake Leman, were drilled daily under the flag of Orange, notwithstanding the expostulations of Louis' agents, and sent to swell the forces of William.

By these means, as well as by energetic efforts at home,[1] William was enabled, by the month of June, 1690, to assemble in the north of Ireland an army of 36,000 men—English, French, Dutch, Danes, and Germans; and putting himself at their head, he at once marched southward.[2] Arrived at the Boyne, about

---

[1] DE FELICE—*History of the French Protestants* (p. 339), says, that "England raised eleven regiments of French volunteers;" but he does not give his authority. It is probable this number is an exaggeration.

[2] William landed at Carrickfergus on the 14th of June, 1690. From thence he proceeded to Belfast. On his way southward to join the army at Loughbrickland, when passing through the village of Lambeg, near Lisburn, he was addressed by one René Bulmer, a Huguenot refugee, then residing in a house now known as The Priory. René explained to his majesty the cause of his being settled there; and as the king was about to pass on, he asked permission to embrace him. To this William at once assented, receiving the Huguenot's salute on his cheek,—after which, stooping from his horse towards Bulmer's wife, a pretty Frenchwoman, he said, "And thy wife too;" and saluted her heartily. The name Bulmer has since been changed to Boomer, but the Christian name Renè or Rainey is still preserved mong the descendants of the family.— *Ulster Journal of Archæology,* i. 135, 286-94.

three miles west of Drogheda, he discerned the combined French and Irish army drawn up on the other side, prepared to dispute the passage of the river. The Huguenot regiments saw before them the flags of Louis XIV. and James II. waving together—the army of the king who had banished them from country, home, and family,—making common cause with the persecutor of the English Protestants ; and when it became known amongst them that every soldier in the opposing force bore the same badge—the white cross in their hats— which distinguished the assassins of their forefathers on the night of St. Bartholomew, they burned to meet them in battle.

On the morning of the 1st of July, the Count Ménard de Schomberg, one of the old marshal's sons, was ordered to cross the river on the right, by the bridge of Slane, and turn the left flank of the opposing army. This movement he succeeded in accomplishing atter a short but sharp conflict ; upon which William proceeded to lead his left, composed of cavalry, across the river, considerably lower down. At the same time, the main body of infantry composing the centre was ordered to advance. The Dutch guards led, closely followed by the Huguenot foot. Plunging into the stream, they waded across and reached the opposite bank under a storm of cannon and musketry. Scarcely had they struggled up the right bank, than the Huguenot colonel, La Caillemote, was struck down by a musket-shot. As he was being carried off the field, covered with blood, through the ranks of his advancing troops, he called out to them, " A la gloire, mes enfans ! à la gloire ! "

A strong body of Irish cavalry charged the advancing infantry with great vigour, shook them until they reeled, and compelled them to give way. Old Marshal Schomberg, who stood eagerly watching the advance of his troops from the northern bank, now saw that the crisis of the fight had arrived, and he prepared to act accordingly. Placing himself at the head of his

15

Huguenot regiment of horse which he had held in
reserve, and pointing with his sword across the river,
he called out, "*Allons, mes amis! rappelez votre
courage et vos ressentements :* VOILA VOS PERSECU-
TEURS !"[1] and plunged into the stream. On reaching
the scene of contest, a furious struggle ensued. The
Dutch and Huguenot infantry rallied; and William,
coming up from the left with his cavalry, fell upon
the Irish flank and completed their discomfiture. The
combined French and Irish army was forced through
the pass of Duleek, and fled towards Dublin—James
II. being the first to carry thither the news of his
defeat.[2] William's loss did not exceed 400 men; but,
to his deep grief, Marshal Schomberg was found
amongst the fallen, the hero of eighty-two having been
cut down in the melée by a party of Tyrconnel's horse;
and he lay dead upon the field, with many other
gallant gentlemen.

---

[1] Rapin, who relates this incident in his *History of England,*
was present at the battle of the
Boyne as an officer in one of the
Huguenot regiments.

[2] On reaching Dublin Castle,
James was received by Lady
Tyrconnel, the wife of his vice-
roy. "Madam," said he, "your
countrymen can run well." "Not
quite so well as your Majesty,"
was her retort, "for I see you
have won the race."

CHAPTER XIII.

IT forms no part of our purpose to describe the military operations in Ireland, which followed the battle of the Boyne. We may, however, mention the principal Huguenot officers who took part in them. Amongst these, one of the most distinguished was Henry, second Marquis de Ruvigny. At the date of the Revocation, he had attained the rank of brigadier in the army of Louis XIV., and was considered an excellent officer, having served with great distinction under Condé and Turenne. Indeed, it is believed that the French army in Germany would have been lost, but for the skill with which he reconciled the quarrels of the contending chiefs who aspired to its command after the death of Turenne.

Louis XIV. desired to retain Ruvigny in his service; but casting in his lot with the exiled Protestants, he left France with his father and settled with him at Greenwich, where he dispensed hospitality and bounty. He did not at first join the British army which fought in Ireland. But when he heard that his only brother, De la Caillemotte, as well as Marshal Schomberg, had been killed at the Boyne, he could restrain his ardour no longer, and offered his services to William. The King appointed him major-general, and also gave him the colonelcy of Schomberg's regiment of Huguenot horse.

Ruvigny joined the army of General Ginkell, while engaged in the siege of Athlone. A Huguenot soldier was the first to mount the breach, where he fell, cheering on his comrades. The place was taken by Ginkell, after which the French general, Saint Ruth, retired with the Irish army to Aughrim, where he took up an almost impregnable position. Notwithstanding this advantage, Ginkell attacked and routed the Irish, the principal share in the victory being attributed to the Marquis de Ruvigny and his horse, who charged impetuously and carried everything before them.

That the brunt of this battle was borne by the Huguenot regiments, is shown by the extent of their loss. Ruvigny's regiment lost 144 men killed and wounded ; that of Cambon 106 ; and that of Belcastle 85—being about one-fifth of the total loss on the side of the victors. "After the battle," says De Bostaquet, " Ginkell came up and embraced De Ruvigny, declaring how much he was pleased with his bravery and his conduct ; then advancing to the head of our regiment, he highly praised the officers as well as the soldiers. M. Causaubon, who commanded, gained great honour by his valour that day." [1] For the services rendered by De Ruvigny on this occasion, William raised him to the Irish peerage, under the title of Earl of Galway,

In 1693, Lord Galway joined William in Flanders, and was with him in the battle of Néerwinden, where the combined Dutch and English army was defeated by Marshal Luxemburg. The Huguenot leader fought with conspicuous bravery at the head of his cavalry, and succeeded in covering William's retreat. He was shortly after promoted to the rank of lieutenant-general.

The war with France was now raging all round her borders,—along the Flemish and the German frontiers, and as far south as the country of the Italian Vaudois. The Vaudois were among the most ancient Protestant people in Europe ; and Louis XIV., not satisfied with exterminating Protestantism in his own dominions,

---

[1] *Memoires Inédits de Dumont de Bostaquet,* p. 303.

sought to carry the crusade against it beyond his own
frontiers into the territories of his neighbours. He accordingly sent a missive to the young Duke of Savoy,
requiring him to extirpate the Vaudois, unless they
conformed to the Roman Catholic religion. The duke
refused to obey the French king's behest, and besought
the heir of the Emperor of Germany and the Protestant
princes of the north, to enable him to resist the armies
of Louis. The Elector of Brandenburg having applied
to William III. for one of his generals, Charles, Duke
of Schomberg, whose father fell at the Boyne, was at
once despatched to the aid of the Savoy prince, with
an army consisting for the most part of Huguenot
refugees. William also undertook to supply a subsidy
of £100,000 a year, as the joint contribution of England and Holland to the cause of Protestantism in
Piedmont.

On Schomberg's arrival at Turin, he found the
country in a state of great consternation, the French
army under Catinat having overrun it in various
directions. With Schomberg's vigorous help, the progress of the French army was for a time checked;
but unfortunately Schomberg allowed himself to be
drawn into a pitched battle on the plains of Marsiglia
in October, 1693, when his army suffered a complete
defeat. At the same time the general received a
mortal wound, of which he died a few days after the
battle.

On this untoward result of the campaign becoming
known in England, the Earl of Galway was despatched
into Savoy to take the command; as well as to repre-
sent England and Holland as ambassador at the court
of Turin. To his dismay, the Earl discovered that the
Duke of Savoy was then engaged in a secret treaty
with the French Government for peace; on which he
at once withdrew with his contingent—the only object
he had been able to accomplish, being to secure a
certain degree of liberty of worship for the persecuted
Vaudois.

On his return to England, the Earl was appointed one of the Lords-Justices of Ireland; and during the time that he held that office, he devoted himself to the establishment of the linen trade, the improvement of agriculture, and the reparation of the losses and devastations from which the country had suffered during the civil wars.

In the meantime, Louis XIV., with that meanness of character that distinguished him in all his dealings with the Huguenots, when he heard of Ruvigny's services to William III., ordered the immediate confiscation of all his property in France. To compensate Ruvigny for this heavy loss, William conferred upon him the confiscated estate of Portarlington; when he at once proceeded to found a Huguenot colony at that place. By his influence he induced a large number of the best class of the refugees—principally exiled officers and gentry, with their families—to settle there; and he liberally assisted them out of his private means in promoting the industry and prosperity of the town and neighbourhood. He erected more than a hundred new dwellings of a superior kind, for the accommodation of the settlers. He built and endowed two churches for their use—one French, the other English,—as well as two excellent schools for the education of their children. Thus the little town of Portarlington shortly became a centre of polite learning, from which emanated some of the most distinguished men in Ireland; while the gentle and industrious life of the colonists exhibited an example of patient labour, neatness, thrift, and orderliness, which exercised a considerable influence on the surrounding population.

Lord Galway was not, however, permitted to enjoy the grant which William III. had made to him, of the Portarlington estate. The appropriation was violently attacked in the English Parliament; and a bill was passed annulling that and all grants of a like kind which had been made by the King. The estate was accordingly taken from Lord Galway, and sold by the Government Commissioners to the London Hollow Sword-Blade Company. The Earl's career as an Irish landlord was thus brought to an end; and Ruvigny, like many of his fellow-exiles, was again left landless. During the time, however, that the Portarlington estate was in his possession, he granted to some of the Huguenot exiles leases for lives, renewable for ever. These leases were not interfered with, and they still continue in force.

While the English Parliament displayed this jealousy of the foreign officers by whom William III. had been so faithfully served, and who contributed so materially to the success of the Revolution of 1688, they entertained an equal jealousy of the Huguenot regiments which still remained in the service of the King. Frequent motions were made in the House of Commons for their disembodiment; and on the 15th of September, 1698, on the motion for going into a committee of supply, the amendment was proposed: " That an address be presented to the Lords-Justices to intercede with His Majesty that the five regiments [1] of French Protestants should be disbanded." In the face of the war which was impending in Europe, William could not agree to the measure; and the regiments continued to be actively employed under different designations down to the middle of the eighteenth century.

---

[1] There were two cavalry regiments, and three infantry, in the Huguenot force, viz. :—

	No. of Companies	Officers.	Non-Commissioned Officers.	Privates	Total.
Galway's Horse . .	9	113	85	531	729
Miremont's Dragoons	8	74	104	480	658
Marton's Foot . . .	13	83	104	780	967
La Melonière's do. .	13	83	104	780	967
Belcastel's do. . . .	13	83	104	780	967
		436	501	3351	4288

Nothing could shake the King's attachment to Lord Galway, or Lord Galway's to him. Being unable, as King of England, to reward his faithful follower, William appointed him general in the Dutch army, and colonel of the Dutch regiment of foot-guards (blue). In 1701, Evelyn thus records in his diary a visit made to the distinguished refugee on his arrival in London from Ireland :—"*June* 22.—I went to congratulate the arrival of that worthy and excellent person, my Lord Galway, newly come out of Ireland, where he had behaved himself so honestly and to the exceeding satisfaction of the people; but he was removed thence for being a Frenchman, though they had not a more worthy, valiant, discreet, and trusty person on whom they could have relied for conduct and fitness. He was one who had deeply suffered, as well as the Marquis his father, for being Protestants."

From this time, Lord Galway was principally employed abroad on diplomatic missions, and in the field. The war against France was now in progress on the side of Spain, where the third Duke of Schomberg, Count Ménard,—who led the attack in the battle of the Boyne,—was, in 1704, placed in command of the British troops, then fighting against the Bourbon Philip V., in conjunction with a Portuguese force. Philip was supported by a French army under command of the Duke of Berwick, the natural son of the dethroned James II. The campaign having languished under Schomberg, and the government at home becoming dissatisfied with his conduct, the Earl of Galway was sent out to Portugal to take the command.

The battles which followed were mostly fought over the ground since made so famous by the victories of Wellington. There was the relief of Gibraltar, the storming of Alcantara, the siege of Badajos—in which the Earl of Galway lost an arm—the capture of Ciudad Rodrigo, and the advance upon Madrid. Then followed the defection of the Portuguese, and a succession of disasters : the last of which was the battle of Almanza, where the British, ill-supported by their Portuguese allies, were defeated by the French army under the Duke of Berwick. Shortly afterwards, the British forces returned home, and the Earl of Galway resided for the rest of his life mostly at Rookley, near Southampton, taking a kindly interest to the last in the relief of his countrymen suffering for conscience' sake.[1]

When the refugees first entered the service of the Elector of Brandenburg, doubts were expressed whether they would fight against their fellow-countrymen. When they went into action at Neuss, one of the Prussian generals exclaimed, " We shall have these knaves fighting against us presently." But all doubts were dispelled by the conduct of the Huguenot musketeers, who rushed eagerly upon the French troops, and by the fury of their attack carried everything before them. It was the same at the siege of Bonn, where a hundred refugee officers, three hundred Huguenot cadets, with detachments of musketeers and horse grenadiers, demanded to be led to the assault ; and on the signal being given, they rushed forward with extraordinary gallantry. " The officers," says Ancillon, " gave proof that they preferred rather to rot in the earth after an honourable death, than that the earth should nourish them in idleness whilst their soldiers were in the heat of the fight." The outer works were carried, and the place was taken.

---

[1] It was when on a visit at Stratton House, that the good Earl of Galway was summoned to his rest. He probably sank under the " bodily pains" to which he was so long subject— namely, gout and rheumatism. His mind was entire to the last. He died on the 3rd of September, 1720, aged seventy-two. He was the last of his family. Lady Russell was his nearest surviving relative, and became his heiress at the age of eighty-four. The property of Stratton has passed out of Russell hands ; and Lord Galway's gravestone [in Micheldever churchyard, where he was buried], cannot now be recognised.—AGNEW—*Protestant Exiles from France in the reign of Louis XIV.*, p. 149.

But nowhere did the Huguenots display such a fury of resentment against the troops of Louis as at the battle of Almanza, above referred to, where they were led by Cavalier, the famous Camisard chief.

Jean Cavalier was the son of a peasant, of the village of Ribaute, near Anduze, in Languedoc. Being an ardent Protestant, he took refuge from the persecutions in Geneva and Lausanne, where he worked for some time as a journeyman baker. But his love for his native land drew him back to Languedoc; and he happened to visit it in 1702, at the time when the Abbé du Chayla was engaged in directing the extirpation of the Protestant peasantry in the Cevennes. These poor people continued, in defiance of the law, to hold religious meetings in the woods, and caves, and fields; in consequence of which they were tracked, pursued, sabred, hanged, or sent to the galleys, wherever found.

The peasants at length revolted. From forty to fifty of the most determined among them assembled at the Abbé du Chayla's house at Pont-de-Montvert, and proceeded to break open the dungeon in which he had penned up a band of prisoners, amongst whom were two ladies of rank. The Abbé ordered his servants to repel the assailants with firearms; nevertheless they succeeded in effecting an entrance, and stabbed the priest to death. Such was the beginning of the war of the Blouses, or Camisards. The Camisards were only poor peasants, driven to desperation by cruelty, without any knowledge of war, and without any arms except such as they wrested from the hands of their enemies. Yet they maintained a gallant struggle against the united French armies for a period of nearly five years.

On the outbreak of the revolt, Jean Cavalier assembled a company of volunteers to assist the Cevennes peasantry; and before long he became their recognised leader. Though the insurrection spread over Languedoc, their entire numbers did not exceed 10,000

men. But they had the advantage of fighting in a
mountain country, every foot of which was familiar
to them. They carried on the war by surprises,
clothing and arming themselves with the spoils they
took from the royal troops. They supplied themselves with balls made from the church-bells. They
had no money, and needed none; the peasantry and
herdsmen of the country supplying them with food.
When they were attacked, they received the first fire
of the soldiers on one knee, singing the sixty-eighth
psalm: "Let God arise, let his enemies be scattered."
Then they rose, precipitated themselves on the enemy,
and fought with all the fury of despair. If they succeeded in their onslaughts, and the soldiers fled, they
then held assemblies, which were attended by the
Huguenots of the adjoining country; and when they
failed, they fled into the hills, in the caverns of which
were their magazines and hospitals.

Great devastation and bloodshed marked the war
carried on against the Camisards. No mercy was
shown either to the peasantry taken in arms, or to
those who in any way assisted them. Whole villages
were destroyed. The order was issued that wherever
a soldier or a priest perished, the village should immediately be burnt down. The punishment of the
stake was revived. Gibbets were erected and kept at
work all over Languedoc. Still the insurrection was
not suppressed; and the peasantry continued to hold
their religious meetings wherever they could.

One day, on the 1st of April, 1703, the intelligence
was brought to Marshal Montrevil, in command of the
royal troops, that some three hundred persons had
assembled for worship in a mill near Nismes. He at
once hastened to the place with a strong force of
soldiers, ordered the doors to be burst open, and the
worshippers slaughtered on the spot. The slowness
with which the butchery was carried on provoked the
marshal's indignation, and he ordered the mill to be
fired. All who had not been murdered were burnt,—

all, excepting one solitary girl, who was saved through the humanity of the marshal's lacquey; but she was hanged next day, and the lacquey who had saved her narrowly escaped the same fate.

Even this monstrous cruelty did not crush the insurrection. The Camisards were from time to time reinforced by burnt-out peasants; and, led by Cavalier and his coadjutor Roland, they beat the detachments of Montrevil on every side—at Nayes, at the rocks at Aubias, at Martignargues, and at the bridge of Salindres. Louis XIV. was disgusted at the idea of a marshal of France, supported by a royal army thoroughly appointed, being set at defiance by a miserable horde of Protestant peasants; and he ordered the recall of Montrevil. Marshal Villars was then sent to take the command.

The new marshal was an honourable man, and not a butcher. He shuddered at the idea of employing means such as his predecessor had employed, to reduce the King's subjects to obedience; and one of the first things he did was to invite Cavalier to negotiate. The quondam baker's boy of Geneva agreed to meet the potent marshal of France, and listen to his proposals. Villars thus described him in his letter to the minister of war: " He is a peasant of the lowest rank, not yet twenty-two years of age, and scarcely seeming eighteen; small, and with no imposing mien, but possessing a firmness and good sense that are altogether surprising. He has great talent in arranging for the subsistence of his men, and disposes his troops as well as the best trained officers could do. From the moment Cavalier began to treat, up to the conclusion of the affair, he has always acted in good faith." [1]

In the negotiations which ensued, Cavalier stipulated for liberty of conscience and freedom of worship,

---

[1] The war against the Camisards is treated at much greater length in *The Huguenots in* *France, after the Revocation of the Edict of Nantes.*

to which, it is said, Villars assented, though the Roman Catholics subsequently denied this. The result, however, was that Cavalier capitulated, accepted a colonel's commission, and went to Versailles to meet Louis XIV.; his fellow-leader, Roland, refusing the terms of capitulation, and determining to continue the struggle. At Paris, the mob, eager to behold the Cevennol rebel, thronged the streets he rode through, and his reception was tantamount to a triumph. At Versailles Louis exhorted him in vain to be converted, Cavalier even daring in his presence to justify the revolt in the Cevennes. He was offered the rank of major-general in the French army, and a pension of 1500 livres for his father; but he refused, and was dismissed from court as " an obstinate Huguenot."

Though treated with apparent kindness, Cavalier felt that he was under constant surveillance; and he seized the earliest opportunity of flying from France and taking refuge in Switzerland. From thence he passed into Holland, and entered the service of William of Orange, who gave him the rank of colonel. The Blouses, or Camisards, who had fled from the Cevennes in large numbers, flocked to his standard, and his regiment was soon full. But a serious difficulty occurred. Cavalier insisted on selecting his own officers, while the royal commissioners required that the companies should be commanded by refugee gentlemen. The matter was compromised by Cavalier selecting half his officers, and the commissioners appointing the other half,—Cavalier selecting only such as had thoroughly proved their valour in the battles of the Cevennes. The regiment, when complete, proceeded to England, and was despatched to Spain with other reinforcements towards the end of 1706.

Almost the only battle in which Cavalier and his Huguenots took part, was at the field of Almanza, where they distinguished themselves in a remarkable manner. Cavalier found himself opposed to one of the French regiments, in whom he recognised his former persecutors in the Cevennes. The soldiers on both sides, animated by a common fury, rushed upon each other with the bayonet, disdaining to fire. The carnage which followed was dreadful. The Papist regiment was almost annihilated, whilst of Cavalier's regiment, 700 strong, not more than 300 survived. Marshal Berwick, though familiar with fierce encounters, never spoke of this tragical event without deep emotion. Cavalier himself was severely wounded, and lay for some time among the slain. He afterwards escaped through the assistance of an English officer. His lieutenant-colonel, five captains, six lieutenants, and five ensigns were killed, and most of the other officers were wounded or taken prisoners.

Cavalier returned to England, where he retired upon a small pension, which barely supported him.[1] He entreated to be employed in active service; but it was not until after the lapse of many years that his application was successful. He was eventually appointed governor of Jersey, and held that office for some time; after which he was made brigadier in 1735, and further promoted to be major-general in 1739. He died at Chelsea in the following year; and his remains were conveyed to Dublin for interment in the French refugee cemetery.

Another illustrious name amongst the Huguenot refugees is that of Paul de Rapin-Thoyras,—better known as the historian of England than as a soldier,—though he bore arms with the English in many a hard-fought field. He belonged to a French noble family, and was lord of Thoyras, near Castres. The persecution drove him and his family into England; but finding nothing to do there, he went over to Holland and joined the army of William as a cadet. He accompanied the

---

[1] While he resided in London, Cavalier employed part of his leisure in dictating to another refugee, Galli of Nismes, the memoirs of his early adventures, which were published under the title of *Memoirs of the Wars of the Cevennes:* London, 1726.

expedition to Torbay, and took part in the transactions which followed.   Rapin was afterwards sent into Ireland with his regiment; and, distinguishing himself by his gallantry at the siege of Carrickfergus, he was promoted to the rank of lieutenant.   He afterwards fought at the Boyne, and was wounded at the assault of Limerick.   At Athlone he was one of the first to enter the place at the head of the assailing force.   He was there promoted to a company; and he remained at Athlone doing garrison duty for about two years.   His intelligence and high culture being well known, Rapin was selected by the King, on the recommendation of the Earl of Galway, as tutor to the Earl of Portland's eldest son, Viscount Woodstock. He accordingly took leave of the army with regret, making over his company to his brother, who afterwards attained the rank of lieutenant-colonel.

From this time, Rapin lived principally abroad, in company with his pupil.   Whilst residing at the Hague, he resumed his favourite study of history and jurisprudence, which had been interrupted by his flight from France at the Revocation.   After completing Lord Woodstock's education, Rapin settled at Wesel, where a number of retired refugee officers resided and formed a very agreeable society.   There he wrote his *Dissertation on Whigs and Torie,* and his well-known *History of England,* founded on Rhymer's *Fœdera,* the result of much labour and research, and long regarded as a standard work. Rapin died in 1725, at the age of sixty-four, almost pen in hand, worn out by hard study and sedentary confinement.

Among the many able Huguenot officers in William's service, John de Bodt was one of the most distinguished.   He had fled from France when only in his fifteenth year, and shortly after joined the Dutch artillery.   He accompanied William to England, and was made captain in 1690.   He fought at the Boyne and at Aughrim, and eventually rose to the command of the Huguenot corps of Engineers. In that capacity he served at the battles of Steinkirk and Néerwinden, and at the siege of Namur he directed the operations which ended in the surrender of the castle to the allied army. The fort into which Boufflers had thrown himself was assaulted and captured a few days later by La Cave at the head of 2000 volunteers; and William III. generously acknowledged that it was mainly to the brave refugees that he owed the capture of that important fortress.

All through the wars in the Low Countries, under William III., Eugene, and the Duke of Marlborough, the refugees bore themselves bravely. Wherever the fighting was hardest, they were there. Henry de Chesnoi led the assault which gave Landau to the allies. At the battles of Hochstedt, Oudenarde, and Malplacquet, and at the siege of Mons, they were conspicuous for their valour. Le Roche, the Huguenot engineer, conducted the operations at Lisle,—" doing more execution," says Luttrell, " in three days than De Meer, the German, in six weeks."

The refugee Ligoniers served with peculiar distinction in the British army. The most eminent was Jean Louis, afterwards Field Marshal Earl Ligonier, who had fled from France into England in 1697. He accompanied the army to Flanders as a volunteer in 1702, where his extraordinary bravery at the storming of Liege attracted the attention of Marlborough. At Blenheim, where he next fought, he was the only captain of his regiment who survived. At Menin he led the grenadiers who stormed the counterscarp. He fought at Malplacquet, where he was major of brigade, and in all Marlborough's great battles. At Dettingen, as lieutenant-general, he earned still higher distinction. At Fontenoy the chief honour was due to him for the intrepidity and skill with which he led the British infantry. In 1746 he was placed in command of the British forces in Flanders, but was taken prisoner at the battle of Lawfield. Restored to England, he was

Effigies Gasparis de Colig. ni. D. de Castillone. Amir alu Franciæ &c.

ADMIRAL COLIGNY

AND A REPRESENTATION OF THE MASSACRE OF ST. BARTHOLOMEW'S DAY.

Reproduced by kind permission of the Court of Directors of the French Hospital from the engraving in their possession.

[*To face p.* 240.

appointed commander-in-chief and colonel of the First
Foot Guards; and in 1770 the Huguenot hero died full
of honours at the ripe age of ninety-two.

Of the thousands of Protestant sailors who left
France at the Revocation, many settled in the ports
along the south and south-east coast of England; but
the greater number entered the Dutch fleet, while some
of them took service in the navy of the Elector of Brandenburg. Louis XIV. took the same steps to enforce
conversion upon his sailors, that he adopted to convert
the other classes of his subjects. So soon, however, as
the sailors arrived in foreign ports, they usually took
the opportunity of deserting their ships and reasserting
their liberty. In 1686, three French vessels which had
put into Dutch ports were entirely deserted by their
crews; and in the same year more than 800 experienced mariners, trained under Duquesne, entered the
navy of the United Provinces. When William sailed
for England in 1688, the island of Zealand alone sent
him 150 excellent French sailors, who were placed, as
picked men, on board the admiral and vice-admiral's
ships. Like their Huguenot fellow-countrymen on
land, the Huguenot sailors fought valiantly at sea
under the flag of their adopted country; and they
emulated the bravery of the English at the great naval
battle of La Hogue, which occurred a few years later.

Many descendants of the refugees subsequently attained high rank in the naval service, and acquired
distinction by their valour on that element which
England has been accustomed to regard as peculiarly
her own. Amongst them may be mentioned "the
gallant, good Riou," who was killed while commanding
the Amazon frigate at Copenhagen in 1801, and the
Gambiers, descended from a refugee family long settled at Canterbury, one of whom rose to be a vice-
admiral, and another an admiral, the latter having also
been raised to the peerage for his distinguished public
services.

16

CHAPTER XIV.

HUGUENOT MEN OF SCIENCE AND LEARNING.

OF the half-million of French subjects who were driven into exile by the Revocation of the Edict of Nantes, more than 120,000 are believed to have taken refuge in England. The refugees were men of all ranks and conditions,—landed gentry, ministers of religion, soldiers and sailors, professional men, merchants, students, mechanics, artizans, and labourers. The greater number were Calvinists, and continued such ; others were Lutherans, who conformed to the English Church ; but many were Protestants merely in name, principally because they belonged to families of that persuasion. But however lightly their family religion might sit upon them, these last offered as strenuous a resistance as the most extreme Calvinists to being dragooned into popery. This was especially the case with men of science, professional men, and students of law and medicine. Hence the large proportion of physicians and surgeons to be found in the ranks of the refugees.

It was not merely free religious thought that Louis XIV. sought to stifle in France, but free thought of all kinds. The blow struck by him at the conscience of France, struck also at its mind. Individualism was crushed wherever it asserted itself. An entire abnegation of the will was demanded. Men must abjure their faith, and believe as they were ordered. They must become part of a stereotyped system—profess adherence to a Church to which they were indifferent, if they did not actually detest it—pretend to believe what they really did not believe,—and in many cases deny their most deeply-rooted convictions.

To indolent minds such a system would no doubt save an infinity of trouble. Only induce men to give up their individuality,—to renounce the exercise of their judgment—to cease to think—and to entertain the idea that a certain set of men, and no other, hold in their hands the keys of heaven and hell,—and conformity becomes easy. But many of the French King's subjects were of another temperament. They would think for themselves in matters of science as well as religion; and the vigorous, the independent, and the self-reliant — Protestant as well as non-Protestant — revolted against the intellectual tyranny which Louis attempted to establish amongst them, and fled for liberty of thought and worship into other lands·

We have already referred to such men as Huyghens and Bayle, who took refuge in Holland, where they found the freedom denied them in their own country. These men were not Protestants so much as philosophers. But they could not be hypocrites, and they would not conform. Hence their flight from France. Others of like stamp took refuge in England. Amongst the latter were some of the earliest speculators as to that wonderful motive power which eventually became embodied in the working steam-engine One of these fugitives was Solomon de Caus, a native of Caux in Normandy. He was a man of encyclopædic knowledge; he had studied architecture in Italy; he was an engineer, a mechanic, and a natural philosopher. Moreover, he was a Huguenot, which was fatal to his existence in France as a free man, and he took refuge in England. There he was employed about the court for a time, and amongst other works he designed and erected hydraulic works for the palace gardens at Richmond. Shortly after he accompanied the Princess Elizabeth to Heidelberg, in Germany, on her marriage to the Elector Palatine, and there he published several works descriptive of the progress he had made in his inquiries as to the marvellous powers of steam.

But still more distinguished among the Huguenot refugees was Dr. Denis Papin, one of the early inventors of the steam-engine, and probably also the inventor of the steamboat.[1] He was born at Blois in 1650, and had studied medicine at the University of Paris, where he took his degree as physician. He began the practice of his profession, in which he met with considerable success. Being attracted to the study of mechanics, and having the advantage of the instruction of the celebrated Huyghens, he made rapid progress, and promised to become one of the most eminent scientific men of his country. But Papin was a Protestant; and when the practice of medicine by Protestant physicians came to be subjected to serious disabilities,—finding the door to promotion or even to subsistence closed against him unless he abjured,—he determined to leave France; and in 1681, the same year in which Huyghens took refuge in Holland, Papin took refuge in England. Arrived in London, he was cordially welcomed by men of science there, and especially by the Honourable Robert Boyle, under whose auspices he was introduced to the Royal Society.

In 1684, Papin was appointed temporary curator of the Royal Society, with a salary of £30 a year. It formed part of his duty, in connection with his new office, to produce an experiment at each meeting of the society; and this led him to prosecute his inquiries into the powers of steam, and ultimately to invent his steam-engine. Papin's reputation having extended abroad, he was invited to fill the office of professor of mathematics in the University of Marburg, which he accepted; and he left England in the year 1687. But he continued until his death, many years later, to maintain a friendly correspondence with his scientific

---

[1] For an account of Solomon de Caus, as well as of the life and labours of Dr. Papin, see "Historical Memoir of the Invention of the Steam-Engine," in *Lives of Boulton and Watt* pp. 8, 30-8.

friends in England; and one of the last things he did was to construct a model steam-engine fitted in a boat —" une petite machine d'un vaisseau à roues "—for the purpose of sending it over to England for trial on the Thames. But, unhappily for Papin, the little vessel never reached England. To his great grief, he found that when it reached Münden on the Weser, it had been seized by the boatmen on the river and barbarously destroyed. Three years later, the illustrious exile died, worn out by work and anxiety, leaving it to other inventors to realise the great ideas which he had conceived as to navigation by steam-power.

Dr. Desaguliers was another refugee who achieved considerable distinction in England as a teacher of mechanical philosophy. His father, Jean des Aguliers, was pastor of a Protestant congregation at Aitré, near Rochelle, from which he fled about the period of the Revocation. His child, the future professor, is said to have been carried on board the ship by which he escaped, concealed in a barrel.[1] The pastor first took refuge in Guernsey, from whence he proceeded to England, took orders in the Established Church, and became minister of the French chapel in Swallow Street, London. This charge he subsequently resigned, and established a school at Islington, at which his son received his first education. From thence the young man proceeded to Oxford, matriculating at Christ Church, where he obtained the degree of B.A., and took deacon's orders. Being drawn to the study of natural philosophy, he shortly after delivered lectures at Oxford on hydrostatics and optics, to which he afterwards added mechanics.

His fame as a lecturer having reached London,

---

[1] This statement is made in the "House and Farm Accounts of the Shuttleworths of Gawthorpe Hall."—*Chetham Society's Papers*, 1856-8. The Shuttleworths were related by marriage to the Desaguliers family; Robert Shuttleworth, one of the successors to Gawthorpe, having married Anne, the second daughter of General Desaguliers (son of the above Dr. Desaguliers), who was one of the equerries of George III.

Desaguliers was pressingly invited thither; and he accordingly removed to the metropolis in 1713. His lectures were much admired, and he had so happy a knack of illustrating them by experiments, that he was invited by the Royal Society to be their demonstrator. He was afterwards appointed curator of the Society; and in the course of his connection with it, he communicated a vast number of curious and valuable papers, which were printed in the Transactions. The Duke of Chandos gave Desaguliers the church living of Edgeware; and the king (before whom he gave lectures at Hampton Court) presented him with a benefice in Essex, besides appointing him chaplain to the Prince of Wales.

In 1734 Desaguliers published his *Course of Experimental Philosophy* in two quarto volumes,—the best book of the kind that had appeared in England. It would appear from this work that the Doctor also designed and superintended the erection of steam-engines. Referring to an improvement which he had made on Savary's engine, he says: "According to this improvement, I have caused seven of these fire-engines to be erected since the year 1717 or 1718. The first was for the late Czar Peter the Great, for his garden at Petersburg, where it was set up." Dr. Desaguliers died in 1749, leaving behind him three sons, one of whom, the eldest, published a translation of the *Mathematical Elements of Natural Philosophy*, by Gravesande, who had been a pupil of his father's; the second was a beneficed clergyman in Norfolk; and the third was a colonel of artillery and lieutenant-general in the army, as well as equerry to George III.

Among other learned refugees who were elected members of the Royal Society, were David Durand, the editor of *Pliny's Natural History, The Philosophical Writings of Cicero,* and other classical works, and the author of a *History of the Sixteenth Century,* as well as of the continuation of *Rapin's History of England;* Peter des Maiseaux, the intimate friend of

St. Evremonde, whose works he edited and translated
into English ; and Abraham de Moivre, the celebrated
mathematician.

De Moivre was the son of a surgeon at Vitry in
Champagne, and received his principal education at
the Protestant seminary of Sedan. From the first
he displayed an extraordinary genius for arithmetic.
His chief delight in his bye-hours was to shut himself
up with Le Gendre's arithmetic and work out its problems. This led one of his classical masters to ask on
one occasion, " What that little rogue meant to do with
all these cyphers ? " When the college of Sedan was
suppressed in 1681, De Moivre went to Saumur to pursue his studies in philosophy, from whence he went to
Paris to prosecute the study of physics. By this time
his father, being prohibited practising as a surgeon
because of his religion, left Vitry to join his son at
Paris; but they were not allowed to remain together.
The agents of the government, acting on their power
of separating children from their parents, and subject-
ing them to the process of conversion, seized young
De Moivre in his nineteenth year, and shut him up in
the priory of St. Martin. There his Jesuit masters
tried to drill him into the Roman Catholic faith; but
the young Protestant was staunch, and refused to
be converted. Being pronounced an obstinate heretic,
he was discharged after about two years' confinement, on which he was ordered forthwith to leave the
country.

De Moivre arrived in London with his father[1] in
1687, at the age of twenty, and immediately bestirred
himself to earn a living. He had no means but his
knowledge and his industry. He first endeavoured to
obtain pupils, to instruct them in mathematics ; and he
also began, like others of the refugees, to give lectures

---

[1] We find, from the *List of
Foreign Protestants,* published
by the Camden Society (1862),
that Abraham and Daniel de
    Moivre obtained letters of natu-
ralisation on the 16th of December, 1687.

on natural philosophy. But his knowledge of English was as yet too imperfect to enable him to lecture with success, and he was, besides, an indifferent manipulator, so that his lectures were shortly discontinued. It happened that the *Principia* of Newton was published about the time that De Moivre arrived in England. The subject offering great attractions to a mind such as his, he entered upon the study of the book with much zest, and succeeded before long in mastering its contents, and arriving at a clear understanding of the views of the author. Indeed, so complete was his knowledge of Newton's principles, that it is said, when Sir Isaac was asked for explanations of his writings, he would say : " Go to De Moivre; he knows better than I do."

Thus De Moivre acquired the friendship and respect of Newton, of Halley, and other distinguished scientific men of the time; and one of the best illustrations of the esteem in which his intellectual qualifications were held, is afforded by the fact that in the contention which arose between Leibnitz and Newton as to their respective priority in the invention of the method of fluxions, the Royal Society appointed De Moivre to report upon their rival claims.

De Moivre published many original works on his favourite subject, more particularly on analytical mathematics. Professor De Morgan has observed of them, that "they abound with consummate contrivance and skill; and one, at least, of his investigations has had the effect of completely changing the whole character of trigonometrical science in its higher departments."[1] One of the works published by him, entitled *The Doctrine of Chances,* is curious, as leading, in a measure, to the development of the science of life assurance. From the first edition, it does not appear that De Moivre intended to do more than illustrate his favourite theory of probabilities. He showed in a

---

[1] Art. " De Moivre " in *Penny Cyclopædia.*

variety of ways the probable results of throwing dice
in certain numbers of throws. From dice throwing he
proceeded to lotteries, and showed how many tickets
ought to be taken to secure the probability of drawing
a prize. A few years later he applied his views to a
more practical purpose—the valuation of annuities on
lives; and though the data on which he based his
calculations were incorrect, and his valuations consequently unreliable, the publication of his *Doctrine of
Chances* applied to the valuation of annuities on lives,
was of much use at the time it appeared; and it
formed the basis of other and more accurate calculations.

De Moivre's books were on too abstruse subjects to
yield him much profit, and during the later years of
his life he had to contend with poverty. It is said
that he derived a precarious subsistence from fees
paid to him for solving questions relative to games of
chance and other matters connected with the value of
probabilities. He frequented a coffee-house in St.
Martin's Lane, of which he was one of the attractions;
and there his customers sought him to work out their
problems. The occupation could not have been very
tolerable to such a man; but he was growing old and
helpless in body, and his powers of calculation formed
his only capital. He survived to the age of eighty-
seven, but during the last month of his life he sank
into a state of total lethargy. Shortly before his
decease, the Academy of Berlin elected him a member.
The French Academy of Sciences also elected him a
foreign associate; and on the news of his death reaching Paris, M. de Fouchy drew up an eloquent *eloge* of
the exiled Huguenot, which was duly inserted in the
records of the Academy.

For the reasons above stated, the number of refugee
physicians and surgeons who sought the asylum of
England was very considerable. Many of them settled
to practise in London and various towns in the south,
while others obtained appointments in the army and

navy. Weiss says it was to the French surgeons especially, that England was in a great measure indebted for the remarkable perfection to which English surgical instruments arrived. The College of Physicians in London generously opened their doors to the admission of their foreign brethren. Between the years 1681 and 1689 we find nine French physicians admitted, amongst whom we observe the name of the eminent Sebastian le Fevre.[1]

Among the literary men of the emigration were the brothers Du Moulin—Louis, for some time Camden professor of history at Oxford, and Peter, prebendary of Canterbury—both authors of numerous works; Henry Justel (secretary to Louis XIV.), who sold off his valuable library and fled to England some years before the Revocation, when he was appointed King's librarian; Peter Anthony Motteaux, an excellent linguist, whose translations of Cervantes and Rabelais first popularised the works of those writers in this country; Maximilian Misson, author of *A New Voyage to Italy, Theatre Sacré des Cevennes*, and other works; Michel de la Roche, author of *Memoirs of Literature*, and *A Literary Journal*, which filled up a considerable gap in literary history;[2] Michel Mattaire, M.A.

---

[1] The family were of long and eminent standing in Anjou as medical men. Joshua le Fevre obtained letters of naturalisation in 1681; but before that date Nicasius le Fevre, a member of the same family, was appointed chemist to Charles II., with a fee of £150 a year.—DURRANT COOPER—*List of Foreign Protestants*, p. xxvi.

[2] In his *Literary Journal*, De la Roche says: "I was very young when I took refuge in England, so that most of the little learning I have got is of an English growth. . . . 'Tis in this country I have learned to have a right notion of religion, an ad-

vantage that can never be too much valued. Being a studious man, it was very natural to me to write some books, which I have done, partly in English and partly in French, for the space of twenty years. The only advantage I have got by them is that they have not been unacceptable, and I hope I have done no dishonour to the English nation by those French books printed beyond sea, in which I undertook to make our English learning better known to foreigners than it was before. I have said just now that I took refuge in England. When I consider the continual fear I was in for a whole

Oxon, one of the masters of Westminster School, an able philologist, the author of several learned works on typography as well as theology; De Souligne, grandson of Du Plessis Mornay (the Huguenot leader), author of *The Desolation of France demonstrated, The Political Mischiefs of Popery*, and other works; John Gagnier, the able Orientalist, professor of Oriental languages at Oxford University, and the author of many learned treatises on Rabbinical lore and kindred subjects; John Cornaud de la Croze, author of *The Bibliothèque Universelle, The Works of the Learned*, and *The History of Learning;* Abel Boyer, the annalist, author of the well-known *French and English Dictionary*, who pursued a successful literary career in England for nearly forty years; Mark Anthony de la Bastide, author of several highly-esteemed controversial works; and Graverol of Nismes, one of the founders of the academy of that city, a poet and jurisconsult, who published in London a history of his native place, addressed to "Messieurs les Refugiés de Nîsmes qui sont établis dans Londres."

The last pages of Graverol's book contain a touching narrative of the sufferings of the Protestants of Languedoc, and conclude as follows:—"We, who are in a country so remote from our own only for the sake of God's word, and for the testimony of Jesus Christ, let us study to render our confession and our faith glorious by discreet and modest conduct, by an exemplary life, and by entire devotion to the service of God. Let us ever bear in mind that we are the sons and the fathers of martyrs. Let us never forget this glory, but strive to transmit it to our posterity."

But the most eminent of the refugees were the Huguenot Pastors, some of whom were men highly distinguished for their piety, learning, and eloquence. Such were Abbadie, considered one of the ablest de-

---

year, of being discovered and imprisoned to force me to abjure the Protestant religion, and the great difficulties I met with to make my escape, I wonder I have not been a stupid man ever since."

fenders of Christianity in his day ; Saurin, one of the
most eloquent of preachers; Allix, the learned philologist and historian, and Delange, his colleague;
Pineton, author of *Les Larmes de Chambrun,* characterised by Michelet as "that beautiful but terrible
recital"; Drelincourt, Marmet, and many more.

Jacques Abbadie was the scion of a distinguished
Bearnese family.   After completing his studies at
Sedan and Saumur, he took his doctor's degree at the
age of seventeen.   While still a young man, he was
invited to take charge of the French church in Berlin,
which he accepted; and his reputation served to attract large numbers of refugees to that city.   His
Treatise on the Truth of the Christian Religion greatly
increased his fame, not only at Berlin, but in France,
and throughout Europe.   Madame de Sévigne, though
rejoicing at the banishment of the Huguenots, spoke
of it in a high strain of panegyric, as the most divine
of all books : "I do not believe," she said, "that any
one ever spoke of religion like this man!"   Even Bussy
Rabutin, who did not pass for a believer, said of the
book : "We are reading it now, and we think it the
only book in the world worth reading."   A few years
later, Abbadie published his *Treatise on the Divinity
of Jesus Christ.*   It is so entirely free from controversial animus, that even the Roman Catholics of
France endeavoured to win him over to their faith.
But they deceived themselves.   For, on the death of
the Elector, Abbadie, instead of returning to France,
accompanied his friend Marshal Schomberg to Holland,
and afterwards to England, in the capacity of chaplain.
He was with the marshal during his campaigns in
Ireland, and suffered the grief of seeing his benefactor
fall mortally wounded at the battle of the Boyne.

Returning to London, Abbadie became attached as
minister to the church of the Savoy, where crowds
flocked to hear him preach.   While holding this position, he wrote his *Art of Knowing One's-self,* in
which he powerfully illustrated the relations of the

human conscience to the duties inculcated by the
Gospel. He also devoted his pen to the cause of
William III., and published his *Defence of the British
Nation*, in which he justified the deposition of James
II., and the Revolution of 1688, on the ground of
right and morality. In 1694 he was selected to
pronounce the funeral oration of Queen Mary, wife of
William III.,—a sermon containing many passages of
great eloquence; shortly after which he entered the
English Church, and was appointed to the deanery of
Killaloe, in which office he ended his days.

Jacques Saurin was the greatest of the Protestant
preachers. He was the son of an advocate at Nismes,
whose three sons all took refuge in England—Jacques,
the pulpit-orator; Captain Saurin, an officer in
William's army; and Louis, some time minister of
the French church in the Savoy, and afterwards Dean
of St. Patrick's, Ardagh.[1] Jacques Saurin was, in the
early part of his life, tempted to the profession of
arms; and when only seventeen years of age he served
as an ensign in the army of Savoy, under the Marquis
de Ruvigny, Earl of Galway. Returning to his studies
at Geneva, he prepared himself for the ministry; and
having proceeded to England in 1701, he was appointed one of the ministers of the French church in
Threadneedle Street. He held that office for four
years, after which he was called to the Hague, and
there developed that talent as a preacher for which
he became so distinguished. He was made minister-
extraordinary to the French community of nobles, and
held that office until his death.

Scarcely less distinguished was Peter Allix, for some
time pastor of the great Protestant church at Charenton, near Paris, and afterwards of the Temple of the
French Hospital in Spitalfields, London. His style of

---

[1] From him were lineally descended the Right Reverend
James Saurin, Bishop of Dromore, and the Right Honourable William Saurin, Attorney-
General for Ireland from 1807
to 1821.

preaching was less ornate, but not less forcible, than that of Saurin. His discourses were simple, clear, and persuasive. The great object which he aimed at, was the enforcement of union among Protestants. Louis XIV. tried every means to induce him to enter the Roman Catholic Church, and a pension was offered him if, in that case, he would return to France. But Allix resisted all such persuasions, and died in exile. His erudition was recognised by the Universities of Oxford and Cambridge, who conferred upon him the degree of Doctor of Divinity; and, on the recommendation of Bishop Burnet, he was made canon and treasurer of Salisbury Cathedral. Allix left behind him many published works, which in their time were highly esteemed.

Jacques Pineton was another of the refugee pastors who illustrated his faith by his life, which was pure and beautiful. He had personally suffered more than most of his brethren, and he lived to relate the story of his trials in his touching narrative entitled *Les Larmes de Chambrun.* He was pastor of a Protestant church in the village of that name, situated near Avignon, in the principality of Orange, when the district was overrun by the troops of Louis XIV. The dragonnade was even more furiously conducted there than elsewhere, because of the hatred entertained by the King towards the Protestant prince who took his title from the little principality. The troops were under the command of the Count of Tessé, a ferocious and profane officer. Pineton was laid up at the time by an attack of gout, the suffering from which was aggravated by the recent fracture of a rib which he had sustained. As he lay helpless on his couch, a party of forty-two dragoons burst into his house, entered his chamber, lit a number of candles, beat their drums round his bed, and filled the room with tobacco-smoke, so as almost to stifle him. They then drank until they fell asleep and snored; but their officers entering, roused them from their stupor by laying about amongst them with their canes. While the men were asleep, Pineton urged his wife to fly, which she attempted to do; but she was taken in the act and brought before Tessé, who brutally told her that she must regard herself as the property of the regiment. She fell at his feet distracted, and would have been lost, but that a priest to whom Pineton had rendered some service, offered himself as surety for her. The priest, however, made it a condition that she and her husband should abjure their religion; and in a moment of agony and despair, both succumbed, and agreed to conform to popery.

Remorse immediately followed, and they determined to take the first opportunity to fly. Upon the plea that Pineton, still in great pain, required surgical aid, he obtained leave to proceed to Lyons. He was placed in a litter, the slightest movement of which caused him indescribable pain. When the people saw him carried away, they wept,—Catholic as well as Protestant. Even the dragoons were moved. The sufferer reached Lyons, where he was soon cured and declared convalescent. It appears that the frontier was less strictly guarded near Lyons; and with the assistance of a friend, Pineton shortly after contrived to escape in the disguise of a general officer. He set out in a carriage with four horses, attended by a train of servants in handsome liveries. At the bridge of Beauvoisin, where a picket of dragoons was posted, he was allowed to cross without interruption, the soldiers having previously been informed that "my lord" was a great officer travelling express into Switzerland. There was, however, still the frontier guard of the Duke of Savoy to pass. It commanded the great road across the Alps, and was maintained for the express purpose of preventing the escape of Huguenots. By the same bold address, and feigning great indignation at the guard attempting to obstruct his passage, Pineton was allowed to proceed, and shortly after he reached Chambery. Next morning he entered the

French gate of Geneva, giving expression to his feelings by singing the eighth verse of the twenty-sixth
Psalm,—

> " Que j'aime ce saint lieu
> Où Tu parois, mon Dieu," etc.

Madame Pineton was less fortunate in her flight.
She set out for the Swiss frontier accompanied by
three ladies belonging to Lyons. The guides whom
they had hired and paid to conduct them, had the
barbarity to desert them in the mountains. It was
winter. They wandered and lost their way. They
were nine hours in the snow. They were driven away
from Cardon, and pursued along the Rhone. The
Lyons ladies, vanquished by cold, fatigue, and hunger,
wished to return to Lyons and give themselves up;
they could endure no longer. But Madame Pineton
hoped that by this time her husband had reached
Geneva; and she found courage for them all. She
would not listen to the proposal to go back ; she must
go forward ; and the contest ended in their proceeding, and arriving at last at Geneva, and there finding
safety and liberty. The pastor Pineton, after remaining for a short time in that city, proceeded towards
Holland, where he was graciously received by the
Prince of Orange. Having been appointed one of the
Princess's chaplains, he accompanied Mary to London,
and was appointed a canon of Windsor. He did not,
however, live long to enjoy his dignity, for he died
in 1689, the year after his arrival in England ; though
he lived to give to the world the touching narrative
of his adventures and sufferings.

Many of the most distinguished of the French
pastors were admitted to degrees in the Universities
of Oxford and Cambridge ; and several, besides the
above, held benefices in the English Church. In 1682,
when the learned Samuel de l'Angle was created D.D.
of Oxford without payment of the customary fees, he
was conducted into the House of Convocation by the
King's professor of divinity, and all the masters stood

up to receive him. De l'Angle had been the chief preacher in the temple of Charenton, near Paris ; and after thirty-five years of zealous work there, he fled from France with his family, to end his days in England. He was afterwards made prebendary of Canterbury and Westminster. Peter Drelincourt, son of the famous French divine, whose work on *Death* [1] has been translated into nearly all the languages of Europe, was another refugee who entered the Church, and became Dean of Armagh. Dr. Hans de Veille, a man of great learning, having also entered the Church, was made library-keeper at Lambeth Palace by Dr. Tillotson, then Archbishop of Canterbury.

Though many of the most eminent French ministers joined the Established Church of England, others equally learned and able became preachers and professors among the Dissenters. While Pierre du Moulin was a prebendary of Canterbury, his brother Louis was a stout Presbyterian. Charles Marie du Veil, originally a Jew, was first converted to Roman Catholicism, next to Protestantism, and ended by becoming a Baptist minister. But the most eminent of the refugees who joined the Dissenters was the Reverend James Capell, who had held the professorship of Hebrew in the University of Saumur at the early age of nineteen. He fled into England shortly after the Revocation, and in 1708 he accepted a professor's chair at the Dissenters' College in Hoxton Square. There he long continued to teach the Oriental languages and their critical application in the study of the Scriptures ; and he performed his duties with such distinguished ability that the institution came to enjoy a very high repute. Many of the ablest ministers of the next generation, Churchmen as well as Dissenters, studied under Mr. Capell, and received from him their best education.

---

[1] *Les Consolations de l'Ame fidelle contre les Frayeurs de la Mort* has been reprinted more than forty times in France, and many times in England in its translated form.

He held the office for fourteen years, and died at eighty-three, the last of his family.

Of the ministers of the French churches in London, besides those already named, the most distinguished were the Reverend Charles Bertheau, minister of the French church in Threadneedle Street, who officiated in that capacity with great ability for a period of forty-six years; the Reverend Henri Chatelain,[1] minister of the French church in St. Martin's Lane; the Reverend Cæsar Pegorier, minister of the Artillery and Tabernacle churches, and author of numerous controversial works; the Reverend Henri Rochblave, minister of the refugee church at Greenwich, and afterwards of the French Chapel-Royal, St. James's; the Reverend Daniel Chamier, minister of the French church in Leicesterfields; and the Reverend Jean Graverol, minister of the French churches of Swallow Street and the Quarré —a voluminous and eloquent writer. The Reverend Antoine Pérès (formerly professor of Oriental languages in the University of Montauban) and Ezekiel Marmet, were ministers of other French churches, and were greatly beloved,—Marmet's book of meditations on the words of Job, " I know that my Redeemer liveth," being prized by devout readers of all persuasions.

The Reverend Claude de la Mothe and Jean Armand du Bourdieu were ministers of the French church in the Savoy, the principal West-end congregation, frequented by the most distinguished of the refugees. Both these ministers were eminent for their learning and their eloquence. The former was of a noble Huguenot family named Grostête. He studied law when a youth at

---

[1] Henri Chatelain was the great-grandson of Simon Chatelain, of Paris, the famous Protestant manufacturer of gold and silver lace. This lace was a much prized article. It procured for the steadfast Huguenot the toleration of his religion, in which he was zealous from the fifteenth year of his age to the eighty-fifth, which was his last. He died in 1675, leaving more than eighty descendants, who all paid fines for openly attending his funeral. —AGNEW— *French Protestant Exiles*, 237.

Orleans, his native city, where he took the degree of Doctor of Civil Law. He was also a member of the Royal Society of Berlin. He practised for some time at Paris as an advocate, but subsequently left law for divinity, and was appointed pastor of the church at Lisy in 1675. At the Revocation he fled to England with his wife, and was selected one of the ministers of the church in the Savoy. He was the author of numerous works, which enjoyed a high reputation in his day. He also devoted much of his time to correspondence, with the object of obtaining the release of Protestant martyrs from the French galleys.

Jean Armand du Bourdieu, the colleague of De la Mothe, though celebrated as a preacher, was still more distinguished as an author. Like himself, his father was a refugee divine, and preached in London until his ninety-fifth year. Jean Armand had been pastor of a church at Montpelier, which he left at the Revocation, and came over to England, followed by a large number of his flock. He was chaplain to the three dukes of Schomberg in succession, and was by the old duke's side when he fell at the Boyne. In 1707 he preached a sermon in London, which was afterwards published, wherein he alluded to Louis XIV. as a Pharaoh to the oppressed Protestants of France. The French king singled him out from the many refugee preachers in England, and demanded, through his minister, that he should be punished. Louis' complaint was formally referred to the Bishop of London —the French church in the Savoy being under his jurisdiction,—and Du Bourdieu was summoned before his Grace at Fulham Palace to answer the charge. After reading and considering the memorial of the French ambassador, the pastor was asked what he had to say to it. He replied that " during the war he had, after the example of several prelates and clergymen of the Church of England, preached freely against the common enemy and persecutor of the Church ; and the greatest part of his sermons being printed with his name affixed, he was far from disowning them; but since the proclamation of the peace [of Utrecht], he had not said anything that did in the least regard the French king." No further steps were taken in the matter.

Du Bourdieu continued indefatigably active on behalf of his oppressed brethren in France during the remainder of his life. His pen was seldom idle, and his winged words flew abroad and kept alive the indignation of the Protestant north against the persecutors of his countrymen. In 1717 he published two works, one "A Vindication of our Martyrs at the Galleys;" another, "A Comparison of the Penal Laws of France against Protestants with those of England against Papists!" and, in the following year, "An Appeal to the English Nation." He was now an old man of seventy; but his fire burned to the last. Two years later he died, beloved and lamented by all who knew him.[1]

There is little reason to doubt that the earnestness, eloquence, and learning of this distinguished band of exiles for conscience' sake exercised an influence, not only on English religion and politics, but also on English literature, which continues to operate to this day.

---

[1] A great-grandson of Du Bourdieu, Captain Saumarez Du-bourdieu, was an officer in the British army at the capture of Martinique from the French in 1762. He received the sword of the French commandant, who said, on presenting it: "My misfortune is the lighter, as I am conquered by a Dubourdieu, a beloved relative. *My* name is Dubourdieu!"

CHAPTER XV.

WE now come to the immigration and settlement in
England of Huguenot merchants, manufacturers, and
artizans, which exercised a still greater influence on
English industry than the immigration of French
literati and divines did upon English literature.

It is computed that about 100,000 French manufacturers and workmen fled into England in consequence of the Revocation, besides those who took
refuge in Switzerland, Germany, and Holland. When
the Huguenot employers of labour shut up their works in
France and prepared to emigrate, their workmen usually
arranged to follow them. Protestant masters and men
converted what they could into money, and made for
the coast, accompanied by their families. The paper-
makers of Angoumois left their mills; the silk-makers
of Touraine left their looms; the tanners of Normandy
left their pits; the vine-dressers and farmers of Saintonge, Poitou, and La Rochelle, left their vineyards,
their farms, and their gardens, and looked into the
wide world, seawards, for a new home and refuge,
where they might work and worship in peace.

The principal immigration into England was from
Normandy and Brittany.[1] Upwards of 10,000 of the

---

[1] FLOQUET, the accredited historian of Normandy (*Histoire du
Parlement de Normandie*), cal-
culates that not less than 184,000
Protestants took advantage of the
vicinity of the sea, and of their
connection with England and
Holland, to abandon their country.

industrial class left Rouen; and several thousand
persons, principally engaged in the maritime trade,
set out from Caen, leaving that city to solitude and
poverty. The whole Protestant population of Cou-
tances emigrated, and the fine linen manufactures of
the place were at once extinguished. There was a
similar flight of masters and men from Elbœuf,
Alençon, Caudebec, Havre, and other northern towns.
The makers of *noyal* and white linen cloths, for which
a ready market had been obtained abroad, left Nantes,
Rennes, and Morlaix in Brittany, and Le Mans and
Laval in Maine, and went over to England to carry
on their manufactures there. The provinces further
north, also largely contributed to swell the stream of
emigration into England: the cloth-makers departed
from Amiens, Abbeville, and Doullens; the gauze-
makers and lace-makers from Lille and Valenciennes;
and artizans of all kinds from the various towns and
cities of the interior.

Notwithstanding the precautions taken by the
French government, and the penalty of death or
condemnation to the galleys for life, to which people
were subject who were taken in the act of flight, the
emigration could not be stopped. The fugitives were
helped on their way by their fellow-Protestants, and
often by Roman Catholics themselves, who pitied their
sad fate. The fugitives lay concealed in barns and
farmyards by day, and travelled by night towards the
coast. There the maritime population, many of whom
were Protestants like themselves, actively connived at
their escape. France presented too wide a reach of
sea-frontier, extending from Bayonne to Calais, to be
effectively watched by any coast-guards; and not only
the French, but the English and Dutch merchant-
ships, which hovered about the coast waiting for the
agreed signal to put in and take on board their freight
of fugitives, had comparatively little difficulty in
carrying them off in safety.

Of those fugitives who succeeded in making good

their escape, the richest took refuge in Holland; while the bulk of those who settled in England were persons of comparatively small means. Yet a considerable sum of ready-money must have been brought over by the refugees, as we find the French ambassador writing to Louis XIV. in 1687, that as much as 960,000 louis d'or had already been sent to the Mint for conversion into English money.[1] This was, however, the property of a comparatively small number of wealthy families; for the greater proportion of those who landed in England were all but destitute.

Prompt steps were taken for the relief of the poorer immigrants. Collections were made in the churches; public subscriptions were raised; and Parliament voted considerable sums from the public purse. Thus a fund of nearly £200,000 was collected and invested for the benefit of the refugees,—the annual interest, about £15,000, being intrusted to a committee for distribution among the most necessitous; while about £2000 a year was applied towards the support of the poor French ministers and their respective churches. The pressure on the relief fund was of course greatest in those years immediately following the Revocation of the Edict of Nantes, before the destitute foreigners had been able to maintain themselves by their respective callings. There was also a large number of destitute landed gentry, professional men, and pastors, to whom the earning of a livelihood was extremely difficult; and these also had to be relieved out of the fund.

From the first report of the French Relief Committee, dated December, 1687—that is, only fourteen months after the Revocation—it appears that 15,500 refugees had been relieved in the course of the year. "Of these," says Weiss, "13,050 were settled in London,

---

[1] MACPHERSON says, "I have seen a computation, at the lowest supposition, of only 50,000 of those people coming to Great Britain, and that, one with another, they brought £60 each in money or effects, whereby they added three millions sterling to the wealth of Britain." —*Annals of Commerce*, ii. 617.

and 2000 in the different seaport towns where they had disembarked. Amongst them the committee distinguishes 140 persons of quality with their families; 143 ministers; 144 lawyers, physicians, traders, and burghers. It designates the others under the general denomination of artizans and workmen. The persons of quality received weekly assistance in money throughout the whole of that year. Their sons were placed in the best commercial houses. About 150 of them entered the army, and were provided, at the cost of the committee, with a complete outfit. The ministers obtained for themselves and their families pensions which were regularly paid. Their sons found employment in the houses of rich merchants or of persons of quality. Weekly assistance was granted to the sick, and to those whose great age prevented them earning their living by labour. The greater part of the artizans and workmen were employed in the English manufactories. The committee supplied them with the necessary implements and tools, and provided, at the same time, for their other wants. Six hundred of them, for whom it could not find employment in England, were sent at its cost to America. Fifteen French churches were also erected out of the proceeds of the national subscription, —three in London, and twelve in the various counties where the greater number of the refugees had settled."[1]

The help thus generously given to the distressed refugees by the nation, was very shortly rendered unnecessary through the vigorous efforts which they made to help themselves. They sought about in all directions for employment; and being ingenious, intelligent, and industrious, they gradually succeeded in obtaining it. French workpeople are better economists than the English, and less sufficed for their wants. They were satisfied if they could keep a roof over their heads, a clean fireside, and the *pot-au-feu* going. What English artizans despised as food they

---

[1] WEISS—*History of the French Protestant Refugees*, p. 224.

could make a meal of. For they brought with them from France the art of cooking—the art of economising nutriment and at the same time presenting it in the most savoury forms—an art almost entirely unknown even at this day in the homes of English workmen, and the want of which occasions enormous national loss. Before the arrival of the refugees, the London butchers sold their bullocks' hides to the fellmongers always with the tails on. The tails were thrown away and wasted. Who could ever dream of eating oxen's tails? The refugees profited by the delusion. They obtained the tails, enriched their *pots-au-feu* with them, and revelled in the now well-known delicacy of ox-tail soup.

The refugees were also very helpful of one another. The richer helped the poorer, and the poorer helped each other. The Marquis de Ruvigny kept almost open house, and was equally ready to open his purse to his distressed countrymen. Those who had the means of starting manufactories and workshops, employed as many hands as they could; and such of the men as earned wages, helped to support those who remained unemployed. Being of foreign birth, and having no claim upon the poor-rates, the French artizans formed themselves into societies for mutual relief in sickness and old age. These were the first societies of the kind established by workmen in England, though they have since been largely imitated;[1] and the Oddfellows, Foresters, and numerous other benefit societies of the labouring class, though they may not know it,

---

[1] One of the oldest of the French benefit societies was the "Norman Society" of Bethnal Green, which only ceased to exist in 1863, after a life of upwards of 150 years. Down to the year 1800, the whole of the society's accounts were kept in French, the members being the descendants of French Protestants, mostly bearing French names; but at length the foreign element became so mixed with the English that it almost ceased to be recognisable, and the society may be said to have died out with the absorption of the distinctive class for whose benefit it was originally instituted.

are but following in the path long since chalked out for
them by the French refugees.

The working-class immigrants very soon settled
down to the practice of their respective callings in
different parts of the country. A large proportion of
them settled in London, and several districts of the
metropolis were almost entirely occupied by them.
Spitalfields, Bethnal Green, and Soho were the principal French quarters, where French was spoken in the
workshops, in the schools and churches, and in the
streets. But the immigrants also distributed themselves in other districts : many of them settled in
Aldgate, Bishopsgate, Shoreditch, and the quarters adjoining Thames Street. A little colony of them settled
in one of the streets leading from Broad Street to the
Guildhall, which came to be called "Petty France,"
from the number of French who inhabited it. Others
settled in Long Acre, the Seven Dials, and the
neighbourhood of Temple Bar. Le Mann, the famous
biscuit maker, opened his shop and flourished near the
Royal Exchange. Some opened shops for the manufacture and sale of cutlery and mathematical and surgical instruments, in the Strand; while others began
the making of watches, the fabrication of articles in
gold and silver, and the cutting and mounting of
jewellery, in which the French artizans were then
admitted to be the most expert in Europe.

France had long been the leader of fashion, and all
the world bought dress and articles of virtu at Paris.
Colbert was accustomed to say that the Fashions were
worth more to France than the mines of Peru were to
Spain. Only articles of French manufacture, with a
French name, could find purchasers amongst people of
fashion in London. "The fondness of the nation for
French Commodities was such," says Joshua Gee, "that
it was a very hard matter to bring them into love with
those made at home."[1]   Goods to the amount of above

---

[1] Joshua Gee—*The Trade and Navigation of Great Britain considered.*

two and a half millions sterling were annually imported from France, whereas the value of English goods exported thither did not amount to a million.

The principal articles imported from France previous to the Revocation, were velvets and satins from Lyons; silks and taffetas from Tours; silk ribands, galloons, laces, gloves, and buttons from Paris and Rouen; serges from Chalons, Rheims, Amiens, and various towns in Picardy; beaver and felt hats from Paris, Rouen, and Lyons; paper of all sorts from Auvergne, Poitou, Limousin, Champagne, Normandy; ironmongery and cutlery from Forrests, Auvergne; linen cloth from Brittany and Normandy; salt from Rochelle and Oleron, Isle of Rhé; wines from Gascony, Nantes, and Bordeaux; and feathers, fans, girdles, pins, needles, combs, soap, aqua-vitæ, vinegar, and various sorts of household stuffs, from different parts of France.

So soon, however, as the French artizans had settled in London, they proceeded to establish and carry on the same manufactures which they had worked at abroad; and a large portion of the stream of gold which before had flowed into France, now flowed into England. They introduced all the manufactures connected with the fashions, so that English customers became supplied with French-made articles, without requiring to send abroad money to buy them; while the refugees obtained a ready sale for all the goods which they could make, at remunerative prices. " Nay," says a writer of the time, " the English have now so great an esteem for the workmanship of the French refugees, that hardly anything vends without a Gallic name."[1] The French beavers, which had before been imported from Caudebec in France, were now made in the borough of Southwark and at Wandsworth, where several hat-makers began their operations on a considerable scale.[2]

---

[1] *History of the Trade in England:* London, 1702.

[2] Hat-making was one of the most important manufactures brought into England by the refugees. In France it had been almost entirely in the hands of the Protestants. They alone

Others introduced the manufacture of buttons, of wool, silk, and metal, which before had been made almost exclusively in France. The printing of calicoes was introduced by a refugee, who established a manufactory for the purpose near Richmond. Other printworks were started at Bromley in Essex, from whence the manufacture was afterwards removed into Lancashire. A French refugee, named Passavant, purchased the tapestry-manufactory at Fulham, originally established by the Walloons, which had fallen into decay. His first attempts at reviving the manufacture not having proved successful, he removed the works to Exeter, where he established them prosperously, with the assistance of some workmen whom he obtained from the Gobelins at Paris.

But the most important branch of manufacture to which the refugees devoted themselves, and in which they achieved both fame and wealth, was the silk manufacture in all its branches. The silk fabrics of France—its satins, brocades, velvets, paduasoys, figured and plain—were celebrated throughout the world, and were eagerly purchased. As much as 200,000 livres worth of black lustrings were annually bought by the English. They were made expressly for their market, and were known as " English taffeties." Shortly after the Revocation, not only was the whole of this fabric made in England, but large quantities were manufactured for foreign exportation.

The English government had long envied France her possession of the silk manufacture, which gave employment to a large number of people, and was a source

---

possessed the secret of the liquid composition which serves to prepare rabbit, hare, and beaver skins. They alone supplied England and Holland with fine hats, principally from Caudebec. After the Revocation, most of the hatmakers went to London, and took with them the secret of their art, which was lost to France for about forty years. During this period, the French nobility, and all persons making pretensions to dress, wore none but English hats. Even the Roman cardinals got their hats from the celebrated manufactory at Wandsworth, established by the refugees !

of much wealth to the country. An attempt was
made in the reign of Elizabeth to introduce the manufacture in England, and it was repeated in the reign of
James I. The corporation of the city of London also
encouraged the manufacture. We find from their records, that, in 1609, they admitted to the freedom of
the city one Robert Therie or Thierry, on account of
his skill and invention; and as "being the first in
England who hath made stuffes of silk, the which was
made by the silkworm nourished here in England."
One M. Brumelach was also invited over from France,
with sundry silk throwsters, weavers, and dyers, and
a beginning was made in the manufacture; but it
was not until the influx of Protestant refugees after
the Revocation, that the silk manufacture took root
and began to flourish.

The workmen of Tours and Lyons brought with
them the arts which had raised the manufactures of
France to such a height of prosperity. They erected
their looms in Spitalfields, and there practised their
modes of weaving,—turning out large quantities of
lustrings, velvets, and mingled stuffs of silk and wool,
of such excellence as to insure for them a ready sale
everywhere. Weiss says that the figured silks which
proceeded from the London manufactories were due
almost exclusively to the skill and industry of three
refugees—Lanson, Mariscot, and Monceaux. The artist
who supplied the designs was another refugee, named
Beaudoin. A common workman named Mongeorge
brought them the secret, recently discovered at Lyons,
of giving lustre to silk taffety; and Spitalfields
thenceforward enjoyed a large share of the trade for
which Lyons had been so famous.

To protect the English manufactures, the import
duties on French silks were at first trebled. In 1692,
five years after the Revocation, the manufacturers of
lustrings and alamode silks were incorporated by
charter under the name of the Royal Lustring Company; shortly after which they obtained from Parlia-

ment an Act entirely prohibiting the importation of
foreign goods of like sorts. Strange to say, one of the
grounds on which they claimed this degree of protection was, that the manufacture of these articles in
England had now reached a greater degree of perfection than was attained by foreigners,—a reason
which ought to have rendered them independent of
all legislative interference in their favour. Certain
it is, however, that by the end of the century the
French manufacturers in England were not only able
to supply the whole of the English demand, but to
export considerable quantities of their goods to those
countries which France had formerly supplied.

One of the most remunerative branches of business
was the manufacture of silk stockings, which the English then shared with the French artizans. This trade
was due to the invention of the stocking-frame by
William Lee, M.A., about the year 1600. Not being
able to find any encouragement for his invention in
England, he went over to Rouen in 1605, on the invitation of the French minister Sully,—to instruct the
French operatives in the construction and working of
the machine. Nine of the frames were in full work,
and Lee enjoyed a prospect of honour and competency,
when, unhappily for him, his protector, Henry IV., was
assassinated by the fanatic Ravaillac. The patronage
which had been extended to him was at once withdrawn, on which Lee proceeded to Paris to press his
claims upon the government. But he had the misfortune to be a foreigner, and, worst of all, a Protestant.
His claims were therefore disregarded, and he shortly
after died at Paris in extreme distress.

Two of Lee's machines were left at Rouen ; the rest
were brought over to England ; and in course of time,
considerable improvements were made in the invention. The stocking-trade became so considerable a
branch of business, that in 1654 we find the frame-
work-knitters petitioning Oliver Cromwell to grant
them a charter of incorporation. The Protector did

not confer upon them the monopoly of manufacture which they sought. Accordingly, when the French refugees settled amongst us, they were as free to make use of Lee's invention as the English themselves were. Hence the manufacture of silk hosiery by the stocking-frame, soon became a leading branch of trade in Spitalfields, and English hose were in demand all over Europe. Keysler, the traveller, writing as late as 1730, remarks that "at Naples, when a tradesman would highly recommend his silk stockings, he invariably protests that they are right English."

In a petition presented to Parliament by the weavers' company in 1713, it was stated that owing to the encouragement afforded by the Crown and by divers Acts of the legislature, the silk manufacture at that time was twenty times greater in amount than it had been in 1664 ; that all sorts of black and coloured silks, gold and silver stuffs, and ribands were made here as good as those of French fabric ; that black silk for hoods and scarfs, which, twenty-five years before, was all imported, was now made here to the annual value of £300,000, whereby a great increase had been occasioned in the exportation of woollen and other manufactured goods to Turkey and Italy, whence the raw silk was imported. Such, amongst others, were the effects of the settlement in London of the French refugee artizans.

Although the manufacture of glass had been introduced into England before the arrival of the French artizans, it made comparatively small progress until they took it in hand. Mr. Pellatt, in his lecture on the manufacture of glass, delivered before the Royal Institution, attributed the establishment of the manufacture to the Huguenot refugees,—most of the technical terms still used in glass-making being derived from the French. Thus, the "found" is the melting of the materials into glass, from the French word *fondre*. The "siege" is the place or seat in which the crucible stands. The "kinney" is the corner of the furnace, probably from *coin* or *cheminée*. The "journey," denoting the time of making glass from the beginning of the "found," is obviously from *journée*. The "foushart," or fork used to move the sheet of glass into the annealing-kiln, is from *fourchette*, The "marmre" is the slab, formerly of marble, but now of iron, on which the ball of hot glass is rolled. And so on with "cullet" (*coule*—glass run off, or broken glass), "pontil" (*pointée*); and other words obviously of French and Flemish origin.

The Parisian glass-makers were especially celebrated for the skill with which they cast large plates for mirrors; and, shortly after the Revocation, when a large number of these valuable workmen took refuge in England, a branch of that manufacture was established by Abraham Thavenart, which proved highly successful. Other works were started for the making of crystal, in which the French greatly excelled; and before long, not only were they able to supply the home market, but to export large quantities of glass of the best sorts to Holland and other European countries.

For the improvement of English paper, also, we are largely indebted to the refugees—to the master manufacturers and their artizans who swarmed over to England from the paper-mills of Angoumois. Before the Revocation, the paper made in this country was of the common "whitey-brown" sort—coarse and inelegant. All the best sorts were imported from abroad, mostly from France. But soon after the Revocation, the import of paper ceased, and the refugees were able to supply us with as good an article as could be bought elsewhere. The first manufactory for fine paper was established by the refugees in London in 1685; but other mills were shortly after begun by them in Kent, at Maidstone and along the Darent, as well as in other parts of England.[1] That

---

[1] The Patent Office Records clearly show the activity of the French exiles in the province of invention, by the numerous pa-

the leading workmen employed in the first fine-paper mills were French and Flemish is shown by the distinctive terms of the trade still in use. Thus, in Kent, the man who lays the sheets on the felts is the *coucher;* the fateman, or vatman, is the Flemish *fassman;* and the room where the finishing operations are performed is still called the *salle.*

One of the most distinguished of the refugee paper-manufacturers, was Henry de Portal. The Portals were an ancient and noble family in the South of France, of Albigeois descent, who stood firm by the faith of their fathers. Several of them suffered death rather than recant. Toulouse was for many generations the home of the Portals, where they held and exercised the highest local authority. Several of them in succession were elected " Capitoul," a position of great dignity and power in that city. When the persecution of the Albigeois set in, the De Portals put themselves at their head; but they were unable to stand against the tremendous power of the Inquisition. They fled from Toulouse in different directions—some to Nismes, and others into the neighbourhood of Bordeaux. Some of them perished in the massacres which occurred throughout France subsequent to the night of Saint Bartholomew at Paris; and they continued to suffer during the century that ended in the Revocation; yet still they remained constant to their faith.

When the reign of terror began in the South of France, under Louis XVI., Louis de Portal was residing

---

tents taken out by them for printing, spinning, weaving, paper-making, and other arts. Such names as Blondeau, Dupin, De Cardonels, Le Blon, Ducleu, Pousset, Gastineau, Couran, Paul, etc., are found constantly recurring in the lists of patentees for many years subsequent to the Revocation. In 1686 we find M. Dupin, A. de Cardonels, C. R. M. de Crouchy, J. de May, and R. Shales, taking out a patent for making writing and printing paper, having " lately brought out of France excellent workmen and already set up several new-invented mills and engines for making thereof, not heretofore used in England."—[See *Abridgment of Specifications relating to Printing*, p. 82.]

18

at his Château de la Portalerie, seven leagues from
Bordeaux. To escape the horrors of the dragonnades,
he set out with his wife and five children to take
refuge on his estate in the Cevennes. The dragoons
pursued the family to their retreat, overtook them, and
cut down the father, mother, and one of the children.
They also burnt to the ground the house in which
they had taken refuge. The remaining four children
concealed themselves in an oven outside the building,
and were thus saved.

The four orphans—three boys and a girl—immediately determined to make for the coast and escape
from France by sea. After a long and perilous journey
on foot—exhausted by fatigue and wanting food—they
at length reached Montauban, where little Pierre, the
youngest, fell down fainting with hunger at the door of
a baker's shop. The humane baker took up the child,
carried him into the house, and fed and cherished
him. The other three—Henry, William, and Mary de
Portal—though grieving to leave their brother behind
them, again set out on foot, and pressed onward to
Bordeaux.

They were so fortunate as to secure a passage by a
merchant-vessel, on board of which they were shipped,
concealed in barrels. They were among the last of
the refugees who escaped, previous to the issue of the
infamous order to fumigate all departing vessels, so as to
stifle any Protestant fugitives who might be concealed
in the cargo. The youthful refugees reached Holland,
where they found friends and foster-parents, and were
shortly in a position to assert the dignity of their
birth. Miss Portal succeeded in obtaining a situation
as governess in the family of the Countess of Finken-
stein. She afterwards married M. Lenormant, a refugee
settled at Amsterdam; while Henry and William followed the fortunes of the Prince of Orange, accompanied him into England, and established the family of
De Portal in this country.[1]

---

[1] William entered the church late in life. He was nominated

Henry, the elder brother, having learnt the art of paper-making, started a mill of his own at Laverstoke on the Itchin, near Whitchurch in Hampshire, where he achieved high reputation as a paper-manufacturer. He carried on his business with great spirit, gathering round him the best French and Dutch workmen. He shortly brought his work to so high a degree of perfection, that the Bank of England gave him the privilege, which a descendant of the family still enjoys, of supplying them with the paper for bank-notes. Henry de Portal had resolved to rebuild the fortunes of his house on English ground ; and he did it nobly by his skill, his integrity, and his industry.

The De Portals of Freefolk Priors re-established themselves among the aristocratic order to which they originally belonged ; and their sons and daughters formed alliances with some of the noblest families in England. The youngest brother, Pierre de Portal, who had been left fainting at the door of the baker at Montauban, was brought up to manhood by the baker, held to his Protestantism, and eventually set up as a cloth-manufacturer in France. He prospered, married, and his sons grew up around him, one of them eventually becoming lord of Pénardières. His grandson Alberèdes, also faithful to the creed of his fathers, rose to high office, having been appointed minister of marine and the colonies, councillor of state, and a peer of France, at the restoration of the Bourbons. The present baron, Pierre Paul Frederick de Portal, maintains the ancient reputation of the family ; and to his highly interesting work, entitled *Les Descendants des Albigeois et des Huguenots, ou Mémoires de la Famille de Portal* (Paris 1860), we are mainly indebted for the above facts relating to the family.

Various other branches of manufacture were either

---

tutor to Prince George, afterwards George III., and held the livings of Clowne in Derbyshire, and Farnbridge in Essex. Abra-ham Portal, whose poetical works were published in 1781, was his grandson.

established or greatly improved by the refugees. At Canterbury they swelled the ranks of the silk-manufacturers; so much so, that in 1694 they possessed 1000 looms, giving employment to nearly 3000 workmen,—though, for the convenience of the trade, the greater number of them subsequently removed to Spitalfields. Many of the immigrants also found their way to Norwich, where they carried on with great success the manufacture of lustrings, brocades, paduasoys, tabinets, and velvets; while others carried on the making of cutlery, clocks, and watches. The fifty years that followed the settlement of the French refugees in Norwich, formed the most prosperous period in the history of that city. Another body of refugees settled at Ipswich in 1681, where they began the manufacture of fine linen, before then imported from France. The elders and deacons of the French church in Threadneedle Street raised the necessary funds for their support until they could maintain themselves by their industry. They were organised and superintended by a refugee from Paris named Bonhomme,[1] one of the most skilled manufacturers in France. To the manufacture of linen, another of sail-cloth was added, and England was enabled entirely to dispense with any further supply of the foreign-made article.

The lace-manufacture, introduced originally by the Walloon refugees, was also increased and improved by the influx of Huguenot lace-makers, principally from Burgundy and Normandy. Some established themselves in London, while others betook themselves to the adjoining counties—settling at Buckingham, Newport-Pagnel, and Stony Stratford, from whence the manu-

---

[1] In 1681, Savil wrote from Paris to Jenkins, then Secretary of State, to announce the approaching departure of Bonhomme and all his family, adding, "This man will be able to give you some lights into the method of bringing the manufacture of sail-cloth in England."

facture extended into Oxford, Northampton, Cambridge, and the adjoining counties.

Some of the exiles went as far north as Scotland, and settled there. Thus, a colony of weavers from Picardy, in France, began the manufacture of linen in a suburb of Edinburgh near the head of Leith Walk, long after known as "Little Picardy,"—the name still surviving in Picardy Place. Others of them built a silk-factory, and laid out a mulberry plantation on the slope of Moultrie Hill, then an open common. The refugees were sufficiently numerous in Edinburgh to form a church, of which the Rev. Mr. Dupont was appointed minister; and William III., in 1693, granted to the city a duty of two pennies on each pint of ale, out of which 2000 marks were to be paid yearly towards the maintenance of the ministers of the French congregation. At Glasgow, one of the refugees succeeded in establishing a paper-mill, the first in that part of Scotland. The Huguenot who erected it escaped from France accompanied only by his little daughter. For some time after his arrival in Glasgow, he maintained himself by picking up rags in the streets. But, by dint of thrift and diligence, he eventually contrived to accumulate sufficient means to enable him to start his paper-mill, and thus to lay the foundation of an important branch of Scottish industry.

In short, there was scarcely a branch of trade in Great Britain, but at once felt the beneficial effects of the large influx of experienced workmen from France. Besides improving those manufactures which had already been established, they introduced many entirely new branches of industry; and by their skill, their intelligence, and their laboriousness, they richly repaid England for the hospitality and the asylum which had been so generously extended to them in their time of need.

CHAPTER XVI.

THE HUGUENOT CHURCHES IN ENGLAND.

THE vast number of French Protestants who fled into England on the Revocation of the Edict of Nantes, led to a large increase in the number of French churches. This was especially the case in London, which was the principal seat of the immigration. It may serve to give the reader an idea of the large admixture of Huguenot blood in the London population, when we state that about the beginning of last century, at which time the population of the metropolis was not one-fourth of what it is now, there were no fewer than thirty-five French churches in London and the suburbs. Of these, eleven were in Spitalfields, showing the preponderance of the French settlers in that quarter.

The French church in Threadneedle Street, the oldest in London, was in a measure the cathedral church of the Huguenots. Thither the refugees usually repaired on their arrival in London, and such of them as had been compelled to abjure their faith, in order to avoid the penalty of death or condemnation to the galleys, there made acknowledgment of their repentance, and were again received into membership. During the years immediately following the Revocation, the consistory of the French church met at least once every week in Threadneedle Street chapel, for the purpose of receiving such acknowledgments or "reconnaissances." The ministers heard the narratives of the trials of the refugees, examined their testimony, and, when judged worthy, received them into communion. At the sitting of the 5th of March, 1686, fifty fugitives from various provinces of France abjured the Roman Catholic religion, to which they had pretended to be converted; and at one of the sittings in May, 1687, not fewer than 497 members were again received into the church which they had, under the force of terror, pretended to abandon.

While the church in Threadneedle Street was thus resorted to by the Huguenot Calvinists, the French Episcopal church in the Savoy, opened about the year 1641, was similarly resorted to by the foreign Protestants of the Lutheran persuasion. This was the fashionable French church of the West-end, and was resorted to by many of the nobility, who were attracted by the eloquence of the preachers who usually ministered there; amongst whom we recognise the great names of Durrel, Severin, Abbadie, Saurin, Dubourdieu, Majendie, and Durand. There were also the following French churches in the western parts of London :—The chapel of Marylebone, founded about the year 1656; the chapel in Somerset House, originally granted by Charles I. to his queen Henrietta as a Roman Catholic place of worship, but which was afterwards appropriated by Parliament, in 1653, for the use of the French Protestants ; Castle Street Chapel in Leicester Square, erected at the expense of the government in 1672 as a place of worship for the refugees; the Little Savoy Chapel in the Strand, granted for the same purpose in 1675 ; and Hungerford Chapel in Hungerford Market, which was opened as a French church in 1687.

After the Revolution of 1688, a considerable addition was made to the French churches at the West-end. Thus, three new congregations were formed in the year 1689,—those of La Patente, in Soho, first opened in Berwick Street, from whence it was afterwards removed to Little Chapel Street, Wardour Street; Glasshouse Street Chapel, Golden Square, from whence it was afterwards removed to Leicester Fields; and La

Quarré (episcopal) Chapel, originally of Berwick Street, and afterwards of Little Dean Street, Westminster.

Another important French church at the West-end was that of Swallow Street, Piccadilly.[1] The congregation had originally worshipped in the French ambassador's chapel in Monmouth House, Soho Square; from whence they removed to Swallow Street in 1690. From the records of the church, which are preserved at Somerset House, it would appear that Swallow Street was in the west, what Threadneedle Street Church was in the east of London,—the place first resorted to by the refugee Protestants to make acknowledgment of their blackslidings, and to claim re-admission to church membership. Hence the numerous " reconnaissances " found recorded in the Swallow Street register.

About the year 1700, there was another large increase in the number of French churches in London, six more being added to those already specified— namely, L'Eglise du Tabernacle, afterwards removed to Leicester Fields Chapel; the French Chapel Royal, St. James's; Les Grecs, in Hog Lane, now Crown Street, Soho; Spring Gardens Chapel, or the Little Savoy; La Charenton, in Grafton Street, Newport Market; and La Tremblade, or West Street Chapel, St Giles's. About the same date, additional church accommodation was provided for the refugees in the city; one chapel having been opened in Blackfriars, and another in St. Martin's Lane, of which the celebrated Dr. Allix was pastor. With the latter chapel, known as the church of St. Martin Ongars, that of Threadneedle Street was eventually united.

But the principal increase in the French churches about that time was in the eastern parts of London, where the refugees of the manufacturing class had for the most part settled. The large influx of foreign Protestants is strikingly shown by the amount of new

---

[1] The chapel was sold to Dr. James Anderson in 1710, and is now used as a Scotch church.

chapels required for their accommodation. Thus, in Spitalfields and the adjoining districts, we find the following :—L'Eglise de St. Jean, Swan Fields, Shoreditch (1687); La Nouvelle Patente, Crispin Street, Spitalfields (1689); L'Eglise de l'Artillerie, Artillery Street, Bishopsgate (1691) ; L'Eglise de Crispin Street, Spitalfields (1693) ; Petticoat Lane Chapel, Spitalfields (1694) ; L'Eglise de Perle Street, Spitalfields (1697), afterwards incorporated with Crispin Street Chapel ; the French Church of Wapping (1700) ; L'Eglise de Bell Lane, Spitalfields (1700); L'Eglise de Wheler Street, Spitalfields (1703), afterwards incorporated with La Nouvelle Patente ; L'Eglise de Swan Fields, Slaughter Street, Shoreditch (1721); L'Eglise de l'Hôpital, afterwards L'Eglise Neuve, Church Street, Spitalfields (1742). Here we have no fewer than eleven French churches opened east of Bishopsgate Street, providing accommodation for a very large number of worshippers. The church last named, L'Eglise Neuve, was probably the largest of the French places of worship in London, being capable of accommodating about 1500 persons. It is now used as a chapel by the Wesleyan Methodists ; while the adjoining church of the Artillery is used as a poor Jews' synagogue.

In addition to the French churches in the city, at the West-end, and in the Spitalfields district, there were several thriving congregations in the suburban districts of London in which the refugees had settled. One of the oldest of these was that of Wandsworth, where a colony of Protestant Walloons settled about the year 1570. Having formed themselves into a congregation, they erected a chapel for worship, which is still standing, nearly opposite the parish church. The building bears this inscription on its front :—" Erected 1573—enlarged 1685—repaired 1809, 1831." Like the other refugee churches, it has ceased to retain its distinctive character, being now used as a Congregational chapel. The Huguenots had also a special burying-ground at Wandsworth, called " Mount Nod "

It is situated on East Hill; and contains the remains of many distinguished refugees—amongst others, of David Montolieu, Baron de St. Hyppolite.

Several other French churches were established in the suburbs after the Revocation. At Chelsea, the refugees had two chapels—one in Cook's Grounds (now used by the Congregationalists), and another in Little Chelsea. There were French churches also at Hammersmith, at Hoxton,[1] at Bow, and at Greenwich. The last named was erected through the influence of the Marquis de Ruvigny, who formed the centre of a select circle of refugee Protestants who long continued to inhabit the neighbourhood. Before their little church was ready for use, the refugees were allowed the use of the parish church, at the conclusion of the forenoon service on Sundays. Evelyn, in his Diary, makes mention of his attending the French service there in 1687, as well as the sermon which followed, in which he says: "The preacher pathetically exhorted to patience, constancy, and reliance on God, amidst all their sufferings." The French church, which was afterwards erected in London Street, not far from the Greenwich parish church, was recently used as a Baptist chapel.

The other French chapels throughout the kingdom, like those of London, received a large accession of members after the Revocation of the Edict of Nantes, and in many cases became too small for their accommodation. Hence a second French church was opened at Canterbury in a place called "The Malthouse," situated within the Cathedral precincts. It consisted at first of about 300 persons; but the Canterbury silk trade having been removed to Spitalfields, the greater number of the French weavers followed it thither; on which the Malthouse Chapel rapidly fell off, and at length became extinct about the middle of last century.

---

[1] Of this church Jacob Bourdillon was the last pastor. Among the names appearing in the Register are those of Romilly, Cossart, Faure, Durand, Hankey, Vidal, and Fargues.

The old French church of "God's House" at
Southampton also received a considerable accession
of members, chiefly fugitives from the provinces of
the opposite sea-board. The original Walloon element
had by this time almost entirely disappeared,—the
immigrants of a century before having become gradually absorbed into the native population. Hence
nearly all the entries in the registers of the church,
subsequent to the year 1685, describe the members
as " François refugiez"; some being from " Basse
Normandie," others from " Haute Languedoc," but the
greater number from the province of Poitou.

Numerous refugee military officers, retired from
active service, seem to have settled in the neighbourhood of Southampton about the beginning of last
century. Henry de Ruvigny, the venerable Earl of
Galway, lived at Rookley, and formed the centre of
a distinguished circle of refugee gentry. The Baron
de Huningue also lived in the town, and was so much
respected and beloved, that at his death he was
honoured with a public funeral. We also find the
families of the De Chavernoys and De Cosnes settled
in the place. The register of " God's House" contains
frequent entries relating to officers in "Colonel Mordant's regiment." On one occasion we find Brigadier
Mordant standing sponsor for the twin sons of Major
François du Chesne de Ruffanes, major of infantry;
and on another, the Earl of Galway standing sponsor
for the infant son of Pierre de Cosne, a refugee
gentleman of La Beauce. From the circumstance of
Gerard de Vaux, the owner of a paper-mill in South
Stoneham, being a member of the congregation, we
also infer that several of the settlers in the neighbourhood of Southampton were engaged in that
branch of manufacture.

Among the new French churches formed in places
where there had been none before, and which mark
the new settlements that followed the fresh influx of
refugees, may be mentioned those of Bristol, Exeter,

Plymouth, Stonehouse, Dartmouth, Barnstaple, and Thorpe-le-Soken in Essex.

The French Episcopal Church at Bristol seems at one time to have been of considerable importance. It was instituted in 1687,[1] and was first held in what is called the Mayor's Chapel of St. Mark the Gaunt; but in 1726 a chapel was built for the special use of the French congregation on the ground of Queen Elizabeth's Hospital for the Red Maids, situated in Orchard Street. The chapel, at its first opening, was so crowded with worshippers, that the aisles, as well as the altar-place, had to be fitted with benches for their accommodation. From the register of the church, it would appear that the Bristol refugees consisted principally of seafaring people—captains, masters, and sailors—from Nantes, Saumur, Saintonge, La Rochelle, and the Isle of Rhé.

The congregations formed at Plymouth and Stone-house, as well as Dartmouth, were in like manner, for the most part composed of sailors; whilst those at Exeter were, on the other hand, principally tradespeople and artizans employed in the tapestry manufacture carried on in the city. M. Majendie, grandfather of Dr. Majendie, Bishop of Chester, was one of the ministers of the Exeter congregation; and Tom D'Urfey, the song-writer, was the son of one of the refugees settled in the place.

The settlement at Thorpe-le-Soken in Essex seems to have been a comparatively small one, consisting principally of refugee gentry and farmers; but they were in sufficient numbers to constitute a church, of

---

[1] The refugees had begun to settle at Bristol in considerable numbers before this time. The reviewer of the first edition of this book in the *Evangelical Magazine* for January, says : " We have noticed among the documents at the Record Office a curious paper, sent up in 1682 from the Corporation of Bristol, proposing that the fines then levied on Dissenters in the city should be appropriated to the relief of French Protestants just settled there. Many readers will regard this as an illustration of the old saying of robbing Peter to pay Paul."

which M. Severin, who afterwards removed to Greenwich, was the first minister. The church was closed
"for want of members" about the year 1726. As was
the case at many other places, the Thorpe-le-Soken
refugees gradually ceased to be French.

There was also a French church at Thorney Abbey,
of the origin of which nothing is known; but it is supposed to have been formed shortly after the breaking
up of the Walloon colony at Sandtoft, Hatfield Chace,
Yorkshire, in the time of the Commonwealth, when
the settlers removed southward. The names of the
colonists are in many instances the same, though there
are others which do not occur in the Sandtoft register,
probably those of new immigrants from the Walloon
provinces and from the northern parts of France. But
it does not appear that the congregation received any
accession of members in consequence of the Revocation
of the Edict of Nantes. Like the other churches of
the same kind, the members gradually became absorbed
in the general population, and the church ceased to
exist in the year 1727.

Year by year the foreign churches declined, even
when they were fed by fresh immigrations from abroad.
It was in the very nature of things that the rising
generation should fall away from them, and desire to
become completedly identified with the nation which
had admitted them to citizenship. Hence the growing
defections in country places, as well as in the towns
and cities where the refuges had settled; and hence
the growing complaints of the falling off in the numbers of their congregations which we find in the
sermons and addresses of the refugee pastors.

About the middle of last century, the thirty-five
French churches in London and its suburbs had become reduced to a comparatively small number; and the
sermons of the French pastors were full of lamentations as to the approaching decadence of those that remained. This feeling was given eloquent utterance to
by the Rev. Jacob Bourdillon, minister of the Artillery

Church in Spitalfields, on the occasion of the jubilee
sermon which he preached there in 1782, in commemoration of his fifty years' pastorate.[1] He had been
appointed minister of the congregation when it was a
large and thriving one in 1731, and he now addressed
but a feeble remnant of what it had been. The
old members had died off; but their places had not
been supplied by the young, who had gone in search
of other pastures. It was the same with all the
other French churches. When M. Bourdillon was
appointed minister of "The Artillery," fifty years
before, there had, he said, been twenty flourishing
French churches in London, nine of which had since
been altogether closed; while of the remaining eleven,
some were fast drawing to their end, others were
scarcely able to exist even with extraneous help, and
very few were in a position to support themselves.

The causes of this decadence of the churches of the
refugees, were not far to seek. The preacher found

---

[1] Men of great eloquence had
been ministers of the Artillery
Church. Amongst these were
Cæsar Pegorier (the first minister),
succeeded by Daniel Chamier,
Pierre Rival, Joseph de la Mothe,
and Ezekiel Barbauld. During
the fifty years of M. Bourdillon's
pastorate, fifty-two ministers of
the London refugee churches had
died,—of whom six had been his
own colleagues. The deceased
pastors, whose names he mentioned, as well as the churches
where they ministered, were as
follows:—

Chapel Royal, St. James's.—
The Revs. M. Menard, Aufrère,
Series, Rocheblanc, De Missy,
Barbauld, Muisson.

The Savoy.—Olivier, Du Cros,
Durand, Deschamps.

*The Walloon Church, Thread-
needle Street.*—Bertheau, Bes-
combes, De St. Colombe, Bonyer,

Barbauld, Couvenant, La Douespe,
Du Boulay.

*Leicester Fields, Artillery,
and La Patente.*—Blanc, Barbauld, Stehelin, Micy, Barnauin.

La Tremblade.—Gillet, Yver.

Castle Street and La Quarré.—
Laval, Bernard, Cautier, Rober
Coderc.

La Patente, Spitalfields. —
Fourestier, Manuel, Balgnarié
Masson.

Brown's Lane.—La Moyne.

St. John's Street. — Vincent
Palairet, Beuzeville.

Wapping.—Sally de Gaujac,
Le Beaupin Say, Guizot, Prelleur.

Swan Fields.—Briel.

Pastors of other French
churches, who had died in London.—Forent, Majendie, Ester-
nod, Montignac, Du Plessis.
Villette, Duval.

them in "the lack of zeal and faithfulness in the heads
of families, in encouraging their children to maintain
them—churches which their ancestors had reared, a
glorious monument of the generous sacrifice which they
had made, of their country, their possessions, and their
employments, in the sacred cause of conscience, for the
open profession of the truth ; whereas now," said he,
"through the growing aversion of the young for the
language of their fathers, from whom they seem almost
ashamed to be descended;—shall I say more?—because
of inconstancy in the principles of the faith, which
induces so many by a sort of infatuation to forsake
the ancient assemblies in order to follow novelties
unknown to our fathers, and listen to pretended
teachers whose only gifts are rapture and babble, and
whose sole inspiration consists in self-sufficiency and
pride. Alas! what ravages have been made here, as
elsewhere, during this jubilee of fifty years ! "

But there were other causes besides these, to account
for the decadence of the refugee churches. Nature
itself was working against them. Year by year the
children of the refugees were becoming less and less
Erench, and more and more English. They lived and
worked amongst the English, and spoke their language. They intermarried with them ; their children
played together; and the idea of remaining foreigners
in the country in which they had been born and bred,
became year by year more distasteful to them. They
were not a "peculiar people," like the Jews; but
Protestants, like the nation which had given them
refuge, and into which they naturally desired to become merged. Hence it was that, by the end of the
eighteenth century, nearly all the French churches, as
such, had disappeared ; and the places of the French
ministers became occupied in many cases by clergymen
of the Established Church, and in others by ministers
of the different dissenting persuasions.

The Church of the Artillery, in which the Rev. J.
Bourdillon preached the above sermon, so full of

lamentations, is now occupied as a poor Jews' syna-
gogue. L'Eglise Neuve is a chapel of the Wesleyan
Methodists. L'Eglise de St. Jean, Swan Fields, Shore-
ditch, has become one of the ten new churches of St.
Matthew, Bethnal Green. Swallow Street Chapel is
used as a Scotch Church. Leicester Fields, now called
Orange Street Chapel, is occupied by a congregation
of Independents. Whereas Castle Street Chapel,
Leicester Square, was, until quite recently, used as a
Court of Requests.

The French churches at Wandsworth and Chelsea
are occupied by the Independents; and those at
Greenwich and Plymouth by the Baptists. The Dutch
church at Maidstone is used as a school; while the
Walloon church at Yarmouth was first converted into
a theatre, and has since done duty as a warehouse.

Among the charitable institutions founded by the refugees for the succour of their distressed fellow-countrymen in England, the French Hospital was the most
important. This establishment owes its origin to M.
De Gastigny, a French gentleman who had been master of the buckhounds to William III. while Prince of
Orange. At his death in 1708, he bequeathed a sum
of £1000 towards founding an hospital in London
for the relief of distressed French Protestants. The
money was placed at interest for eight years, during
which successive benefactions were added to the fund.
In 1716, a piece of ground in Old Street, St. Luke's,
was purchased of the Ironmongers' Company, and a
lease was taken from the city of London of some adjoining land, forming altogether an area of about four
acres, on which a building was erected and fitted up
for the reception of eighty poor Protestants of the
French nation. In 1718, George I. granted a charter
of incorporation to the governor and directors of the
hospital, under which the Earl of Galway was appointed the first governor. Shortly after, in November,
1718, the opening of the institution was celebrated by
a solemn act of religion; and the chapel was conse-

crated amidst a great concourse of refugees and their descendants, the Rev. Philip Menard, minister of the French chapel of St James's, conducting the service on the occasion.

From that time the funds of the institution have steadily increased. The French merchants of London, who had been so prosperous in trade, liberally contributed towards its support; and legacies and donations multiplied. Lord Galway bequeathed £1000 to the hospital at his death in 1720; and, in the following year, Baron Hervart de Huningue gave a donation of £4000. The corporation were thus placed in the posssesion of ample means: and they proceeded to erect additional buildings, in which they were enabled, by the year 1760, to give asylum to 234 poor people.[1]

Among the distinguished noblemen and gentlemen of French Protestant descent, who have officiated as governors of the institution since the date of its foundation, may be mentioned the Earl of Galway, the Baron de Huningue, Robethon (privy councillor), the Baron de la Court, Lord Ligonier, and several successive Earls of Radnor; whilst among the lists of directors we recognise the names of Montolieu, Baron de St. Hippolite, Gambier, Bosanquet, Columbies, Magendie (D.D.), Colonel de Cosné, Dalbiac, Gaussen, Dargent, Blaquiere, General Ruffane, Lefevre, Boileau (Bart.), Colonel Vignoles, Romilly, Turquand, Pechel (Bart.), Travers, Lieut.-General de Villetes, Major-General Montressor, Devisme, Chamier (M.P.), Major-General Layard, Bouverie, Captain Dumaresq (R.N.), Duval, the Hon. Philip Pusey, André (Bart.), De Hochepied Larpent (Bart.), Jean Sylvestre (Bart.), Cazenove, Dolland, Petit (M.D.), Le Mesurier, Landon, Martineau,

---

[1] The French hospital has recently been removed from its original site to Victoria Park, where a handsome building has been erected as an hospital for the accommodation of 40 men and 20 women, after the designs of Mr. Robert Lewis Roumieu, architect, one of the directors; Mr. Roumieu being himself descended from an illustrious Huguenot family—the Roumieus of Languedoc.

Baron Maseres, Chevalier, Durand, Hanbury, Labouchere, De la Rue (F.R.S.); and many other names well
known and highly distinguished in the commerce,
politics, literature, and science of England.

One of the most interesting relics of the Huguenot
immigration, which has survived the absorption of
the refugees into the general population, is the French
church which still continues to exist in the Under Croft
of Canterbury Cathedral. Three hundred years have
passed since the first body of exiled Walloons met to
worship there,—three hundred years, during which
generations have come and gone, and revolutions have
swept over Europe; and still that eloquent memorial
of the religious history of the middle ages survives,
bearing testimony alike to the rancour of the persecutions abroad, the steadfastness of the foreign Protestants, the liberal spirit of the English Church, and the
free asylum which England has provided in past times
for fugitives from foreign oppression and tyranny.

The visitor to the cathedral, in passing through
the Under Croft, has usually pointed out to him the
apartment still used as "the French Church." It is
walled off from the crypt in the south side-aisle; and
through the windows which overlook the interior
the arrangements of the place can easily be observed.
It is plainly fitted up with pews, a pulpit, and pre-
centor's desk, like a dissenting place of worship; and
indeed it is a dissenting place of worship, though
forming part of the High Cathedral of Canterbury.
The place also contains a long table, at which the
communicants sit when receiving the sacrament of
the Lord's Supper, after the manner of the Geneva
brethren.

And here the worship still continues to be conducted
in French, and the psalms are sung to the old Huguenot
tunes, almost within sound of the high choral service
of the Established Church of England overhead.
"Here," says the German Dr. Pauli, "the early
refugees celebrated the services of their Church; and

here their descendants, who are now reduced to a very small number, still carry on their Presbyterian mode of worship in their own tongue, immediately below the south aisle of the high choir, where the Anglican ritual is observed in all its prescribed form—a noble and touching concurrence, the parallel to which cannot be met with in any other cathedral church in England."[1]

The French church at Canterbury would doubtless long since have become altogether extinct, like the other churches of the refugees, but for an endowment of about £200 a year, which has served to keep it alive. The members do not now amount to more than twenty, of whom two are elders and four deacons.

The Dutch congregation at Norwich has also continued to exist in name, for the same reason. There is an endowment belonging to it of some £70 a year; and to preserve this, an annual service is held in the choir of the Black Friars' Church, still called the Dutch Church, —the nave of the building being known as St. Andrew's Hall, and used for holding public meetings and festivals. The annual sermon, preached in Dutch, is a mere form, and the congregation has become a shadow without substance.

But though these ancient churches are now the mere vestiges and remnants of what they once were, they are nevertheless of genuine interest, and serve to mark an epoch of memorable importance in the history of England.

---

[1] PAULI, *Pictures of Old England,* 29.

CHAPTER XVII.

HUGUENOT SETTLEMENTS IN IRELAND.

It was long the favourite policy of the English monarchs to induce foreign artizans to settle in Ireland and establish new branches of trade. It was hoped that the Irish people, inhabiting so rich a land, and needing only peace and industry to make it prosper, might be induced to follow their example; and that the abundant population of the country, instead of being a source of poverty and idleness, might be rendered a source of national wealth and strength.

Elizabeth encouraged such settlements in Ireland, though the disturbed state of the country prevented her intentions being carried into effect. While many Flemish settlements were established in England during her reign, almost the only one of a similar kind established in Ireland, of which we have any account, was that of Swords, near Dublin.

It was not until the early part of the reign of James I. that any considerable progress was made in the settlement of foreign artizans and merchants in Ireland. In 1605, John Vertroven and John Van Dale of Brabant, Gabriel Behaes and Matthew Derenzie of Antwerp,— in 1607, William Baell of Antwerp,—in 1608, James Marcus of Amsterdam, and Derrick Varveer of Dort, —and in 1613, Wybrant Olferston and John Olferston of Holland,—obtained grants of naturalisation, and settled in Ireland, mostly at Dublin and Waterford, where they carried on business as merchants. It is supposed that the Vanhomrigh and Vandeleur families entered Ireland about the same period. The strangers made good their footing, and eventually established themselves as landed proprietors in the country.

When the Earl of Strafford was appointed chief deputy in the reign of Charles I., he applied himself with much zeal to the establishment of the linen-manufacture ; sending to Holland for flax-seed, and inviting Flemish and French artizans to settle in Ireland. In order to stimulate the new industry, the earl himself embarked in it, and expended not less than £30,000 of his private fortune in the enterprise. It was afterwards made one of the grounds of his impeachment that "he had obstructed the industry of the country by introducing new and unknown pro-cesses into the manufacture of flax." It was neverthe-less greatly to the credit of the earl that he should have endeavoured to improve the industry of Ireland by introducing the superior processes employed by the foreign artizans; and had he not attempted to turn the improved flax-manufacture to his own advantage by erecting it into a personal monopoly, he would have been entitled to great regard as a genuine bene-factor of Ireland.

The Duke of Ormond followed the example of Strafford in endeavouring to induce foreigners to settle in Ireland. Only two years after the Restoration, he had a bill carried through the Irish Parliament en-titled " An Act for encouraging Protestant strangers and others to inhabit Ireland," which duly received the royal assent. The Duke actively encouraged the settlement of the foreigners, establishing about four hundred Flemish artizans at Chapel Izod, in Kilkenny, under Colonel Richard Lawrence. He there built houses for the weavers, supplying them with looms and raw material ; and a considerable trade in cordage, sail-cloth, and linen shortly grew up. The Duke also settled Walloon colonies at Clonmel, Kilkenny, and

---

[1] FOSTER, *Lives of Eminent British Statesmen.* ii. 385.

Carrick-on-Suir, where they established, and for some time successfully carried on, the making of woollen cloths and other branches of manufacture.

The refugees were prosperously pursuing their respective trades when the English Revolution of 1688 occurred, and again Ireland was thrown into a state of civil war, which continued for three years, but was at length concluded by the peace of Limerick in 1691.

No sooner was the war at an end, than William III. took active steps to restore the prostrate industry of the country. The Irish Parliament again revived their bill of 1674 (which the Parliament of James II. had suspended), granting naturalisation to such Protestant refugees as should settle in Ireland, and guaranteeing them the free exercise of their religion. A large number of William's foreign officers at once availed themselves of the privilege, and settled at Youghal, Waterford, and Portarlington; whilst colonies of foreign manufacturers at the same time planted themselves at Dublin, Cork, Lisburn, and other places.

The refugees who settled at Dublin established themselves for the most part in "The Liberties," where they began the manufacture of tabinet, since more generally known as "Irish Poplin." [1] The demand for the article became such, that a number of French masters and workmen left Spitalfields, and migrated to Dublin, where they largely extended the manufacture. The Combe, Pimlico, Spitalfields, and other streets in Dublin, named after corresponding streets in London, were built for their accommodation; and Weaver's Square became a principal quarter in the

---

[1] There are no certain records for fixing the precise date when silk-weaving was commenced in Dublin; but it is generally believed that an ancestor of the present respected family of the Latouches commenced the weaving of tabinets or poplins and tabbareas, in the liberties of Dublin, about the year 1693.— Dr. W. Cooke Taylor, in *Statistical Journal* for December, 1843, p. 354.

city. For a time the trade was very prosperous,
and gave employment to a large number of persons;
but about the beginning of the present century, the
frequent recurrence of strikes among the workmen
paralysed the employers of labour. The manufacture
became almost entirely lost, and "The Liberties,"
instead of the richest, became one of the poorest quarters
of Dublin. So long as the French colony prospered,
the refugees had three congregations in the city. One
of these was an Episcopal congregation, attached to
St. Patrick's Cathedral, which worshipped at St. Mary's
Chapel, granted them by the dean and chapter; and it
continued in existence until the year 1816. The other
two were Calvinistic congregations, one of which had a
chapel in Peter Street,[1] and the other in Lucas Lane.
The refugees had special burying-places assigned to
them; the principal one adjoined St. Stephen's Green,
the other was situated on the southern outskirts of
the city.

But the northern counties of Down and Antrim
were, more than any other parts of Ireland, regarded
as the sanctuary of the refugees. There they found
themselves amongst men of their own religion,—
mostly Scotch Calvinists, who had fled from the Stuart
persecutions in Scotland to take refuge in the comparatively unmolested districts of Ulster. Lisburn,
formerly called Lisnagarvey, about ten miles south-
west of Belfast, was one of their favourite settlements. The place had been burnt to the ground in
the civil war of 1641; but with the help of the refugees, it was before long restored to more than its
former importance, and became one of the most prosperous towns in Ireland.

The government of the day, while they discouraged
the woollen-manufacture of Ireland because of its
supposed injury to England, made every effort to en-

---

[1] The old French church in Peter Street is now used as the
Molyneux asylum for the blind.

courage the trade in linen. An Act was passed with
the latter object in 1697, containing various enactments calculated to foster the growth of flax and the
manufacture of linen cloth. Before the passing of
this Act, William III. invited Louis Crommelin, a
Huguenot refugee, then temporarily settled in Holland,
to come over into Ireland and undertake the super-
intendence of the new branch of industry.

Crommelin belonged to a family that had carried
on the linen-manufacture in its various branches in
France for upwards of 400 years. He had himself
been engaged in the business for more than thirty
years at Armancourt, near Saint Quentin in Picardy,
where he was born. He was singularly well fitted for
the office to which the King called him. He was a
man of admirable business qualities, excellent good
sense, and remarkable energy and perseverance. Being
a Protestant, and a man of much foresight, he had
quietly realised what he could of his large property
in the neighbourhood of St. Quentin, shortly before
the Revocation of the Edict of Nantes; and he had
migrated across the frontier into Holland before the
bursting of the storm.

In 1698, Crommelin, having accepted the invitation
of William, left Holland, accompanied by his son, and
shortly after his arrival in England he proceeded into
the north of Ireland to fix upon the site best adapted
for his intended undertaking. After due deliberation,
he pitched upon the ruined village of Lisnagarvey as
the most suitable for his purpose.[1] The King approved
of the selection, and authorised Crommelin to proceed
with his operations, appointing him "Overseer of the
Royal Linen Manufactory of Ireland." In consideration of Crommelin advancing £10,000 out of his own
private fortune to commence the undertaking, a grant
of £800 per annum was guaranteed to him for twelve

---

[1] Crommelin's first factory was
at the foot of the wooden bridge
over the Lagan, and his first
bleaching-ground was started at
the place called Hilden.

years—being at the rate of 8 per cent. on the capital invested.   At the same time, an annuity of £200 was granted him for life, and £120 a year for two assistants, whose duty it was to travel from place to place and superintend the cultivation of the flax, as well as to visit the bleaching-grounds and see to the proper finishing of the fabric.

Crommelin sent invitations abroad to the Protestant artizans to come over and join him, and numbers of them responded to his call.   A little colony of refugees of all ranks and of many trades was soon planted at Lisburn, and the place exhibited an appearance of returning prosperity.   With a steadiness of purpose which distinguished Crommelin through life, he devoted himself with unceasing zeal to the promotion of the enterprise which he had taken in hand.   He liberally rewarded the toil of his brother exiles, and cheered them on the road to success.   He imported from Holland a thousand looms and spinning-wheels of the best construction, and gave a premium of £5 for every loom that was kept going.   Before long, he introduced improvements of his own in the looms and spinning-wheels, as well as in the implements and in the preparation of the material.   Every branch of the operations made rapid progress under the Huguenot chief—from the sowing, cultivating, and preparing of the flax through the various stages of its manipulation, to the finishing of the cloth at the bleach-field.   And thus by painstaking, skill, and industry, zealously supported as he was by his artizans, Crommelin was shortly enabled to produce finer sorts of fabrics than had ever before been made in Britain.

Crommelin, amongst his other labours for the establishment of the linen trade, wrote and published a-Dublin, in 1705, *An Essay towards the Improving of the Hempen and Flaxen Manufactures of the Kingdom of Ireland*, so that all might be made acquainted with the secret of his success, and enabled to follow his example.   The treatise contained many useful instructions for the cultivation of flax, in the various stages of its planting and growth, together with directions for the preparation of the material, in the several processes of spinning, weaving, and bleaching.

Though a foreigner, Crommelin continued throughout his life to take a warm interest in the prosperity of his adopted country; and his services were recognised, not only by King William, who continued his firm friend to the last, but by the Irish Parliament, who from time to time voted grants of money to himself, his assistants, and his artizans, to enable him to prosecute his enterprise; and in 1707, they voted him the public thanks for his patriotic efforts towards the establishment of the linen trade in Ireland, of which he was the founder. Crommelin died in 1727, and was buried beside other members of his family, in the churchyard at Lisburn.

The French refugees long continued a distinct people in the neighbourhood. They clung together, associated and worshipped together, frequenting their own Huguenot church, in which they had a long succession of French pastors.[1] They carefully educated their children in the French language, and in the Huguenot faith; cherishing the hope of being enabled some day to return to their native land. But that hope at length died out, and the descendants of the Crommelins eventually mingled with the families of the Irish, and became part and parcel of the British nation.

---

[1] The Rev. Saumarez Dubourdieu, grandson of the celebrated French Pastor of the Savoy Church in London, was minister of the French church at Lisburn for forty-five years, and was so beloved in the neighbourhood that, at the insurrection of 1798, he was the only person in Lisburn whom the insurgents agreed to spare. The French congregation having become greatly decreased, by deaths as well as intermarriages with Irish families, the chapel was at length closed. It is now used as the court-house of Lisburn. The pastor Dubourdieu joined the Established Church, and was presented with the living of Lambeg. His son, rector of Annahelt, County Down, was the author of *A Statistical Survey of the County Antrim*, published in 1812.

Among the other French settlers at Lisburn, was
Peter Goyer, a native of Picardy. He owned a large
farm there, and also carried on an extensive business
as a manufacturer of cambric and silk, at the time of
the Revocation. When the Dragonnades began, he
left his property behind him, and fled across the
frontier. The record is still preserved in the family, of
the cruelties practised upon Peter's martyred brother
by the ruthless French soldiery, who tore a leaf from
his Bible, and forced it into his mouth before he died.
From Holland, Goyer proceeded to England, and from
thence to Lisburn, where he began the manufacture of
the articles for which he had acquired so much reputation in his own country. After a short time, he resolved on returning to France, in the hope of being able
to recover some of his property. But the persecution was
raging more fiercely than before, and he found that, if
captured, he would probably be condemned to the galleys for life. He again contrived to make his escape,
having been carried on board an outward-bound ship
concealed in a wine-cask. Returned to Lisburn, he
resumed the manufacture of silk and cambric, in which
he employed a considerable number of workmen. His
silk manufacture was destroyed by the rebellion of
1798, which dispersed the workpeople; but that of
cambric survived, and became firmly founded at
Lurgan, which now enjoys a high reputation for the
perfection of its manufactures.

Other colonies of the refugees were established in
the south of Ireland, where they carried on various
branches of manufacture. William Crommelin, a
brother of Louis, having been appointed one of his
assistants, superintended the branch of the linen trade
which was established at Kilkenny through the instru-
mentality of the Marquis of Ormonde. At Limerick,
the refugees established the lace and glove trades,
which still flourish. At Bandon, they carried on
cloth-manufacturing, the names of the colonists indicating a mixture of Walloons and Huguenots,—the

Garretts, De Ruyters, and Minhears being Flemish, and the Beaumonts, Willises, and Baxters, being French immigrants, from the banks of the Loire.

Another settlement of French refugees was formed at Cork, where they congregated in a quarter of the town forming part of the parish of St. Paul, the principal street in which is French Church Street, so called from the place of worship belonging to them, where the service was performed in French down to the beginning of the present century.[1] Though the principal refugees in Cork were merchants and traders, there was a sufficient number of them to begin the manufacture of woollen cloth, ginghams, and other fabrics, which they carried on for a time with considerable success. Another body of Huguenot refugees endeavoured to introduce the silk manufacture at Inneshannon, about three miles below Bandon, where they built houses recognisable by their ornamental brickwork and lozenge-shaped windows, and which is still known as "the colony." But their efforts to rear silkworms failed; the colonists migrated to Spitalfields; and all that remains of their enterprise is " The Mulberry Field," which still retains its name.

The woollen-manufacture at Cork was begun by James Fontaine, a member of the noble family of De la Fontaine in France, a branch of which embraced Protestantism in the sixteenth century, and continued to adhere to it down to the period of the Revocation. The career of James Fontaine was singularly illustrative of the times in which he lived. His case was only one amongst thousands of others, in which persons of

---

[1] A Cork correspondent says: "The Irish could never pronounce the French names, and some curious misnomers have been the consequence, now identified with the topography of the city. For example, there is a wretched cul-de-sac off the north main street, now called in the *Post-Office Directory,* 'Coach-and-Six Lane.' A Huguenot of the name of Couchancex having resided here more than a century ago, when it was a fashionable quarter, the place was called after him, and has thus become metamorphosed **into** 'Coach-and-Six.'"

rank, wealth, and learning, were suddenly stripped of
their all, and compelled to become wanderers over the
earth for conscience' sake. His life further serves to
show how a clever and agile Frenchman, thrown upon
a foreign shore, a stranger to its people and its language,
without any calling or resources, but full of energy and
courage, could contrive to earn an honest living and
achieve an honourable reputation.

James Fontaine was the son of a Protestant pastor
of the same name, and was born at Royan in Saintonge,
a famous Huguenot district. His father was the first
of the family to drop the aristocratic prefix of " de ia,"
which he did from motives of modesty. When a child
Fontaine met with an accident through the carelessness
of a nurse, which rendered him lame for life. When
only eight years old, his father died, so that little was
done for his education until he arrived at about the
age of seventeen, when he was placed under a com-
petent tutor, and eventually took the degree of M.A.,
at the College of Guienne, in his twenty-second year.
Shortly after, his mother died, and he became the
possessor of her landed property near Pons, in the
Charente.

Young Fontaine's sister, Marie, had married a
Protestant pastor named Forestier, of St. Mesme
in Angoumois. Jacques went to live with them for a
time, and to study theology under the pastor. The
persecutions having shortly set in, Forestier's church
was closed and he himself compelled to fly to England.
The congregation of St. Mesme was consequently left
without a minister. Young Fontaine, though he well
knew the risks he ran, nevertheless encouraged the
Protestants to assemble in the open air, and occasionally conducted their devotions. On being informed
against, he was cited to appear before the local
tribunals. He was charged with the crime of attending a Protestant meeting in 1684, contrary to
law; and though he had not been present at the meeting specified, he was condemned and imprisoned. He

appealed to the Parliament at Paris, whither he carried his plea of *alibi*, and was acquitted.

When the intelligence reached him in the following year, that the Edict of Revocation was proclaimed, he at once determined to make his escape. A party of Protestant ladies had arranged to accompany him, consisting of Janette Forestier, the daughter of the pastor of St. Mesme (already in England), his niece, and the two Mesdemoiselles Boursignot, to one of whom Fontaine was betrothed.

At Marennes, the captain of an English ship was found, willing to give the party a passage to England. It was at first intended that they should rendezvous on the sands near Tremblade, and then proceed privily on shipboard. But the coast was strictly guarded, especially between Royan and La Rochelle, where the Protestants of the interior were constantly seeking outlets for escape ; and this part of the plan was given up. The search of vessels leaving the ports had become so strict, that the English captain feared that even if Fontaine and his ladies succeeded in getting on board, it would not be possible for him to conceal them or prevent their falling into the hands of the King's detectives. He therefore proposed that his ship should set sail, and that the fugitives should put out to sea and wait for him, when he would take them on board. It proved fortunate that this plan was adopted ; for, scarcely had the English merchantman left Tremblade, than she was boarded and searched by a French frigate on the look-out for fugitive Protestants. No prisoners were found ; and the captain of the merchantman was ordered to proceed at once to his destination.

Meanwhile, the boat containing the fugitives having put out to sea, as arranged, lay to, waiting the approach of the English vessel. That they might not be descried from the frigate, which was close at hand, the boatman made them lie down in the bottom of the boat, covering them with an old sail. They all knew the penalties to which they were liable if detected in

the attempt to escape—Fontaine, the boatman, and
his son, to condemnation to the galleys for life; and
the three ladies to imprisonment for life. The frigate
bore down upon the boat and hailed the boatman,
who feigned drunkenness so well that he completely
deceived the captain, who, seeing nothing but the old
sail in the bottom of the boat, ordered the frigate's
head to be put about, when it sailed away in the direc-
of Rochefort. Shortly after, while she was still in
sight, though distant, the agreed signal was given by
the boat to the merchantman (that of dropping the sail
three times in the apparent attempt to hoist it), on
which the English vessel lay to, and took the exiles on
board. After a voyage of eleven days, they reached
the welcome asylum of England, and Fontaine and
his party landed at Barnstaple, North Devon,—his sole
property consisting of twenty pistoles and six silver
spoons, which had belonged to his father, and bore upon
them his infantine initials, I. D. L. F.—Jacques de la
Fontaine.

Fontaine and the three ladies were hospitably received by Mr. Donne of Barnstaple, with whom they
lived until a home could be provided for their reception. One of the first things which occupied Fontaine's
attention was, how to earn a living for their support.
A cabin-biscuit, which he bought for a halfpenny,
gave him his first hint. The biscuit would have cost
twopence in France; and it at once occurred to him
that, such being the case, grain might be shipped from
England to France at a profit. Mr. Donne agreed to
advance the money requisite for the purpose, taking
half the profits. The first cargo of corn exported
proved very profitable; but Fontaine's partner afterwards insisting on changing the consignee, who proved
dishonest, the speculation eventually proved unsuc-
cessful.

Fontaine had by this time married the Huguenot
lady to whom he was betrothed, and who had accompanied him in his flight to England. After the failure

of the corn speculation, he removed to Taunton in
Somerset, where he made a shift to live. He took
pupils, dealt in provisions, sold brandy, groceries, stockings, leather, tin and copper wares, and carried on
wool-combing, dyeing, and the making of calimancoes.
In short, he was a "jack-of-all-trades." He followed
so many callings, and occasioned so much jealousy in
the place, that he was cited before the mayor and
aldermen as an interloper, and required to give an
account of himself. This and other circumstances
determined him to give up business in Taunton—not,
however, before he had contrived to save about £1000
by his industry—and to enter upon the life of a pastor.
He had already been admitted to holy orders by the
French Protestant synod at Taunton, and in 1694 he
left that town for Ireland, in search of a congregation.

Fontaine's adventures in Ireland were even more
remarkable than those which he had experienced in
England. The French refugees established at Cork
had formed themselves into a congregation, of which
he was appointed pastor in January, 1695. They
were, however, as yet too poor to pay him any stipend;
and, in order to support himself, as well as turn to
account the money which he had saved by his industry
and frugality at Taunton, he began a manufactory of
broadcloth. This gave much welcome employment to
the labouring poor of the city, besides contributing
towards the increase of its general trade,—in acknowledgment of which the corporation presented him
with the freedom. He still continued to officiate as
pastor; but, one day, when expounding the text of
"Thou shalt not steal," he preached so effectively as
to make a personal enemy of a member of his congregation, who, unknown to him, had been engaged in a
swindling transaction. The result was, that so much
dissension was occasioned in the congregation, that he
eventually gave up the charge.

To occupy his spare time,—for Fontaine was a man
of an intensely active temperament, and most unhappy

when unemployed,—he took a farm at Bearhaven, situated at the entrance to Bantry Bay, nearly at the extreme south-west point of Munster, the very Land's End of Ireland, for the purpose of founding a fishery. The idea occurred to him, as it has since occurred to others, that there were many hungry people on land waiting to be fed, and shoals of fish at sea waiting to be caught,—and that it would be a useful enterprise to form a fishing-company, and induce the idle people to put to sea and catch the fish, selling to others the surplus beyond what was necessary to feed them. Fontaine succeeded in inducing some of the French merchants settled in London to join him in the venture ; and he himself went to reside at Bearhaven to superintend the operations of the company.

Fontaine failed, as other Irish fishing-companies have since failed. The people would rather starve than go to sea—for Celts are by nature averse to salt water ; and the consequence was, that the company made no progress. Fontaine had even to defend himself against the pillaging and plundering of the natives. He then induced some thirteen French refugee families to settle in the neighbourhood, having previously taken small farms for them, including Dursey Island ; but the Irish gave the foreigners no peace nor rest, and they left before the end of three years. The local court would not give Fontaine any redress when an injury was done to him. If his property was stolen, and he appealed to the court, his complaint was referred to a jury of papists, who invariably decided against him ; whereas, if the natives made any claim upon him, they were sure to recover what they demanded.

Notwithstanding these great discouragements, Fontaine held to his purpose, and determined, if possible, to establish a fishing station. He believed that time would work in his favour, and that it might yet be possible to educate the people into habits of industry. He was well supported by the Government, who, observing his zealous efforts to establish a new branch of industry, and desirous of giving him increased influence in his neighbourhood, appointed him Justice of the Peace. In this capacity he was found very useful in keeping down the "Tories," and breaking up the connection between them and the French privateers who occasionally frequented the coast. Knowing his liability to attack, Fontaine converted his residence at Bearhaven into a sod fort; and not without cause, as the result proved.

In June, 1704, a French privateer entered Bantry Bay, and proceeded to storm the sod fort; when the lame Fontaine, by the courage and ability of his defence, showed himself a commander of no mean skill. John Macliney, a Scotchman, and Paul Roussier, a French refugee, showed great bravery on the occasion; while Madame Fontaine, who acted as aide-de-camp and surgeon, distinguished herself by her quiet courage. The engagement lasted from eight in the morning until four in the afternoon, when the French decamped with the loss of three killed and seven wounded, spreading abroad a very wholesome fear of Fontaine and his sod fort. When the refugee's gallant exploit was reported to the government, he was rewarded by a pension of five shillings a day for beating off the privateer, and supplied with five guns, which he was authorised to mount in his battery.

Fontaine was not allowed to hold his post unmolested. It was at the remotest corner of the island, far from any town, and surrounded by a hostile population in league with the enemy, whose ships were constantly hovering about the coast. In the year succeeding the above engagement, while Fontaine himself was absent in London, a French ship entered Bantry Bay, and cautiously approached Bearhaven. Fontaine's wife was, however, on the look-out, and detected the foreigner. She had the guns loaded and one of them fired off to show that the little garrison was on the alert. The Frenchman then veered off and made for Bear Island, where a party of the crew landed, stole some cattle, which they put on board, and sailed away again.

A more serious assault was made on the fort about two years later. A company of soldiers was then quartered at the Half Barony in the neighbourhood, the captain of which boarded with the refugee family. On the 7th of October, 1708, during the temporary absence of Fontaine as well as the captain, a French privateer made his appearance in the haven, and hoisted English colours. The ensign residing in the fort at the time, deceived by the stratagem, went on board, when he was immediately made prisoner. He was plied with drink and became intoxicated, when he revealed the fact that there was no officer in command of the fort. The crew of the privateer were principally Irish, and they determined to attack the place at midnight, for which purpose a party of them landed.

Fontaine had by this time returned, and was on the alert. He hailed the advancing party through a speaking-trumpet, and, no answer being returned, he ordered fire to be opened on them. The assailants then divided into six detachments, one of which set fire to the offices and stables; the household servants, under the direction of Madame Fontaine, protecting the dwelling-house from conflagration. The men within fired from the windows and loopholes, but the smoke was so thick that they could only fire at random. Some of the privateer's men succeeded in making a breach with a crowbar in the wall of the house, but they were saluted with so rapid a fire through the opening that they suspected there must be a party of soldiers in the house, and they retired. They advanced again, and summoned the besieged to surrender, offering fair terms. Fontaine approached the French for the purpose of parley, when one of the Irish lieutenants took aim and fired at him. This treachery made the Fontaines resume the defensive,

which was continued without intermission for some
hours; when, no help arriving, Fontaine found himself
under the necessity of surrendering, conditional upon
himself and his two sons, with their two followers,
marching out with the honours of war. No sooner,
however, had the house been surrendered, than Fontaine, his sons, and their followers, were at once made
prisoners, and the dwelling was given up to plunder.

Fontaine protested against this violation of the
treaty, but it was of no use. The leader of the French
party said to him, "Your name has become so notorious among the privateers of St. Malo, that I dare
not return to the vessel without you. The captain's
order was peremptory, to bring you on board, dead or
alive." Fontaine and his sons were accordingly taken
on board prisoners; and when the Huguenot hero
appeared on deck, the crew set up a shout of "Vive
le Roi." On this, Fontaine called out, "Gentlemen,
how long is it since victories have become so rare in
France, that you must needs make a triumph of such
a poor affair as this? A glorious feat indeed! Eighty
men, accustomed to war, have succeeded in compelling
a lame pastor, four cowherds, and five children, to
surrender upon terms!" Fontaine again expostulated
with the captain, and informed him that, being held a
prisoner in breach of the treaty under which he had
surrendered, he must be prepared for the retaliation of
the English government upon French prisoners of war.
The captain would not, however, give up Fontaine
without a ransom, and demanded £100. Madame
Fontaine contrived to borrow £30, and sent it to the
captain, with a promise of the remainder. The captain could not wait, but he liberated Fontaine, and
carried off his son Pierre to St. Malo, as a hostage for
the payment of the balance.

When the news of this attack on the fort at Bearhaven reached the English Government, and they were
informed of the violation of the conditions under
which Fontaine had surrendered, they ordered the

French officers at Kinsale and Plymouth to be put in irons until Fontaine's son was sent back. This produced an immediate effect. In the course of a few months Pierre Fontaine was set at liberty and returned to his parents, and the balance of the ransom was never claimed. The commander of the forces in Ireland made Fontaine an immediate grant of £100, to relieve him from the destitution to which he had been reduced by the plunder of his dwelling. The county of Cork afterwards paid him £800 as damages, on its being proved that Irishmen had been principally concerned in the attack and robbery; and Fontaine's two sons were awarded the position and rights of half-pay officers, while his own pension was continued. The fort at Bearhaven, having been completely desolated, was abandoned ; and Fontaine, with the grant made to him by government, and the sum awarded by the county, left the lawless neighbourhood which he had so long laboured to improve and to defend, and proceeded to Dublin, where he settled for the remainder of his life as a teacher of langauges, mathematics, and fortification. His undertaking proved successful, and he ended his days there in peace. His noble wife died in 1721, and he himself followed her shortly after, respected and beloved by all who knew him.[1]

---

[1] Nearly all Fontaine's near relatives took refuge in England. His mother and three of his brothers were refugees in London. One of them afterwards became a Protestant minister in Germany. One of his uncles, Peter, was pastor of the Pest House Chapel in London. Two aunts—one a widow, the other married to a refugee merchant—were also settled in London. Fontaine's sons and daughters mostly emigrated to Virginia, where their descendants are still to be found. His daughter Mary Anne married the Rev. James Maury, Fredericksville Parish, Louisa County, Virginia, from whom Mathew Fontaine Maury, LL.D., lately Captain in the Confederate States Navy, and author of *The Physical Geography of the Sea*, is lineally descended. The above particulars are for the most part taken from the "*Memoirs of a Huguenot Family* ; translated and compiled from the original Autobiography of the Rev. James Fontaine, and other family manuscripts, by ANN MAURY" (another of the descendants of Fontaine) : New York, 1853.

We return to the subject of the settlements made by
other refugees in the southern parts of Ireland. In
1697, about fifty retired officers, who had served in the
army of William III., settled with their families at
Youghal, on the invitation of the mayor and corporation, who offered them the freedom of the town on
payment of the nominal sum of sixpence each. It
does not appear that the refugees were sufficiently
numerous to maintain a pastor, though the Rev. Arthur
d'Anvers for some time privately ministered to them.
Most probably, from the circumstance of their comparatively small number, they speedily ceased to exist
as a distinctive portion of the community, though
names of French origin are still common in the
town.

The French refugee colony at Waterford was of
considerably greater importance. Being favourably
situated for trade near the mouth of the river Suir,
with a rich agricultural country behind it, Waterford
offered many inducements to the refugee merchants
and traders to settle there. In the Act passed by the
Irish Parliament in 1662, and re-enacted in 1672, "for
encouraging Protestant strangers and others to inhabit
Ireland," Waterford is specially named as one of the
cities selected for the settlement of the refugees. Some
twenty years later, in 1693, the corporation of Waterford, being desirous not only that the disbanded
Huguenot officers and soldiers should settle in the
place, but also that persons skilled in the arts and
manufactures should become citizens, ordered, "that
the city and liberties do provide habitations for fifty
families of the French Protestants to drive a trade of
linen-manufacture,—they bringing with them a stock
of money and materials for their subsistence until flax
can be sown and produced on the lands adjacent;
and that the freedom of the city be given them *gratis*."
At the same time, the choir of the old Franciscan
monastery was assigned to them, with the assent of
the bishop, Dr. Nathaniel Foy, himself descended from

a Protestant refugee, for the purposes of a French church, the corporation guaranteeing a stipend of £40 a year towards the support of their pastor, the Rev. David Gervais, afterwards a prebendary of Lismore Cathedral.

These liberal measures had the effect of inducing a considerable number of refugees to establish themselves at Waterford, and carry on various branches of trade and manufacture. Some of them became leading merchants in the place, and rose to wealth and distinction. Thus, John Espaignet was sheriff of the city in 1707; Jeremy Gayot in 1709; and the two brothers Vashon served, the one as mayor in 1726, the other as sheriff in 1735. James Henry Reynette afterwards held office both as sheriff and mayor. The foreign wine-trade of the south of Ireland was almost exclusively conducted through Waterford by the French wine-merchants, some of their principal stores being in the immediate neighbourhood of the French church. The refugees also made vigorous efforts to establish the linen-manufacture in Waterford, in which they were materially assisted by Louis Crommelin and John Latrobe in the first instance, and by Bishop Chenevix in the next; and for many years linen was one of the staple trades of the place, although it ceased shortly after the introduction of power-looms.

Another colony of the refugees was established at Portarlington, which town they may almost be said to have founded. The first settlers consisted principally of retired French officers as well as privates, who had served in the army of King William. We have already referred to the circumstances connected with the formation of this colony by the Marquis de Ruvigny, created Earl of Galway, to whom William granted the estate of Portarlington, which had become forfeited to the crown by the treason and outlawry of Sir Patrick Grant, its former owner. Although the grant was revoked by the English Parliament, and the Earl ceased to own the Portarlington estate, he nevertheless continued to take the same warm interest as before in the prosperity of the refugee colony.[1]

Among the early settlers at Portarlington were the Marquis de Paray, the Sieur de Hauteville, Louis le Blanc, Sieur de Pierce, Charles de Ponthieu, Captain d' Alnuis and his brother, Abel Pelissier, David d' Arripe, Reuben de la Rochefoucauld, the Sieur de la Boissere, Guy de la Blachière, De Bonneval, De Villier, Fleury, Champagne, De Bostaquet, Franquefort, Châteauneuf, La Beaume, Montpeton du Languedoc, Vicomte de Laval, Pierre Goulin, Jean la Ferriere, De Gaudry, Jean Lafaurie, Abel de Ligonier, De Vignoles, Anthoine de Ligonier, and numerous others.

The greater number of these noblemen and gentlemen had served with distinction under the Duke of Schomberg, La Melonniere, La Caillemotte, Cambon, and other commanders, in the service of William III. They had been for the most part men of considerable estates in their own country, though they were now content to live as exiles on the half-pay granted them by the country of their adoption. When they first came into the neighbourhood, the town of Portarlington could scarcely be said to exist. The village of Cootletoodra, as it was formerly called, was only a collection of miserable huts unfit for human residence ; and until the

---

[1] The *Bulletin de la Société de l'Histoire du Protestantisme Français* (1868, p. 69), contains a letter addressed by the Earl of Galway to David Barbut, a refugee residing at Berne, in January, 1693, wherein he informs him that King William is greatly concerned at the distress of the French refugees in Switzerland, and desires that 600 families should proceed to Ireland and settle there. He adds that the King has recommended the Protestant Princes of Germany, and the States-General of Holland, to pay the expense of the transport of these families to the sea-board ; after which, the means would be provided for their embarkation for Ireland. "The King," he says, "is so touched at the misery with which these families are threatened where they are, and perceives so clearly how valuable their settlement would be in his kingdom of Ireland, that he is resolved to provide all the money that may be required for the purpose. We must not lose any time on this matter ; and I hope that by the month of April, or May at the latest, these families will be on their way to join us."

dwellings designed for the reception of the exiles by the Earl of Galway could be built, they resided in the adjoining villages of Doolough, Monasterevin, Cloneygown, and the ancient village of Lea. Portarlington shortly became the model town of the province. The dwellings of the strangers were distinguished for their neatness and comfort. Their farms and gardens were patterns of tidiness and good management. They introduced new fruit-trees from abroad; amongst others the black Italian walnut and the jargonelle pear,—specimens of which still flourish at Portarlington in vigorous old age. The planter of these trees fought at the Boyne as an ensign in the regiment of La Melonniere. The immigrants also introduced the "espalier" with success; and their fruit of all kinds became widely celebrated. Another favourite branch of cultivation was flowers, of which they imported many new sorts; while their vegetables were unmatched in Ireland.

The exiles formed a highly select society, composed, as it was, of ladies and gentlemen of high culture, of pure morals, and of gentle birth and manners,—so different from the roystering Irish gentry of the time. Though they had suffered grievous wrongs at the hands of their own countrymen, they were contented, cheerful, and even gay.[1] Traditions still exist of the military refugees, in their scarlet cloaks, sitting in groups under the old oaks in the market-place, sipping tea out of their small china cups. They had also their balls, and ordinaries, and "ridottos" (places of pleasant resort); and a great deal of pleasant visiting went on amongst them. They continued to enjoy their favourite wine of Bordeaux, which was imported for them in

[1] An Irish correspondent, however, extensively acquainted with the descendants of the Huguenots, says that, "so far as his observation goes, they, for the most part, bear a pensive, not to say melancholy, cast of countenance,—the same sort of sad expression which may be observed in the Polish Jews, doubtless the result of long persecution and suffering."

considerable quantities by their fellow-exiles, the French wine-merchants of Waterford and Dublin.

There were also numerous refugees of a humbler class settled in the place, who carried on various trades. Thus the Fouberts carried on a manufacture of linen. Many of the minor tradesmen were French—bakers, butchers, masons, smiths, carpenters, tailors, and shoemakers. The Blancs, butchers, transmitted the business from father to son for more than 150 years; and they are still recognisable at Portarlington under the name of Blong. The Micheaus, farmers, had been tenants on the estates of the Robillard family in Champagne: they were now tenants of the same family at Portarlington. One of the Micheaus was sexton of the French church of the town, until within the last few years. La Borde the mason, Capel the blacksmith, and Gautier the carpenter, came from the neighbourhood of Bordeaux; and their handiwork, much of which still exists at Portarlington and the neighbourhood, bears indications of their foreign training and artistic culture.

The refugees, as was their invariable practice where they settled in sufficient numbers, early formed themselves into a congregation, and a church was erected for their accommodation, in which a long succession of able ministers officiated, the last of whom was Charles de Vignoles, afterwards Dean of Ossory.[1] The service was conducted in French down to the year 1817; since

---

[1] The Register of the French church is still preserved. The entries begin in 1694. The Register contains the names, families, and localities in France, from whence the exiles came. The first volume still wears the coarse brown paper cover with which it was originally invested by its foreign guardians nearly 190 years ago. The following is a list of the pastors of the Portarlington Church :—

Calvinists.

Depuis 1694—96 Gillet

5 Octr.	1696—	Belagniere
1 Decr.	1696—98	Gillet
15 May	1698—	Durassus
,, ,,	,,	Ducasse
26 June	1698—1702	Daillon.

Anglicans.

3 Octr.	1702—29	De Bonneval
14 Aug.	1729—39	Des Vœux
17 Feb.	1739—67	Caillard
2 Sep.	1767—93	Des Vœux
Jan.	1793—1817	Vignoles *père*
	1817—	Charles Vignoles *fils.*

then it has been discontinued, the language having by that time ceased to be understood in the neighbourhood.

Besides a church, the refugees also possessed a school, which long enjoyed a high reputation for the classical education which it provided for the rising generation. At an early period, the boys seem to have been clothed as well as educated, the memorandum-book of an old officer of the Boyne containing an entry, April 20, 1727, " making six sutes of cloths for ye blewbois, at 18 pce. per sute, 00 : 09 : 00." M. Le Fevre, founder of the Charter Schools, was the first schoolmaster in Portarlington. He is said to have been the father of Sterne's " poor sick lieutenant."[1]   The Bonnevaux and Tersons were amongst the subsequent teachers, and many sons and daughters of the principal Protestants in Ireland passed under their hands.   Among the more distinguished men who received the best part of their education at Portarlington, may be mentioned the Marquis of Wellesley and his brother the Earl of Mornington, the Marquis of Westmeath, the Right Hon. John Wilson Croker, Sir Henry Ellis (of the British Museum), Daniel W. Webber, and many others.

Lady Morgan, referring in her *Memoirs* to the French colony at Portarlington, observes : " The dispersion of the French Huguenots, who settled in great numbers in Ireland, was one of the greatest boons conferred by the misgovernment of other countries upon our own.   Eminent preachers, eminent lawyers, and clever statesmen, whose names are not unknown to the literature and science of France, occupied high places in the professions in Dublin.   Of these I may mention,

[1] The Portarlington Register contains the following record :— " Sépulture du Dimanche 23e Mars, 1717-18. Le Samedy 22e du présent mois entre minuet et une heure, est mort en la foy du Seigneur et dans l'espérance de la glorieuse résurrection, Monsieur Favre, Lieutenant à la pention, dont l'ame estait allée à Dieu, son corps a été enterré par Monsieur Bonneval, ministre de cette Eglise dans le cemitière de ce lieu. A Ligonier Bonneval min. Louis Buliod."

as personal acquaintances, the Saurins, the Lefanus, Espinasses, Favers, Corneilles, Le Bas, and many others whose families still remain in the Irish metropolis."[1]

It may here be noted that the social standard of the Huguenot immigration into Ireland was generally higher than that of the same immigration into England, principally because of the large number of retired French officers, most of them of noble and gentle blood, who settled at Portarlington, Waterford, and the other southern Irish towns, shortly after the conclusion of the peace of Utrecht. Some of these retired veterans bore the noblest historic names in France. Their sons and their daughters intermarried, and thus kept up the Huguenot line, usually to the second and third, and often to the fourth generation. Their martial instincts survived their separation from the country of their birth; and to this day a large proportion of the descendants of the Huguenot settlers in Ireland are to be found serving as officers in the British army; whilst many others belong to the Church and the learned professions. Thus, among the MSS [2] left by Dr. Letablère, Dean of Tuam—son of René de la Douespe, representative of the illustrious family of L'Establere in Picardy —we find lists of persons descended from Huguenot refugees in Ireland; among whom there were two generals, six colonels, five majors, and twenty-four captains, besides subaltern officers. At the same time there were then serving in the Irish Church, one bishop of Huguenot extraction (Dr. Chevenix), three deans (Brocas, Champagne, and Letablère), and thirty-three clergymen, besides nineteen ministers of French churches in different parts of Ireland. The Dean's papers also contain a list of about a hundred persons established in Dublin in 1763, carrying on business there as bankers, physicians, attorneys, merchants,

---

[1] LADY MORGAN—*Memoirs*, i. 106.

[2] These papers have been kindly submitted for our inspec-

by R. W. Litton, Esq., one of the surviving representatives of Dr. Letablère by the female line goldsmiths, manufacturers, and traders of various kinds.

It is to be regretted that the industrial settlements of the refugee French and Flemings in Ireland, were generally so much smaller than those which they effected in different parts of England,—otherwise the condition of that unfortunate country would probably have been very different from that in which we now find it. The only part of Ireland in which the Huguenots left a permanent impression was in the north, where the branches of industry which they planted took firm root, and continue to flourish with extraordinary vigour to this day. But in the south it was very different. Though the natural facilities for trade at Cork, Limerick, and Waterford, were much greater than those of the northern towns, the refugees never obtained any firm footing or made any satisfactory progress in that quarter. Their colonies at first maintained only a sickly existence, and they gradually fell into decay. The last blow was given to them by Strikes.

One has only to look at Belfast and the busy hives of industry in that neighbourhood, and to note the condition of the northern province of Ulster—existing under precisely the same laws as govern the south,— to find how seriously the social progress of Ireland has been affected by the want of that remunerative employment which the refugees were always so instrumental in providing in the districts in which they settled,— wherever they found a population willing to be taught by them, and to follow in the path which they undeviatingly pursued—of peaceful, contented, and honourable industry.

CHAPTER XVIII.

DESCENDANTS OF THE REFUGEES.

ALTHOUGH 300 years have passed since the first religious persecutions in Flanders and France compelled so large a number of Protestants to fly from those countries and take refuge in England, and although nearly 200 years have passed since the second great emigration from France took place in the reign of Louis XIV., the descendants of the "gentle and profitable strangers" are still recognisable amongst us. In the course of the generations which have come and gone since the dates of their original settlement, they have laboured skilfully and diligently, for the advancement of British trade, commerce, and manufactures; while there is scarcely a branch of literature, science, or art, in which they have not honourably distinguished themselves.

Three hundred years form a long period in the life of a nation. During that time many of the distinctive characteristics of the original refugees must necessarily have become effaced in the persons of their descendants. Indeed, by far the greater number of them before long became completely Anglicised, and ceased to be traceable except by their names; and even these have for the most part become converted into names of English sound.

So long as the foreigners continued to cherish the hope of returning to their native country, on the possible cessation of the persecutions there, they waited and worked on, with that end in view. But as the persecutions only waxed hotter, they at length gradually gave up all hope of returning. They claimed and obtained letters of naturalisation; and though many of them continued for several generations to worship in their native language, they were content to live and die as English subjects. Their children grew up amidst English associations, and they desired to forget that their fathers had been fugitives and foreigners in the land. They cared not to remember the language or to retain the names which marked them as distinct from the people amongst whom they lived ; and hence many of the descendants of the refugees, in the second or third generation, abandoned their foreign names, and gradually ceased to frequent the distinctive places of worship which their fathers had founded.

Indeed, many of the early Flemings had no sooner settled in England and become naturalised, than they threw off their foreign names and assumed English ones. Thus, as we have seen, Hoek, the Flemish brewer in Southwark, assumed the name of Leeke; while Haestricht, the Flemish manufacturer at Bow, took that of James. Mr. Pryme, formerly professor of political economy in the University of Cambridge, and representative of that town in Parliament, whose ancestors were refugees from Ypres in Flanders, has informed us that his grandfather dropped the " de la " originally prefixed to the family name, in consequence of the strong anti-Gallican feeling which prevailed in this country during the Seven Years' War of 1756-63, though his son has since assumed it ; and the same circumstance doubtless led many others to change their foreign names to those of an English sound.

Nevertheless, a large number of purely Flemish names are still to be found in various parts of England and Ireland, where the foreigners originally settled. They have been on the whole better preserved in the rural districts than in London, where the social friction was greater, and rubbed off the foreign peculiarities more quickly. In the lace towns of the west of England such names as Raymond, Spiller, Brock, Stocker, Groot, Rochett, and Kettel, are still common; and the same trades have continued in some of their families for generations. The Walloon Goupés, who settled in Wiltshire as clothmakers more than 300 years since, are still known there as the Guppys, and the Thunguts as Dogoods and Toogoods.

In the account of the early refugee Protestants given in the preceding pages, it has been pointed out that the first settlers in England came principally from Lille, Turcoing, and the towns situated along both sides of the present French frontier—the country of the French Walloons, though then subject to the crown of Spain. Among the first of these refugees was one Laurent des Bouveryes,[1] a native of Sainghin, near Lille. He first settled at Sandwich as a maker of serges, in 1567; after which, in the following year, he removed to Canterbury to join the Walloon settlement there. The Des Bouveryes family prospered greatly. In the third generation we find Edward, grandson of the refugee, a wealthy Turkey merchant in London. In the fourth generation the head of the family was created a baronet; in the fifth, a viscount; and in the sixth, an earl; the original Laurent des Bouveryes being at this day represented in the House of Lords by the Earl of Radnor.

About the same time that the Des Bouveryes came into England from Lille, the Hugessens arrived from Dunkirk, and settled at Dover. They afterwards removed to Sandwich, where they prospered; and in the course of a few generations, we find them enrolled among the county aristocracy of Kent, and their name borne by the ancient family of the Knatchbulls. It is not the least remarkable circumstance connected with this family, that a member of it now represents the

---

[1] The Bouveryes were men of mark in their native country. Thus, in the *Histoire de Cambray et du Cambrensis*, published in 1664, it is stated, "La famille de Bouverie est reconnu passer plusieurs siècles entre les patricés de Cambray."

borough of Sandwich, one of the earliest seats of the refugees in England.

Among other notable Flemish immigrants may be numbered the Houblons, who gave the Bank of England its first governor, and from one of whose daughters the late Lord Palmerston was lineally descended.[1] The Van Sittarts, Jansens, Courteens, Van Milderts, Vanlores, Corsellis, and Vannecks,[2] were widely and honourably known in their day as London bankers or merchants. Sir Matthew Decker, besides being eminent as a London merchant, was distinguished for the excellence of his writings on commercial subjects, then little understood. He made an excellent member of Parliament: he was elected for Bishop's Castle in 1719.

Various members of the present landed gentry trace their descent from the Flemish refugees. Thus Jacques Hoste, the founder of the present family (represented by Sir W. L. S. Hoste, Bart.), fled from Bruges, of which his father was governor in 1569; the Tyssens (now represented by W. G. Tyssen Amhurst, Esq., of Foulden) fled from Ghent; and the Cruses of Norfolk fled from Hownescout in Flanders. All of them took refuge in England.

Among artists, architects, and engineers of Flemish descent we find Grinling Gibbons, the wood-sculptor; Mark Gerrard, the portrait-painter; Sir John Vanbrugh, the architect and play-writer; Richard Cosway, R.A.,[3] the miniature-painter; and Vermuyden and Westerdyke, the engineers employed to reclaim the drowned lands in the Fens. The Tradescants, the celebrated antiquarians, were also of the same origin.[4]

---

[1] Anne, sister and heir of Sir Richard Houblon, was married to Henry Temple, created Lord Palmerston in 1722.

[2] The Vanneck family is now represented in the peerage by Baron Huntingfield.

[3] Cosway belonged to a family, originally Flemish, long settled at Tiverton, Devon. His father was master of the grammar-school there.

[4] *The Tatler*, vol. i., ed. 1786, p. 435, in a note, says: "John

One of the most distinguished families of the Netherlands was that of the De Grotes or Groots, of which Hugo Grotius was an illustrious member. When the Spanish persecutions were at their height in the Low Countries, several of the Protestant De Grotes, who were eminent merchants at Antwerp, fled from that city, and took refuge, some in England and others in Germany. Several of the Flemish De Grotes had before then settled in England. Thus, among the letters of Denization mentioned in Mr. Brewer's *Calendar of State Papers*, Henry VIII., we find the following :—

"Ambrose de Grote, merchant of the Duchy of Brabant (Letters of Denization, Patent 11th June, 1510, 2 Henry VIII.)

"12 Feby., 1512-13.—Protection for one year for Ambrose and Peter de Grote, merchants of Andwarp, in Brabant, going in the retinue of Sir Gilbert Talbot, Deputy of Calais."

One of the refugee Grotes is supposed to have settled as a merchant at Bremen, from which city the grandfather of the late George Grote, the historian of Greece, came over to London early in last century, and established a mercantile house, and afterwards a banking house, both of which flourished. Mr. Grote was also of Huguenot blood through his mother, who was descended from Colonel Blosset, commander of "Blosset's Foot," the scion of an ancient Protestant family of Touraine. He was an officer in the army of Queen Anne, and the proprietor of a considerable estate in the county of Dublin.

The great French immigration, which occurred at the Revocation of the Edict of Nantes, having been the most recent, has left much more noticeable traces

---

Tradescant, senior, is supposed to have been of Dutch or Flemish extraction, and to have settled in this kingdom probably about the end of Queen Elizabeth's reign, or in the beginning of the reign of James I." Father and son were very ingenious persons, and were held in esteem for their early promotion and culture of botany and natural history. The son formed the Tradescant museum at Oxford.

in English family history and nomenclature, notwithstanding the large proportion of the refugees and their descendants who threw aside their French names, or, rather, translated them into English. Thus, L'Oiseau became Bird; Le Jeune, Young; Du Bois, Wood; Le Blanc, White; Le Noir, Black; Le Maur, Brown; Le Roy, King; Lacroix, Cross; Le Monnier, Miller; Tonnelier, Cooper; Le Maitre, Masters; Dulau, Waters; Sauvage, Savage and Wild. Some of the Lefevres changed their name to the English equivalent of Smith, as was the case with the ancestor of Sir Culling Eardley Smith, Bart., a French refugee whose original name was Le Fevre. Many names were strangely altered in their conversion from French into English. Jolifemme was freely translated into Pretyman [1]—a name well known in the Church; Momerie became Mummery, a common name at Dover; and Planché became Plank, of which there are still instances at Canterbury and Southampton. At Oxford, the name of Willamise was traced back to Villebois; Taillebois became Talboys; Le Coq, Laycock; Bouchier, Butcher or Boxer; Boyer, Bower; Bois, Boys; Mesurier, Measure; Mahieu, Mayhew; Bourgeois, Burgess; Souverain, Suffren; De Vere, Weir; Coquerel, Cockerill; Drouet, Drewitt; D'Aeth, Death; D'Orleans, Dorling. Other pure French names were dreadfully vulgarised. Thus Condé became Cundy; Chapuis, Shoppee; De Preux, Diprose; De Moulins, Mullins; Pelletier, Pelter; Huyghens, Huggins or Higgins; and Beaufoy, Boffy! [2]

---

[1] A correspondent informs us, that some years since he saw over a shop door at Dover the words "Susanne Handsomebodie," probably a rough rendering of the same name of "Jolifemme."

[2] Mr. Lower, in his *Patronymica Britannica*, suggests that Richard Despair, a poor man buried at East Grinstead in 1726,

was, in the orthography of his ancestors, a Despard.

Among other conversions of French into English names may be mentioned the following :— Letellier, converted into Taylour; Brasseur into Brassey; Batchelier into Bachelor; Lenoir into Lennard; De Lean into Dillon; Pigou into Pigott; Breton into Britton; Dieudonn into Dudney; Bau-

Many pure French names have, however, been preserved; and one need only turn over the pages of a
London Directory to recognise the large proportion
which the descendants of the Huguenots continue to
form, of the modern population of the metropolis.
But a short time since, in reading the report of a
meeting of the district board of works at Wandsworth
—where the refugees settled in such numbers as to
form a considerable congregation—we recognised the
names of Lobjoit, Baringer, Fourdrinier, Poupart, and
others, unmistakably French. Such names are constantly " cropping out " in modern literature, science,
art, and manufactures. Thus we recognise those of
Delaine and Fonblanque in the press; Rigaud and
Roget in science; Dargan (originally Dargent) in
railway construction; Pigou in gunpowder; Gillot in
steel pens; Courage in beer; and Courtauld in silk.

That the descendants of the Huguenots have vindicated and continued to practise that liberty of thought
and worship for which their fathers sacrificed so much,
is sufficiently obvious from the fact that among them
we find men holding such widely different views as
the brothers Newman, Father Faber and James Martineau, Dr. Pusey and the Rev. Hugh Stowell. Dr.
Arnold's mother was a Delafield, and the Rev. Sidney
Smith's a D'Olier. The latter was accustomed to at-
tribute much of his constitutional gaiety to his mother,
whom he characterised as a woman " of noble countenance and as noble a mind."

From the peerage to the working classes, the descendants of the refugees pervade, to this day, the
various ranks of English society. The Queen of
England herself is related to them, through her
descent from Sophia Dorothea, grand-daughter of the

doir into Baudry; Guilbert into
Gilbert; Koch into Cox; Re-
nalls into Reynolds; Merineau
into Meryon; Petit into Pettit;
Reveil into Revill; Saveroy into
Savery; Gebon into Gibbon;
Scardeville into Sharwell; Leve-
reau into Lever; and so on with
many more.

Marquis d'Olbreuse, a Protestant nobleman of Poitou. The Marquis was one of the numerous French exiles who took refuge in Brandenburg on the Revocation of the Edict of Nantes. The Duke of Zell married his only daughter, whose issue was Sophia Dorothea, the wife of George Louis, Elector of Hanover, afterwards George I. of England. The son of Sophia Dorothea succeeded to the English throne as George II., and her daughter married Frederick William, afterwards King of Prussia; and thus the Huguenot blood continues to run in the royal families of the two great Protestant states of the north.

Several descendants of French Huguenots have become elevated to the British peerage. Of these the most ancient is the family of Trench, originally De la Tranche, the head of which is the Earl of Clancarty. Frederick, Lord of La Tranche in Poitou, took refuge in England about the year 1574, shortly after the Massacre of St. Bartholomew. He settled for a time in Northumberland, from whence he passed over into Ireland. Of his descendants, one branch founded the peerage of Clancarty, and another that of Ashtown. Several members of the family have held high offices in church and state; among whom may be mentioned Power le Poer Trench, the last Archbishop of Tuam, and the present Archbishop of Dublin, in whom the two Huguenot names of Trench and Chenevix are honourably united.

Among other peers of Huguenot origin are Lord Northwick, descended from John Rushout, a French refugee established in London in the reign of Charles I.; Lord de Blaquiere, descended from John de Blacquire, a scion of a noble French family, who settled as a merchant in London shortly after the Revocation; and Lord Rendlesham, descended from Peter Thelusson, grandson of a French refugee who about the same time took refuge in Switzerland.

Besides these elevations to the peerage of descendants of Huguenots in the direct male line, many of the daughters of distinguished refugees and their offspring formed unions with noble families, and led to a further intermingling of the blood of the Huguenots with that of the English aristocracy.   Thus the blood of the noble family of Ruvigny mingles with that of Russell[1] (Duke of Bedford) and Cavendish (Duke of Devonshire) ; of Schomberg with that of Osborne (Duke of Leeds) ; of Champagné (*née* De la Rochefoucauld) with that of Forbes (Earl of Granard); of Portal and Boileau with that of Elliott (Earl of Minto) ; of Auriol with that of Hay Drummond (Earl of Kinnoul) ; of D'Albiac with that of Innes-Ker (Duke of Roxburghe); of La Touche with that of Butler-Danvers (Earl of Lanesborough); of Montolieu with that of Murray (Lord Elibank) ; and so on in numerous other instances.

Among recent peerages are those of Taunton, Eversley, and Romilly, all direct descendants of Huguenots.   The first Labouchere who settled in England was Peter Cæsar Labouchere.   He had originally taken refuge from the persecution of Louis XIV. in Holland, where he joined the celebrated house of Hope at Amsterdam ; and he came over to London as the representative of that firm.   He eventually acquired wealth and distinction; and the head of the family now sits in the House of Lords as Baron Taunton.

The Lefevre family came originally from Normandy, where they held considerable landed property.   Peter Lefevre, born in 1650, had scarcely succeeded to his paternal estates, when he was forced to fly with his

---

[1] Rachel, daughter of Daniel de Massue, Seigneur de Ruvigny, married Thomas Wriothesley, Earl of Southampton, in 1634. The Countess died in 1637, leaving two daughters, one of whom, Elizabeth, afterwards married the Earl of Gainsborough, and the other, Rachel, married, first Lord Vaughan, and secondly William Lord Russell, known as "patriot." Every one has heard of his celebrated wife, the daughter of a Ruvigny, whose son afterwards became second Duke of Bedford, and whose two daughters married, one the Duke of Devonshire, and the other the Marquis of Granby.

family into England, rather than renounce his faith.
He first settled at Canterbury, and there embarked in
trade with the capital he had brought with him. One
of his sons, John, entered the army, and rose to the
rank of Lieutenant-Colonel, serving under Marlborough
through his campaigns in the Low Countries. He
afterwards resided at Walthamstow, and held the office
of High Sheriff of Essex. The younger brother, Isaac
(from whom Lord Eversley, late Speaker of the House
of Commons, is lineally descended), was put apprentice
to trade at Canterbury; and, after his father's death,
he removed to Spitalfields, where he set up for himself
as a scarlet dyer, and was very successful. His son
John possessed considerable property at Old Ford and
Bromley, which is still in the family; and his only
daughter Helena having married Charles Shaw of
Lincoln's Inn, in 1789, their descendants have since
borne the name and arms of the Lefevres.

The story of the Romilly family is well known
through the autobiography left by the late Sir Samuel
Romilly and published by his sons.[1] The great-grand-
father of Sir Samuel was a considerable landed proprietor in the neighbourhood of Montpellier. Though
a Protestant by conviction, he conformed to Roman
Catholicism, with the object of saving the family property for the benefit of his only son. Yet he secretly
worshipped after his own principles, as well as brought
up his son in them. The youth indeed imbibed Protestantism so deeply, that in the year 1701, when only
seventeen, he went to Geneva for the sole purpose of
receiving the sacrament,—the administration of the
office by Protestant ministers in France still rendering
them liable, if detected, to death or condemnation to
the galleys for life. At Geneva, young Romilly met
the celebrated preacher Saurin, then in the height of
his fame, who happened to be there on a visit. The

---

[1] *Memoirs of the Life of Sir Samuel Romilly written by himself.*
Edited by his Sons. 3 Vols. London. 1840.

result of his conversations with Saurin was the formation in his mind of a fixed determation to leave for
ever his native country, his parents, and the inheritance
which awaited him, and trust to his own industry
for a subsistence in some foreign land, where he might
be free to worship God according to conscience.

Young Romilly accordingly set out for London; and
it was not until he had landed in England that he
apprised his father of the resolution which he had formed.
After a few years' residence in London, where he
married Judith de Monsallier, the daughter of another
refugee, Mr. Romilly began the business of a wax-
bleacher at Hoxton, his father supplying him from
time to time with money. But a sad reverse of fortune
ensued on the death of his father. A distant relative,
who was a Catholic, took possession of the family estate,
and further remittances from France were stopped.
Then followed difficulty, bankruptcy, and distress;
and the landowner's son, unable to bear up under his
calamities, sank under them at an early age, leaving a
widow and a family of eight children almost entirely
unprovided for.

The youngest son, Peter, father of the future Sir
Samuel, was bound apprentice to a French refugee
jeweller, named Lafosse, whose shop was in Broad
Street. On arriving at manhood he went to Paris,
where he worked as a journeyman, saving money
enough to make an excursion as far south as Montpellier,
to view the family estate, now in the possession of
strangers and irrecoverably lost, since it could only be
redeemed, if at all, by apostasy. The jeweller eventually returned to London, married a Miss Garnault,—descended like himself from a Protestant refugee,—and
began business on his own account. He seems to have
enjoyed a moderate degree of prosperity, living carefully and frugally, bringing up his family virtuously
and religiously, and giving them as good an education as
his comparatively slender means would admit, until
the death of a rich relative of his wife, a Mr. de la

Haize,—who left considerable legacies to each member of the family,—enabled Mr. Romilly to article his son Samuel to a clerk in chancery, and to enter upon the profession in which he acquired so much distinction. It is unnecessary to describe his career, which has been so simply and beautifully related by himself, or to trace the further history of the family, the head of which now sits in the House of Lords, under the title of Baron Romilly.

The baronetage, as well as the peerage, includes many descendants of the Huguenots. Jacques Boileau was Lord of Castlenau and St. Croix, near Nismes, in the neighbourhood of which the persecution long raged so furiously. He was the father of a family of twenty-two children, and could not readily leave France at the Revocation; but, being known as a Protestant, and refusing to be converted, he was arrested and placed under restraint, in which condition he died. His son Charles fled, first into Holland, and afterwards into England, where he entered the army, obtained the rank of captain, and commanded a corps of French gentlemen under Marlborough at the battle of Blenheim. He afterwards settled as a wine-merchant at Dublin, and was succeeded by his son. The family prospered; and the great-grandson of Marlborough's captain was promoted to a baronetcy,—the present wearer of the title being Sir John Boileau.

The Crespignys also belonged to a noble family in Lower Normandy. Claude Champion, Lord of Crespigny, was an officer in the French army; but at the Revocation he fled into England, accompanied by his wife, the Comtesse de Vierville, and a family of eight children,—two of whom were carried on board the ship in which they sailed, in baskets. De Crespigny entered the British army, and served as colonel under Marlborough. The present head of the family is Sir C. W. Champion Crespigny, Bart.

Elias Bouhérau, M.D., an eminent physician in Rochelle, being debarred the practice of his profession

by the edict of Louis XIV., fled into England with his
wife and children, and settled in Ireland, where his
descendants rose to fame and honour; the present representative of the family being Sir E. R. Borough,
Bart.

Anthony Vinchon de Bacquencourt, a man eminent
for his learning, belonged to Rouen, of the parliament
of which his father was President. He was originally
a Roman Catholic, but being incensed at the pretended
miracles wrought at the tomb of the Abbé Paris, he
embraced Protestantism, and fled from France. He
settled in Dublin under the name of Des Vœux (the
family surname), and became minister of the French
church there. He afterwards joined the Rev. John
Peter Droz, another French refugee, in starting the
first literary journal that ever appeared in Ireland.
The present representative of the family is Sir C.
Des Vœux, Bart.

Among other baronets descended from French
refugees, may be mentioned Sir John Lambert, descended from John Lambert of the Isle of Rhé; Sir J.
D. Legard, descended from John Legard, of ancient
Norman lineage; Sir A. J. de Hochepied Larpent, descended from John de Larpent of Caen; and Sir G. S.
Brooke Pechell, descended from the Pechells of Montauban in Languedoc. One of the members of the last-
mentioned family having embraced Roman Catholicism,
his descendants still hold the family estate in France.

Many of the refugees and their descendants have
also sat in Parliament, and done good service there.
Probably the first Huguenot member of the House
of Commons was Phillip Papillon, who sat for the
city of London in 1695. The Papillons had suffered
much for their religion in France, one of them having
lain in gaol at Avranches for three years. Various
members of the family have since represented Dover,
Romney, and Colchester.

Of past members of Parliament, the Pechells have
sat for Essex; the Fonneraus for Aldborough; the

Durants for St. Ives and Evesham; the Devagnes for Barnstaple; the Maugers for Poole; the La Roches for Bodmin; and the Amyands for Tregony, Bodmin, and Camelford. The last member of the Amyand family was a baronet, who assumed the name of Cornewall on marrying Catherine, the heiress of Velters Cornewall, Esq., of Moccas Court, Herefordshire; and his only daughter having married Sir Thomas Frankland Lewis, became the mother of the late Sir George Cornewall Lewis, Bart.

Many descendants of the Huguenots who settled in Ireland, also represented constituencies in the Irish Parliament. Thus, the La Touches sat for Carlow; the Chaigneaus for Gowran; and the Right Hon. William Saurin, who filled the office of Irish Attorney-General for fourteen years, may be said to have represented all Ireland. He was a man of great ability and distinguished patriotism; and but for his lack of ambition, would have been made a judge and a peer, both of which dignities he refused. Colonel Barré, who belonged to the refugee family of that name settled in Ireland, is best known by his parliamentary career in England. He was celebrated as an orator and a patriot, resisting to the utmost the passing of the American Stamp Act, which severed the connection between England and her American colonies. In 1776 he held the office of Vice-Treasurer of Ireland, and afterwards that of Paymaster to the Forces for England.

Among more recent members of Parliament may be mentioned the names of Dupré, Gaven, Hugessen, Jervoise, Labouchere, Layard, Lefevre, Lefroy, Paget (of the Leicestershire family, formerly member for Nottingham), Pusey, Tomline, Rebow, and Vandeleur. Mr. Chevalier Cobbold is descended by the female side from Samuel le Chevalier, minister of the French church in London in 1591; one of whose descendants introduced the well-known Chevalier barley. Mr. Du Cane is descended from the same family to which the great admiral belonged. The first Du Cane or Du Quesne who fled into England for refuge, settled at Canterbury, and afterwards in London. The head of this family was an Alderman of the City in 1666, and in the next century his grandson Richard sat for Colchester in Parliament; the present representative of the Du Canes being the member for North Essex.

Of the descendants of refugees who were distinguished as divines, may be mentioned the Majendies, one of whom—John James, son of the pastor of the French church at Exeter—was Prebendary of Sarum, and a well-known author; and another, son of the Prebendary, became Bishop of Chester, and afterwards of Bangor. The Saurins also rose to eminence in the Church,—Louis Saurin, minister of the French church in the Savoy, having been raised to the Deanery of St. Patrick's, Ardagh; whilst his son afterwards became Vicar of Belfast, and his grandson Bishop of Dromore. Roger Du Quesne, grandson of the Marquis Du Quesne, was Vicar of East Tuddenham in Norfolk, and a Prebendary of Ely.

One of the most eminent scholars of Huguenot origin was the Rev. Dr. Jortin, Archdeacon of London. He was the son of René Jortin, a refugee from Brittany, who served as secretary to three British admirals successively, and went down with Sir Cloudesley Shovel in the ship in which he was wrecked off the Scilly Isles in 1707. The son of René was entered a pupil at the Charter-House, and gave early indications of ability, which were justified by the distinction which he shortly after achieved at Cambridge. On the recommendation of Dr. Thirlby, young Jortin furnished Pope with translations from the commentary of Eustathius on Homer, as well as with notes for his translation of the *Iliad;* but though Pope adapted them almost verbatim, he made no acknowledgment of the assistance of his young helper. Shortly after, on a fellowship becoming vacant at Cambridge by the death of William Rosen, the descendant of another refugee,

Jortin was appointed to it. A few years later, he was appointed to the vicarage of Swavesey, in Cambridgeshire, from whence he removed to the living of Kensington near London. There he distinguished himself as the author of many learned works, of which the best known is his able and elaborate *Life of Erasmus.* He was eventually made Archdeacon of London, and died in 1770 at Kensington, where he was buried.

Another celebrated divine was the Rev. George Lewis Fleury, Archdeacon of Waterford—" the good old archdeacon," as he was called—widely known for his piety, his charity, and his goodness. He was descended from Louis Fleury, pastor of Tours, who fled into England with his wife and family at the Revocation. Several of the Fleurys are still clergymen in Ireland.

The Maturins also have produced some illustrious men. The pastor Gabriel Maturin, from whom they are descended, lay a prisoner in the Bastile for twenty-six years on account of his religion. But he tenaciously refused to be converted, and he was at length, discharged, a cripple for life,—having lost the use of his limbs during his confinement. He contrived, however, to reach Ireland with some members of his former flock, and there he unexpectedly found his wife and two sons, of whom he had heard nothing during the long period of his imprisonment. His son Peter arrived at some distinction in the Church, having become Dean of Killala ; and his grandson Gabriel James became Dean of St. Patrick's, Dublin. From him descended several clergymen of eminence, one of them an eloquent preacher, who is perhaps more widely known as the author of two remarkable works— *Melmoth the Wanderer,* and the tragedy of *Bertram.*

There were numerous other descendants of the refugees, clergymen and others, besides those already named, who distinguished themselves by their literary productions. Louis Dutens, who held the living of Elsdon in Northumberland, produced a successful

tragedy, *The Return of Ulysses,* when only about
eighteen years of age. In his later years, he was the
author of numerous works of a more solid character, of
which one of the best known is his *Researches on the
Origin of Discoveries attributed to the Moderns*—a
work full of learning and labour. He also wrote an
Appeal to Good Sense, being a defence of Christianity
against Voltaire and the Encyclopædists, besides
numerous other works.

The Rev. William Romaine, Rector of St. Ann's,
Blackfriars, was the son of a French refugee who had
settled at Hartlepool as a merchant and corn-dealer.
Mr. Romaine was one of the most popular of London
clergymen, and his *Life, Walk, and Triumph of Faith*
is to this day a well-known and popular book among
religious readers. Romaine has been compared to " a
diamond—rough often, but very pointed ; and the more
he was broken by years, the more he appeared to
shine." Much of his life was passed in polemical
controversy, and in maintaining the Calvinistic views
which he so strongly held. He was a most diligent
improver of time ; and besides being exemplary and
indefatigable in performing the duties of his office, he
left behind him a large number of able works, which
were collected and published in 1796 in eight octavo
volumes.

We have already spoken of the distinction achieved
by Saurin and Romilly at the Irish and English bar.
But they did not stand alone. Of the numerous lawyers descended from the refugees, several have achieved
no less eminence as judges than as pleaders. Of these,
Baron Mazeres, appointed Curzitor Baron of the Exchequer in 1773, was one of the most illustrious. He was
not less distinguished as a man of science and an antiquarian, than as a lawyer. Justice Le Blanc, Sir John
Bayley, and Sir John Bosanquet, were also of French
extraction, the latter being descended from Pierre
Bosanquet, of Lunel in Languedoc. Chief Justice
Lefroy and Justice Perrin, of the Irish bench, were in

like manner descended from Huguenot families long
settled in Ireland.

A long list might be given, in addition to those
already mentioned, of persons illustrious in literature,
science, and the arts, who sprang from the same stock;
but we must be content with mentioning only a few.
Peter Anthony Motteaux was not less distinguished for
his enterprise as an East India merchant, than for his
ability as a writer; and Sir John Charden, the traveller
and author, afterwards jeweller to the court, was esteemed in his time as a man of great parts and of
noble character. Garrick, the great English actor, was
of Huguenot origin, his real name being Garrigue.
The French D'Aubignés have given us several eminent
men, bearing the name of Daubeny, celebrated in
natural history. Among other men of science, we note
the names of Rigaud, Sivilian professor of astronomy
at Oxford, and Roget, the physiologist, author of one
of the Bridgewater treatises. The Martineaus, so well
known in English literature, are descended from
Gaston Martineau, a surgeon of Dieppe, who settled at
Norwich in 1685; and the Barbaulds are sprung from
a minister of the French church of La Patente in
London. Some of our best novelists have also been of
French extraction. Captain Marryatt and Captain
Chamier, whose nautical tales have charmed so many
readers, were both descended from Huguenots, as was
also Tom D'Urfey, the English song-writer. It has also
been supposed that the family of De Foe (or Vaux)
was of Huguenot origin.

Several men of considerable distinction in science
and invention emanated from the Huguenot settlers in
Spitalfields, which long continued to be the great
French quarter of London. The French handloom
weavers were in many respects a superior class of
workmen, though their earnings were comparatively
small in amount. Their employment was sedentary,
and entirely of a domestic character,—the workshop
being almost invariably situated over the dwelling,

and approached through it. All the members of the family took part in the work, which was of such a nature as not to prevent conversation; and when several looms were worked on the same floor, this was generally of an intellectual character. One of the young people was usually appointed to read to those at work—it might be a book on history, or frequently a controversial work,— the refugee divines being among the most prolific authors of their time. Nor were the sufferings of the Huguenots at the galleys and in the prisons throughout France forgotten in the dwellings of the exiles, who often spoke of them to their children, and earnestly enjoined them to keep steadfast in the faith for which their fathers had suffered so much.

The circumstances in which the children of the Huguenot workmen were thus brought up—their domestic training, their religious discipline, and their school culture—rendered them for the most part intelligent and docile, while their industry was proverbial. The exiles indulged in simple pleasures, and were especially noted for their love of flowers. They vied with one another in the production of the finest plants; and wherever they settled, they usually set up a floricultural society to exhibit their products. One of the first societies of the kind in England, was that established by the exiles in Spitalfields; and when a body of them went over to Dublin to carry on the manufacture of poplins, they proceeded to set on foot the celebrated Flower Club which still exists in that city. Others of them, who settled in Manchester and Macclesfield, carried thither the same love of flowers and botany, which still continues to characterise their descendants.

Among the handloom weavers of Spitalfields were also to be found occasional inquirers in physical science, as well as several distinguished mathematicians. They were encouraged in these studies by the societies which were established for their cultivation,—a philosophical hall having been founded with that object in Crispin

Street, Spitalfields.[1] Though Simpson and Edwards, both professors of mathematics at Woolwich, were not of French extraction, they were both silk-weavers in Spitalfields, and taught mathematics there. The Dollonds, however, were of pure French origin. The parents of John Dollond were Protestant refugees from Normandy,—from whence they came shortly after the Revocation. His father was a silk-weaver, to which trade John was also brought up. From an early age he displayed a genius for construction, and embraced every opportunity of reading and studying books on geometry, mathematics, and general science. He was, however, unable to devote more than his spare moments to such objects; and when he reached manhood and married, his increasing family compelled him to work at his loom more assiduously than ever. Nevertheless, he went on accumulating information, not only on mathematics, but on anatomy, natural history, astronomy, and optics, reading also extensively in divinity and ecclesiastical history. In order to read the New Testament in the original, he even learnt Greek; and to extend his knowledge of foreign literature, he also learnt Latin, French, German, and Italian.

John Dollond apprenticed his eldest son Peter to an optician; and on the expiry of the young man's apprenticeship, at the age of twenty, he opened a shop in Vine Street, Spitalfields. The business proved so prosperous that, shortly after, the elder Dollond was induced to leave his loom at the age of forty-six, and enter into partnership with his son as an optician. He was now enabled to devote himself wholly to his favourite studies, and to pursue as a business the art which before had occupied him chiefly as an amusement.

One of the first subjects to which Dollond devoted himself was the improvement of the refracting tele-

---

[1] The building, which still exists, is now used as an earthenware-store.

scope. He entered on a series of experiments which
extended over several years, at first without results ;
but at length, after " a resolute perseverance " (to use
his own words), he made the decisive experiment which
showed the error of Newton's conclusion as to the
supposed law of refraction. The papers embodying
Dollond's long succession of experiments were printed
in the Transactions of the Philosophical Society, and
for the last of them he was awarded the Royal Society's
Copley medal. The result of the discovery was an
immediate great improvement in the powers and
accuracy of the telescope and microscope, of which the
Dollond firm reaped the result in a large increase of
business, which still continues in the family.

Many other descendants of the Huguenots distinguished themselves by their inventions in connection
with chronometry, paper-making (Fourdrinier for
example), turning and tool-making, and spinning and
carding machinery. Of the latter class, it may suffice
to mention the name of Louis Paul, the original inventor of spinning by rollers, subsequently revised and
successfully applied by Sir Richard Arkwright,—an
invention which has exercised an extraordinary influence on the manufacturing system of England and
the world at large.

This invention, together with that of the steam-
engine and the power-loom, gave almost the death-
blow to hand-loom weaving. From that time, the
manufactures of Spitalfields, Dublin, and the other
places where the descendants of the refugee workmen
had principally settled, fell into comparative decay.
Many of the artizans, following the current of trade,
left their looms in London, and migrated to Coventry,
Macclesfield, Manchester, and other northern manufacturing towns, then rising in importance. The stronger
and more self-reliant pushed out into the world ; the
more quiescent and feeble remained behind. The
hand-loom trade could not be revived, and no amount
of patient toil and industry could avert the distress

that fell upon the poor silk-weavers, which, even to this day, from time to time sends up its wail in the eastern parts of London.

Owing to these circumstances, as well as to the gradual intermingling of the foreign with the native population, the French element year by year became less marked in Spitalfields ; and in the course of a few generations the religious fervour which had distinguished the original Huguenot refugees, entirely died out in their descendants. They might continue to frequent the French churches, but it was in constantly decreasing numbers. The foreign congregations which had been so flourishing about the beginning of the eighteenth century, towards the end of it became the mere vestiges of what they had been, and at length many of them were closed altogether, or turned over to other denominations.

Sir Samuel Romilly, in his *Autobiography*, gives a touching account of the domestic life of his father's family,—their simple pleasures, their reading, society, and conversation. Nearly all the visitors and friends of the family were of French descent. They associated together, worshipped together, and intermarried with each other. The children went to a school kept by a refugee. On Sunday mornings, French was exclusively spoken in the family circle; and at least once in the day the family pew in the French Artillery Church was regularly filled. "My father," says Sir Samuel, "had a pew in one of the French chapels, which had been established when the Protestant refugees first emigrated into England, and he required us to attend alternately there and at the parish church [this was about the year 1730]. It was a kind of homage which he paid to the faith of his ancestors, and it was a means of rendering the French language familiar to us ; but nothing was ever worse calculated to inspire the mind of a child with respect for religion than such a kind of religious worship. Most of the descendants of the refugees were born and

bred in England, and desired nothing less than to
preserve the memory of their origin; and the chapels
were therefore ill-attended. A large uncouth room,
the avenues to which were crowded courts and dirty
alleys, and which, when you entered it, presented to
the view only irregular unpainted pews and dusty un-
plastered walls; a congregation consisting principally
of some strange-looking old women, scattered here
and there, two or three in a pew; and a clergyman
reading the service and preaching in a monotonous
tone of voice, and in a language not familiar to me,
was not likely either to impress my mind with much
religious awe, or to attract my attention to the doctrines which were delivered.   In truth, I did not once
attempt to attend to them; my mind was wandering
to other subjects, and disporting itself in much gayer
scenes than those before me, and little of religion was
mixed in my reveries." [1]

Very few of the refugees returned to France. They
long continued to sigh after the land of their fathers,
hoping that the religious persecutions abroad would
abate, so that they might return to live and die there.
But the persecutions did not abate. They flared up
again from time to time with increased fury, even
after religion had become almost prostrate throughout
France.   Protestantism, though proscribed, was not,
however, dead; and meetings of the Huguenots continued to be held in "the Desert,"—by night, in caves,
in the woods, among the hills, by the sea-shore, where
a body of faithful pastors ministered to them at the
hourly peril of their lives.   The "Church in the
Desert" was even regularly organised, had its stated
elders, deacons, and ministers, and appointed circuit
meetings.   Very rarely were their secrets betrayed;
yet they could not always escape the vigilance of the
Jesuits, who continued to track them with the aid of
the soldiery and police, and succeeded in sending fresh

[1] *Life of Sir Samuel Romilly*, i., 15.

victims to the galleys so long as they retained power in France.

Down even to the middle of last century the persecution of the Protestants continued unabated. Thus, at Grenoble, in the years 1745 and 1746, more than three hundred persons were condemned to death, the galleys, or perpetual imprisonment, because of their religion. Twenty-nine nobles were condemned to be deprived of their nobility; fourteen persons were banished; four were condemned to be flogged by the common hangman; six women were sentenced to have their heads shaved by the same functionary, and to be imprisoned, some for different periods, others for life; two men were condemned to be placed in the pillory; thirty-four were sent to the galleys for from three to five years, six for ten years, and a hundred and sixteen, amongst whom were forty-six gentlemen and two chevaliers of the order of Saint Louis, were sent to the galleys for life; and four were sentenced to death.[1] The only crime of which these persons had been guilty was, that they had been detected attending Protestant worship contrary to law.

The peace of Aix-la-Chapelle, in 1750, which gave a brief repose to Europe, brought no peace to the Huguenots. There was even an increase in their persecutions for a time; for a large body of soldiery had been thereby set at liberty, who were employed to hunt down the Protestants at their meetings in "the Desert." Between the years 1750 and 1762, fifty-eight persons were condemned to the galleys, many of them for life. In the latter year more than six hundred fugitives fled across the frontier into Switzerland, and passed down the Rhine, through Holland and England, into Ireland, where they settled. It is a somewhat remarkable circumstance, that, according to M. Coquerel, one of the last women imprisoned for her religion was condemned by an Irish Roman Catholic,

---

[1] ANTOINE COURT—*Mémoires Historiques*, pp. 94 *et seq*

then in the service of France:—"Marguerite Robert, wife of Joseph Vincent, of Valeirarques, in the diocese of Uzès, was arrested in her house, because of having been married by a Protestant pastor; and condemned in 1759, by *Monseigneur de Thomond . . . ce Lord Irlandois.*"[1]

The punishment of the galleys was also drawing to an end. The mutterings of the coming revolution were already beginning to be heard. The long uncontrolled rule of the Jesuits had paved the way for Voltaire and Rousseau, whose influence was about to penetrate French society. In 1764, the Jesuits were suppressed by Parliament, and the persecutions in a great measure ceased. In 1769, Alexander Chambon, of Praules in the Viverais, the last galley-slave for the faith, was discharged from the convict-prison at Toulon, through the intervention of the Prince of Beauvau. Chambon was then eighty years old, and had passed twenty-seven years at the galleys, to which he had been condemned for attending a religious meeting.

The last apprehension of a Protestant minister was that of M. Broca, of La Brie, as late as the year 1773; but the spirit of persecution had so much abated that he was only warned and required to change his residence. It began to be felt that, whilst materialism and atheism were being openly taught even by priests and dignitaries of the French Church—by the Abbé de Prades and others—the persecution of the Protestants could no longer be consistently enforced; and they accordingly thenceforwards enjoyed a degree of liberty in the exercise of their worship, such as they had not experienced since the death of Mazarin.

But this liberty came too late to be of any use to the exiled Huguenots and their descendants settled in England, who had long since given up all hope of returning to the land of their fathers. The revolutionary period shortly followed, after which came the wars of

---

[1] CHARLES COQUEREL—*Histoire des Eglises du Desert*, ii., p. 428.

the republic, and the revival of the old feud between France and England. Many of the descendants of the exiles, no longer desiring to remember their origin, adopted English names, and ceased to be French. Since that time the fusion of the exiles with the English people has become complete, even in Spitalfields. There are whole quarters of streets there, in which the glazed garrets indicate the dwellings of the French silk weavers. There are still some of their old mulberry-trees to be seen in the gardens near Spital Square. Many pure French names may still be observed over the shop-doors in that quarter of London; and several descendants of the French manufacturers still continue to carry on the business of silk-weaving. Even the *pot-au-feu* is still known in Spitalfields, though the poor people who use it know not of its origin. And although there are many descendants of the French operatives still resident in the east of London, probably by far the largest proportion of them have long since migrated to the more prosperous manufacturing districts of the north.

Throughout the country there was the same effacement of the traces of foreign origin among the descendants of the exiles. Everywhere they gradually ceased to be French.[1] The foreign manners, customs, and language, probably held out the longest at Portarlington, in Ireland, where the old French of Louis Quartorze long continued to be spoken in society. The old French service was read in the Huguenot church down to the year 1817, when it was finally supplanted by the English.

Thus, the refugees of all classes at length ceased to exist as a distinctive body among the people who had given them refuge. They were eventually absorbed into, and became an integral part of the British nation.

---

[1] The French mercantile houses in England and Ireland, who did business in London, long continued to have their special London bankers, amongst whom may be mentioned those of Bosanquet, Puget, etc. The house of Puget and Co. in St. Paul's Churchyard, recently wound up, kept all their books in French down to the beginning of the present century.

CHAPTER XIX.

CONCLUSION.—THE FRENCH REVOLUTION.

WHILE such were the results of the settlement of the Protestant refugees in England, let us briefly glance at the effect of their banishment upon the countries which drove them forth.

The persecutions in Flanders and France succeeded, after a sort. Philip II. crushed Protestantism in Flanders, as had been done in Spain, to the temporary ruin of the one country and the debasement of the other. Flanders eventually became lost to the Spanish crown, though it has since entered upon a new and prosperous career under the constitutional government of Belgium; but Spain sank until she reached the very lowest rank among the nations of Europe. The Inquisition flourished, but the life of the nation decayed. Spain lost her commerce, her colonies, her credit, her intellect, her character. She became a country of émeutes, revolutions, pronunciamentos, repudiations, and intrigues. We have only to look at Spain now. If it be true that in the long run the collective character of a nation is fairly represented by its government and its rulers, the character of Spain must have fallen very low indeed.[1]

---

[1] Will Spain establish constitutional government, and thus vindicate her recent revolution? It is doubtful. Why? Let Castelar, her greatest orator, supply the answer. "It is said," he observed in a recent speech, "that our people are not instructed; and it is true. Yet, for fifteen centuries the Catholic Church has had the instructing of them. There is not a single

And how fared it with France after the banishment of her Huguenots? So far as regarded the suppression of Protestantism, Louis XIV. may also be said to have succeeded. For more than a century, that form of religion visibly ceased to exist in France. The Protestants had neither rights nor privileges, nor any vestige of liberty. They were placed entirely beyond the pale of the law. Such of them as would not be dragooned into conformity to the Roman Catholic religion, were cast into prison or sent to the galleys. If the Protestants were not stamped wholly out of existence, they were at least stamped out of sight; and if they continued to worship, it was in secret only—in caves, among the hills, or in "the Desert." Indeed, no measure of suppression could have been more complete. But see with what results.

One thing especially strikes the intelligent reader of French history subsequent to the Act of Revocation,—and that is, the almost total disappearance of great Frenchmen. After that date, we become conscious of a dull, dead level of subserviency and conformity to the despotic will of the King. Louis trampled under foot individuality, strength, and genius; there remained only mediocrity, feebleness, and flunkeyism. This feature of the time has been noted by writers so various as De Felice, Merivale, Michelet, and Buckle—the last of whom goes so far as to say that Louis XIV. " survived the entire intellect of the French nation."

progressive principle but has been cursed by the Catholic Church. Not a constitution has been born, not a single progress made, not a solitary reform effected, which has not been under the terrible anathema of the Church. We are a great charnel - house, which extends from the Pyrenees to the sea of Cadiz, and we have been sacrificed on the altar of Catholicism. Our religious intolerance has given rise to that apathy which, in spite of our character, is felt respecting us throughout Europe. Oh, there is nothing more abominable than that Spanish empire which extends itself like a winding-sheet all over the planet!" Though the government of Spain may for a time be changed, while the power of the priests remains as it is, there is comparatively little hope for Spain.

The Protestant universities of Saumur, Montauban, Nismes, and Sedan were suppressed, and their professors departed into other lands. All Protestant schools were closed, and the whole educational organization of the nation was placed in the hands of the Jesuits. War was declared against Books forbidden by the Church of Rome. Domiciliary visits were paid by the district commanders to every person suspected of possessing them; and all devotional books of sermons and hymns, as well as Bibles and Testaments, that could be found, were ruthlessly burnt.

There was an end for a time of political and religious liberty in France. Freedom of thought and freedom of worship were alike crushed; and the new epoch began,—of mental stagnation, political depravity, religious hypocrisy, and moral decay. With the great men of the first half of Louis XIV.'s reign, the intellectual greatness of France disappeared for nearly a century. The Act of Revocation of 1685 cut the history of his reign in two: everything before, nothing after. There was no great statesman after Colbert. At his death in 1683, the policy which he had so laboriously initiated was summarily overthrown. The military and naval genius of France seemed alike paralysed. The great victories of Condé and Turenne on land, and of Duquesne at sea, preceded the Revocation. After that, Louis' army was employed for years in hunting and dragonnading the Huguenots, which completely demoralised them; so that his next campaign, that of 1688, began in disaster and ended in disgrace.

The same barrenness fell upon literature. Molière, the greatest of French comedians, died of melancholy in 1674. Racine, the greatest of French poets and dramatists, died in 1697; but his genius may be said to have culminated with the production of *Phædre* in 1676. Corneille died in 1684, but his last, though not his greatest work, *Surena*, was produced in 1676. La Fontaine published his last fables in 1679.

With Pascal, a man as remarkable for his piety as

for his genius, expired, in 1662, the last free utterance of the Roman Catholic Church in France. He died protesting to the last against the immorality and despotism of the principles of the Jesuits. It is true, after the Revocation, there remained, of the great French clergy, Bossuet, Bourdaloue, and Fénélon. They were, however, the products of the first half of Louis' reign, and they were the last of their race. For we shall find that the effect of the King's policy was to strike with paralysis the very Church which he sought exclusively to establish and maintain.

After this period, we seem to tread a dreary waste in French history. True loyalty became extinguished, and even patriotism seems to have expired. Literature, science, and the arts almost died out, and there remained a silence almost as of the grave, broken only by the noise of the revelries at court, amidst which there rose up from time to time the ominous wailings of the gaunt and famishing multitude.

The policy of Louis XIV. had succeeded, and France was at length "converted"! Protestantism had been crushed, and the Jesuits were triumphant. Their power over the bodies and souls of the people was as absolute as law could make it. The whole education of the country was placed in their hands; and what the character of the next generation was to be, depended in a great measure upon them. Not only the churches and the schools, but even the national prisons, were controlled by them. They were the confessors of the bastiles, of which there were twenty in France, where persons could be incarcerated for life on the authority merely of *lettres de cachet*, which were given away or sold. Besides the bastiles and the galleys,[1]

---

[1] In the reign of Louis XV., "The Well-Beloved," the galleys still contained many Protestants, besides persons who had been detected aiding Protestants to escape. They were regarded as veritable slaves, and were occasionally sold ; the price of a galley-slave in The Well-Beloved's reign being about £120. Voltaire was presented with a galley-slave by M. de Choiseul.

over which the Jesuits presided, there were also the
state prisons, of which Paris alone contained about
thirty, besides convents,—where persons might be
immured without any sentence. " Surely never," says
Michelet, " had man's dearest treasure, liberty, been
more lavishly squandered."

The Church in France had grown immensely rich
by the property of the Protestants which was transferred to it, as well as by royal grants and private
benefactions. So far as regards money, it had in its
hands the means and the power of doing all that it
could, to mould the mind and conscience of the French
nation. The clergy held in their hands one-fifth ot the
whole landed property of the country, estimated to be
worth about £160,000,000; and attached to these lands
were the serfs whom they continued to hold until the
Revolution.

And now, let us see what was the outcome of the
action of this Church, so rich and so powerful,—after
enjoying a century of undisputed authority in France.
All other faiths had been compelled to make way for
it. Protestantism had been put down with a strong
hand. Free thought of all kinds had shrunk for a
time out of sight.

What was the result of this exclusive action on
the mind and conscience of the French people ? The
result was utter emptiness : to use the words of
Carlyle, " emptiness of pocket, of stomach, of head, and
of heart." The church which had claimed and obtained the sole control of the religious education of
France, saw itself assailed by its own offspring,—so
desperate, ignorant, and ferocious, that in some places,
they even seized the priests and indecently scourged
them in front of their own altars.

The nation that would not have the Bayles, and
Claudes, and Saurins of a century before, now cast
themselves at the feet of the Voltaires, Rousseaus, and
Diderots. Though France would not have the God of
the Huguenot's Bible, she now accepted the Evangel of

Jean Jacques! A poor bedizened creature, clad in tawdry, was led through the streets of Paris in the character of the Goddess of Reason!

Even the Roman Catholic clergy themselves had, to a large extent, ceased to believe in the truth of their doctrines. They had become utterly corrupted and demoralised. Their monasteries were the abodes of idleness and self-indulgence. Their pulpits were mute: their books were empty. The doctors of the Sorbonne still mumbled their accustomed jargon, but it was now powerless. Instead of the great churchmen of the past—Bossuet, Bourdaloue, and Fénélon—there were such blind leaders of the blind as the Cardinal de Rohan,—the profligate confederate of Madame la Motte in the affair of the diamond necklace; the Abbé Sieyes,—the constitution-monger; the Abbé Raynal,—the open assailant of Christianity in every form; and Father Lomenie,—the avowed atheist.[1]

The corrupt, self-condemned institution, became a target for the wit of Voltaire and the encyclopædic philosophy of Diderot. It was assailed by the clubs of Marat, Danton, and Robespierre. Then the unfed, untaught, victims of centuries of oppression and misguidance rose up as one man, and cried, "Away with it"—*Ecrasez l'Infame.* The churches were attacked

---

[1] At the Revolution, many of the priests openly abjured Christianity, and were applauded accordingly. The Bishop of Perigaux presented the woman whom he had married to the Convention, saying, "I have taken her from amongst the sans-culottes." His speech was hailed with immense applause. Gobel, Archbishop of Paris, presented himself at the bar of the Convention, with his vicars and many of his curates, and desired to lay at the feet of the Assembly their sacerdotal garments. "Citizens," said the President in reply, "you are worthy of the Republic, because you have sacrificed at the altar of your country these Gothic baubles." Gobel and the priests donned the *bonnet rouge* in token of fraternisation with the "Friends of Men." Numbers of priests came daily and gave up to the Convention their letters of priesthood. Puaux says, "Those of their predecessors who distinguished themselves in the crusades against the Huguenots, had slipped their foot in blood; but these fell lower—their foot slipped in mud."

and gutted, as those of the Huguenots had been a century before. The church-bells were cast into cannon;
the church-plate coined into money; and at length
Christianity itself was abolished by the Convention,
which declared the Supreme People to be the only
Supreme God!

The Roman Catholic clergy, who had so long persecuted the Huguenots, were now persecuted in turn by
their own flocks. Many of them were guillotined;
others, chained together as the Huguenots had formerly
been, were sent prisoners to Rochelle and the Isle of
Aix. As a body of them passed through Limoges, on
their way to the galleys, they encountered a procession
of asses clothed in priests' dresses, a mitred sow marching at their head. Some 400 priests lay riding in Aix
roads, where the Huguenot galley-slaves had been before them—"ragged, sordid, hungry, wasted to shadows,
eating their unclean rations on deck, circularly, in parties of a dozen, with finger and thumb; beating their
scandalous clothes between two stones; choked in horrible miasmata, under close hatches, seventy of them
in a berth through the night, so that the aged priest is
found lying dead in the morning in an attitude of
prayer."[1]

Such was the outcome of the Act of Revocation of
Louis the Great—Sans-culottism and the Reign of
Terror! There was no longer the massacre and banishment of Huguenots, but there was the guillotining
and banishment of the successors of the priests whom
Louis had set up. There was one other point in
which 1793 resembled 1685. The fugitive priests fled
in precisely the same direction in which the Huguenot
pastors had done; and again the persecuted for religion's sake made for the old free land of England, to
join the descendants of the Huguenots, driven out of
France for altogether different reasons a century
before.

---

[1] CARLYLE—*French Revolution*, ii. 338.

But the Roman Catholic priests did not fly alone. They were accompanied by the nobles, the descendants of those who had superintended the dragonnades. Never, since the flight of Huguenots which followed the Revocation of the Edict of Nantes, had there been such an emigration of Frenchmen from France. But there was this difference between the emigrations of 1685 and 1793—that whereas in the former period the people who emigrated consisted of the industrious classes, in the latter period they consisted for the most part of the idle classes. The men who now fled were the nobles and priests, who had so misguided and mis-taught the people entrusted to their charge, that in nearly all parts of France they rose up in rebellion against them.

The great body of the people had become reduced to absolute destitution. They had no possession whatever but their misery. They were literally dying of hunger. The Bishop of Chartres told Louis XV. that in his diocese the men browsed like sheep. For want of food, they filled their stomachs with grass. The dragoons, who had before been employed to hunt down the Huguenots because of their attending religious meetings, were now employed on a different duty. They were stationed in the market-places where meal was exposed for sale, to keep back the famishing people.

In Paris alone, there were 200,000 beggars prowling about, with sallow faces, lank hair, and hung in rags. In 1789, crowds of them were seen hovering about the Palais Royal—spectral-looking men and starving women, delirious from fasting. Some were said not to have eaten for three whole days. The women wandered about like hungry lionesses; for they had children. One Foulon, a member of the King's council, on being told of the famine endured by the people, said—" Wait till I am minister : I will make them eat hay ; my horses eat it." The words were bitterly avenged. The hungry mob seized Foulon, hanged him *à la lanterne,* and carried his head about the streets, his mouth filled with hay.

From the provinces, news came that the starving Helots were everywhere rising, burning down the châteaus of the nobles, tearing up their title-deeds, and destroying their crops. On these occasions, the church-bells were rung by way of tocsin, and the population of the parish turned out to the work of destruction. Seventy-two châteaus were wrecked and burnt in the Maconnais and Beaujolais alone; and the conflagration spread throughout Dauphiny, Alsace, and the Lyonnais,—the very quarters from which the Huguenots had been so ferociously driven out a century before.

There was scarcely a district in which the Huguenots had pursued their branches of industry,—now wholly suppressed,—in which the starving and infuriated peasantry were not working wild havoc, and taking revenge upon their lords. They had learned but too well the lessons of the sword, the dungeon, and the scaffold, which their rulers had taught them; and the Reign of Terror which ensued, was but the natural outcome of the massacre of Saint Bartholomew, the wars of the dragonnades, and the ineffable cruelties which followed the Act of Revocation. But the victims had now changed places. Now it was the nobles who were persecuted, burnt out, had their estates confiscated, and were compelled to fly for their lives.

The dragonnades of the Huguenots were repeated in the noyades of the Royalists; and again Nancy, Lyons, Rouen, Bordeaux, Montauban, and numerous other places witnessed a repetition of the cruelties of the preceding century. At Nantes, where the famous Edict of Toleration (afterwards revoked) was proclaimed, the guillotine was worked until the headsman sank exhausted; and to hasten matters, a general fusillade in the plain of St. Mauve followed, of men, women, and children. At Paris, the hideous Marat called for "eight hundred gibbets," in convenient rows, to hang the enemies of

the people.   He would be satisfied with nothing short
of " two hundred thousand aristocratic heads."

It is unnecessary to pursue the dreadful story
further.   Suffice it to say that the nobles, like the
priests, fled out of France to escape the fury of the
people, and they too made for England, where they
received the same asylum which had been given to
their clergy.   To prevent the flight of the noblesse, the
same measures were adopted by the Convention which
Louis XIV. had adopted to prevent the escape of
the Huguenots.   The frontiers were strictly guarded,
and all the roads patrolled which led out of France.
Severe laws were passed against emigration ; and the
estates of fugitive aristocrats were declared to be confiscated to the state.   Nevertheless, many succeeded in
making their escape into Switzerland, Germany, and
England.

It fared still worse with Louis XVI. and his beautiful
queen, Marie Antoinette.   They were the most illustrious victims of the barbarous policy of Louis XIV.
That monarch had sowed the wind, and they were
now reaping the whirlwind.   A mob of starving men
and women, the genuine offspring of the Great King,
burst in upon Louis and his consort at Versailles,
shouting " Bread ! bread !"   They were very different
from the plumed and garlanded courtiers accustomed
to worship in these gilded saloons.   They insisted on
the king and queen accompanying them to Paris,
virtually as their prisoners.   The royal family tried to
escape, as the Huguenots had done before them, across
the frontier into Germany.   But in vain !   The king's
own highway was closed against him ; and the fugitives were led back to Paris and the guillotine.

The last act of the unfortunate Louis was his attempt
to address a few words to his subjects ; when the drums
were ordered to be beaten, and his voice was drowned
by the noise.   It was remembered that the last occasion on which a like scene had occurred in France, was
that of the execution of the young Huguenot pastor

23

Fulcran Rey, at Beaucaire. When he opened his mouth publicly to confess his faith, the drummers posted round the scaffold were ordered to beat, and his dying speech remained unheard. The slaughter of the martyred preacher was thus terribly avenged.

We think we are justified in saying, that but for the persecution and expulsion of the Huguenots at the Revocation of the Edict of Nantes in 1685, the Revolution of 1789 most probably never would have occurred. The Protestants supplied that enterprising and industrious middle class which gives stability to every state. They provided remunerative employment for the population, while at the same time they enriched the kingdom by their enterprise and industry. Moreover, they furnished that virtuous and religious element in society without which a nation is but as so much chaff that is driven before the wind. When they were suppressed or banished, there was an end of their industrial undertakings. The further growth of a prosperous middle class was prevented ; and the misgovernment of the ruling class being unchecked, the great body of the working order were left to idleness, nakedness, and famine. Faith in God and in good died out ; religion, as represented by the degenerate priesthood, fell into contempt ; and the reign of materialism and atheism began. Frightful distress at length culminated in revolution and anarchy ; and there being no element of stability in the state,—no class possessing moral weight to stand between the infuriated people at the one end of the social scale, and the king and nobles at the other,—the imposture erected by the Great Louis was assailed on all sides, and king, church, and nobility were at once swept away.

As regards the emigration of the Huguenots in 1685, and of the nobles and clergy in 1789, it must be acknowledged that the former was by much the most calamitous to France. "Was the one emigration greater than the other ?" says Michelet. "I do not know. That of 1685 was probably from three to four hundred thousand persons. However this may be, there was this great difference between them : France, at the emigration of '89, lost its idlers; at the other, its workers. The terror of '89 struck the individual, and each feared for his life. The terror of the dragonnades struck at heart and conscience ; then men feared for their all."

The one emigration consisted for the most part of nobles and clergy, who left no traces of their settlement in the countries which gave them asylum ; the other emigration comprised all the constituent elements of a people—skilled workmen in all branches, manufacturers, merchants, and professional men ; and wherever they settled they founded numerous useful establishments which were a source of prosperity and wealth.

Assuredly England has no reason to regret the asylum which she has in all times so freely granted to fugitives flying from religious persecution abroad. Least of all has she reason to regret the settlement within her borders of so large a number of industrious, intelligent, and high-minded Frenchmen, who have made this country their home since the Revocation of the Edict of Nantes, and thereby not only stimulated, but in a measure created, British industry ; while, at the same time they have influenced, in a remarkable degree, our political as well as our religious history.

DISTINGUISHED HUGUENOT REFUGEES

AND THEIR

DESCENDANTS.

DISTINGUISHED HUGUENOT REFUGEES

AND

THEIR DESCENDANTS.

ABBADIE, JAMES, D.D. : a native of Nay, in Bearn, where he was born in 1654. An able preacher and writer ; first settled in Berlin, which he left to accompany the Duke of Schomberg into England. He was for some time minister of the Church of the Savoy, London, and afterwards became Dean of Killaloe, in Ireland. He died in London, 1727. For notice see p. 252.

A'LASCO : see p. 116.

ALLIX, PETER : an able preacher and controversialist. Born at Alençon, 1641 ; died in London, 1717. He was one of the ministers of the great church at Charenton, near Paris. At the Revocation he took refuge in England, where he was appointed canon and treasurer to the Cathedral of Salisbury. For notice see p. 253.

AMAND, or AMYAND : a Huguenot refugee of this name settled in London in the beginning of last century. His son Claude was principal surgeon to George II. ; and the two sons of the latter were Claudius, Under Secretary of State, and George (created a baronet in 1764), who sat in Parliament for Barnstaple. The second baronet assumed the name of Cornewall. His daughter married Sir Gilbert Frankland Lewis, Bart., and was the mother of the late Sir Cornewall Lewis, Bart., M.P. William Henry Haggard of Bradesham, Norfolk, married Miss Frances Amyand, who belonged to a younger branch of the family, in right of whom the present Mr. Haggard now possesses Amyand House, Twickenham.

ANDRÉ: the name of a French refugee family settled in Southampton, to whom the celebrated and unfortunate Major André belonged,—though the latter was brought up at Lichfield.

ARNAUD : a Huguenot family of noble descent. In Monstrelet's continuation of Froissart's *Chronicles*, translated by Thomas Jones, an ancestor of the Arnauds is described in a note (i. 348) as " Guillem-Arnaud, baron of Barbazan in Bigorre, first Chamberlain to Charles VII., afterwards Governor of Champagne and the Lionnais," etc. The king gave him the title of *Chevalier sans reproche,* and permitted him to take the fleur-de-lys for his arms. He was killed at Belleville in 1432, and buried with the highest honours." Shakespeare, in his play of Henry V., alludes to him as a "devil," *i.e.* to the English army to which he was opposed. A descendant of his was the Marquis de Pompone (Simon Arnaud), Secretary of State for Foreign Affairs to Louis XIV. In the sixteenth century a branch of the family became Huguenot, and emigrated to England. The ancestor of the English Arnauds was, when quite a child, smuggled out of France in a hamper, and brought across the English Channel in an open boat. Elias Arnaud, his son, subsequently became a thriving merchant at Portsmouth, and was appointed deputy - lieutenant for the county of Hants. His son Elias Bruce Arnaud was also a deputy - lieutenant, and a very active magistrate. In 1804, when England was threatened with invasion by the French, he raised a regiment of infantry at Portsmouth, and commanded it as colonel. His second son, John, was a lieutenant in the 11th Regiment at Toulouse, where (according to Sir Wm. Napier, in his *History of the Peninsular War,* vi. 169) two British regiments, the 11th and 91st, came up and turned the tide of battle, which, until then, had gone in favour of the French. He died a few years ago, a major - general, K.H. His eldest son Elias, for many years collector of customs at Liverpool, was the father of Henry Bruce Arnaud, now a member of the English bar. The present representative of the second or junior branch of the Arnauds, is John Macaulay Arnaud, related, through his maternal grandfather John Macaulay, formerly of Ardincaple in Dumbartonshire, to the late Lord Macaulay, and through the ancient family of the Oliphants of Gask in Perthshire, to several noblemen and persons of distinction, including the celebrated Lady Nairne. The Arnauds are also related to Sir George Bowyer, Sir Maziere Brady, ex-Lord Chancellor of Ireland, and the late Sir Lucius Curtis, admiral of the fleet.

ARNAULD, JOHN: James Fontaine, in his Autobiography, frequently makes mention of his cousin, John Arnauld, settled in London.

AUBERTIN: This family originally belonged to Metz, in Lorraine. The original emigrant fled from France at the Revocation, leading his grandchild, a little boy, by the hand. They arrived at Neuchâtel, in Switzerland; other members of the family joined them; and they settled there for a time. But the great-grandson of the original emigrant, not finding a small place like Neuchâtel to his taste, left it about a century ago, and naturalized himself in England. His son, the late Rev. Peter Auberton, vicar of Chepstead, Surrey, died in 1861, in his 86th year, leaving a numerous family. The Rev. Edmund Auberton, of Chalon-sur-Marne, a famous Protestant divine, author of the famous work on the Eucharist, which so much disturbed Rome at the time of its publication, was a collateral ancestor of the same family.

AUFRERE, GEORGE, M.P. : descended from a Huguenot refugee ; sat for Stamford in Parliament from 1761 to 1768.

AURIOL, PETER : a refugee from Lower Languedoc, who rose to eminence as a London merchant. The Archbishop of York, the Hon. and Most Rev. R. N. Drummond, married his daughter and heiress, Henrietta, and afterwards succeeded to the peerage of Strathallan. The refugee's daughter thus became Countess of Strathallan. The present head of the family is the Earl of Kinnoul, who continues to bear the name of Auriol. The Rev. Edward Auriol is rector of St. Dunstan's-in-the-West, London.

BACQUENCOURT : See *Des Vœux.*

BARBON : A French Huguenot family of this name lived at Wandsworth. The name was changed to Barbone, or Barebone. In Mount Nod, the French burying-ground at Wandsworth, is a tombstone bearing this inscription: *"Sarai, daughter of Praise Barbone, was buried 13th April, 1635."* Praise-God Barebone, the leather-seller in Fetter Lane, belonged to this family.

BARON, PETER : Professor in the University of Cambridge about 1575. He was originally from Etampes, and fled to England after the massacre of

Saint Bartholomew. He died in London, leaving behind him an only son, Samuel, who practised medicine at Lyme-Regis in Norfolk.

BARRÉ: a Protestant family of Pont-Gibau, near Rochelle, several members of which settled in Ireland. Peter Barré married Miss Raboteau, also a refugee. He was an alderman of Dublin, and carried on a large business as a linendraper. His son Isaac, educated at Trinity College, Dublin, entered the army, in which he rose to high rank. He was adjutant-general of the British forces under Wolfe at Quebec. He afterwards entered Parliament, where he distinguished himself by his eloquence and his opposition to the American Stamp Act. In 1776 Colonel Barré was made Vice-Treasurer of Ireland and Privy Councillor. He subsequently held the offices of Treasurer of the Navy and Paymaster of the Forces, in both of which he displayed eminent integrity and ability. He died in 1802. See also pp. 173, 331.

BASNAGE : Few families in France have produced so many persons of literary distinction and moral worth, as the Basnages. Nicholas Basnage was driven by the persecutions which followed the massacre of St. Bartholomew, to take refuge in England, where he for some time officiated as pastor of the French Walloon Church at Norwich. He afterwards returned to France. His son Benjamin succeeded his father as minister of Charenton, and was head of the Protestant assembly held at Rochelle, in 1622. He was sent over to England on a mission, to solicit aid from James I. for the Protestants. He was the author of several able works, and during his lifetime was regarded as one of the chief luminaries of the Protestant Church. Antoine, son of Benjamin, was minister of Bayeux, and was long imprisoned because of his faith, in the prison of Havre de Grace. After the Revocation, he escaped to Zutphen, in Holland, where he was minister of a French congregation, and died in 1681. Samuel Basnage, son of Antoine, was a minister, like his father, and, like him, escaped to Zutphen, succeeding him in his charge. He was the author of numerous works, greatly prized in their time. Henri Basnage was one of the most able and eloquent advocates in the Parliament of Rouen. His learning was great, and his integrity unsullied. But his eldest son, Jacques Basnage, was the most eminent member of the family. He was a man of immense learning. At the early age of 23, he was appointed minister of the great Protestant church at Grand Queville, near Rouen, capable of accommodating 10,500 persons. When that church was demolished, and the persecution waxed very hot, he took refuge at the Hague. While there he was often employed in delicate state affairs, which he skilfully conducted ; and Voltaire said of him, that he was better fitted to be a minister of state than

of a parish. He published eleven learned historical works in his lifetime, some of which passed through many editions. His younger brother, Henri, was also an esteemed author. Like Jacques, he took refuge in Holland, and died there.

BATZ: the name of a Huguenot family, the head of which was seigneur of Monan, near Nerac, in Guyenne. Three of the sons of Joseph de Batz, seigneur of Guay, escaped from France into Holland, and entered the service of the Prince of Orange, whom they accompanied in his expedition to England. Two of them, captains of infantry, were killed at the Boyne.

BAUDOUIN: This family is descended from Jacques Baudouin, whose tombstone, in Mount Nod burying-ground at Wandsworth, relates all that we know of him : "James Baudouin, Esq., born at Nismes, in France ; but in the year 1685, fled from France to avoid Tyranny and Persecution, and enjoyed a Protestant Liberty of Conscience, which he sought, and happily found, and was gratefully sensible of, in the Communion of the Church of England. He constantly answered this pious Resolution in his life, and went to enjoy the blessed Fruits of it, by his death on the 2nd day of Feb., 1738-9, aged 91."

BAYLEY, Sir JOHN, Bart. : the late distinguished Judge of the Court of Queen's Bench, (1808-30), afterwards a Baron of the Court of Exchequer and Privy Councillor, was fourth in descent from Philippe de Bailleul, a French Protestant refugee, who settled in the neighbourhood of Thorney Abbey about the year 1656. It is believed that the family originally came from the neighbourhood of Lille, where there are still many of the same name ; and that they joined the Walloon colony, which in the first place settled at Sandtoft in Yorkshire, but migrated from thence to Thorney Abbey during the wars of the Commonwealth. The above Philippe de Bailleul, or his son Daniel, purchased a small estate at Willow Hall, near Peterborough, which still belongs to the family. These two married daughters of Protestant refugees ; but Daniel's son, Isaac Bayley, married Orme Bigland, a member of the ancient family of Bigland of Bigland ; and their second son, John Bayley, married Sarah Kennet, granddaughter and heir of White Kennet, Bishop of Peterborough, by whom he became father of Sir John Bayley, and grandfather of the late Judge Bayley, of the Westminster County Court. The original name of De Bailleul has undergone many transmutations,—passing through Balieu, Balieul, Bayly, Bailly, and ultimately arriving at Bayley.

BEAUFORT, DANIEL CORNELIS DE : a controversial writer. He was pastor of the church of New Patente in 1728 ; of the Artillery in 1728 ; and of the Savoy, and probably Spring Gardens, in 1741. He afterwards went to Ireland, where he held the living of Navan, and was appointed Dean of Tuam. Admiral Sir Francis Beaufort, Hydrographer Royal, belonged to the family, as also does Lady Strangford and the rector of Lymm, Cheshire.

BEAUVOIR, DE : the name of one of the most ancient families in Languedoc, several branches of which were Protestant. Francis, eldest son of Scipio du Roure, took refuge in England at the Revocation, and obtained a company in a cavalry regiment. His two sons also followed the career of arms with distinction. Alexander, the eldest, was colonel of the 4th Foot, Governor of Plymouth, Lieutenant-General, Commander-in-Chief in Scotland, etc. He especially distinguished himself at the battle of Dettingen. He went into France for the benefit of his health, and died at Baréges, where he had gone for the benefit of the waters. The French Government having refused his body Christian burial, in consequence of his being the son of a Protestant refugee, the body was embalmed and sent to England to be buried. The second son, Scipio, was also the colonel of an English Infantry regiment, and was killed at the battle of Fontenoy.—Another family of the same name is sprung from Richard de Beauvoir, Esq., of the island of Guernsey, who purchased the manor of Balmes, in the parish of Hackney, and thus gave its name to De Beauvoir Town.

BELCASTEL DE MONTVAILLANT, PIERRE : a refugee officer

from Languedoc, who entered the service of William of Orange. After the death of La Caillemotte at the Boyne, he was made colonel of the regiment. Belcastel took a prominent part in the Irish campaigns of 1690-91. He was eventually raised to the rank of major-general in the Dutch army. He was killed at the battle of Villa Viciosa, Spain, in 1710.

BENEZET, ANTOINE : one of the earliest and most zealous advocates of negro emancipation. He was born in London in 1713, of an honest refugee couple from Saint-Quentin, and bred to the trade of a cooper. He accompanied his parents to America, and settled at Philadelphia. There he became a Quaker, and devoted himself with great zeal to the question of emancipation of the blacks, —for whose children he established and supported schools in Philadelphia. He died there in 1784.

BENOIT, N. : a refugee silk-weaver settled in Spitalfields. He was the author of several controversial works, more particularly relating to baptism ; Benoit being of the Baptist persuasion.

BERANGER : a branch of the Huguenot family of this name settled in Ireland and another in Holland, but both dwindled in numbers until, in 1750, they became reduced to two—one the only surviving son of the Dutch refugee, and the other the only surviving daughter of the Irish refugee. The Dutchman, Gabriel Beranger, came over to Dublin and married his Irish cousin. She died without issue, and the widower next married a Mademoiselle Mestayer, also of French descent.—Beranger was a very clever, observant man. He was employed by an antiquarian society in Dublin, under Burton, Conyngham, and Vallancy, to travel through Ireland in company with the celebrated Italian architect, Signor Bigari, and describe and draw the various antiquities of Ireland. A considerable collection of his drawings and MSS. recently came into the possession of the late Sir W. R. Wilde, who contributed an illustrative memoir of Beranger to the *Kilkenny Journal of Archæology.* He died in St. Stephen's Green, Dublin, in 1817, and was interred in the French burying-ground there.

BERTHEAU, Rev. CHARLES: refugee pastor in London : a native of Montpellier. He was expelled from Paris, where he was one of the ministers of the great Protestant church of Charenton, at the Revocation. He became minister of the Walloon church in Threadneedle Street, which office he filled for forty-four years. Several volumes of his sermons have been published.

BERNIÈRE, JEAN ANTOINE DE: a refugee officer who served under the Earl of Galway in Spain. He lost a hand at the battle of Almanza. His son was captain in the 30th Foot ; his grandson (Henry Abraham Crommelin de Bernière), was a major-general in the British army ; and his great-grandson, married to the sister of the late Archbishop of Canterbury, rose to the same rank.

BION, JEAN FRANÇOIS : a native of Dijon, Roman Catholic curate of Ursy, afterwards appointed chaplain to the galley *Superbe* at Toulon, which contained a large number of galley-slaves condemned for their faith. Touched by their sufferings, as well as by the patience and courage with which they bore them, Bion embraced Protestantism, exclaiming, "Their blood preaches to me!" He left France for Geneva in 1704, and afterwards took refuge in London, where he was appointed rector of a school, and officiated as minister to the French church at Chelsea. He subsequently proceeded to Holland, where he exercised the functions of chaplain to an English church. He was the author of several works, —the best known being his *Relation des Tourmens que l'on fait souffrir aux Protestans qui sont sur les Galères de France*, published at London in 1708.

BLANC, ANTHONY : pastor of the French church of La Nouvelle Patente in 1692. Theodore and Jean Blanc were two other French refugee pastors in London about the same time, the latter being pastor of L'Artillerie. The Blancs were from Saintonge and Poitou.

BLAQUIÉRE, DE : a noble family of Limousin, of whom John de Blaquiére, a zealous Huguenot, took refuge in England in 1685. He married Mary Elizabeth de Varennes, the daughter of a refugee, by whom he had issue. One of his sons became eminent as a London merchant; another settled at Lisburn, where his sister married John Crommelin, son of Louis. The fifth son, John, entered the army, and became lieutenant-colonel of the 17th Light Dragoons. He held various public offices : was Secretary of Legation at Paris; secretary to the Lord-Lieutenant of Ireland ; was made a baronet in 1784 ; and raised to the peerage in 1800 as Lord de Blaquiére of Ardkill in Ireland.

BLONDEL, MOSES : a learned refugee scholar in London about 1621, author of a work on the Apocryphal writings.

BLONDEL, JAMES AUGUSTUS : a distinguished refugee physician in London, as well as an able scholar. The author of several learned and scientific treatises. He died in 1734.

BLOSSET : a Nivernais Protestant family, the head of which was the Sieur de Fleury. Several Blossets fled into Holland and England at the Revocation. Colonel Blosset, of "Blosset's Foot," who settled in Ireland, was the owner of a good estate in the county of Dublin. Serjeant Blosset, afterwards Lord Chief-Justice of Bengal, belonged to the family. For his connection with Mr. Grote, see p. 322.

BOCHART, FRANÇOIS : Haag says that amongst the Protestant refugees in Scotland, Francis Bochart has been mentioned, who, in conjunction with Claude Paulin, established in 1730 the manufacture of cambric at Edinburgh.

BODT or BOTT, JOHN DE : a refugee French officer : appointed captain of artillery and engineers in the British service in 1690. He distinguished himself by the operations conducted by him at the siege of Namur—to which William III. mainly attributed the capture of the place. Bodt afterwards entered the service of the King of Prussia, who made him brigadier and chief engineer. He was also eminent as an architect, and designed some of the principal public buildings in Berlin.

BOESMER DE LA TOUCHE : pastor of the French congregation at Winchelsea in 1700-6. His son, of the same name, was a surgeon in London in 1764.

BOEVEY, ANDREW : a Protestant refugee from Courtray, in Flanders. He fled into England during the persecutions carried on in the reign of Philip II., and settled in London in 1572. He was a successful merchant ; and at his death, he left legacies to the Dutch congregations in London, Norwich, and Haarlem. His successors became landed proprietors and intermarried with the aristocracy ; Sir Thomas Hyde Crawley Boevey, Bart., Flaxley Abbey, being the present head of the family.

BOILEAU DE CASTELNAU : an ancient Languedoc family, many of whose members embraced Protestantism and remained faithful to it. Jacques Boileau, fifth Baron, counsellor of Nismes, born 1657, died in prison in France, after a confinement of ten years and six months, for his adherence to the Protestant religion. His son Charles took refuge in England, served in the English army as captain of infantry, and died at Dublin. His son Simeon, born at Southampton, was succeeded by Solomon Boileau, who had sons, from the eldest of whom, Simeon Peter, the present Major-General Boileau is descended ; Sir John Boileau, Bart., being descended from John Peter, the fifth son. See also p. 329.

BOILEAU : see *Bouherau.*

BOISBELAU DE LA CHAPELLE, usually known as Armand de la Chapelle. He left France at the Revocation. He was destined for the ministry from an early age. At eighteen he was sent into Ireland to preach to the French congregations, and after two years, at the age of twenty, he was appointed pastor of the French church at Wandsworth. He subsequently officiated as minister of the Artillery church, and of the French church at the Hague. He was a voluminous writer.

BONHOMME : a Protestant draper from Paris, who settled at Ipswich, and instructed the artizans there in the manufacture of sail-cloth, which shortly became a considerable branch of British industry.

BONNELL, THOMAS : a gentleman of good family near Ypres, in Flanders, who took refuge in England from the Duke of Alva's persecutions, and settled at Norwich, of which he became mayor. His son was Daniel Bonnell, merchant, of London, father of Samuel Bonnell, who served his apprenticeship with Sir William Courteen (a Flemish refugee), and established himself as a merchant at Leghorn. He returned to England, and at the Restoration was appointed accountant-general for Ireland. He died at Dublin, and was succeeded in the office by his son, a man eminent for his piety, and whose life has been fully written by Archdeacon Hamilton, of Armagh.

BOSANQUET, DAVID : a Huguenot refugee, naturalised in England in 1687. His grandson, Samuel, was a director of the Bank of England. Mary, the sister of the latter, was the celebrated wife of the Rev. Mr. Fletcher, vicar of Madeley. Other members occupied illustrious positions in society. One, William, founded the wellknown bank in London. Sir John B. Bosanquet, the celebrated judge, also belonged to the family, which is now represented by Samuel Richard Bosanquet, of Dingestow Court, Monmouth.

BOSQUET, ANDREW: a refugee from Languedoc, who escaped into England after suffering fourteen years' slavery in the French King's galleys. He was the originator of the Westminster French Charity School, founded in 1747, for the education of children of poor French refugees.

BOSTAQUET, DUMONT DE : for notice see pp. 202-28.

BOUFARD, see *Garric.*

BOUHERAU, ELIAS, M.D., D.D.: son of one of the Protestant pastors of La Rochelle, from which port he escaped at the Revocation, carrying with him the records of the Consistory, of which his father was president. He settled in Dublin, where he was appointed librarian to the Marsh Library (now known as St. Patrick's Library), and deposited the above-mentioned papers in a strong box. He afterwards officiated as secretary to the Earl of Galway. When the Earl left Ireland, Dr. Bouherau became pastor of one of the French congregations in Dublin ; but, having been officially ordained, he afterwards officiated as chantor of St. Patrick's Cathedral. One of his sons, John, entered the church ; another was "Townmajor of Dublin." The latter altered his name to Borough ; and from him the present Sir E. R. Borough, of Baseldon Park, Berkshire, is lineally descended. Within the last few years the original box, containing the records of the church of La Rochelle previous to the Revocation, brought over by Dr. Bouherau in 1685, was opened, and a paper found in it in the doctor's handwriting, directing that, in the event of the Protestant Consistory at La Rochelle ever becoming reconstituted and reclaiming the papers, they were to be given up. A communication was accordingly forwarded to the Consistory of La Rochelle, offering to restore the papers : and they were duly forwarded to Pastor Delmas, the president, who has since published, with their assistance, a history of the Protestant church of La Rochelle.

BOURDILLON, JACOB: an able an eloquent pastor of several French churches in London. For notice, see pp. 285-7.

BOURGEOIS, BURGESS : an ancient Protestant family of Picardy (seigneurs of Gamache and d'Oye, and of de la Fossé), a member of which, Valéry or Valérien de Bourgeois, came over to England with one of the first bodies of immigrants, and settled with the earliest congregation at Canterbury. Births, deaths, and marriages of members of the family appear in the registers of the Huguenot church there, from the year 1592 downwards. In that year Rolin Bourgeois " de Gamache en Picardie," son of the original refugee, married Marie Gambier ; and successive intermarriages took place with members of the De Moncy, Le Cornue, La Motte, and Fournier families, down to the middle of last century, when the Huguenot identity became almost unrecognisable, and Bourgeois was changed to Burgess. The tradition, however, continued to exist in the family, that they were of Huguenot extraction ; and since the publication of the first edition of this book, Lieutenant Burgess, late of the 46th Regiment, has, with the assistance of the Heralds' College of France and the Canterbury Registers, clearly traced the pedigree of his family back to the seigneurs of Gamache.

BOUVERIES, LAURENCE DES :

a refugee from Sainghen, near Lille, in 1568. He settled first at Sandwich, and afterwards at Canterbury, where he began the business of a silk weaver. Edward, the grandson of Laurence, established himself in London as a Levant merchant ; and from that time the family greatly prospered. William was made a baronet in 1711 ; and Jacob was created a peer, under the title of Viscount Folkestone, in 1747. His son Philip assumed the name of Pusey on his marriage in 1798. The Rev. Dr. Pusey, of Oxford, is one of the sons by this marriage. For further notice see p. 320.

BOYER, ABEL : a refugee from Castres, where he was born in 1664. He died, pen in hand, at Chelsea, in 1729. He was the author of the well-known *French and English Dictionary*, as well as of several historical works.

BREVIN, COSME : a Huguenot pastor, who took refuge in Guernsey, after the St. Bartholomew massacre. He was made minister of the island of Sark. His grandson, Daniel Brevin, D.D., was prebendary of Durham and Dean of Lincoln ; and the author of several important religious works.

BRIOT, NICOLAS : one of the first coin-engravers of his age, supposed to have been the inventor of the coining-press. He was a native of Lorraine, a gentleman born, and possessed of the genius of a true artist. He was Graver of the Mint to Louis XIII., king of France ; but being a Protestant, and thereby placed under serious disabilities, he fled from his native country and took refuge in England, where he introduced his coining-press, and was appointed chief engraver to the Mint by Charles I. in the year 1626. His first published work was a fine medal of the King, exhibited in Evelyn, with the artist's name, and the date 1628. In 1632 we find Briot engaged coining money upon the regular establishment, by means of his press, instead of by hammering, as was the previous practice. In 1633, he was sent down to Scotland to prepare and coin the coronation pieces of Charles I. On the death of Sir John Foulis, Master of the Mint in Scotland, Briot was appointed to the office in 1635, and superintended the coinage for several years. Sir John Falconer, brother of Sir Alexander Falconer, one of the Senators of the College of Justice (created Lord Halkerton in 1647), having married Esther Briot, daughter of Nicolas Briot, in 1637, was from that year conjoined with him in the office, which he held until the outbreak of the civil war. The coronation-medal of Charles I., executed by Briot, and struck at Edinburgh on the 18th June, 1633, was the first piece struck in Britain with a legend on the edge, and, it is supposed, was the only gold one ever coined in Scotland. Three only of these fine medals are known to exist, one of which is in the British Museum. Briot was recalled to England by the

King ; and, at the time of the rebellion, he took possession of the punches, roller instruments, and coining apparatus at the Tower, by order of his Majesty, and had them removed, trussed up in saddles, at the hazard of his life, for the purpose of continuing the coining operations in the cause of the King. The tradition in the family—which survives in the Falconers, his descendants —is, that he died of grief on the death of Charles I. In the Museum at Oxford are two small carvings on wood—representing Christ on the Cross, and the Nativity — with the cypher N.B. on each, which are understood to have been the work of this accomplished artist.

BRISSAC, B. DE : a refugee pastor from Châtellerault, who fled from France at the Revocation. We find one of his descendants, Captain George Brissac, a director of the French Hospital in London in 1773. Haag says that one of the female Brissacs became famous at Berlin for her sausages, and especially for her black puddings, which continue to be known there as " boudins français."

BROCAS : a noble family, holding numerous lordships in the south of France, mostly in the neighbourhood of Bordeaux. The Very Reverend Theophilus Brocas, D.D., was a scion of the family. He escaped from France at the Revocation, and, having taken holy orders, he was appointed by the Crown to the deanery of Killala and vicarage of St. Anne's, Dublin.

He was a highly distinguished divine, and for his valuable services in promoting the arts and manufactures of Ireland, he was presented with the freedom of the city of Dublin in a gold box, accompanied by a suitable address. He died in 1766, and was interred in St. Anne's churchyard, Dublin. He was succeeded in the deanery by his only son and heir, the Rev. John Brocas, D.D., rector of Monkstown, and chaplain of the military chapel at Rings-end. He died in 1806, and left issue, the Rev. Theophilus Brocas, rector of Strabane, in the diocese of Derry, and an only sister, Georgiana, who married, in 1804, Robert Lindesay, Esq., captain of the Louth Militia. The Rev. Theophilus Brocas dying without issue, this noble family has become extinct in the male line, but survives, through the female line, in the person of Walter Lindesay, Esq., of Glenview, County Wicklow, J.P., who is its present representative.

BROS : see *De Brosses.*

BRUNET : a numerous Protestant family in Saintonge. N. Brunet, a privateer of La Rochelle, was in 1662 condemned to suffer corporal punishment, and to pay a fine of 1000 livres, unless within a given time he produced before the magistrates thirty-six young Protestants whom he had carried over to America. Of course the refugee youths were never produced. At the Revocation the Brunets of Rochelle nearly all emigrated to London. We find frequent baptisms of children of the name recorded in the registers of the churches of Le Quarré and La Nouvelle Patente, as well as marriages at the same place, and at Wheeler Street Chapel and La Patente in Soho.

BUCER, MARTIN : a refugee from Alsace ; one of the early reformers, an eloquent preacher as well as a vigorous and learned writer. He accepted the invitation of Archbishop Cranmer to settle in England, where he assisted in revising the English liturgy, excluding what savoured of popery, but not going so far as Calvin. He was appointed professor of theology at Cambridge, where he was presented with a doctor's diploma. But the climate of England not agreeing with him, Bucer returned to Strasburg, where he died, 1551.

BUCHLEIN, otherwise called FAGIUS : a contemporary of Martin Bucer, and, like him, a refugee at Cambridge University, where he held the professorship of Hebrew. While in that office, which he held for only a few years, he fell ill of fever, of which he died, but not without a suspicion of having been poisoned.

BURGESS : see *Bourgeois.*

BUSSIÉRE, PAUL : a celebrated anatomist, F.R.S., and corresponding member of various scientific societies. He lived for a time in London, but eventually settled at Copenhagen, where he achieved a high reputation. We find one Paul Buissiére governor of the French Hospital in London in 1729, and Jean Buissiére in 1776.

CAILLEMOTTE, LA : younger son of the old Marquis de Ruvigny; he commanded a Huguenot regiment at the battle of the Boyne, where he was killed. See *Massue*, and notices, pp. 222, 225.

CAMBON : a refugee French officer, who commanded one of the Huguenot regiments raised in London in 1689. He fought at the Boyne and at Athlone, and died in 1693.

CAPPEL, LOUIS: characterized as " the father of sacred criticism." He was born at Saint Elier in 1585 ; at twenty he was selected by the Duke de Bouillon as tutor for his son. Four years later the church at Bordeaux furnished him with the means of visiting the principal academies of England, Holland, and Germany. He passed two years at Oxford, during which he principally occupied himself with the study of the Semitic languages. He subsequently occupied the chair of theology in the university of Saumur until his death, which occurred in 1658. Bishop Hall designated Louis Cappel " the grand oracle of the Hebraists." Louis' son James was appointed professor of Hebrew in the same university at the early age of nineteen. At the Revocation he took refuge in England, and became professor of Latin in the Nonconformist College, Hoxton Square, London. For notice see p. 257.

CARBONEL, JOHN : son of Thomas Carbonel, merchant of Caen ; John was one of the secretaries of Louis XIV. He fled to England at the Revocation. His brother William became an eminent merchant in London.

CARLE, PETER : a native of Valleraugue in the Cevennes, born 1666 ; died in London 1730. He fled from France at the Revocation, passing by Geneva through Switzerland into Holland, and finally into England. He entered the corps of engineers in the army of William, and fought at the Boyne. He afterwards accompanied the army through all its campaigns in the Low Countries. He rose to be fourth engineer in the British service, and retired upon a pension in 1693. He afterwards served under Lord Galway in Spain, after which the king of Portugal made him lieutenant-general and engineer-in-chief. In 1720 he returned to England, and devoted the rest of his life to the improvement of agriculture, on which subject he wrote and published many useful works.

CARRÉ : a Protestant family of Poitou, of which several members emigrated to England and others to North America. A. M. Carré officiated as reader in the French church at Hammersmith ; and another of the same name was minister of La Patente, London. We also find one Francis Carré a member of the consistory of New York in 1772.

CARTAUD, or CARTAULT, MATTHEW : a Protestant minister who fled from France at the time of the Bartholomew massacre, and officiated as pastor of the little church of fugitives at Rye, afterwards returning to Dieppe ; and again (on the revival of the persecution) finally settling and dying in England. One of his sons was minister of La Nouvelle Patente, London, in 1696.

CASAUBON, ISAAC : son of a French refugee from Bourdeaux settled at Geneva, where he was born in 1559. His father returned to Paris on the temporary cessation of the persecution, became minister of a congregation at Crest, and proceeded with the education of his son Isaac, who gave signs of extraordinary abilities. At nine years of age he spoke Latin with fluency. At the massacre of Saint Bartholomew the family fled into concealment ; and it was while hiding in a cavern that Isaac received from his father his first lesson in Greek. At nineteen he was sent to the academy of Geneva, where he studied jurisprudence under Pacius, theology under De Beza, and Oriental languages under Chevalier ; but no branch of learning attracted him more than Greek, and he was, at the age of twenty-four, appointed professor of that language at Geneva. His large family induced him to return to France, and accept the professorship of civil laws in the university of Montpellier ; and there he settled for a time. On the revival of persecution in France after the assassination of Henry IV., Casaubon emigrated to England. He was well received by James I., who gave him a pension, and ap-

pointed him prebendary of Westminster. He died at London in 1614, leaving behind him twenty sons and daughters, and a large number of works written during his lifetime, chiefly on classical and religious subjects. His son Florence Stephen Casaubon, D.D., having accompanied his father into England, was entered a student at Christ Church, Oxford, in 1614, where he greatly distinguished himself. In 1622 he took the degree of M.A. He was appointed rector of Ickham, and afterwards prebendary of Canterbury. He was the author of many learned works. He died at Canterbury in 1671.

CAUX, DE : many refugees of this name fled from Normandy into England. Several of them came over from Dieppe and settled in Norwich, their names frequently occurring in the registers of the French church there, in conjunction with those of Martineau, Columbine, Le Monnier, De la Haye, etc. Solomon de Caus, the engineer, whose name is connected with the first invention of the steam-engine, spent several years as a refugee in England ; after which he proceeded to Germany in 1613, and ultimately died in France, whither he returned in his old age. For notice, see p. 243.

CAVALIER, JOHN : tne Cevennol leader, afterwards brigadier-general in the British army, and lieutenant-governor of Jersey. For notice, see p. 234.

CAZENOVE : The family of

De Cazenove de Pradines, at Marmande, in Guienne, were well-known Huguenots at the time of the Revocation. Several members of the family took refuge in England. One of its present representatives, Philip Cazenove, is well known as a large-hearted benefactor in every good undertaking.

CHABOT, JAMES: The head of this family in England, was sent over from France, when about seven years of age, concealed in a hamper or basket. This was during the persecutions which followed the Revocation of the Edict of Nantes. It is supposed that his parents sent him over to England to prevent him being taken from them and brought up as a Roman Catholic. They doubtless intended to follow him, but were unable to make their escape. Nothing is known of them, excepting that they were nobles, and possessed of large estates. For this reason, they may have been murdered. Or, the father may have been sent to the galleys, and the mother immured in a convent for life. But as regards the child who had escaped to England, he was brought up in the household of the Duke of Bolton. On the death of his patron, and after arriving at man's estate, he married, and settled at High Wycombe, Bucks,—being described, in the registers of his two sons, as "of the Borough of Chepping Wycombe." His eldest son, James, carried on the business of a Calendarer and Tabby Waterer in Moorfields, London,—whose third

son, Philip, the grandfather of Philip James, settled in Spitalfields as a silk dyer,—the firm continuing for three generations. Philip James Chabot, M.A., F.R.A.S., was for about twenty years Secretary of the Old Mathematical Society of Crispin Street (a society mainly supported by the descendants of French refugees), until its incorporation with the Royal Astronomical Society in 1845. He was then made, in common with the other remaining members, a fellow of the latter society. M. Chabot was for many years a director of the French Hospital. It was mainly owing to his exertions that the Conditioning of Silk, as practised in all continental cities, was established in London. His first cousin, James Chabot, Esq., of Manchester, eldest son of the late James Chabot, Esq., of Malta, is now the head of the family.

CHAIGNEAU, LOUIS, JOHN, AND STEPHEN: refugees from St. Sairenne, in the Charente, where the family held considerable landed estates. They settled in Dublin, and prospered. One of the sons of Louis sat for Gowran in the Irish Parliament ; another held a benefice in the Church. John had two sons—Colonel William Chaigneau, and John, Treasurer of the Ordnance. The great-grandson of Stephen was called to the Irish bar in 1793. He eventually purchased the estate of Benown, in county Westmeath.

CHAMBERLAYNE, PETER, M.D. : a physician of Paris,

who fled into England at the massacre of St. Bartholomew. He was admitted a member of the College of Physicians, and obtained an extensive practice in London, where he died.

CHAMIER : an eminent Protestant family, originally belonging to Avignon. Daniel Chamier, who was killed in 1621 in the defence of Montauban, then besieged by Louis XIII., was one of the ablest theologians of his time, and a leading man of his party. He drew up for Henry IV. the celebrated Edict of Nantes. Several of his descendants settled in England. One was minister of the French church in Glass-House Street, London, and afterwards of the Artillery church. His eldest son, also called Daniel, emigrated to Maryland, U.S., where he settled in 1753. A younger son, Anthony, a director of the French Hospital, sat for Tamworth in Parliament in 1772. See also *Des Champs.*

CHAMPAGNÉ, ROBILLARD DE : a noble family in Saintonge· Several of the members took refuge in England and Ireland. The children of Josias de Robillard, chevalier of Champagné, under charge of their mother, escaped from La Rochelle concealed in empty wine casks, and arrived safe at Plymouth. Their father went into Holland and took service with the Prince of Orange. He afterwards died at Belfast, on his way to join his regiment in Ireland. Madame de Champagné settled at Portarlington with her family.

One of Champagné's sons, Josias, was an ensign in La Melonniére's regiment of French infantry, and fought at the Boyne. He afterwards became major of the 14th Foot. Several of his descendants have served with distinction in the army, the church, and the civil service ; while the daughters of the family have intermarried with various titled families in England and Ireland.

CHAMPION : see *Crespigny.*

CHARDEVENNE : a Protestant family belonging to Casteljaloux. The first eminent person of the name was Antoine, doctor of medicine, who afterwards became a famous preacher and pastor, first at Caumont, and afterwards at Marennes. At the Revocation, the members of his family became dispersed. Some of them went to North America ; in 1724 we find Pierre (son of the pastor above named) a member of the French church at New York ; while others fled to England, and established themselves at Hungerford.

CHARLOT, CHARLOTTI: Three brothers of this name emigrated from Picardy, after the Revocation of the Edict of Nantes, and settled in Edinburgh, where they established the manufacture of cambric muslin. They built a factory and dwelling-house at the head of Leith Walk. The place on which it was built (for it has long since been pulled down) is now known as Picardy Place. Another brother of the same family was murdered in France because of his religion.

CHARLOT, CHARLES, better known under the name of d'Argenteuil, was a Roman Catholic curé converted to Protestantism, who took refuge in England, and officiated as pastor in several of the London churches. In 1699 he was minister of the Tabernacle, with Pierre Rival and Cæsar Pegorier for colleagues. He published several works through Duchemin, the refugee publisher.

CHARPENTIER, of Ruffec, in Angoumois : a martyr to the brutality of the dragoons of Louis XIV. To force him to sign his abjuration, they made him drink from twenty-five to thirty glasses of water ; but this means failing, they next dropped into his eyes the hot tallow of a lighted candle. He died in great torture, 1685. His son John took refuge in England, and was minister of the Malthouse Church, Canterbury, in 1710.

CHASTELET, HIPPOLYTE : a monk of La Trappe, who left that monastery in 1672, and took refuge in England, where he acquired great fame as a Protestant preacher, under the name of Lusancy. He officiated for a time as pastor of the church of the Savoy, and was afterwards appointed to the charge of the French church at Harwich. Lusancy wrote and published a life of Marshal Schomberg, together with other works, principally poetry.

CHATELAIN, SIMON : a famous Protestant manufacturer of gold and silver lace in Paris. His lace procured for him the toleration of his religion. He was even allowed to be buried without disgrace, though eighty of his descendants paid fines for openly attending his funeral. After his death, his son Zacharie was harassed with a view to his forced apostasy ; but at length, in 1685, he fled to Holland in disguise. For this he was hanged in effigy, and his house at Villiers-Le-Bel was razed to the ground. His son, also named Zacharie, was thrown into the Bastile, in 1686, and on being set at liberty, removed to Holland, where he introduced the manufacture of gold and silver lace. His eldest son, Henry, studied for the ministry, and removed to England in 1709, when he was ordained by the Bishop of London. He was pastor of the Church of St. Martin Orgas (St. Martin's Lane), for ten years, after which he returned to Holland. His sermons were published in six volumes.

CHENEVIX : a distinguished Lorraine family, which became dispersed at the Revocation. The Béville branch of the family settled in Brandenburg, and the Eply branch in England. Two brothers belonging to the latter, Paul and Philip Chenevix, were both Protestants ; the former—a gentleman, illustrious for his learning and piety—was councillor of the king in the court of Metz ; the latter was pastor of the church of Limay, near Nantes. It happened that in 1686, the year after the Revocation, the elder brother fell dangerously ill, when the curate of the parish, forcing himself into his presence, importuned him to confess. The councillor replied that he declined to confess to any but God, who alone could forgive sin. The Archbishop next visited him, urging him to communicate before he died, at the same time informing him of the penalty (refusal of Christian burial) decreed by the King against such as died without receiving the sacrament. He refused, declaring that he would never communicate after the popish manner. At his death, shortly after, orders were given that his body should be removed by the executioner ; and his corpse was accordingly seized, dragged away on a hurdle, and cast upon a dunghill. About four hundred of his friends proceeded thither by night to fetch the body away. They wrapped it in linen ; four men bore it aloft on their shoulders, and they buried it in a garden. While the corpse was being let down into the grave, the mourning assembly sang the 79th psalm. The Rev. Philip Chenevix, brother of the above, fled into England at the Revocation, and the family afterwards settled in Ireland. The refugee's son entered the King's Guards, of which he became colonel ; and his grandson rose to eminent dignity in the church—being made Bishop of Killaloe in 1745, and afterwards of Waterford and Lismore. The present Archbishop of Dublin, Richard Chenevix Trench, is his great-grandson by the mother's side,— being also descended, by the

father's side, from another Huguenot family, the Trenches or De la Tranches, of whom the Earl of Clancarty is the head. The first La Tranche emigrated from France and settled in England at the massacre of St. Bartholomew. Another member of the family, Richard, was a distinguished chemist, member of the Royal Society in 1801, and author of many able works on science, including an *Essay on National Character.*

CHEROIS : see *De la Cherois.*

CHERON, LOUIS : a painter and engraver who took refuge in England at the Revocation, and died in London in 1723.

CHEVALIER, ANTOINE-RO-DOLPHE : a zealous Huguenot, born at Montchamps in 1507. When a youth he was compelled to fly into England for life. He completed his studies at Oxford, and being recommended to the Duke of Somerset, he was selected by him to teach the Princess (afterwards Queen) Elizabeth the French language. Chevalier subsequently held the professorship of Hebrew at Cambridge, but resigned it in 1570 to return to France. He was again compelled to fly by the renewed persecutions at the time of the Bartholomew massacre, and died in exile at Guernsey in 1572. He was a voluminous writer on classical subjects. During his short residence abroad, he left his son Samuel at Geneva, for the purpose of being educated for the church, under Theodore de Beza. On the revival of the persecutions in France, Samuel took refuge in England, was appointed minister of the French church in London in 1591, and afterwards of the Walloon church at Canterbury in 1595. Mr. Chevalier Cobbold, M.P., belongs to this family.

CLAUDE, JEAN-JACQUES : a young man of remarkable talents, grandson of the celebrated French preacher at the Hague. He was appointed pastor of the Walloon church in Threadneedle Street in 1710, but died of small-pox a few years later, aged only twenty-eight.

COËTLOGEN : a Breton family who emigrated to England at the Revocation. The village of Coëtlogon is some ten miles from Loudeac, and the château, where the family lived, is now in ruins. The estate passed into other hands. The son of the first emigrant—the Chevalier Dennis de Coëtlogen,— published a Dictionary of the Arts and Sciences (London, 1745), and many other works. He was a physician, Knight of St. Lazare, etc. His son was Rector of Godstone, in Surrey, celebrated alike as an author and a preacher. The present representative of the family is the Rev. Charles de Coëtlogon, British Chaplain at Aix-la-Chapelle.

COLIGNON, ABRAHAM DE : minister of Mens. At the Revocation he and several of his sons took refuge in Hesse, while Paul became minister of the Dutch church in Austin Friars, London. His son Charles was professor of anatomy and medicine at Cambridge, and was known as the author of several able works on these subjects.

COLLOT DE L'ESCURY : a refugee officer from Noyon, who escaped from France through Switzerland into Holland at the Revocation, and joined the army of William of Orange. He was major in Schomberg's regiment at the Boyne. His eldest son David was a captain of dragoons ; another, Simeon, was colonel of an English regiment ; both of their sons were captains of foot. Their descendants still survive in Ireland.

COLOMÉS, JEROME: the great pastor and preacher of Rochelle, belonged to a Bearnese family. His grandson, Paul, the celebrated author, came over to England in 1681, and was first appointed reader in the French church of the Savoy. Sancroft, Archbishop of Canterbury, afterwards made him his librarian. Paul Colomiès was the author of numerous learned works, the titles of nineteen of which are given by Haag in *La France Protestante.* He died in London, 1692.

CONANT, JOHN : son of a Protestant refugee, probably from Normandy, who settled in Devonshire. John was born at Yeatenton in 1608. He studied at Oxford, and in 1633 obtained a fellowship of Exeter College, which he resigned in 1647 because of declining to sign the Covenant. Two years later, he accepted the rectorship of the same college ; and though he declined pledging his fidelity to the Commonwealth,

Cromwell confirmed the appointment. In 1654 he was elected professor of theology, and in 1657 vice-chancellor of the University. He was one of the Commissioners for the Review of the Liturgy in 1661. In 1676 he was appointed Archdeacon of Norwich, and in 1681 prebendary of Worcester. He died in 1693. Sir Nathaniel Conant, who was chief magistrate of London early in the present century, was Dr. Conant's great-grandson. Sir Nathaniel's grandson, Edward Conant, Esq., of Lyndon, Rutlandshire, is the present representative of the family. There is a good memoir of Dr. Conant in *Aikin's Biography.*

CONDAMINE : see *La Condamine.*

CONSTANT : a Protestant family of Artois. At the Revocation, several of them fled into Switzerland, and others into Holland, where they took service under the Prince of Orange. Samuel, known as Baron de Constant, served as adjutant - general under Lord Albemarle in 1704 ; and afterwards fought under Marlborough in all the great battles of the period. His son David-Louis, an officer in the same service, was wounded at Fontenoy. Benjamin Constant, the celebrated French author, belonged to this family.

CONTÉ : see *Morell.*

CORCELLIS, NICHOLAS : son of Zeager Corcellis of Ruselier, in Flanders, who took refuge in England from the persecutions of the Duke of Alva. Nicholas became a prosperous London merchant. James was a physician in London, 1664.

CORNAUD DE LA CROZE : a learned refugee, author of *The Works of the Learned, The History of Learning,* and numerous other works.

COSNE, PIERRE DE: a refugee gentleman from La Beauce, Orleans, who settled at Southampton. His son Ruvigny de Cosne entered the Coldstream Guards, and rose to be lieutenant-colonel in the British army. He was afterwards secretary to the French embassy, and ambassador at the Spanish court.

COSNE-CHAVERNEY, DE: another branch of the same family. Captain de Cosne - Chaverney came over with the Prince of Orange in command of a company of gentlemen volunteers. He was lieutenant-colonel of Belcastel's regiment at the taking of Athlone in 1691.

COSSÉ ; an old French family of Brissac, who settled in England at the Revocation. A granddaughter of the refugee married Captain Dickinson, R.N., whose son was the great paper manufacturer. The writer of an obituary notice of the late Mr. John Dickinson, in the *Times,* says : " It is probable that, as has been the case in many other instances, it was by this infusion of French blood that much of the inventive faculty to which Mr. Dickinson owed his subsequent success was due. He was associated in his patent with Henry Fourdrinir, the grandson of another French refugee."

COTTEREAU, N. : a celebrated

Protestant horticulturist, who fled into England at the Revocation, and was appointed one of the gardeners of William III. Having gone into France to look after a manufactory of pipes which he had established at Rouen, he was detected encouraging the Protestants there to stand fast in the faith. He had also the imprudence to write something about Madame de Maintenon in a letter, which was construed into a libel. He was thereupon seized and thrown into the Bastile, where he lay for many years, during several of which he was insane. The converters offered him liberty if he would abjure his religion. At last he abjured ; but he was not released. " It was deemed just, as well as necessary, that Cottereau should remain in the Bastile and be forgotten there." He accordingly remained there a prisoner for eighteen years, until he died.

COULAN, ANTHONY : a refugee pastor from the Cevennes. He was for some time minister of the Glass-house Street French church in London. He died in 1694.

COUR : see *De la Cour.*

COURAYER : see *Le Courrayer.*

COURTAULD : a family from the neighbourhood of Saintonge. The first settler in England was Augustin, who came over at Revocation. Shortly after his arrival, he married Anne Bardine, daughter of another French refugee, and began the trade of a gold and silver smith in Cornhill. His son Samuel (who married Miss Ogier, also of Huguenot descent) carried on the same business ; and his son, the grandson of Augustin, having been bred to the silk trade, was the founder of the modern manufacturing house of Courtauld. He was the first to introduce silk throwing into the county of Essex. He built throwing-mills at Pebmarsh and Braintree, the latter of which is now one of the largest establishments in England for the manufacture of silk crape. The present head of the Courtauld firm—Samuel Courtauld, Esq., of Gosfield Hall, Essex—is widely known as the staunch friend of civil and religious liberty.

COURTEEN, WILLIAM : the son of a tailor at Menin in Flanders, who took refuge in England from the persecutions of the Duke of Alva. He established himself in business, with his son Peter Boudeau, in Abchurch Lane, and is said to have owed his prosperity to the manufacture of French hoods. His son became Sir William Courteen, a leading merchant of the city of London. His descendants married with the Bridgewater and other noble families.

COUSIN, JEAN : a refugee pastor from Caen ; he was one of the first ministers of the Walloon church in London, about the year 1562. He returned to France, but again fled back to England after the massacre of St. Bartholomew, and died in London. A correspondent at Melrose, in Scotland, bearing the same name, informs us that the tradition exists in his family, settled in Fife, that they were originally driven out of France by religious persecution—which is by no means improbable, as the name is peculiarly French. It is also believed that Cousin, the engraver, belonged to the same family.

CRAMAHÉ : a noble family of La Rochelle. The three brothers, Cramahé, De L'Isle, and Des Roches, made arrangements to escape into England at the Revocation. The first two succeeded, and settled in this country. Des Roches was less fortunate ; he was detected under the disguise in which he was about to fly ; he was flogged, maltreated, stripped of all the money he had, put into chains, and cast into a dungeon. After being transferred from one prison to another, undergoing many cruelties, and being found an obstinate heretic, he was, after twenty-seven months' imprisonment, banished the kingdom.

CRAMER : a refugee Protestant family of Strasburg, some of whom settled in Geneva, where Gabriel Cramer, a celebrated physician, became Dean of the College of Medicine in 1677. Jean-Louis Cramer held the rank of captain in the English army, and served with distinction in the Spanish campaign. When the French army occupied Geneva at the Revolution, Jean-Antoine, brother of the preceding, came over to England and settled. His second son, Jean-Antoine, was a professor at Oxford and Dean of Carlisle. He was the author of several geographical works. Another member of this family was Gabriel Cramer, of Geneva, the celebrated mathematician.

CREGUT : a refugee pastor from Montélimar, who officiated as minister of the French church in Wheeler Street, and afterwards in that of La Nouvelle Patente, London.

CRESPIGNY, CLAUDE CHAMPION DE : a landed proprietor in Normandy, who fled from France into England with his family, at the Revocation. He was related by marriage to the Pierpoints, who hospitably received the fugitives. Two of his sons entered the army ; Gabriel was an officer in the Guards, and Thomas captain in Hotham's Dragoons. The grandson of the latter had two sons: Philip Champion de Crespigny, M.P. for Aldborough, 1803 ; and Sir Claude Champion de Crespigny, created Baronet in 1805.

CROMMELIN, LOUIS : royal superintendent of the linen-manufacture in Ireland, to which office he was appointed by William III. For notice of him, see p. 296. A correspondent (A. V. Kirwan, Esq.), says: " I knew well a descendant of the Crommelins, Nicolas de la Cherois Crommelin, a gentleman of good landed estate. Like all the descendants of the Huguenots whom I have known, he bore a pensive, not to say melancholy, cast of countenance. The same sense of sadness may be observed in the expression of the Jews in Poland."

CROZE : see *Cornaud de la Croze.*

CRUSO, JOHN : a refugee from Hownescoat in Flanders, who settled in Norwich. His son Timothy became a prosperous merchant in London, and founded the present Norfolk family of the Crusos.

DAILLON, JAMES DE : a member of the illustrious family of Du Lude. He entered the English Church, and held a benefice in Buckinghamshire towards the end of the 17th century ; but having declared in favour of James II., he was deposed from his office in 1693, and died in London in 1726. His brother Benjamin was also a refugee in England, and held the office of minister in the church of La Patente, which he contributed to found.

D'ALBIAC : this family is said to derive its name from Albi, the capital of the country of the Albigenses, which was destroyed in the religious crusade against that people in the thirteenth century. The D'Albiacs fled from thence to Nismes, where they suffered heavily for their religion, especially after the Revocation. Two youthful D'Albiacs were sent to England, having been smuggled out of the country in hampers. They both prospered and founded families. We find the names of their descendants occurring amongst the directors of the French Hospital. The late Lieutenant-General Sir J. C. Dalbiac, M.P., was lineally descended from one of the sons, and his only daughter became Duchess of Roxburghe by her marriage with the Duke in 1836.

DALECHAMP, CALEB : a refugee from Sedan, who entered the English Church, and became rector of Ferriby in Lincolnshire.

DAMPIER : the navigator, is said to have belonged to an old Huguenot family settled in Somersetshire. There is a glover of the same name in Yeovil, who claims to be of like French descent.

DANSAYS, FRANCIS : a French refugee at Rye in Sussex. William was a jurat of that town ; he died in 1787. The family is now represented by the Stonhams.

D'ALTERA : The ancestors of this family possessed large estates near Nismes, in Languedoc. They emigrated to England early in the sixteenth century, and afterwards took refuge in the county of Cork, Ireland. The only surviving member of the family is a Surgeon-Major in the British army.

D'ARANDA : originally a Spanish family, supposed to have been driven out of Flanders by the persecutions of the Duke of Alva. In 1617, Elie D'Aranda was minister of the Walloon church at Southampton ; in 1619, " modérateur de colloques " at Norwich. He was grandfather of Paul D'Aranda, Amsterdam, sometimes called " the merchant prince," and, by the female line, to the Rev. William Coxe, archdeacon of Wilts and canon of Salisbury, author of the " Life of Sir R. Walpole," " House of Austria," etc. The male branch of the D'Aranda family is now extinct.

DARGENT OR DARGEN : a refugee family from Sancerre, some of the members of which settled in England and Ireland at the Revocation. Two of them served as officers in William III.'s Guards. Two brothers were directors of the French Hospital—John in 1756, and James in 1762.—Dargan, the late railway contractor in Ireland, is supposed to have belonged to this family.

D'ARGENTEUIL : see *Charlot.*

DAVID : a Protestant family of Rochelle, many members of which fled from France, some into England, and others to the United States of America. One, John David, was a director of the French Hospital in London in 1750.

DAUDÉ, PETER : a member of one of the best families of Maruéjols in the Gévaudan. He came to England in 1680, and became a tutor in the Trevor family ; afterwards he accepted a clerkship in the Exchequer, which he held for twenty-eight years. He was a very learned, but an exceedingly diffident and eccentric man. His nephew, also named Peter, was a minister of one of the French churches in London.

DE BROSSES : One of the descendants of the distinguished refugee of this name officiated as secretary of the Bank of England under the name of Bros. His son is a barrister on the Oxford circuit.

DE FOE : Charles Philarète, in *Notes and Queries,* for March 7th, 1868, says : " The real patronymic of Daniel De Foe appears to have been De Foy, or De Foix, which belongs to an old Huguenot family of Provence. His progenitors were refugees who adopted the false orthography of De Foe in order to avoid having the name pronounced in the English fashion, which would have lent to the syllable *oi* a sound analogous to that of *hoist, moist,* etc."

DE JEAN, LOUIS : descended from a Fench refugee, was colonel of the 6th Dragoon Guards, and eventually lieutenant-general.

DE LA CHEROIS, SAMUEL : scion of a noble Huguenot family of the Gatinais, whose two sons, Nicolas and Bourjouval, officers in the French army, being Protestants, left France at the Revocation, and took service under the Prince of Orange. They were afterwards joined by their elder brother Daniel, and their two sisters, Judith and Louisa, who had succeeded in escaping from France in disguise. The two first-named brothers entered the service of William III., and both distinguished themselves at the battle of the Boyne. The second was killed at the siege of Dungannon ; but Nicolas served the King through all his wars, and afterwards under Marlborough, rising to the rank of lieutenant-colonel. Having married Marie Crommelin, a sister of Louis Crommelin, he left a family whose descendants still survive in the north of Ireland. The eldest of the three brothers, Daniel, held the office of governor of Pondicherry in the East Indies, to which he was nominated by King William ; and in that capacity he realized a considerable fortune. His only daughter married for her second husband Count Montgomery, of Mount Alexander. Judith, one of the girls who had fled from France in disguise, lived to the age of 113, and died at Mount Alexander in the full possession of her faculties.

DE LA COUR : an illustrious Huguenot family, many members of which filled places of high trust under the French kings, as indicated by the billets on their coat of arms. The first of the family that emigrated on account of religion, was a distinguished officer of the French army, who settled in the neighbourhood of Portarlington, from whence his descendants afterward removed to the county of Cork. The motto of the branch of the family settled in Ireland, *Au Ciel de la Cour*, was adopted on their leaving France, intimating that they had left a high position at Court for the sake of the religion which they professed.

DE LAINE, PETER : a French refugee, who fled into England before the Revocation, and obtained letters of denisation dated 1681. He was appointed French tutor to the children of the Duke of York, afterwards James II. We are informed by a correspondent, that J. T. Delane, editor of the *Times*, is collaterally descended from this refugee.

DE LA MOTHE : see *Mothe.*

DELAMOTTE, JOSEPH : born at Tournay, of Roman Catholic parents, about the middle of the sixteenth century, while the Low Countries were under the dominion of Spain. He was apprenticed to a silkman, who was a Protestant, and becoming informed as to the truth of the new views, he embraced Protestantism. When the persecution began under the Duke of Alva, young Delamotte went to Geneva, studied for the ministry, was ordained, and returned to Tournay, where he privily officiated as minister to the flock there, at the same time working with his old master as a silkman. But his profession and calling having been discovered, he was forced to fly across the frontier into France. The following account is contained in a MS. in the possession of his family :—" An information having been given against him to the Inquisition, they sent their officers in the night to apprehend him ; they knocked at the door and told his master (who answered them) that they wanted his man. He, judging who they were, called Joseph, and he immediately got on his clothes and made his escape over the garden wall, with his Bible, and travelled away directly into France, to St. Malo. They, believing him to be gone the nearest way to the sea-coast, pursued toward Ostend, and missed him. From St. Malo he got over to Guernsey (then in the possession of Queen Elizabeth), and from thence to Southampton, where, his money being all gone, he applied himself to the members of the French church there, making his condition known to them. Their minister being just dead, they desired that he would preach to them the next Sabbath day, which accordingly he did, and they chose him for their minister." He married and had a large family, most of whose descendants also have had large families, so that the Southampton Delamottes now form a very numerous body. Some members of the family have been distinguished as merchants and manufacturers, and others as clergymen.

DELAUNE : a refugee family from Normandy, who took refuge in England as early as 1599, when a Delaune officiated as minister of the Walloon Church in London. Another, in 1618, held the office of minister of the Walloon church at Norwich. Thomas Delaune was a considerable writer on religious and controversial subjects.

DE LAVAL, VICOMTE : possessor of large estates in Picardy, who, after heavy persecution, fled at the Revocation, and took refuge in Ireland, settling at Portarlington. His son was an officer in the British army : and descendants of the family are still to be met with in Ireland.

DE LAVALADE : this family possessed large estates in Languedoc. Several members of them succeeded in escaping into Holland, and afterwards proceeded to Ireland, settling in Lisburn. M. De Lavalade was forty years pastor of the French church there.

DELEMAR, DE LA MER, DELMER : a Protestant refugee family at Canterbury, whose names are of frequent occurrence in the register of that church. Their descendants are numerous, and enjoy good positions in society.

DELMÉ, PHILIP : minister of the Walloon congregation, Canterbury, whose son Peter settled in London as a merchant, and whose grandson, Sir Peter, ancestor of the present family of Delmé Radcliffe, was Lord Mayor of London in 1723.

DEMOIVRE, ABRAHAM, F.R.S.: notice, p. 231.

DESAGULIERS, DR. : notice p. 247.

DES CHAMPS JOHN : a native of Bergerac, belonging to an ancient family established in Perigord. At the Revocation he took refuge, first in Geneva, and then in Prussia. Of his sons, one became minister of the church at Berlin ; while another came over to England and became minister of the church of the Savoy, in which office he died in 1767. The son of the latter, John Ezekiel, entered the civil service of the East India Company, and became member of Council of the Presidency of Madras. He ultimately took the name of *Chamier*, having been left sole heir to Anthony Chamier, the descendant of another refugee. By his marriage with Georgiana Grace, daughter of Admiral Burnaby, he had a numerous family. One of his sons is Captain Frederick Chamier, the novelist and nautical annalist

DES MAISAUX, PETER : a native of Auvergne, born 1666; the son of a Protestant minister, who took refuge in England. Little is known of Des Maisaux's personal history, beyond that he was a member of the Royal Society, a friend of St. Evremond, and a voluminous author. He died in 1745.

DES ORMEAUX, also named COLIN DES ORMEAUX : of a Rochelle family. At the Revocation several members of it settled at Norwich. One Catherine Colin was married to Thomas le Chevalier in 1727. Gabriel Colin was minister of Thorpe-le-Soken from 1707 to 1714. A member of the family, Jacques Louis des Ormeaux, was elected a director of the French Hospital in 1798.

DE REGIS : the head of this family emigrated to England at the Revocation. In his will, De Regis stated that he was "entitled by primogeniture to an abbey, and to paternal and maternal estates in Dauphiny." His son, the Rev. Balthazar Regis, was educated at Trinity College, Dublin; was D.D. of Cambridge, 1721; Canon of Windsor, 1751 ; Chaplain to the King ; Rector of Adisham, Kent; and died 1757.

DESBOIS : a farmer of Autun, in Burgundy, born in 1646. He married Lazarin Paulet, by whom he had Lazarus, born 1670, Martin, and a daughter. At his death, in 1679, the property was taken in charge by his wife's father, who induced his daughter to put the children into the Convent of St. Lazare, Autun, under protection of the abbess. Lazarus assisted as singing boy in the chapel, and in the work of the convent ; but finding it irksome, he left for Paris, and became apprenticed to a joiner. While in this service, he became acquainted with some Protestants, and adopted their faith. The monks, observing that he no longer attended confession and mass, reproached him for his conduct. Finding it unsafe to remain in Paris, he set out for Amsterdam. He remained there for seven years, after which, in 1699, he passed over into England, and settled himself in Crompton Street, Soho, where he pursued the trade of a joiner and cabinet-maker. In 1701 he married Margaret Loizel, a Protestant refugee from St. Quentin, in Brittany, by whom he had a family, and his descendants still survive.

DE SCHIRAC : a Huguenot family from Bergeral, in Guienne. The first refugee had the greatest difficulty in escaping from France, after the Revocation of the Edict of Nantes. He was compelled to comply with the outward ceremony of abjuring his faith. Then he arranged to send his family out of the country. The ship in which his wife embarked was burnt, and the report reached him that none on board had escaped but a few sailors. The two eldest daughters, who could not escape with their mother, were sent on board another vessel. One of them, when the ship was searched, was obliged to con-

25

ceal herself in a coil of ropes. At length, after visiting numerous seaports, and finding that he was unable to escape by sea, De Schirac and his son managed to cross the Swiss frontier accompanied by a party of recruits. After remaining at Zurich for a few days, he and his son set out for England. M. De Schirac eventually became minister of the French church at Bristol. The late Professor Rigaud drew out an abstract of his history, which concludes with the following words : " He died in his pulpit at Bristol ; he had a lap-dog with him at the time, which could not be driven from his corpse. His daughter married M. Triboudet Demainbray, himself a refugee from France in consequence of the Revocation of the Edict of Nantes, —and their granddaughter was my mother."

D'ESPAGNE, JEAN : a Huguenot pastor, who fled from Dauphiny, shortly after the assassination of Henry IV. He was one of the most able divines of the refugee churches in England. He died in 1659.

D'ESPARD : PHILIP D'ESPARD escaped to England from the massacre of St. Bartholomew, abandoning his title and estate rather than abjure Protestantism. He was sent to Ireland on civil service by Queen Elizabeth. His grandson, William, was colonel of engineers in the army of William III., and in 1715 his eldest son represented the borough of Thomastown, and afterwards the County Kilkenny, in the Irish House of Commons. Many members of the family have served in the church and the army : two were generals, one governor of Newfoundland, three were High-Sheriffs of Queen's County, and several were magistrates there and elsewhere. The name has been written " Dispard " without the apostrophe for about 150 years. There are still numerous D'Espards in the south of France. Several of them reside on the banks of the Loire near Tours.

DES VŒUX, VINCHON: second son of De Bacquencourt, president of the parliament of Rouen. He took refuge in Dublin, where he became minister of the French church. In conjunction with the Rev. Peter Droz, he commenced, about 1742, the publication of the first literary journal which appeared in Ireland. He afterwards removed to Portarlington. The present head of the family is Sir C. Des Vœux, Bart.

DEVAYNES, WILLIAM, M.P. : descended from a Huguenot refugee. He was a director of the East India Company, a director of the French Hospital, and was elected for Barnstaple in 1774.

DE VEILLE HANS: a refugee who entered the English Church, and was made library keeper at Lambeth by Archbishop Tillotson. His son Thomas entered the English army as a private, and was sent with his regiment to Portugal. There he rose by merit to the command of a troop of dragoons. On his return to London, he was appointed a London justice—an office then paid by fees ; and his conduct in the riots of 1735 was so much approved, that he received the honour of knighthood. He was also colonel of the Westminster militia.

D'OLIER : see *Olier.*

DIBON : HENRY DE DIBON, a Huguenot landed proprietor in the Isle of France, was arrested in 1685 by order of Louis XIV., and thrown into prison and tortured. He contrived to escape into Holland, where he entered the service of William III. His granddaughter Margaret became the wife of the Rev. Dr. Traviss, vicar of Snape, in Yorkshire, whose eldest daughter, Anne, married, in 1772, the Rev. Thomas Faber, vicar of Calverley, and was the mother of the late George Stanley Faber, prebendary of Salisbury, whose family still possess the much-prized Bible with which the orginal refugee fled out of France. The Fabers are themselves supposed to be of Huguenot descent by the male side, as is indicated by their name. The families of Buck of Townhall and Denham Park, Cooke of Swinton, and Atkinson of Bradford, are descended by intermarriages from the Dibon family. See notice, p. 167.

DOBRÉE: the ancestor of this family fled to the island of Guernsey during the massacre of St. Bartholomew. From him descended Peter Dobrée, merchant of London, father of the Rev. William Dobrée, rector of St. Saviour, Guernsey ; and the Rev. Peter Paul Dobrée, Regius Professor of Greek at the University of Cambridge. Dobrée Bonamy, the well-known author and political economist, belongs to this family.

DOLLOND, JOHN : for notice, p. 337.

DOMBRAIN, D'EMBRUN, D'AMBRAIN : a Protestant Huguenot family of high extraction, the head of which, Jacques d'Embrun, fled from the town of Embrun, near Gap, in the Hautes-Alpes, in 1572. Escaping to Rouen, his family, with six others, De Cafour, Le Gyt, De Lasaux, Beaufort, Le Pine, and La Grande, crossed the Channel in an open boat on the 19th August, 1572, and settled at Canterbury. The head of the family is Sir James D'ombrain, Kt., Bt., R.N., now resident in Ireland. His son, the Rev. Henry Honywood D'ombrain, is vicar of Westwell, Kent, and his grandson, the Rev. James D'ombrain, is rector of St. Benedict's, Norwich.—Some years since there was an eminent surgeon of the same name settled in Edinburgh.

DRELINCOURT, PETER : son of Charles Drelincourt, one of the ablest preachers and writers among the French Protestants. He was educated at Geneva, and afterwards came to England, where he entered the English Church, and eventually became dean of Armagh.

DU BEDAT : the head of this family was the Marquis Du Bédat. One of his descendants is secretary to the Bank of Ireland.

DU BOIS or DU BOUAYS : a

Protestant family of Brittany, of whom many members came over to England and settled at an early period at Thorney, Canterbury, Norwich, and London. Others of the name came from French Flanders.

DUBOIS, FRANÇOIS: fled from the massacre of St. Bartholomew into England. He settled at Shrewsbury, where he founded a ribbon manufactory. Mr. Agnew says that his descendants removed to Wolverhampton, where they purchased coalmines, and built extensive iron forges. In the fourth generation, the Dubois changed their name to *Wood.* William Wood, born in 1671, was the manufacturer of "Wood's halfpence," the circulation of which caused such a *fureur* in Ireland. William Wood's fourth son was Charles Wood,—the discoverer of platinum. He built the Lowmill Iron Works, near Whitehaven, and the Cyfarthon Works, near Merthyr-Tydvil. Mrs Mary Howitt (wife of William Howitt) is the granddaughter of Charles Wood.

DUBOUCHET : an illustrious Huguenot family of Poitou, several of whose members took refuge in England. One of them, Pierre, officiated as minister of the French church at Plymouth between 1733 and 1737.

DU BOULAY : a family descended from the Marquis d'Argencon de Boulay, a Huguenot refugee in Holland in 1658. His grandson was minister of the French church in Threadneedle Street, London. The family is now represented by Du Boulay, of Donhead Hall, Wiltshire. Mr. Agnew says : " This family is at present largely represented in the church, and is established in the Southern Counties. It exemplifies the manner in which the French colony clung together,—though perhaps it is only a coincidence,—that by the marriage of the widow of the Rev. J. T. H. Du Boulay, of Heddington, with the Rev. G. J. Majendie, son of the Bishop of Bangor, the Rev. Henry William Majendie, at present the representative of the Majendies, is half-brother to the present head of the Du Boulays."

DUBOURDIEU : a noble Protestant family of Bearn. Isaac was for some time minister of the Savoy church, London. His son, John Armand, after having been minister at Montpellier, took refuge in England, and also became one of the ministers of the church in the Savoy. His grandson was the last pastor of the French church at Lisburn, and afterwards rector of Annahilt, in Ireland. For notice of the Dubourdieus, see p. 258.

DU BUISSON, FRANCIS: a doctor of the Sorbonne. Becoming converted to Protestantism, he fled into England at the time of the massacre of St. Bartholomew, and became minister of the French church at Rye. Another emigrant of the same name was Pierre Grostête du Buisson. His grandson bought an estate in South Wales, which one of the branches of the family still occupies.

DUCANE : see *Du Quesne.*

DU CAREL, ANDREW-COLTÉE :
a refugee who accompanied his
parents from Caen into England, at the revival of religious
persecution in France in 1724.
He studied at Eton and Oxford.
In 1757 he was appointed archbishop's librarian at Lambeth,
and in the following year he
was sent to Canterbury, where
he held an important appointment in the record office. He
was a man of great antiquarian
learning, and published numerous works on classical antiquities.

DU CROS, JOHN : a refugee
from Dauphiny. In 1711 his
son John was minister of the
Savoy.

DU JON : a noble family of
Berri, several members of which
took refuge in England. Francis, son of a refugee at Leyden,
where he studied, was appointed
librarian to the Earl of Arundel,
and held the office for thirty
years. He was one of the first
to devote himself to the study
of Anglo-Saxon literature, and
published several works on the
subject.

DU MOULIN : an ancient and
noble family of the Isle of
France, that has furnished dignitaries to the Roman Church
as well as produced many
eminent Protestant writers.
Charles du Moulin, the eminent
French jurisconsult, declared
himself as Protestant in 1542.
Pierre du Moulin belonged to
another branch of the family.
He was only four years old at
the massacre of Bartholomew,
and was saved by an old servant of his father, who picked
him up from amongst the
dead and dying. In his youth
he studied at Sedan and
afterwards at Oxford and Leyden. At the latter university
he was appointed professor of
philosophy when only in his
twenty-fourth year. Grotius
was among his pupils. Seven
years later, he was "called"
by the great Protestant church
at Charenton near Paris, and
accepted the invitation to be
their minister. He officiated
there for twenty-four years,
during which he often incurred
great peril, having had his
house twice pillaged by the
populace. At the outbreak of
the persecution in the reign of
Louis XIII. he accepted the
invitation of James I. to settle
in England, where he was received with much honour. The
King appointed him prebendary
of Canterbury, and the university of Cambridge conferred
upon him the degree of D.D.
He afterwards returned to Paris,
to assist in the conferences of
the Protestant church, and
died at Sedan at the age of
ninety. His two sons, Peter
and Louis, both settled in England. The former was preacher
to the university of Oxford in
the time of the Commonwealth.
In 1660 Charles II. appointed
him one of his chaplains, as well
as prebendary of Canterbury.
Louis, on the other hand, who
had officiated as Camden professor of history at Oxford
during the Commonwealth, was
turned out of his office on the
Restoration, and retired to
Westminster, where he continued for the rest of his life

an extreme Presbyterian. Both brothers were voluminous authors.

DUNCAN : a Scotch family naturalised in France at the beginning of the seventeenth century. Mark Duncan was Protestant Professor of philosophy and Greek at Saumur. One of his sons, Sainte-Hélène, took refuge in London, where he died in 1697. Another descendant of the family, Daniel, was celebrated as a chemist and physician, and wrote several able works on his favourite subjects. His son Daniel was the last pastor of the French church at Bideford, where he died in 1761. He was also celebrated as a writer on religious subjects.

DUPIN, PAUL : an eminent paper-manufacturer who established himself in England after the Revocation, and carried on a large paper-mill with great success.

DU PLESSIS, JACQUES ; chaplain to the French Hospital in 1750. Another of the name, Francis, was minister of La Nouvelle Patente and Wheeler Street chapels, London—of the latter in 1720.

DU PORT : a Protestant family of Poitou, several members of which took refuge in England. One of them, James, was pastor of the French Walloon church in London in 1590. His son, of the same name, filled the office of professor of Greek at the University of Cambridge with great distinction. In 1660 he was appointed dean of Peterborough and chaplain to the King. He was

the author of several learned works : he died in 1679.

DUPUY : a Protestant family of Languedoc. At the Revocation, the brothers Philip and David entered the army of William of Orange. They were both officers in his guards, and were both killed at the Boyne. Another brother, Samuel, was also an officer in the British army, and served with distinction in the Low Countries.

DU QUESNE, ABRAHAM : second son of the celebrated admiral, lieutenant in the French navy, settled in England after the Revocation, and died there. His son Thomas Roger was prebendary of Ely, and vicar of East Tuddenham, Norfolk. Another branch of the family of Du Quesne or Du Cane, settled in England in the sixteenth century. One of their descendants was an alderman of London. From this branch the Du Canes of Essex are descended. Charles Du Cane, M.P., of Braxted Park, is the representative of the family.

DURAND, FRANCOIS GUILLAUME : a native of Montpellier, born 1649. On arriving at maturity he became an ordained minister of the French Protestant Church ; and was appointed to a cure at Genuillac, in Lower Languedoc. In 1680 he married the Demoisell de Brueyx de Fontcouverte, daughter of the Baron of that name, residing in the diocese of Usez. Durand lived at Genuillac for two or three years, until the persecutions began, and then he was compelled to fly from France, leaving behind him his son Francis. He fled into Westphalia, where he lived for a year, and then proceeded to Schaffhausen in Switzerland. He afterwards settled at Copet, near Geneva. There we find him acting as captain in the service of William III. of England. That monarch was then raising Huguenot regiments abroad, to enable him to carry on his contest with James II. in Ireland. Durand succeeded in raising in the Canton of Vaux the 2nd and 3rd Battalions of the Regiment of Loches, and the Dragoon Regiment of Baltasar. The ministers of Geneva, however, having given it as their opinion that the duties of Captain and Minister were incompatible, he resigned the former office, and remained Chaplain of the Regiment of Baltasar. He served with the English army in Savoy, under the Duke of Schomberg, after which he journeyed northward to Nimuegen, in Holland, where he was appointed minister of the Walloon church. His son Francis there joined him; the old refugee died at the advanced age of eighty-four. Francis Durand de Fontcouverte, after the flight of his father, had been apprehended and educated by the Jesuits of Montpellier, and was accordingly brought up a Roman Catholic. He afterwards left France, joined his father at Nimuegen, and was permitted to practise at the bar in Holland. He had doubtless returned to the faith of his fathers, for we find him bringing up his son as a minister of the Reformed Church. His son, Francis William Isaiah Durand, proceeded to Norwich in England, with his Huguenot wife, where he was appointed minister of the Dutch church in 1743. In 1751 he was ordained Deacon and Priest by Benjamin, Bishop of Winchester. Four days after his reordination, he was inducted into the United Parishes of St. Sampson and the Vale in the Island of Guernsey. Some time after, he was made minister of the French church held in the Crypt, Canterbury,—still retaining his Guernsey livings. He died at Canterbury in 1789. One of his sons was Dean of Guernsey. His descendants have filled various public offices of importance. Charles James Durand, Captain of the Bengal Staff Corps, has favoured us with the above particulars.

DURAND : a noble family of Dauphiny. Several ministers of the name officiated in French churches in England—one at Bristol and others in London.

DURANT : several members of this Huguenot family sat in Parliament. Thomas sat for St. Ives in 1768, and George for Evesham.

DURAS, BARON: see *Durfort.*

DURFEY, THOMAS : born at Exeter about the middle of the seventeenth century. He was the son of a French refugee from Rochelle, and is well known as a song writer and dramatic author.

DURFORT DE DURAS : an ancient Protestant family of Guienne. Louis, Marquis of Blanquefort, came over to England in the reign of Charles II., and was well received by that monarch, who created him Baron de Duras and employed him as ambassador-extraordinary at Paris. James II. created him, though a Protestant, Earl of Faversham, and gave him the command of the army which he sent against the Duke of Monmouth. He died in 1709. The French church which he founded at Faversham did not long survive him.

DUROURE, FRANCIS : scion of an ancient family in Languedoc. His two sons were officers in the English army. Scipio was lieutenant-colonel of the 12th Foot, and was killed at Fontenoy. Alexander was colonel of the 4th Foot, and rose to be lieutenant-general.

DURY, PAUL : an eminent officer of engineers, who entered the service of William III., from which he passed into that of the Elector of Hesse. Two of his sons served with distinction in the English army ; the elder, of the regiment of La Melonniére, was killed at the Boyne.

DU SOUL, MOSES : a refugee from Tours, known in England as a translator and philologist, about the beginning of the eighteenth century.

DUTENS, LOUIS : a refugee from Tours, historiographer to the king of England, member of the Royal Society and of the French Academy of Inscriptions. Having entered the English Church, he was presented with the living of Elsdon in Northumberland. He was the author of many well-known works ; amongst others, of the learned treatise entitled *Origine des Découvertes attribuées aux Modernes.*

DUVAL : many refugees from Rouen of this name settled in England, and several were ministers of French churches in London. Several have been governors of the French Hospital.

DU VEIL : three brothers of this name, Jews by birth, were won over by the Roman Catholic Church. Daniel Du Veil, the eldest, was baptised under Royal sponsorship at the palace of Compiègne. After further study the three brothers became Protestants ; two took refuge in England, the third in Holland. Charles Marie Du Veil came to England about the year 1677. He was ordained a minister of the Church of England ; but, having abjured the theory of infant baptism, he eventually became a Baptist minister. He published several works on religious subjects.

EMERIS : a refugee family of this name fled out of France at the massacre of St. Bartholomew, and purchased a small property in Norfolk, which descended from father to son, and is still in the possession of the family,—at present represented by W. R. Emeris, Esq., of Louth, Lincolnshire.

EVREMOND, CHARLES DE ST. DENYS, SEIGNEUR DE STE. EVREMOND : a refugee gentleman of wit and bravery, who served with distinction under Turenne and Condé. His satiric humour lost him the friendship of his patrons, and provoked the enmity of Louis XIV., who ordered his arrest. Having received timely notice, Evremond fled first into Germany and Holland, and afterwards into England, where he became a great favourite with Charles II., who gave him a pension. In 1678, an order in Council was passed directing returns to be made of foreigners then in England, and amongst them appears the following, doubtless that of our French seigneur :—"Nov. 23, 1678. S^te· Evremond chassé de France il y a long temps, est venu d'abord en Angleterre, de la il est allé en Flandre, de Flandre en Allemagne, d'Allemagne en Hollande, de Hollande il est revenu en Angleterre, ou il est presentemente, ne pouvant retourner en son pais ; il n'a qu'un valet nommé Gaspard Girrard, Flammand de nation. Je suis logé dans St. Albans Street au coin.—S^r. Evremond."—[*State Papers, Domestic, various,* No. 694.] Ste. Evremond was not a Protestant, nor would he be a Catholic. Indeed, he seems to have been indifferent to religion. His letters are among the most brilliant specimens of that style of composition in which the French so much excel ; but his other works are almost forgotten. Des Maiseaux, another refugee, published them in three vols. quarto, in 1705 ; afterwards translating the whole into English.

EYNARD : a refugee family of Dauphiny. Anthony entered the British army, and served with distinction, dying in 1739.

His brother Simon began business in London, and acquired a considerable fortune by his industry. A sister, Louise, married the refugee Gideon Ageron, who also settled in England.

FABER : see *Dibon.*

FARGUES, JACQUES DE : a wealthy apothecary belonging to one of the best families of Montpellier. In 1569 his house was pillaged by the populace, while he himself was condemned to death because of his religion, and hanged. His family fled into England, where their descendants still exist.

FAUSSILLE, RENE DE LA : belonged to an ancient Angevine family, and was captain of the Royal Regiment of La Ferté previous to the Revocation. He left the French king's service, and first emigrated to Switzerland, from whence he proceeded to Holland and entered the service of the Prince of Orange. He became captain of grenadiers in the regiment of Caillemotte-Ruvigny, and fought with it at the battle of the Boyne, where he received six severe wounds, which disabled him for life. King William, who personally witnessed his bravery in the battle, rewarded him by appointing him governor of the port, town, and county of Sligo, and conferring on him a pension of 10s. a day. He left behind him a family of two sons and three daughters. Both sons became officers in the army ; one saw much service in Flanders, was brigade-major at Fontenoy and Dettingen, and subsequently became major-general and colonel of the 66th

Regiment. He was present at the capture of Havannah, and died on board ship on the voyage home. The general left only one daughter ; his brother, a captain in the army, died unmarried. The general's daughter married a member of the Torriano family, and had two sons, one a captain in the Artillery, the other a lieutenant in the 71st Regiment ; the Torrianos in England being also descended from another victim of religious persecution, who fled from Milan and settled in London in 1620.

FLEURY, LOUIS : Protestant pastor of Tours, who fled into England in 1683. His son, Philip Amuret, went over to Ireland as a Protestant minister, and settled there. His son, grandson of the refugee, became vicar-choral of Lismore; and the great-grandson of the refugee, George Lewis Fleury, became archdeacon of Waterford. See p. 333.

FONBLANQUE : the original name of this refugee family was Grenier, of the estate of Fonblanque, in the department of Tarn et Garonne. The Greniers, says a writer in *Notes and Queries* [4th S. iv. 247], "appear to have been of considerable antiquity; noble, though not titled, and enjoyed the privilege of glass-making as Gentilshommes Verriers,—a monopoly granted by St. Louis on his return from the Crusades, as an indemnification for the loss of their patrimony in that service. Part of the family, having embraced the Reformed faith, were in consequence exposed to neglect and persecution, and the elder branch was extinguished by the death of the three brothers Grenier, who were decapitated on the accusation of harbouring the Protestant minister Rochette in their house and favouring his escape. All the principal family documents of importance were destroyed during the dragonnades of Louis XIV. and XV." The late Albany Fonblanque was for many years editor of the *Examiner*. His brother J. S. Fonblanque was one of the commissioners of Bankruptcy.

FONNEREAU : three members of this family, descended from a Huguenot refugee—Zachary Philip, Thomas, and Martin— sat in Parliament successively for Aldborough in 1768, 1773, and 1774.

FONTAINE, DE LA FONTAINE : many members of this family settled in England.—James Fontaine, son of James de la Fontaine, pastor of Vaux and Royan, married for his first wife an Englishwoman, a Miss Thompson, in 1628, and had by her five children ;—of whom Judith, married to a M. Sinermot, was left a widow with four children. After being herself shut up in a convent, and compelled to make abjuration of her religion, she succeeded in escaping with her daughters to London, where they maintained themselves by needlework. —James, pastor of Archiac, in Saintonge, died and left a widow, who, after being confined in a dungeon for three years because of her faith, succeeded in reaching

London with her three sons, one of whom became a Protestant minister in Germany.— Elizabeth, married to M. Santreau, pastor of Saujon, in Saintonge, who first emigrated to Ireland, and left it for America with his family, but their vessel being wrecked, they were all drowned within sight of Boston.—Peter, pastor of Vaux, who, after imprisonment for six months, escaped to England, and settled in London, where he became minister of the Pest House chapel. One of Peter's daughters married John Arnauld, a London merchant.—James Fontaine married for his second wife Marie Chaillon, in 1641, by whom he had two sons and three daughters; — of whom Mary married Peter Forestier, a zealous pastor, who took refuge in London, and whose son was a celebrated chronometer maker; Ann, who married Leon Testard Sieur des Meslars, and escaped to Plymouth with her husband, but died shortly after reaching England; James (see narrative at p. 301); and Peter, who, under the influence of his wife, abjured his religion, became a Roman Catholic, and remained in France. James Fontaine, so celebrated for his exploits at Bearhaven, died in Dublin, but nearly all his family subsequently emigrated to Virginia, and settled there. His eldest daughter, Mary Anne, married Matthew Maury, of Castel Mauron, Gascony, who for a time settled in Dublin, but afterwards left for America; and from this branch the

Maurys of Virginia are descended. The only one who remained in this country was Moses, who pursued the calling of an engraver, in London, in which he acquired considerable reputation. A lady in Australia writes to us as follows: "My great-great-grandfather Fontaine, or De la Fontaine, was at one time Lord of the Manor of Nismes. He was greatly persecuted for his faith. For a long time he preached to the people in the mountain gorges of the Cevennes. He ultimately escaped from France with his betrothed and his sister. After reaching London, one of his sons was employed in the Bank of England."

FORESTIER, or FORESTER: there were several refugees of this name in England. Peter Forester was minister of the French church, La Nouvelle Patente, 1708. Paul was minister of the French church at Canterbury; and another was minister of that at Dartmouth. Alexander was a director of the French Hospital in 1735; and James was a captain in the British army.

FORET, MARQUIS DE LA: a major-general in the British army, who served in the Irish campaign of 1699.

FOURDRINIER, HENRY: the inventor of the paper-making machine. He was descended from one of the numerous industrial families of the north of France, who fled into Holland at the Revocation. From Holland, Fourdrinier's father passed into England about the middle of the eighteenth century, and established a paper-manufactory. The first idea of the paper-making machine belonged to France, but Four-drinier fully developed it and embodied it in a working plan. He laboured at his invention for seven years, during which he was assisted by his brother Sealy and John Gamble. It was perfected in 1809. Several of the Fourdrinier family are buried in the French burying-ground at Wandsworth.

GABRIEL, GABRIELLE: a Huguenot family of this name settled in London after the Revocation of the Edict. Sir Thomas Gabriel, a recent Lord Mayor, is descended from them.

GAGNIER, JOHN : a celebrated Orientalist scholar, who, becoming converted to Protestantism, fled from France into England. The Bishop of Worcester appointed him his chaplain. In 1715 he was appointed professor of Oriental languages at Oxford. His son took the degree of M.A., and was appointed rector of Stranton in the diocese of Durham.

GALWAY, EARL OF : see p. 227.

GAMBIER : a French refugee family settled at Canterbury, the name very frequently occurring in the registers of the French church there. James Gambier, born 1692, became distinguished as a barrister : he was a director of the French Hospital in 1729. He had two sons, James and John. The former rose to be a vice-admiral, the second became governor of the Bahama Islands, where his son James, afterwards Lord

Gambier, was born, 1756. He early entered the royal navy, and rose successively to the ranks of post-captain, vice-admiral, and admiral. He was created a peer for his services in 1807. His elder brother, Samuel, was a commissioner of the navy ; and other members of the family held high rank in the same service.

GARENCIÉRES, THEOPHILUS DE : a doctor of medicine, native of Caen, who came over to England as physician to the French ambassador, and embraced Protestantism. He was the author of several medical works.

GARENCIÉRES, THE REV. DUDLEY: probably the son of the preceding. A minor canon of Chester, he was made rector of Handley, Cheshire, in 1684, also rector of Waverton, Cheshire, in 1696. According to Ormerod, in his *History of Cheshire*, the Rev. Mr. Garenciéres was the only minor canon who was promoted to a prebendal stall in Chester Cathedral. His son Theophilus was educated on the foundation of the King's School, Chester ; he went from thence to Oxford, and was afterwards rector of a church in Yorkshire.

GARRET, MARK : afterwards called Gerrard, the portrait-painter, a refugee from Bruges in Flanders, from whence he was driven into England by the religious persecutions in the Low Countries. He was king's painter in 1618.

GARRIC, GARRICK, GARRIGUE: an ancient family possessing estates near Castres, south of

Bourdeaux, of which Pierre Bouffard, Sieur de la Garrigue, was the head. Two of the scions of this family, Pierre and David, being Protestants, fled at the Revocation, the former to Holland, and the latter to England, both adopting, according to the usual custom, the name of the family estate. David fled from Bourdeaux and travelled by Saintonge, Poitou, and Brittany, to St. Malo, from whence he sailed for Guernsey, and afterwards reached London in October, 1685. He left his wife and his infant son, Peter (then only five months old), behind him, his wife arriving in London about two months after him, having come by sea in a little Guernsey vessel of only 14 tons, and her son about eighteen months later, accompanied by his nurse. This boy, on arriving at manhood, entered the army, was lieutenant of Dragoons, afterwards captain of the Old Buffs; and it was while recruiting at Hereford, in 1716, that his son David, afterwards the celebrated actor, was born, in the Angel Inn there. While abroad on foreign service, the captain's family resided at Lichfield, to which his wife belonged —Arabella Clough, daughter of one of the vicars of the cathedral. On arriving at manhood, Peter, the captain's eldest son, and his brother David, began the business of wine-merchants in London ; but the latter, not taking kindly to a business life, and probably conscious of the power within him, eventually left the wine trade and took to the stage, on which he displayed such extraordinary genius. See also notice at p. 174.

GASTIGNY : founder of the French Hospital in London. See p. 288.

GAUSSEN : there were several branches of this distinguished Protestant family in France. Haag mentions those of Saumur, Burgundy, Guienne, and Languedoc. David Gaussen, who took refuge in Ireland in 1685, belonged to Lunel in Languedoc. His descendants still flourish at Antrim, Belfast, and Dublin. The Gaussens who settled in England, were also from Languedoc. About the period of the Revocation, John Gaussen, son of Pierre (noble), emigrated from Lunel to Geneva, where he married Marie Bosanquet (also an emigré family still existing in England), by whom he had six children ; of these Francis emigrated to London, where he died, unmarried, in 1744 ; and Peter, who married in London a Mademoiselle Molet, died at Geneva without issue. Paul Gaussen emigrated from France after the Revocation, and died at Geneva in 1774. He married Catherine Salat, widow of Jacques de Beaumont (noble), and had issue, Jean Pierre and four other sons. Jean Pierre joined his two uncles in London, and became governor of the Bank of England, which he administered for many years. He married, in 1775, Anna Maria Bosanquet, daughter of Samuel Bosanquet, Esq., of Forest House, in Essex ; and died in 1778, leaving five children. The eldest, Samuel Robert Gaussen, of Brookman's Park, Herts, married Eliza Bosanquet, daughter of James Bosanquet, Esq. He was High-Sheriff of Herts, M.P. for Warwick, and a lieutenant-colonel of the militia. He died in 1812, leaving issue, of whom Peter, a captain in the Cold-stream Guards, died of fever contracted in the Walcheren expedition; Eliza married Mr. Whatman, of Vinters, near Maidstone; and Harriet married Colonel Best. Samuel Robert, the second son, who succeeded to the family estate in Herts, was also High-Sheriff of the county; he died in 1818, and left issue, Robert William Gaussen, Esq., of Brookman's Park, the present representative of the family, who was High-Sheriff in 1841. The same year he married Elizabeth, daughter of James Casamayor, Esq., by whom he has two sons—Robert George, and Casamayor William, the former of whom is captain in the Grenadier Guards. A Roman Catholic branch of the Gaussens, who remained in France, still holds large property in the neighbourhood of Montpellier; and many members of the family have distinguished themselves in the French military and diplomatic services. Other members of the Protestant branch are still resident in Geneva; the famous Pasteur Gaussen, the friend of Merle d'Aubigné, being one of them. It may be mentioned, as a singular illustration of how the Huguenot refugee families kept together, that the Gaussens, while neighbours of the Bosanquet family in France, twice intermarried with them there, and have, since the families settled in England, intermarried with them no less than four times.

GAUTIER, N : a physician of Niort, who took refuge in England at the Revocation. He was the author of several religious books.

GENESTE, LOUIS : the owner of a large estate in Guienne, which he forfeited by adhering to the Protestant religion. He first fled into Holland and took service under the Prince of Orange, whom he accompanied into England and Ireland, and fought in the battle of the Boyne in the regiment of Lord Lifford. After the pacification of Ireland, Geneste settled at Lisburn, and left behind him two sons and a daughter, among whose descendants may be mentioned Hugh Stowell, and Geneste, well known in the Christian world.

GEORGES, PAUL : two refugees of this name were ministers of the French church at Canterbury. One of them, from Chartres, was minister in 1630. The other, a native of Picardy, died in 1689, after a ministry of 42 years.

GERVAISE, LOUIS : a large hosiery merchant at Paris, elder of the Protestant church there. At the Revocation of the Edict, though seventy years of age, he was incarcerated in the Abbey of Gannat, from which he was transferred to that of Saint Magloire, then to the Oratory, and after that to the convent of Lagny and the castle of Angoulême. All methods of converting him having failed, he was finally banished from France in 1688, when he took refuge in London with his brother and his son, who had succeeded in escaping before him.

GIBERT, ETIENNE : one of the last refugees from France for conscience' sake. He laboured for some time as a pastor of the "Church in the Desert;" but the Bishop of Saintes having planned his capture, he fled into Switzerland. Afterwards, in 1763, we find him attending a secret synod in France, as deputy of Saintonge ; but at length, in 1771, he fled into England. He was minister of the French church of La Patente, in London, in 1776, and afterwards of the Chapel Royal of St. James. He was finally presented with the rectory of St. Andrew's in the island of Guernsey, where he died in 1817.

GOSSET : a Huguenot family, originally from Normandy ; they first settled in Jersey. Some of the younger branches passed over into England, where the first of the name that distinguished himself was Isaac, born 1683, celebrated for his skill in the fine arts ; amongst others, for his exquisite modelling of portraits in wax. He was buried in St. Marylebone churchyard, 1744. His grandson, Dr. Gosset, D.D., was a famous classical scholar and book collector, died 1812; he was father of the Rev. Isaac Gosset, for many years vicar of Windsor and Datchet, and chaplain to four successive sovereigns. Among the members of the elder branch of the family may be mentioned Matthew, for many years Vicomte of Jersey, who died 1842 ; Major - General Sir William Gosset, C.B., R.C.A., who held the office of Under-Secretary of State for Ireland ; was for some time M.P. for Truro ; and for several years sergeant-at-arms to the House of Commons: he died in 1848. Admiral Henry Gosset is now the eldest survivor of the senior branch of the family.

GOST, JOHN : the son of Daniel Gost, a French Protestant refugee, settled in Dublin about 1684. His son John was born in that city about 1715, and graduated in the University there. Having taken priest's orders, he was selected to perform the duty of pastor to the French Protestant congregation at Portarlington ; he was honoured with the degree of D.D., and appointed to the archdeaconry of Glendalough and rectory of Arklow. Besides sermons and other writings, Dr. Gost published a History of Greece.

GOULARD, JAMES, MARQUIS OF VERVANS : a Huguenot refugee in England, who died there in 1700. The marchioness, his wife, was apprehended when about to set out to join her husband. She was shut up in the convent of the Ursulines at Angoulême, from which she was successively transferred to the Abbey of Puyberlan, in Poitou, to the

Abbey of the Trinity at Poitiers, and finally to Port-Royal. Her courage at length succumbed, and she conformed, thereby obtaining possession of the estates of her husband.

GOYER, PETER : a refugee manufacturer from Picardy, who settled at Lisburn in Ireland. His son was English master in the Belfast academy. For notice see p. 299.

GRAVEROL, JOHN : born at Nismes, 1647, of a famous Protestant family. He early entered the ministry, and became pastor of a church at Lyons. He fled from France at the Revocation, and took refuge in London. He was pastor of the French churches in Swallow Street and the Quarré. Graverol was a voluminous author.

GROSTETE, CLAUDE : a refugee pastor in London, minister of the French church in the Savoy.

GROTE or DE GROOT : for notice, see p. 322.

GUALY : a Protestant family of Rouergue. Peter, son of the Sieur de la Gineste, fled into England at the Revocation, with his wife and three children—Paul, Francis, and Margaret. Paul entered the English army, and died a major-general. Francis also entered the army, and eventually settled at Dublin, where his descendants still live.

GUERIN : a French refugee family long settled at Rye, now represented by the Crofts.

GUIDE, PHILIP : a French physician of Paris, native of Châlons-sur-Saône, who took refuge in London at the Revocation. He was the author of several medical works.

GUILL, GEORGE : a refugee from the neighbourhood of Tours. He abandoned an estate and property in France of the value of £12,000. He left the following notice inscribed on his family Bible : "On Thursday, Oct. 11, 1685, we set out from Tours, and came to Paris on the 15th of the same month. On the 17th came out the King of France's declaration to drive out the Protestants, who had notice in Paris, in four days,—which, falling on the 21st, was just the day whereon our places in the waggon for Calais were retained ; and the day before, I was warned, by letters from Tours, that upon false accusations I was sought by the Intendant and other magistrates ; and that they had written to the Chancellor of France to send after me and arrest me. But it pleased God that, immediately after his signing and sealing the declaration, he fell sick and died, while we were on our journey." Guill arrived safely in London. His daughter afterwards married the Rev. Daniel Williams, D.D., the founder of the Williams Library ; and a great friend of the banished Huguenots.

GUILLEMARD, JOHN : a refugee in London from Champdeniers, where he had been minister. His descendants have been directors of the French Hospital at different times.

GUILLOT : several members of this family were officers in the navy of Louis XIV.

They emigrated to Holland at the Revocation, and were presented by the Prince of Orange with commissions in his navy. Their descendants settled at Lisburn in Ireland. Others of the same name—Guillot and Gillett—of like French extraction, settled in England, where their descendants are still to be found at Birmingham (everybody knows the " Gillott pens") and Sheffield, as well as at Glastonbury, Exeter, and Banbury.

GUYON DE GEIS, WILLIAM DE: son of the Sieur de Pampelona, a Protestant, who fled into Holland at the Revocation. He took service under William of Orange, and saw much service in the campaigns in Piedmont and Germany, where he lost an arm. William III. gave him a retiring pension. He settled at Portarlington, and died there in 1740. Several of his descendants have been officers in the English army. The last Count Guyon entered the Austrian service, and distinguished himself in the Hungarian rebellion of 1848.

HAESTRICHT: a Flemish refugee, who fled into England during the persecutions of the Duke of Alva in the Low Countries. He became a well-known manufacturer at Bow; and afterwards assumed the English name of James. The Flemings were given a site in Austin Friars, on which to build a Dutch church; and adjoining the church the James family still continue to hold their house property on a nominal ground rent from the Trustees.

The property has been in their possession since 1656.

HAMON : an ancient Normandy family. There were Hamons in Baccaville and Rouen who claimed descent from the great Hamon Dentatus, Earl of Corbeil, in that historic province. To this illustrious family belonged Hector Hamon, one of the first ministers of a Huguenot congregation that settled in England. He is described as *minister verbi Dei* to the little flock of refugees that worshipped nearly three hundred years ago in the crypt of Canterbury cathedral. The two brothers Hamon who settled at Portarlington in Ireland about the middle of the following century were descended from him. There are Hamons still in Ireland, though the name has in some cases been changed to Hammond.

HARENC: a refugee family from the south of France. Benjamin was a director of the French Hospital in 1765. He bought the estate of Footscray, Kent; his son married the daughter of Joseph Bernes, Esq., and was a prominent county magistrate. The family is at present represented by C. J. Harenc, Esq., barrister, on the Home Circuit.

HAZARD or HASAERT, PETER : a refugee in England from the persecutions in the Low Countries under the Duke of Parma. Returning on a visit to his native land, he was seized and burnt alive in 1568. His descendants still survive in England and Ireland under the name of Hassard.

HENZELL : a foreign Protest-

26

ant who settled at Newcastle-on-Tyne, about the time of the massacre of St. Bartholomew. He was joined by two other refugees, named Tysack and Tittory ; and the three established glassworks which long continued to flourish. To preserve their nationality, the members of the three families intermarried with each other ; and so much were they isolated from the other inhabitants of the district, that they were generally known as " the Pilgrims," or "the Strangers." In course of time, two of the families, the Tysacks and Tittorys, became extinct ; but the Henzells remained in possession of the glassworks until the commencement of the present century, when the owner died, and the works passed into other hands. Mr. Alderson, Town Hall, Manchester, married the granddaughter of the last owner of the works, of the name of Henzell ; but there are other members of the family still living in different parts of the country.

HERAULT, LOUIS : a refugee pastor from Normandy, who obtained a benefice in the English Church in the reign of Charles I. But he was found so zealous a Royalist that he was forced to fly again into France, from which, however, he returned at the Restoration, and obtained a canonry at Canterbury, which he enjoyed until his death.

HERVART, PHILIBERT, BARON DE HUNINGUE : a refugee of high character and station. In 690 William III. appointed him his ambassador at Geneva.

He afterwards settled at Southampton. He became governor of the French Hospital in 1720, to which he gave a sum of £4000, dying in the following year.

HEURTELEU, CHARLES ABEL : a native of Rennes, who came into England before the Revocation. The name has since been changed to Heurtley. The present representative of the family, Dr. Heurtley, Margaret Professor of Divinity, and Canon of Christ Church, Oxford, informs us that, among other family records, he possesses a passport to one of his ancestors, described as " Le Sieur du Creux, controlleur de la Maison de Monsieur le Prince." It is dated July, 1613, and is signed by Marshal Turenne, the father of the more eminent person who bore the name. Dr Heurtley does not know at what time the original refugee came into England. He had a daughter who returned to France, and who must have been born between 1684 and 1690. His son, probably by a second marriage, was born in England in 1707. He was baptized at Les Grecs, the French church in Soho. He was an officer in the English army, and served against the Pretender in 1745-6.

HIPPOLITE, STE. : see *Montolieu.*

HOUBLON, PETER : a refugee from Flanders because of his religion, who settled in England about the year 1568. His son John became an eminent merchant in London, his grandson James being the "father" of the Royal Exchange. Two sons of the latter, Sir James and Sir John, were aldermen of London. While the former represented the city in Parliament in 1698, the latter served it as Lord Mayor in 1695. Sir John was the first governor of the Bank of England ; he was also a commissioner of the Admiralty. Another brother, Abraham, was also a director and governor of the bank. His son, Sir Richard, left an only daughter, who married Henry Temple, created Lord Palmerston, 1722, from whom the late Lord Palmerston was lineally descended.

HUDEL or UDEL : a pastor of " Les Grecs " French church, London, the eldest son of a zealous Huguenot. He was confined in prison for a quarter of a century, and was only released at the death of Louis XIV.

HUGESSEN, JAMES : a refugee from Dunkirk, who settled at Dover. The family is now represented by E. Knatchbull-Hugessen, M.P. For notice, see p. 320.

JANSEN, THEODORE, youngest son of the Baron de Heez. The latter was a victim to the cruelty of the Duke of Alva in the Netherlands, and suffered death at the hands of the public executioner. Theodore took refuge in France, from whence the family fled into England. His grandson, also named Theodore, was knighted by William III., and created a baronet by Queen Anne. The family were highly distinguished as merchants and bankers in London. Three of

Sir Theodore's sons were baronets, two were members of Parliament, and one, Sir Stephen Theodore, was Lord Mayor of London in 1755.

JEUNE, LE JEUNE : George Le Jeune emigrated from France about the time of the massacre of St. Bartholomew, and settled in Jersey, where the family long continued to flourish, intermarrying with the families of St. Croix, De Carteret, Le Fevre, La Chappelain, etc. The Le Jeunes belonged originally to La Marche, from which they afterwards removed to Montpellier, the head-quarters of the Huguenot party in the south of France. They became sieurs of Chambson, one of them subsequently officiating as judge-royal of Villeneuve. In the sketch of the family pedigree which we have seen, George Jeune was settled in the parish of St. Brelade, Jersey, in 1570, in which year he married Marie Hubert. One of the last and most distinguished members of the family was the late Dr. François Jeune, Dean of Jersey 1838, and Bishop of Peterborough 1864. His father was the owner of a small estate in Jersey, long in the possession of the family.

JORTIN, RENE : a refugee from Brittany. For notice, see p. 332.

JUSTEL, HENRY : a great Protestant scholar, formerly secretary to Louis XIV., but a fugitive at the Revocation. On his arrival in England in 1684, the king appointed him royal librarian. He was the author of numerous works.

KERK, DAVID : a celebrated sea-captain, born in Dieppe, who took refuge in England about 1620 because of his religion, and entered the English naval service. When Charles I. declared war against France, in 1620, Kerk was put in command of a squadron of six ships, and sent out to Quebec, then a French fortress, to besiege and if possible reduce it. Kerk appeared before the fortress in July 1628, but with his weak squadron he failed to make any impression on it. He learnt, however, that the garrison were in great straits for want of provisions, and that a French fleet was on its way from France for their relief. He then dropped down the St. Lawrence, to lie in wait for the French squadron ; and on its making its appearance, he suddenly attacked, surprised, and captured the relieving ships. Again ascending the river, he summoned the garrison, now reduced to the last extremity ; and though Governor Champlain held out for a few weeks longer, he was at length compelled to surrender. Kerk was then appointed Governor of Quebec, and he held the office until the conclusion of a peace with France, when it was restored to its former owners.

LABAT, LABATT : a branch of this very ancient Normandy family, related to the Sabatiers and Chateauneufs, has been long settled in Ireland. The first Labat came over with William III., in whose army he was an officer. He was afterwards at the siege of Derry, on board the "Mount-joy," which burst the boom across the harbour mouth, and led to the raising of the siege. He eventually settled in King's County. The representative of the family is the Rev. Edward Labat, M.A., Rector of Kilcar, County Donegal.

LABILLIERE : the ancestor of the family, Peter de Labilliere, fled from France at the Revocation. He was naturalized along with Peter Bagneol, Daniel Souault, and others. He was described in his letters of naturalization as " Peter de Labilliere, son of Charles de Labilliere and François his wife, born in Languedoc, in France." He belonged to a noble family. From Hozier's *Armorial General ou Regestres de la Noblesse de France*, it appears that the De la Cours are lineally descended from Bernard de la Cour Damoiseau, born early in the fifteenth century. The fourth in descent from him was the "Noble Fulcrand de la Cour, Seigneur de Labilliere." In his will he declared that he belonged to the Reformed Faith. From his time until the Revocation the family continued Protestant ; but, on the perpetration of that great injustice, the Labillieres fled, but De la Cour de Montcamp and De la Cour de Viala abjured Protestantism and remained in France. The French general who fell defending Quebec belonged to the former branch. The "Noble Pierre de la Cour, Seigneur de la Gardoile," who was sponsor to Peter and Paul de Labilliere, died in London on the 3rd of

October, 1705. Peter de Labilliere was married in London
to Margue Francoise Reynaud.
He and Paul became officers in
the British army. The present
representative of the family is
a member of the English bar.

LABOUCHERE : an ancient distinguished Bearnese Protestant
family, whose original name
was Barrier. In 1621, Jean-
Guyon Barrier, notary-royal,
married Catherine de la Broue,
and from this union sprang
Francis, seigneur of Labouchere,
practitioner of law at Stranniac,
in the department of Commin-
gues. His son Peter, who was
a merchant at Orthez, being a
Protestant, sent his son and
daughter, Matthew and Susan,
to London to be educated by
their relative, Dr. Majendie,
pastor of the French church in
St. Martin's Lane, who was also
from Orthez. The children did
not return to France. Matthew went to Holland, where
he married and settled. He
had several sons, of whom
Peter-Cæsar established the
branch of the family which ultimately settled in England ;
while Samuel-Peter continued
the descent in Holland. The
former was born at the Hague
in 1772. After undergoing
some preliminary training in
the office of his uncle Peter at
Nantes, he entered the great
commercial house of Hope at
Amsterdam, in which he became
a partner at the age of twenty-
two, together with Mr. Alexander Baring, whose sister he
married. On the invasion of
Holland by Pichegru, in 1793,
the head-quarters of the house

of Hope were removed to London, where Mr. Labouchere
settled in 1799, and superintended the business for many
years, conducting many large
financial operations. Strange to
say, he possessed the confidence
in a large degree of Napoleon
Bonaparte, who employed him
privately in 1810, to sound the
British Government as to the
conditions on which they would
agree to a general peace. Mr. Labouchere retired from business
in 1822. His eldest son, Henry,
who took honours at Oxford,
sat in the House of Commons
for many years, was President
of the Board of Trade and Secretary for Ireland, and has since
been raised to the peerage under
the title of Baron Taunton.
His second son, who married a
Miss Dupré, also descended
from a Huguenot family, and
was for a long time one of the
principal partners in the London
banking house of Williams,
Deacon, Labouchere, and Co.

LABRUNE : see *Riou.*

LA CONDAMINE : an ancient
and noble family belonging to
the neighbourhood of Nismes.
André, the eldest, was a Protestant, and held to his religion ; Charles Antoine abjured,
and obtained possession of the
family estate. André fled with
his family, travelling by night
only,--his two youngest children swung in baskets across
a horse or mule. They succeeded in reaching the port of
St. Malo, and crossed to Guernsey. The boy who escaped in
the basket founded a family of
British subjects. His son John
became King's Comptroller of

Guernsey, and colonel of the Guernsey militia ; and his descendants still survive in England and Scotland.

LALO : of the house of De Lalo in Dauphiny, a brigadier in the British army, killed at the battle of Malplaquet.

LA MELONNIÉRE, ISAAC DE MONCEAU, SIEUR DE : a lieutenant-colonel in the French army, who fled from France at the Revocation, and joined the army of the Prince of Orange. He raised the regiment, called after him, "Lameloniére's Foot." He served throughout the campaigns in Ireland and Flanders, and was raised to the rank of major-general. Several of his descendants have been distinguished officers in the British army.

LA MOTTE, FRANCIS : a refugee from Ypres in Flanders, who settled at Colchester as a manufacturer of bays and sayes. His son John became an eminent and wealthy merchant of London, of which he was an alderman.

L'ANGLE, DE : for notice, see p. 256.

LANGLOIS : Benjamin Langlois, Under Secretary of State for the Home Department, who died in 1802, was youngest son of Pierre Langlois, by Julie de la Melonniére, sister of Lieutenant-colonel de la Melonniére, mentioned above. The family was from Montpellier, but originally from Normandy, and was naturalised in England in 1702. Pierre Langlois left four sons, three of whom died unmarried. Of these Peter Langlois rose to great distinction in

the Austrian service, and died in 1788, Governor of Trieste, a Feld Zuegmeister, and high in the favour of the Emperor Joseph II. He left an only daughter, who married Anthony Lefroy of Leghorn. See *Lefroy.*

LA PIERRE : a Huguenot family of Lyons. Marc-Conrad was a magistrate, and councillor to the Parliament of Grenoble —a man highly esteemed for his learning and integrity. He left France at the Revocation, and settled in England. One of his sons was minister of Spring Gardens French church in 1724 ; and Pierre de la Pierre was a director of the French Hospital in 1740.

LA PILLONIERE : a Jesuit converted to Protestantism, who took refuge in England about 1716. He was the author of several works relating to his conversion, and also on English history.

LA PRIMAUDAYE : a noble Protestant family of Anjou. Several of them took refuge in England. In 1740 Pierre de la Primaudaye was a governor of the French Hospital, and others of the same name afterwards held that office.

LA RIVE : a refugee settled in Ireland, who escaped with his wife, by pretending to be sellers of oranges, and going about with a donkey and panniers. On reaching Holland the Prince of Orange gave him a commission in his troops, and he acquitted himself bravely in the Irish campaigns. He afterwards became agent to Sir C. Wandersforde at Castle

Corner, where he died, and his tombstone is to be seen in the churchyard of that place.

LA ROCHE : a refugee from Bordeaux, originally named Crothaire, whose son became M.P. for Bodmin in 1727. His grandson, Sir James Laroche, Bart., also sat for the same borough in 1768.

LAROCHEFOUCAULD, FREDE-RICK CHARLES DE, Count de Roye : an able officer of Louis XIV., field-marshal under Turenne, who served in the great campaigns between 1672 and 1683. He left France at the Revocation, first entering the Danish service, in which he held the post of grand-marshal. He afterwards settled in England. He died at Bath in 1690. His son Frederick William was a colonel of one of the six French regiments sent to Portugal under Schomberg. He was promoted to the rank of major-general, and was raised to the peerage (for life) under the title of Earl of Lifford in Ireland.

LAROCHEFOUCAULD, FRANCIS DE : son of the Baron de Montendre. He escaped from the abbey of the Canons of Saint Victor, where he had been shut up for "conversion," and fled to England. He entered the English army, served in Ireland, where he was master-general of artillery, and rose to the rank of field-marshal.

LA ROCHE-GUILHAM, MELLE DE : a voluminous writer of romances of the Scuderi school. He was a Protestant, and first took refuge in Holland, and afterwards settled in England

about 1697, though his works were still published abroad, mostly in Amsterdam.

LARPENT, JOHN DE : a refugee from Caen in Normandy, who fled into England at the Revocation. His son and grandson were employed in the Foreign Office. The two sons of the latter were F. S. Larpent, judge advocate-general in Spain under the Duke of Wellington, and Sir George Gerard De Hochepied Larpent, Bart.

LA TOMBE, THOMAS : a Protestant refugee from Turcoigne, in the Low Countries, who settled at Norwich about 1558. His son, of the same name, was a thriving merchant in London in 1634.

LA TOUCHE : a noble Protestant family of the Blesois, between Blois and Orleans, where they possessed considerable estates. The eldest son of the family, Paul de la Touche, having conformed, retained possession of the estates, and also obtained those of his uncle, Digues de la Brosse, who had refused to conform, and fled to Amsterdam, where he settled. Paul's young brother, David, also remained staunch to the Protestant faith, and fled to join his uncle, taking with him a Bible which is still preserved in the family. Shortly after reaching Amsterdam, his uncle obtained for him a commission in Caillemotte's Dragoons, with which he afterwards served in the Irish campaigns ; his gallant conduct at the Boyne securing his promotion. At the close of the war, the regiment was disbanded in Dublin, where many of the officers settled, amongst others, Digues de la Touche. "Having a little money," says his biographer, "he and another Huguenot established a silk, poplin, and cambric manufactory, articles which were produced in high perfection, and soon acquired celebrity. For the sale of them, a shop was opened in the High Street. Many of his countrymen had to visit the provinces with the view of ascertaining eligible places of settlement. The refugees usually left with him what money and other valuables they had, beyond what was required for travelling expenses, that it might be in safe custody till their return. Thus a considerable amount of property came into his hands." To employ the money at profitable interest, advances were made on good security, or remittances were sent to London for the purpose; hence the origin of the Latouche Bank. At his death, his eldest son, David, succeeded to the Bank, and his younger son, James, to the poplin trade, both of which prospered. Both brothers founded families, from which have come the Latouches of Bellevue, Marlay, Harristown, and Sans-Souci. Many members of the family have held high offices, sat in Parliament, and intermarried with the landed aristocracy. — N. Latouche, a refugee in London, but unconnected with the above, was the author of an excellent French grammar.

LA TRANCHE, FRÉDÉRIC DE : a Huguenot gentleman, who took refuge in England shortly after the massacre of St. Bartholomew. He first settled in Northumberland, from whence his descendants removed to Ireland, and founded the Trench family, the head of which is the Earl of Clancarty. Many high dignitaries of the church, and officers in the army and civil service, have belonged to this family. The present Archbishop of Dublin is a Trench as well as a Chenevix (which see), being thus doubly a Huguenot by his descent. The Power-Keatings are a branch of the Trench family. The Earl of Ashtoun is the head of another branch.

LA TREMOUILLE, CHARLOTTE DE : wife of James Stanley, Earl of Derby. The Countess was a Protestant—the daughter of Claude de la Tremouille and his wife, the Princess of Orange. Sir Walter Scott incorrectly makes the Countess to have been a Roman Catholic.

LA TROBE, JEAN : a Huguenot refugee from the south of France shortly after the Revocation of the Edict of Nantes. He came to Ireland by way of Holland, and settled in Waterford about the year 1690. He was of a noble family (originally of Villemur, near Montauban in Languedoc), which had early become attached to the doctrines of the Reformation, and had shared in all the vicissitudes of the party both before and after the accession of Henri IV. Jean La Trobe died in Dublin at an advanced age. Among his descendants are names which have since been of note in literature, science, and art, both in England and in the United States of America. The grandson of Jean la Trobe, Benjamin la Trobe, married into a Protestant refugee family, who had emigrated from the Palatinate after its devastation by Louis XIV., and had taken refuge in the British plantations in Pennsylvania. The name, originally *Von Blume*, was changed to *Antes*, which it still bears ; and there is no doubt but that it is from this family that the very marked engineering talent which has distinguished many of the descendants of Benjamin La Trobe, both in England and America, is derived. The name of La Trobe has been more particularly and honourably associated, for the last hundred years, with Protestant missionary work among the heathen in the British dependencies, in consequence of the connection of the elder branch of the family with the church of the United Brethren or Moravians.

LAVAL, ETIENNE-ABEL : author of a *History of the Reformation and of the Reformed Churches of France*, and minister of the French church in Castle Street, London, about the year 1730.

LA VALLADE : pastor of the French church at Lisburn, in Ireland, during forty years. He left an only daughter, who married, in 1737, George Russell, Esq., of Lisburn, whose descendants survive.

LAYARD : an ancient Albigensian family, whose original name was Raymond "de Lay-

arde" (near Montpellier), being merely their *nom de terre*, as in so many similar cases. Pierre Raymond de Layarde, born 1666, left France about the period of the Revocation. He attended William III. into England as major in General Verey's Regiment of Foot. The family settled first at Canterbury, of which Pierre de Layarde was mayor ; and we find in the church register there the baptism of his son Gaspard, in 1725. Another son, Daniel-Peter, was a celebrated doctor, and held the appointment of physician to the Dowager Princess of Wales. He was the author of numerous works on medicine ; amongst others, of a treatise on the cattle distemper, which originally appeared in the *Philosophical Transactions*, and has since been frequently reprinted. The doctor had three sons—Charles-Peter, afterwards prebendary of Worcester and dean of Bristol ; Anthony-Louis and John-Thomas, who both entered the army, and rose, the one to the rank of general, and the other to that of lieutenant-general. Austin Layard, lately M.P., so well known for his exploration of the ruins of Nineveh, and Colonel F. P. Layard, are grandsons of the above dean of Bristol. Two cousins are in the church. The head of the family is Brownlow Villiers Layard, Esq., of Riversdale, near Dublin.

LE BAS, PETER : a Protestant refugee naturalised in 1687, from whom descended the late eminent divine, the Rev.

Charles Webb Le Bas, LL.B., president of the East India College at Haileybury.

LE COURRAYER, PIERRE-FRANCOIS : a canon of St. Geneviève at Paris, afterwards canon of Oxford. He was a very learned man and a voluminous author. Having maintained, as a Roman Catholic, the validity of ordination by the bishops of the Anglican Church because of their unbroken succession from the apostles, he was denounced by his own Church as a heretic, and excommunicated. In 1728 Le Courrayer took refuge in England, and was cordially welcomed by Wake, then Archbishop of Canterbury. The university of Oxford conferred upon him the degree of D.D. Although he officiated as canon of Oxford, he avowed to the last that he had not changed his religion ; and that it was the Roman Catholic Church and not he that was in fault, in having departed from the doctrines and practices of the early church. Le Courrayer died in London in 1776.

LE FANU : a Norman Protestant family. Etienne Le Fanu, of Caen, having, in 1657, married a lady who professed the Roman Catholic religion, her relatives claimed to have her children brought up in the same faith. Le Fanu nevertheless had three of them baptized by Protestant ministers. The fourth was seized and baptized by the Roman Catholic vicar. At the mother's death, the maternal uncle of the children claimed to bring them up, and to set aside their father, because of his being a Protestant ; and the magistrates of Caen ordered Le Fanu to give up the children accordingly. He appealed to the parliament of Rouen in 1671, and they confirmed the decision of the magistrates. Le Fanu refused to give up his children, and was consequently cast into prison, where he lay for three years. He afterwards succeeded in making his escape into England, and eventually settled in Ireland, where his descendants still survive.

LE FEVRE : many refugees of this name settled in England. The Lefevres of Anjou were celebrated as chemists and physicians. Nicholas, physician to Louis XIV. and demonstrator of chemistry at the Jardin des Plantes, was invited over to England by Charles II., and made physician and chemist to the king in 1660. Sebastian Lefevre, M.D., of Anjou (one of whose sons, Pierre, suffered death for his religion), was admitted licentiate of the London College of Physicians in 1684. Another family of the same name, from Normandy, settled in Spitalfields, where they long carried on the silk manufacture. From this line, the present Lord Eversley is descended. For notice, see p. 326.

LEFROY : Antoine Leffroy, a native of Cambray, took refuge in England from the persecutions in the Low Countries about the year 1587, and settled at Canterbury, where his descendants followed the business of silk-dyeing, until the death of Thomas Leffroy in1723. The family appears to have been originally from Picardy, where the name Leffroy is still to be found. The sole descendant of this Antoine established himself in business. Anthony Lefroy settled at Leghorn in 1728, and died there in 1779. He was a great antiquarian, and possessed one of the most extensive collections of coins ever made by a private person, numbering over 6600 pieces, many of them of the utmost rarity : *vide Catalogus numismaticus Musei Lefroyani.* He left two sons, Lieutenant-Colonel Anthony Lefroy, of Limerick, father of the Right Hon. Thomas Lefroy, ex-Chief Justice of the Court of Queen's Bench, Ireland, and from whom is the Irish branch ; and the Rev. I. P. G. Lefroy, Rector of Ashe, Hants, from whom is the English branch of the family of this name. The present Brigadier-General, J. H. Lefroy, R.A., F.R.S., has compiled a private monograph " relating to the family of Leffroy."

LE GOULAN : a pupil of Vauban, and a refugee at the Revocation ; general of artillery in the army of William III. He served with distinction in Ireland, Germany, and Italy, and died abroad.

LE KEUX : the celebrated architectural engraver, was descended from a Huguenot refugee, his father being a manufacturer of pewter in London. His master Basire

was also a Huguenot, whom Le Keux greatly excelled in his breadth and boldness of style. His son inherited much of his father's genius.

LE MOINE, ABRAHAM : son of a refugee from Caen. He was chaplain to the Duke of Portland, rector of Eversley, Wilts, and the author of numerous works. He died in 1760.

L'ESCURY : see *Collot.*

LESTANG : a Protestant family of Poitou, one of whom acted as aide-de-camp to the Prince of Orange on his invasion of England. Another, Louis de Lestang, settled at Canterbury with his family.

LE SUEUR : the refugee sculptor who executed the fine bronze equestrian statue of Charles I. at Charing Cross. Another work of his, still preserved, is the bronze statue of the Earl of Pembroke in the picture-gallery at Oxford. The statue of Charles was sold by Parliament for old metal, when it was purchased by Jean Rivet, supposed to be another refugee, and preserved by him until after the Restoration.—A refugee named Le Sueur was minister of the French church at Canterbury.

LETABLÉRE or DE L'ESTABLÉRE : an ancient family, of large landed possessions in France, several members of which emigrated at the Revocation of the Edict of Nantes, and settled in England and Ireland. Of these, René de la Douespe, lord of the manor of Letablére, in the parishes of Saint Germain and Mouchamps, near Fontenai, in Lower Poitou, left France in 1685, at the age of 22, "on the dragoons coming to his mother's," as expressed in the records of the family. He arrived in Holland the same year, when he entered the military service of the Prince of Orange. He was an officer in Du Cambon's Foot at the battle of the Boyne, and afterwards in Lifford's Horse. It appears from a manuscript account in the possession of his descendants, that René received remittances at various times (amounting to 5570 livres) from his relatives in France, who succeeded to the estates which he had renounced for the sake of his religion. In 1723, when about 60 years old, he returned to the scenes of his youth, and visited his numerous relations in Poitou. On that occasion the heirs of those who had succeeded to his ancestral possessions presented him with 4000 livres. Returning to Dublin, he settled, and died there in 1729, at the age of 66. His son. Dr Daniel Letablére, Dean of Tuam, to whose memory a monument has been erected in St. Patrick's Cathedral, was a divine eminent for his piety and learning. He was a great promoter of the Dublin silk-manufacture, and was presented by the Mason's Guild with the Freedom in a silver snuff-box, still in the possession of the family. The dean's youngest daughter, Esther Charlotte Letablére, the eventual heiress of the family, married Edward Litton, Esq., an officer in H.M. 37th Foot, who served with distinction in the first American war, and was wounded at Bunker's Hill. Of this marriage there are three surviving sons—Daniel Litton, Esq., of Dublin ; Edward Litton, Esq., of Altmore, County Tyrone, a Master in Chancery, for some time leader of the bar in Ireland, formerly M.P. for Coleraine ; and John Litton, Esq., J.P., of Ardavilling, County Cork.

LE THIEULLIER, JOHN : a Protestant refugee from Valenciennes. His grandson was a celebrated London merchant, who was knighted in 1687.

LE VASSOR, MICHAEL : a refugee from Orleans, who entered the English Church, and held a benefice in the county of Northampton, where he died. He was the author of several works,—amongst others of a *History of Louis XIII.*, which gave great offence to Louis XIV.

LIGONIER : a Protestant family of Castres. Jean Louis was a celebrated general in the English service; he was created Lord Ligonier and Baron Inniskillin. During his life he was engaged in nineteen pitched battles and twenty-three sieges, without ever having received a wound. One of his brothers, Antoine, was a major in the English army; and another, who was raised to the rank of brigadier, was mortally wounded at the battle of Falkirk. For further notice of Lord Ligonier, see p. 240.

LOGIER, JEAN-BERNARD : a refugee musician, inventor of the method of musical notation which bears his name. He settled as a teacher of music at Dublin, where he died.

LOMBART, PIERRE: a celebrated French Engraver, who took refuge in England in the reign of Charles I., and remained there until the early period of the Restoration. During that time he produced a large number of highly esteemed engravings. He died at Paris, and was interred in the Protestant cemetery at Charenton a few years before the Revocation.

LUARD, ROBERT ABRAHAM: a Huguenot refugee from Caen, who settled in London. His son, Peter Abraham, became a great Hamburg merchant. George Augustus Luard, Esq., of Blyborough Hall, is the present head of the family, to which Major Luard, of the Mote, Tunbridge, also belongs.

LUSANCY: see *Chastelet.*

MAITTAIRE, MICHAEL: a celebrated philologist, linguist, and bibliographer, — one of the masters of Westminster School at the beginning of the eighteenth century. He was an able writer, principally on classical and religious subjects. Haag gives a list of sixteen of his works.

MAJENDIE: Several refugees from Bearn of this name fled into England at the Revocation. One of them became pastor of the French church at Exeter. His son, Jean-Jacques Majendie, D.D., was pastor of the French church in St. Martin's Lane, and afterwards of the Savoy. The son of this last became Bishop of Bangor, and afterwards of Chester. The present head of the family is —— Majendie, Esq., of Hedingham Castle.

MANGIN: several refugees of this name from Metz settled in Ireland. Paul became established at Lisburn, where he married Madelaine, the daughter of Louis Crommelin.

MARCET: a refugee family from Meaux, originally settled at Geneva, from whence Alexander came over to London about the end of last century, and settled as a physician. He was one of the founders of the Medico-Chirurgical Society, Physician to Guy's Hospital, and the author of many valuable works on medicine and chemistry. Mrs. Marcet was also the author of some excellent popular works on political economy and natural history.

MARIE, JEAN: minister of the Protestant church at Lion-sur-Mer, who took refuge in England after the massacre of St. Bartholomew, and became pastor of the French church at Norwich. His son Nathaniel was minister of a French church in London.

MARION, ELIÉ: a refugee from the Cevennes. He joined his friend Cavalier in England. Francis Marion, the celebrated general in the American War of Independence, is said to have been one of his descendants.

MARTINEAU, GASTON: a surgeon of Dieppe, who fled into England at the Revocation, and settled at Norwich. His son David was also a skilful surgeon. Many of their descendants still exist, and some of them are highly distinguished in modern English literature.

MASERES, FRANCIS : a celebrated judge and mathematician. At the Revocation, the grandfather of Maseres escaped into Holland, took service in the army of William of Orange, and came over to England in the regiment of Schomberg, in which he served as a lieutenant. He was afterwards employed in Portugal, where he rose to the rank of colonel. His son studied medicine at Cambridge, took his degree of doctor and practised in London. Francis Maseres, the grandson of the refugee, also studied at Cambridge ; and after distinguishing himself in mathematics, he embraced the profession of the law. Besides his eminence as a judge, he was an able and industrious author. Haag gives the titles of fifteen books published by him on different subjects. His *Historiæ Anglicanæ Selecta Monumenta* is a mine of antiquarian learning.

MASSUE, HENRI DE, Marquis de Ruvigny : for notice of, see p. 219; and his son Henry, Earl of Galway, pp. 227-33, 265, 311.

MATHY, MATTHEW : a celebrated physician and author. After a residence in Holland, he settled in England about the middle of last century. He was admitted a fellow of the Royal Society, of which he was appointed secretary in 1758. He was afterwards appointed librarian of the British Museum, in which office he was succeeded by his son.

MATURIN, GABRIEL : a refugee pastor who escaped from France after having been shut up in the Bastile for twenty-six years. He settled in Ireland, where he arrived a cripple. His son Peter became dean of Killala, and his grandson dean of St. Patrick's, Dublin. From him descended the Rev. C. Maturin, senior fellow, Trinity College, Dublin, rector of Fanet ; the Rev. C. R. Maturin, an eloquent preacher, author of *Bertram ;* and Gabriel Maturin, Esq., Washington.

MAUDUIT, ISAAC : descended from a Norman refugee settled at Exeter as a merchant. Isaac was a dissenting minister at Bermondsey. He was the father of Jasper Mauduit, Esq, of Hackney.

MAURY, MATTHEW : a refugee gentleman from Castle Mauron in Gascony, who settled in London for a time. His son James was ordained a minister there. The family afterwards emigrated to Virginia, U.S., where their descendants survive. Captain Maury, LL.D., belonged to the family.

MAYERNE, THEODORE DE : a celebrated physician, belonging to a Lyons family, originally from Piedmont. He studied medicine at Heidelberg and Montpellier, where he took his degree of M.D. in 1595. He opened a medical school at Paris, in which he delivered lectures, and obtained an extensive practice. Henry IV. appointed him his first physician. After the assassination of the King, Marie de Medicis endeavoured to convert Mayerne from Protestantism ; but he was firm, and consequently lost the patronage of the court. James I. invited him over to England, and appointed him his first physician. The universities of Oxford and Cambridge conferred honorary degrees upon him, and he obtained a large practice in London. After the execution of Charles I. he retired into private life, and died at Chelsea in 1655.

MAZIERES, DE : a Protestant family of Aunis, north of Saintonge, several members of which fled from France at the Revocation. Peter was a lieutenant in the French army, and afterwards joined the army of William of Orange. He settled at Youghal, in Ireland, where he died in 1746. Other members of the family settled at Cork, where they left numerous descendants.

MERCIER, JEAN LE : born at Usez in Languedoc. A famous Hebrew scholar. He married one of the Morell family. His descendants survive in England.

MERCIER, PHILIP : a portrait-painter, born at Berlin, of French refugee origin. He afterwards settled in London, where he died in 1760. He was patronised by Frederick Prince of Wales. Many of his portraits were engraved by Simon, Faber, Avril, and Heudelot (refugee engravers in London), as well as by English artists.

MESNARD, JEAN : one of the pastors of the Protestant church of Charenton at Paris,

from which he fled into Holland at the Revocation. His brother Philip, pastor of the Church of Saintes, was fined 10,000 livres and condemned to perpetual banishment ; his church was demolished and a cross set up on its site. Mesnard was invited to Copenhagen by the queen, Charlotte Amelia, and appointed pastor of the French church there. He afterwards came over to England, and became minister of the Chapel-Royal of St. James in 1700. He was appointed a director of the French hospital in 1718 ; and died in 1727.

METTAYER, JOHN : minister of the Patente in Soho ; afterwards minister of the French church at Thorpe-le-Soken, where he died in 1707.

MEUSNIER, PHILIP : a refugee painter of architectural subjects, who studied under Nicholas de Larquillière, another refugee artist.

MISSON, MAXIMILIEN : one of the Protestant judges in the " Chamber of the Edict," at the Parliament of Paris. At the Revocation he fled into England, and was selected by the Duke of Ormond as tutor to his grandson. Misson travelled with him through Europe, and afterwards published several books of travels.

MISSY, CÆSAR DE : son of a refugee merchant from Saintonge established at Berlin, who studied for the ministry, and came over to England in 1731, where he was appointed minister of the French church of the Savoy, in London, and afterwards of St. James's. He was the author of many able works.

MOIVRE, ABRAHAM : see *De Moivre.*

MOLENIER, STEPHEN : a refugee pastor from the isle of Jourdain, who fled into England and became minister of the French church at Stonehouse, Plymouth.

MONCEAU, ISAAC DE : see *La Melonniére.*

MONTENDRE, DE : see *Larochefoucauld.*

MONTOLIEU, DE SAINT HIPPOLITE : Of this noble family, David came to England with the army of William III., under whom he also served in Flanders. He was made a colonel and afterwards a brigadier-general. His descendants still survive in several noble and gentle families.

MORELL, DANIEL ; born in a village in Champagne about the period of the Revocation ; he lost his parents , supposed to have been murdered, at an early age. He was brought up from his infancy by a Protestant nurse, Madame Conté, whose son—Morell's foster-brother—fled with him into Holland, under the guidance of a party of refugee Protestants of distinction. When Daniel Morell and Stephen Conté grew up to manhood, they entered the army of William III., and fought under him through the Irish campaigns. The foster-brothers settled in life, married, and saw themselves united again in their old age, in the persons of their children. Young Daniel Morell married the daughter of Conté, and the

issue was Stephen Morell, who entered the navy, served under Hawke and Boscawen, and died at Maldon, in Essex, at an advanced age, leaving behind him three sons, all of whom became eminent as dissenting ministers. The eldest son, Stephen, was minister of an Independent congregation at Little Baddon, Essex ; the second, Dr. John, was minister of a Unitarian congregation at Brighton ; and the youngest son, Thomas, was for twenty years theological tutor of the Independent Academical Institution known as Coward College. Dr. Morell, author of *The History of Philosophy,* and other well-known works, belongs to this family. See further incidental notice at p. 167.

MOTHE, CLAUDE DE LA : refugee minister of the church in the Savoy. For notice of, see p. 258.

MOTTEUAX, PETER ANTHONY : poet and translator ; a refugee from Rouen, who fled into England and settled in London in 1660. He first translated and published Don Quixote and Rabelais into English, which were received with great favour. He also published several volumes of poetry and a tragedy, "Beauty in Distress." Notwithstanding his success as an English author, he abandoned literature for commerce, and made a considerable fortune by a series of happy speculations. He died in 1717.

NADAULD : a Huguenot family who settled at Ashford-in-the-Water, in Derbyshire, shortly after the Revocation. The grandson of the original refugee was the Rev. Thomas Nadauld, for upwards of fifty years incumbent of Belper and Turnditch. One of the members of the family was a celebrated watchmaker and silversmith. Another was a sculptor, who was employed by the Duke of Devonshire to execute some of the most important works at Chatsworth Palace. Others were clergymen, surgeons, and officers in the British army.

NICHOLAS, ABEL: descended from an ancient family in Brittany. He left France at the Revocation, and settled at East Looc in Cornwall. His eldest son, Paul, was twice mayor of the town, and left descendants. Nicholas was major in a dragoon regiment, and John, captain in the Royal Marines, afterwards mayor of East Looe. Other descendants of the family have been officers in the army and navy.

NOODT, NOOTH : an ancient family of North Brabant, frequently mentioned in Dutch history under the name of Van der Noodt. One of them, a colonel, distinguished himself greatly at the siege of Ostend. One branch of the family remained Roman Catholics, and their descendants still exist in Belgium ; another became Protestant, and emigrated into England in the 17th century. In 1712 we find James Nooth vicar-choral of Wells Cathedral. He married Miss Winchcombe, cousin of Lady Bolingbroke, and his son, Colonel Nooth, marrying Miss Anne

Assheton Yates, heiress of the Vavasours of Spaldington, Co. York, he assumed the name of Vavasour, now represented by Sir H. M. Vavasour, Bart.— Another member of the same family informs us that his branch came into Cumberland in the time of Henry I., and that they migrated into Pembrokeshire, where they were settled for centuries, at Easthook Hall, near Haverford West.—One of the Van der Noodts was high in office at Brussels. He was Burgomaster of the city, and his arms are carved on the Hotel de Ville. He was a great benefactor of the city.

OLIER, D'OLIER : an ancient, powerful, and noble family in the south of France, whose names are of constant occurrence in French history. Bertrand Olier was Capitoul of Toulouse as early as 1364. Members of the family held high offices under the French kings ; intermarrying with the Colberts, Malherbes, Beauregards, and other illustrious lines. Edouard Olier, secretary to the king and councillor of parliament, was made Marquis of Nointel in 1656. His eldest son, Charles Edouard, was French Ambassador at Constantinople in 1673. The second son, Paul, was a chevalier of Malta ; and it was intended that Pierre Olier (of Collegnes near Montauban), the third son, should enter the same order, but having embraced the doctrines of the Reformation, he was precluded from doing so. He married, 1665, Genevieve Genoud de Guiberville, by whom he had issue, Isaac Olier; he fled from France at the Revocation and entered the service of William, Prince of Orange, who afterwards, in acknowledgment of his valuable services, bestowed upon him a grant of land. In the year 1686, he was made a free burgess of the city of Amsterdam. He eventually settled in Dublin, with the freedom of which he was also presented in 1697. He now assumed the name of D'Olier. His grandson, Jeremiah, was high-sheriff in the year 1788,— one of the principal streets in the city being named after him, D'Olier Street. He was one of the founders of the Bank of Ireland, of which he was a governor, as was also his relative, the late Isaac M. D'Olier of Collegnes, Co. Dublin. A second branch of the Olier family in France held the Marquisate of Verneuil, and numbered many illustrious names.— The late Rev. Sydney Smith's mother was Maria Olier, daughter of a Huguenot refugee from Languedoc, but it is not known that she belonged to the above family.

ONWHYN : see *Unwin.*

OUVRY, JAMES : a refugee from the neighbourhood of Dieppe about the period of the Revocation. His family became settled in Spitalfields, and, were owners of freeholds there in the early part of last century. Frederic Ouvry, treasurer of the Society of Antiquaries, belongs to the family ; also Francisca I. Ouvry, author of *Henri de Rohan, or the Hu-*guenot *Refugee,* and other works.

PAGET, VALERAIN : a refugee from France after the massacre of St. Bartholomew, who settled in Leicestershire and founded a flourishing family, the head of which is Thomas Paget, Esq., of Humberstown. Charles, lately M.P. for Nottingham, belongs to the family.

PAIN, ELIE : a merchant in Paris, who fled from France at the Revocation and settled in London, where he greatly prospered. Numerous French Protestants of the same name fled into England, where their descendants still survive under the names of Pain, Paine, or Payne. At Deal and Sandwich, at Rye, and in the southern counties, the Paines are numerous. One of the ministers of the French church at Bristol was a M. Pain. Louis Pain was a well-known author, and William was an architect in London.

PALAIRET, ELIE : descended from a refugee family settled at Rotterdam, from whence he passed over into England. He became minister of the French church at Greenwich, and afterwards of St. John's Church, London. He was the author of numerous able philological works. Another of the name, John, born at Montauban, 1697, emigrated to England, and became French master to the royal family ; he was also the author of numerous works.

PAPILLON, DAVID : a refugee from Avranches, where he was imprisoned for three years because of his religion. Le Sieur Papillon took refuge in England in 1685, but several members of the family had settled here before the Revocation. In 1695, Philip Papillon represented the city of London in Parliament, and other members of the family have since represented London, Dover, Romney, and Colchester. The present head of the family is David Papillon, Esq., of Crowhurst, Sussex.

PAPIN, DENIS : for notice, see p. 244.

PARMENTIER, JACQUES : a refugee portrait and historical painter. He was employed, with several other refugee artists, in the decoration of Montague House (now the British Museum), after which he worked at the decoration of the palace of King William at Loo, in Holland. Returning to England, he obtained commissions to paint altar-pictures for Holy Trinity Church, Hull, and St. Peter's, Leeds ; as well as pictures for Worksop Manor, and Painter's Hall, London. He died in 1730.

PASSAVANT, JEAN-ULRIC : a refugee from Strasburg, where he was born in 1678. Settling in England, he purchased the manufactory of Gobelin tapestry for some time established at Fulham, and removed it to Exeter, where it long continued to flourish.

PAUL, LEWIS : inventor of spinning by rollers, son of a French refugee who settled in England, and practised as a physician shortly after the Revocation.

PECHEL, SAMUEL DE : lord of La Buissonade, near Montauban. He was subjected to cruel persecution at the period of the Revocation, having been thrown into prison, where he was kept for eighteen months. His wife, near her confinement, fled from her home with four children ; and the house was given up to pillage by the dragoons. De Pechel, after long imprisonment, was at length transported to the island of St. Domingo, from which he contrived to escape. He arrived in England, and there found his wife, bereft of her children. They had all been taken from her and sent to convents to be educated as Roman Catholics. These daughters afterwards succeeded to the family estates, which their descendants still hold. The Pechel family, however, greatly prospered in England. Several of them have been directors of the French Hospital. Samuel Pechell was a Master in Chancery, and Lieutenant-Colonel Paul Pechell, of Pagglesham, Essex, was created a baronet in 1797. Two other descendants of the family have been rear-admirals and occupied seats in the House of Commons. The present head of the family is Sir G. S. Brooke Pechell, Bart.

PEGORIER, CÆSAR : a native of Roujan, in Languedoc, minister of the church of Sénitot, in Normandy, until the Revocation, when he fled into England. He was for some time minister of the Artillery Church, Spitalfields, and afterwards of the Tabernacle.

PELESSIER, ABEL : a refugee Huguenot officer who settled at Portarlington. His two sons were clergymen, and other members of the family have been officers in the army.

PERRIN, COUNT : a Huguenot refugee from Nouere, where he had large possessions. He originally settled at Lisburn, in Ireland, from which he afterwards removed to Waterford, and founded the family to which Justice Perrin of the Irish Bench belonged.

PERRONET : a French refugee pastor settled at Chateaux d'Oex, in the Canton of Berne, Switzerland, whose son David came into England about the year 1680, settled in London, and married a Miss Philothea Arthur. Their son Vincent, born in 1693, was educated for the church. He graduated at Oxford at twenty-four, took orders, and was curate of Sandwich, in Kent, for nine years. He was afterwards presented to the vicarage of Shoreham, which he served for more than half a century, dying in 1785. The Rev. Vincent Perronet was one of the few regular clergy who openly joined John Wesley. From him, by the mother's side, was descended the late General Perronet Thompson, author of the *Cornlaw Catechism* and numerous other works. Perronet, the celebrated French engineer, was cousin of the David Perronet who first settled in England.

PETIT, LE SIEUR : an officer in the Red Dragoons of the Prince of Orange on his expedition to England. Many descendant of the family have served in the British army, and held offices in church and state.

PETITOT, JEAN : an excellent painter in enamel, patronised by Charles I., who knighted him, and gave him apartments at Whitehall to live in. At the King's death, Petitot returned to France to practise his art. Being a Protestant, he was thrown into jail, and kept there until he consented to abjure, when he was set at liberty. But he took the first opportunity of flying to Geneva, where he died. Of his numerous sons, Francis, who followed his father's art of painting in enamel, settled in London. His descendants for the most part removed to Ireland, where the family still exists.

PHILIPPONNEAU : a Protestant family belonging to Normandy, several members of which took refuge in Holland, where they entered the Dutch service. They afterwards accompanied William III. into England. Francis, Sieur de la Motte, was raised to the rank of colonel in the English army ; John, Sieur de Boispré, was a lieutenant-colonel ; and Gabriel, Sieur de Bélét, was captain in Ruvigny's dragoons.

PHILIPOT, ELISEE : a refugee from Bordeaux who settled at Norwich in 1672, and there established a soap-manufactory which proved eminently successful. Towards the close of his life he filled with honour the office of high-sheriff of the county of Norfolk.

PIERREPONT, ANTOINE and ETIENNE : descended from a noble Norman family, who took refuge in England after the Revocation. Several of their descendants emigrated to New England (U.S.); and from one of them came John Pierpont, the celebrated American poet, born at Newhaven in 1785. Philip Fresnau, Jefferson's secretary, was another of the American poets of Huguenot descent.

PILOT, JOSUE : a refugee of this name settled in Ireland, several of whose descendants occupied high positions. Josué, the original refugee, possessed lands in Poitou, which he lost by his flight for conscience' sake. He commanded an independent company at the siege of Derry. By intermarriages his descendants are connected with the families of Hamon, Champagné, Bouherau (Burrowes), Des Vœux, etc. His son, Dr. Pilot, was doctor of Battereau's Regiment of Foot, and served through the Duke of Cumberland's northern campaign of 1745-6.

PINETON, Rev. JAMES, DE CHAMBRUN : for notice of, see p. 254.

PLANCHÉ : the first refugee of this name is said to have escaped from France concealed in a tub. Pierre Antoine Planché, one of his grandsons, was an East India merchant in London. Another grandson, Paul, married Marie Anne Fournier, and had five sons. One of these, Andrew, was the first maker of porcelain in Derby. From him is descended the present James Robinson Planché, the distinguished antiquarian and author. He is

now Somerset Herald, with the title of *Rouge Croix.* See his "Recollections and Reflections," published in 1872.

PLIMSOLL : several refugees of this name fled from Brittany at the Revocation, and took refuge in the southern counties of England. One of the families settled at Bristol. It is from this branch that Mr. Plimsoll, M.P., the friend of the merchant seamen, is descended. There are still many Plimsolls in Brittany.

PORTAL : an ancient noble Protestant family of Toulouse. For notice of refugees of the name in England, see p. 273.

PRELLEUR, PETER : a musical composer, born in London of a French refugee family. He began life as a writing-master in Spitalfields, after which he applied himself exclusively to music. He composed a number of pieces for the theatre in Goodman's Fields, in which David Carrick, or Garrigue, the son of another French refugee, made his first appearance as an actor. Prelleur also held the office of organist of the church of St. Albans, and afterwards of Christ Church, Middlesex.

PRIMROSE, GILBERT: of Scotch origin, who settled in France in 1601, as minister of the Protestant church of Mirambeau, and afterwards of Bourdeaux. In 1623, Louis XIII. ordered his banishment from France, when he proceeded to London and became minister of the French church in Threadneedle Street; after which we find him appointed chaplain to the king, then canon of Windsor, and eventually bishop of Ely. His two sons, David and James, were remarkable men in their time—the one as a theologian, the other as a physician. Both were authors of numerous works.

PROVOST : a refugee family who settled at Thorney Abbey about 1652. One of this name was a large occupier of land in "French Drove," so called because farmed principally by French colonists ; and the farm to this day continues to be occupied by one of his descendants, the uncle of our informant.

PRYME, MATTHEW DE LA : a refugee from Ypres in Flanders during the persecutions of the Duke of Alva. He settled, with many others of his countrymen, in the Level of Hatfield Chace, after the same had been drained by Vermuyden. His son was the Rev. Abraham de la Pryme. George Pryme, Esq., late M.P., and professor of political economy at Cambridge, was lineally descended from the above.

PUGET : a Huguenot refugee, who settled in London, and founded the banking house of Puget, Bainbridge, and Co., St. Paul's Churchyard, whose establishment was formerly the medium of monetary transactions between the British Government and Ireland. They had a large connection with the commercial class of French settlers ; and their books were kept in French down to the beginning of the present century. Mr. Digges La Touche, one of the bankers of Dublin, married Miss Grace Puget.

Admiral Puget also belonged to the family.

PUISSAR, LOUIS JAMES, Marquis of : was appointed colonel of the 24th regiment in 1695, and afterwards served in Flanders.

PUSEY : see *Bouveries.*

RABOTEAU, JOHN CHARLES : a refugee from Pont-Gibaud, near Rochelle, who settled in Dublin, and prospered as a wine-merchant. For notice of his nieces, the Misses Raboteau, see p. 172.

RADNOR, EARL OF : see *Bouveries.*

RAPIN DE THOYRAS, PAUL : for notice of, see p. 238.

RAVENEL, SAMUEL DE : son of a Protestant gentleman of Picardy who came into England before the Revocation. He afterwards married the niece of Marlborough. Hozier supposes that Edward Ravenel, director of the French Hospital in 1740, was his son.

REBOW : a refugee of this name, from Flanders, settled at Colchester, from whom Sir Isaac Rebow, knighted by King William (whom he entertained), was descended. Several members of the family have since represented the town in Parliament.

REGIS : see *De Regis.*

RENOUARD : a distinguished Huguenot family from Sancerre, near Orleans. At the Revocation the members fled into Holland and England. David Renouard became a well-known merchant at Amsterdam. His son entered the army of William III., and was colonel of the 1st Royal Dragoons. He was a brave and distinguished officer. His son Peter was captain in the 10th Dragoons ; also a man of considerable military reputation. Colonel Renouard married Miss St. Pierre, daughter of Colonel St. Pierre, also of a refugee family, a distinguished soldier, colonel of the 1st Dragoons. The late Rev. Mr. Renouard, rector of Swanscombe, Kent, was also a descendant of the original refugee.

REYNET, or DE REYNET : a refugee family who held landed estates in the Vivarais, from whence they emigrated at the Revocation, and settled at Waterford. Henri de Reynet had a family of five or six sons, two only of whom remained in Ireland. The youngest returned to France, and, having professed the Roman Catholic religion, he was put in possession of the family estate, which his descendants in the female line still hold. Another of the sons became a distinguished traveller. The freedom of the city of Waterford was conferred in perpetuity on the descendants of Henri de Reynet. The Rev. Henry Reynet, D.D., and General Sir James Henry Reynet, K.C.B., K.C.H., belonged to the family, whose descendants survive.

RIGAUD : the late distinguished Professor of Astronomy at Oxford, Stephen Peter Rigaud, F.R.S., was descended from a Huguenot gentleman, Monsieur Rigaud, whose wife was a daughter of M. La Brue, a celebrated military engineer under Henri IV. His maternal grandfather, D. S. Demain-bray, was at the head of the Kew Observatory, as King's Observer, in which office he was succeeded by Professor Rigaud's father. Major-General Rigaud is the head of the family.

RIOU, RIEUX : an ancient family, whose estates at Vernoux, in Languedoc, were forfeited at the Revocation. Estienne Riou, who was born after his father's death, left France with his uncle Matthieu Labrune, when only eleven years old, and took refuge with him at Berne in Switzerland. Labrune there established himself as a merchant. In his nineteenth year Estienne joined the English army in Piedmont under the Duke of Schomberg, —entering the Huguenot regiment of Lord Galway as a cadet, and serving at the siege of Cassale. His uncle being anxious for his return to Berne, Estienne left the regiment after about two years' service. In 1698, the uncle and nephew left Berne and came to London, accompanied by Pastor Bermondsey, formerly pastor of Vernoux. Matthieu Labrune brought with him a capital of £8000, and taking his nephew into partnership, they began business as merchants in 1700, in which they were very successful. Estienne, when in his fortieth year, married Magdalen, daughter of Christopher Baudoin, a refugee gentleman from Tourraine, and left issue. His son Stephen entered the army, served as a captain of horse, and afterwards accompanied Sir R. K. Porter in his embassy to Constantinople.

His sons were distinguished officers. The eldest, Philip, served in the Royal Artillery, and died senior colonel at Woolwich in 1817. The second, Edward, entered the navy at twelve years old, and in 1776 was appointed to the "Discovery," which accompanied the "Resolution" (Captain Cook) round the world. He also subsequently served in the the "Resolution" itself. After twenty-seven years of very distinguished and honourable service, Captain Riou—"the gallant good Riou"—was killed while commanding the "Amazon" frigate at the battle of Copenhagen, April 2nd, 1801. The only surviving daughter of Stephen Riou married Colonel Lyde Browne, of the 21st Fusileers, who was assassinated at Dublin on the night of the 23rd July, 1803, when hastening to the assistance of Lord Kilwarden, who was killed on the same night. Colonel Browne's only daughter married G. Benson, Esq., of Lutwyche Hall, Salop.

RIVAL, PETER : pastor of several of the French churches in London, and lastly of that of the Savoy. He was a copious author and a vehement controversialist. He died about 1728.

RIVE : see *La Rive.*

ROBETHON, the Right Hon. John : a French refugee in London. His brother remained in Paris, and was attorney-general of the Mint in 1722. William III. made John Robethon his private secretary. He was afterwards made secretary to the Embassies, and privy

councillor. In 1721 he was elected governor of the French Hospital. He died in the following year.

ROCHE, LOUIS : a refugee manufacturer who settled in Lisburn at the same time that Louis Crommelin established himself there. He became an extensive merchant, and his descendants are now among the first inhabitants of Belfast.

ROCHEBLAVE, HENRY DE : pastor in succession of the French churches of Greenwich, Swallow Street, Hungerford, the Quarré, St. James's, and, last of all, of Dublin, where he died in 1709.

ROMAINE : a Huguenot refugee who settled at Hartlepool as a corndealer ; father of the celebrated Rev. W. Romaine, author of the *Triumph of Faith.* One of his sisters married one of the Callenders of Manchester. The late M.P. for Manchester was called after him—W. Romaine Callender. The Rev. W. Romaine had two sons. One, Captain Romaine, died in India. The other was the Rev. Dr. Romaine, of Reading : his two daughters married clergymen— the eldest, the Rev. J. B. Storey, of Great Tey, Essex, the youngest the Rev. Romaine Govett, for 49 years vicar of Staines, Middlesex, and a great blessing to the place. One of the sons of the latter is now vicar of All Saint's, Newmarket ; his brother, W. Govett Romaine, was late secretary to the Admiralty.

ROMILLY : for notice of this family see p. 327.

Rou, Roux, Le Rou, etc. : there were many refugees of this name, some of whom were long settled at Canterbury. There was another but more aristocratic refugee Rou, Sieur de la Butte, some members of whose family emigrated to the United States, while others settled in England. In the early part of last century, a lineal descendant of the Sieur de la Butte, named Louis Rou, officiated as minister of the French church at New York. Several of his daughters married and came to England, where their descendants survive.

ROUBILLIAC, LOUIS-FRANCIS: the sculptor; born at Lyons about 1595. Haag says he was probably the son of a "new convert," and that he only returned to the religion of his fathers. His works in England are well known. He was buried in the French church of St. Martin's-le-Grand in 1762.

ROUBILLARD : see *Campagné*.

ROUMIEU : a Huguenot refugee in England, descended from Romieu, the Albigensian hero. The present representative of the family is Robert Lewis Roumieu, the celebrated architect.

ROUQUET, JAMES : son of a French Protestant condemned to the galleys for life. The young man reached London, and was educated at Merchant Taylors' school. He entered the church, but became a follower of Wesley, and superintended Wesley's school at Kingswood. He eventually accepted the curacy of St. Werburgh, Bristol, where he laboured with great zeal in reclaiming outcasts, and died in 1776.

ROUQUET, N. : a painter in enamel, belonging to a French refugee family of Geneva, who spent the greater part of his life in England. He was an artist, and wrote an account of *The State of Art in England*, which was published at Paris in 1755.

ROUSSEAU, JAMES : an excellent landscape-painter, mostly in fresco, son of a joiner at Paris, where he was born in 1630. He studied art in Italy, and on his return to France his reputation became great. He was employed in decorating the palaces at Versailles and Marley, and other important works. In 1662 he was admitted a member of the Royal Academy of Painting, and was afterwards elected a member of the council. But in 1681, when the persecution of the Protestants set in with increased severity, Rousseau was excluded from the Academy because of his being a Huguenot. At the same time, eight other Protestant artists were expelled. At the Revocation of the Edict, Rousseau first took refuge in Switzerland, from whence he proceeded to Holland, and afterwards to England, where he settled. The Duke of Montague employed him to execute the decorations of his townhouse, on the site of the present British Museum. It is also said that he superintended the erection of the buildings. He executed other fresco-paintings on the walls of Hampton

Court, where they are still to beseen. He diedin London in 1693.

ROUSSEAU, SAMUEL : an Orientalist scholar, the son of a French refugee settled in London. He was an extensive contributor to the *Gentleman's Magazine* on classical subjects, as well as the author of several works on the Persian and Hindostanee languages.

ROUSSELL, ISAAC : a French Protestant refugee from Quillebœu, in Normandy, who fled into England in 1699. He settled in London, and became a silk-manufacturer in Spitalfields. The present representative of the family is John Beuzeville Byles, Esq., of Henley-on Thames.

ROYE, DE : see *Larochefoucauld.*

RUVIGNY, Marquis of : see *Massue.*

SARAVIA : a family of Spanish Protestants, who fled from the Low Countries in the time of the Duke of Alva's persecution. Dr. Hadrian Saravia, one of the translators of the Bible into English, was for some time master of the Free Grammar School at Southampton ; and, taking orders in the church, he was afterwards appointed a prebendary of Canterbury.

SAURIN, JACQUES : for notice of, as well as other members of the family, see pp. 253, 331.

SAVARY : the family of Tanzia was originally of considerable importance in the province of Perigord, in the south-west of France. In the latter part of the sixteenth century a younger brother, holding the lands of Savary, becoming Protestant, was under the necessity of fleeing from France and taking refuge at Antwerp. His elder brother transmitted to him money for the maintenance of his family. The lineal descendant of this Tanzia de Savary entered the service of William of Orange, and came over with him to England, where he afterwards held the rank of colonel of horse. William made him a grant of land ; he also owned property at Greenwich, on part of which the French church was built. Several tombstones erected to members of the family are still to be found in the churchyard of St. Alphage at Greenwich. There are still descendants of the Savary family in England, bearing the name. One of them informs us that "there are many interesting anecdotes and legends in the family :—of a buried Bible, afterwards recovered, and patched on every leaf ; of a beautiful cloak made by a refugee, and given to my great-great-grandfather as a token of gratitude for help given by him in time of need ; besides many others." The lands of the family in Perigord were afterwards held by Savary, created by Napoleon I. Duc de Ruvigo.

SAY : a French Protestant family of Languedoc, of whom several members settled in England. One of them, Samuel Say, who died in 1743, was a dissenting minister in London ; another, Francis-Samuel, was minister of the French church in Wheeler Street. Thomas

Say emigrated to America and joined the Quakers ; and his son was the well-known natural historian of the United States. Jean Baptiste Say, the celebrated writer on political economy, belonged to the same family.

SCHOMBERG, Dukes of : for notices of Frederick Armand, 1st duke, see pp. 200, 221; Charles, 2nd duke, p. 229 ; Menard, 3rd duke, pp. 225, 231.

SIMON : a family of artists originally from Normandy, who belonged to the Protestant church of Charenton, near Paris. John, a refugee in London, acquired great reputation as an engraver. He was employed by Sir Godfrey Kneller to engrave the portraits painted by him, a long list of which, as well as of his other works, is given by Haag. Simon died at London in 1755.

ST. PIERRE : see *Renouard*.

TAHORUDIN, GABRIEL : a Protestant refugee from the province of Anjou, who came to England on the Revocation of the Edict of Nantes, leaving behind considerable landed property, which was confiscated. He was naturalised in 1687, and, settling in London, became a wealthy merchant. He died 29th November, 1730, and is still represented by his descendants, one of whom is an eminent London solicitor.

TANZIA : see *Savary*.

TASCHER ; several refugees of this name were ministers of French churches in London at the beginning of the eighteenth century. Pierre de Tascher was a director of the French Hospital in 1727.

TERROT : the De Terrots belonged to the petite noblesse, and held property in the neighbourhood of 'La Rochelle. They were Protestants, and fled into England at the Revocation. Many members of the family have held high offices in the army and the church. Among the former were Captain Charles Terrot (first commission dated 1716) ; Captain Samuel Terrot, R.A. ; Captain Elias Terrot (killed in India) ; Captain C. E. Terrot, 63rd Regiment; and Colonel Elias Terrot (Indian service). And among the churchmen of the family may be mentioned the Rev. W. Terrot, vicar of Grindon, Durham ; the Rev. C. P. Terrot, vicar of Wispington ; and the Hon. and Rev. Dr. Charles Terrot, Bishop of Edinburgh. The Rev. William Terrot, above mentioned, was chaplain to the Royal Naval Asylum at Greenwich, and died more than thirty years since. When once asked to sign a petition in favour of Roman Catholic Emancipation, he declined, with the remark that "the Roman Catholics had kicked his family out of France, and he had no wished to be kicked back again."

TEXTARD, LEON, SIEUR DES MESLARS : a refugee who feigned to abjure under the terror of the dragonnades, and at length fled to England with his wife, a sister of James Fontaine, whom no terrors could shake. They settled in London, together with other members of the family.

TEXTAS ; two ministers of this name, related to the family of Chamier, took refuge in England after the Revocation.

TEULON OR THOLON : an ancient family of Nismes, descended from Marc Tholon, Sieur de Guiral. Peter and Anthony fled from France at the time of the Revocation, and settled at Greenwich. Peter went into Ireland, and founded the Cork branch of the family. In the last generation there were three brothers— George, Charles, and Peter— who each attained the rank of lieutenant-colonel. Charles served with the 28th Regiment in the Peninsula and at Waterloo, where he was captain, and brought the regiment out of action. The present representatives are G. B. Teulon, Esq., of Bandon ; Thomas, a major in the army ; and Charles Peter, a barrister.—Anthony Teulon, of Greenwich, married Marie de la Roche, and left descendants. Among the present representatives of this branch may be named Seymour Teulon, Esq., of Limpsfield, Surrey, and Samuel Saunders and William Milford Teulon, the eminent architects. The Wagners of Sussex are also descended from Anthony Teulon, through the female line.—Another branch is settled in Scotland, represented by John Hall Teulon, son of Melchior Seymour Teulon, resident at Greenock, and Captain James Teulon.—Pierre Emile Teulon of Nismes, president of the council under the government of Louis Phillipe, belonged to a branch of the family remaining in France.

THELUSSON ; originally a Protestant family of Lyons, which took refuge in Geneva. Peter Thelusson, son of John (an illustrious citizen of the Republic) settled in London in 1750, and acquired a large fortune by trade. He sat in Parliament— some time for Malmesbury. His son, Peter-Isaac, was created Baron Rendlesham.

THORIUS, RAPHAEL : a physician and celebrated Latin poet, born in France, but a refugee in England because of his religion. He died in 1625, leaving behind him a son, John, who studied medicine at Oxford and became fellow of the College of Physicians of Dublin in 1627. He was the author of several medical works.

TRADESCANT : the distinguished naturalist of this name belonged to a Protestant refugee family, originally from Flanders.

TRENCH : see *La Tranche* and *Chenevix.*

TURQUAND, PETER : a Protestant refugee from Châtelherault, near Poitiers, who settled in London, where his descendants still flourish.

TYRON, PETER : a wealthy refugee from Flanders, driven out by the persecutions of the Duke of Alva. He succeeded in bringing with him to England as large a sum as £60,000. The family made many alliances with English families of importance. Samuel, son of the original refugee, of Layer Marney in Essex, was made a baronet in 1621. The baronetcy expired in 1724.

TYSSEN, FRANCIS : a refugee from Ghent in Flanders. His son of the same name became a thriving merchant in London. The family is at present represented by W. G. Tyssen Amhurst of Foulden in Norfolk, lord of the manor of Hackney.

UNWIN, ONWHYN : several refugees of this name came from the Low Countries in the time of the persecutions of the Duke of Alva ; and there are three branches of them now settled in England,—one, the most numerous, in Essex and the eastern counties, another in Leicestershire, and the third in the neighbourhood of Sheffield. One of their descendants, settled in Yorkshire, thus writes : " They were from the first engaged in textile manufactures, and some members of the family still keep up that connection. I am not aware that any of the Unwins have risen to high eminence as public men ; but there have never been wanting to the family men and women who have maintained its good name and standing, and who have been widely known and looked up to in those parts of the country where they have lived. The members of this family with whom the poet Cowper was on such intimate terms, and who brought so much comfort into his life, will be remembered by all English readers."

VALLANCEY : the predecessors of this noble family emigrated into England at the Revocation. They were originally known as De Vallencey, or L'Estampes de Vallencey.

General Vallencey was an eminent military engineer, who served England ably during the late continental war.

VALLENTIN : the De Vallentins of Eschepy, in Normandy, were among the refugees who settled in London after the Revocation. One of their descendants, James Vallentin, was recently Sheriff of London and Middlesex.

VANACKER, JOHN : a refugee from Lille in Flanders, who became a merchant in London. His grandson Nicolas, a Turkey merchant, was created a baronet in 1700.

VANBRUGH : the original name of the family was Vandenbergh. They were from Antwerp, from whence they fled during the persecutions of the Duke of Alva. They first took refuge in Holland, and afterwards passed into England in the reign of Elizabeth. Some members of the family settled in Chester (of which the Rev. G. Vanburgh, rector of Aughton, Lancashire, was the last descendant bearing the name), and others in London. Sir John Vanburgh, the architect and dramatist, descended from the latter branch. His father, William Vandenbergh, was a merchant in Laurence-Pountney Lane, City.

VANDERPUTT, HENRY : born in Antwerp; he fled to England from the religious persecution in the Low Countries in 1568, and became a London merchant. His great-grandson Peter, also a London merchant, was sheriff of London in 1684, and created a baronet in 1723.

VANLORE, PETER : a Protestant refugee from Utrecht. He became a celebrated London merchant, and was created a baronet in 1628.

VARENNES, JOHN DE : a French refugee, whose descendants remain in England. Ezekiel G. Varennes was recently a surgeon in Essex.

VERNEUIL, JOHN : a native of Bourdeaux, from which city he fled, on account of his religion, to England. He was a learned man, and was appointed sub-librarian at Oxford, where he died in 1647.

VICOSE, GUY DE, Baron de la Court : a Protestant noble, who suffered frightful cruelties during the dragonnades. He took refuge in London, where we find him a director of the French Hospital in 1718, and governor in 1722.

VICTORIA, QUEEN : for notice of her Huguenot descent, see p. 324.

VIGNOLES : a noble Protestant family in Languedoc. Charles de Vignoles, fourth son of Jacques de Vignoles, seigneur de Prades, near Nismes, fled with his wife into Holland at the Revocation. He afterwards accompanied the Prince of Orange into England, fought in the Irish campaigns, and settled at Portarlington. Many members of the family have distinguished themselves in the army, the church, and the civil service. Dr. Vignoles, dean of Ossory, and Charles Vignoles. F.R.S., the eminent engineer, were presentatives of the family.

VILETTES, SEBASTIAN DE: a country gentleman, lord of Montledier, near Castres. Like his ancestors, he was a Protestant, and suffered serious persecutions at the Revocation. The family fled from France, and took refuge in foreign lands; some in England, and others in Germany. The names of the De Vilettes frequently occur in the list of directors of the French Hospital. Amongst others, we observe those of Lieut.-General Henry Clinton de Vilettes in 1777, and of Major William de Vilettes in 1779.

VILLETTE, C. L. DE : a minister of the French church in Dublin, and the author of numerous religious works.

WALDO : Mr. Agnew gives particulars of this family. A person of this name fled from the Low Countries during the Duke of Alva's persecutions, and settled near London. His son Robert founded a family at Deptford. Edward Waldo, in 1677, received the honour of knighthood from Charles II. There have been numerous clergymen, authors, knights, and members of Parliament, in this family. The late Colonel Sibthorp bore their name and arms.

WITTENRONG, JACOB ; a Protestant refugee from Ghent, in Flanders, who practised in London as a notary. His son became a brewer in London, and greatly prospered. He was knighted by Charles I. in 1640, and created a baronet, of Stantonbury, county Bucks, in 1662.

YVER, JOHN : a refugee pastor, who officiated as minister in several of the churches of the Refuge in London. He afterwards went to Holland, where he died.

APPENDIX.

BACOT, PETER: a refugee from near Tours, after the Revocation. He was then Baron de Romand ; but being a Protestant, the estates were confiscated, and afterwards made over to his brother, who became a Roman Catholic. He is said to have been smuggled over to England in a cask. He had two sons, Peter and John. The latter left his property to his three nephews, Peter, John Stephen, and William. Peter was a jeweller and a watchmaker. The present representative of the family says : " I have a watch with his name on the works, and the family story goes that he was apprenticed to this trade because jewellers were at that time the only tradesmen who wore swords. The present Baron Bacot visited London at the first Exhibition in Hyde Park, called upon my father, and the relationship which existed was fully acknowledged. Curiously enough, the Heralds College acknowledged my father's right to bear the arms of Bagot, for the Bacot family is said to have sprung from a Bagot who was Lieutenant-Governor of Calais while the town was in the possession of England. A brother officer,—one of the Bagots,—who was in the Guards while my father served as surgeon from Corunna to the abdication of Napoleon (prior to Waterloo), acknowledged my father's claim. My father retired from the army in 1817, to commence private practice in London, where he was well known. He died a few years ago, in his ninetieth year."

BEAUFORT, DANIEL CORNELIS DE [additional memoir] : He was minister of La Savoy and other French Protestant churches and chapels from 1728 to 1741, when he was appointed rector of East Barnet. He was naturalized in 1842, and in the following year went to Ireland with Lord Harrington. He was rector of Navan and Clonenagh and provost and archdeacon of Tuam. In 1788, at the age of eighty-eight, he published a small work on the errors of Rome Upon naturalization he dropped the "de" from his name. His son, Daniel Augustus Beaufort, rector of Navan and vicar of Collon and LL.D., was the author of the well-known map of Ireland with the accompanying memoir of the civil and ecclesiastical state of the country. The

Royal Irish Academy owed its formation in great measure to his exertions. Born in 1739 he died in 1821 [see an obituary notice in the *Times* of June 18th, 1821]. His two sons were : William Louis Beaufort, rector of Glanmire and prebendary of Rathcooney, co. Cork, 1814 to 1849 ; and Admiral Sir Francis Beaufort, K.C.B., Hydrographer of the Admiralty, 1829 to 1855. He was a highly distinguished scientific man and the inventor (1805) of the " Beaufort notation," now used universally for recording the force of the wind and the state of the weather. Born in 1774, he died in 1857. Among his children were : Daniel Augustus Beaufort, sometime rector of L y m m - c u m - W a r b u r t o n, Cheshire, author of sundry works ; Francis Lestock Beaufort of the Bengal Civil Service, author of a well-known " Digest of Criminal Law Procedure in Bengal," and the Viscountess Strangford, author of " Egyptian Sepulchres and Syrian Shrines," and " The Eastern Shores of the Adriatic. '

BOILEAU [*additional memoir*] : Jacques Boileau de Castelnau, tenth baron, was great-grandson of Jean Boileau, the first Protestant of the family. He was imprisoned on account of his faith, from 1687 to 1697, when he died. He had sixteen children, of whom three sons may be noted : Henri, born 1665, left France in 1685 ; entered the "mousquetaires " of Brandenbourg, where he remained until 1689, when he was made captain of Horse Grenadiers, which were reduced in 1697. He then attached himself to M. le Comte Christophe de Dona, marshal-general and minister of state at Brandenbourg, whom he followed in his embassy to England. He was at the siege of Huy in 1694, at the siege and taking of Namur in 1695 by William III. of England ; at the taking of Kenisewort, de Veuls, Kempen, and Linn, in 1702. He was made captain-lieutenant of the Marquis de Vignole's company in Schoening's regiment, and eventually captain of that regiment of cavalry in the service of Brandenbourg in 1705. He was at the battle of Oudenarde, where he was the first who attacked the French troops with his squadron. He was killed by a blow from a fusil on the head, in the trenches before Tournay, whilst watching the attack of General de Saxe Schuberbourg, and was interred before the Standard.—Jean Louis, born 1667, left France in 1685. He was an ensign in Corneau's regiment in 1687, whence he was drawn for the mousquetaires of Brandenbourg, and remained with them until 1693 ; when he purchased an ensigncy in Luc's regiment of infantry, in the service of the Duke of Brunswick-Lunenberg-Zell ; and soon after he was presented with the lieutenancy of Schnau's company in the same regiment. In 1702 he was present at the assault on the town and citadel of Liége. On the 2nd of July, 1704, he was at the battle of Donawitz on the Danube, which was gained by the Duke of Marlborough over the Comte d'Arcot. In the same year he was wounded at the battle of Blenheim, gained by the duke over the French and Bavarians, who lost 20,225 killed and 15,000 prisoners. He was then promoted to a captaincy in Luc's regiment ; but he died at Northingen in Suabia of his wounds. He had been pierced from his chest to his spine, and two of his ribs were broken.— Charles Boileau was born 10th February, 1673, at Nismes. On the death of his brother Henri he was the rightful heir to the family titles and estates. Having, however, escaped from France at the time of his father's imprisonment in 1687, he took refuge in England, where he entered the British army, determining not to return to the land where his father had been martyred. By a formal deed he renounced his rights in favour of his next brother, Maurice : the deed was proved in the Prerogative Court of Canterbury in 1733. Charles was for some time in Farringdon's regiment. He was still an ensign at the Peace of Ryswick in 1697. He then went to Ireland, where he remained until 1701, when Farringdon's regiment having been disbanded he re-entered the army as lieutenant in 1703. In the following year he was enrolled in the Brandenbourg army, and served as a Grand Mousquetaire. He was taken prisoner at Lunengen, but was exchanged at Valenciennes in 1709. He returned to England in charge of his company. He left the army in 1711 and retired—at first to Southampton, but afterwards, in 1722, left the place for Dublin, where he died in 1733. He had married, in 1704, the daughter of Daniel Collot d'Escury, a captain of cavalry, who had served under Marshal Turenne. (For additional particulars, see pp. 329 and 366.)

BONBONOUS : a refugee family settled near Cork. John Bonbonous lived in Cork, and made a considerable fortune as a woollen manufacturer. (Where are the woollen manufacturers of Cork now?) He bequeathed several thousand pounds to his sons and daughters, and a legacy to the poor of the French church in the city of Cork. His son, Peter Bonbonous, practised as a physician in the same city. His daughter married the Rev. W. Nash, a beneficed clergyman in the diocese of Cloyne—a gentleman of good private property. Our informant says that "from the time of the great French Revolution, and the wars growing out of it, Frenchmen became so unpopular in this country, that few cared to keep up the recollection that they were of French origin." It is believed that Bonbonous was of the same family as Bombomoux, who distinguished himself so much in the wars of the Camisards.

BORDES : a well-known Huguenot family. Their descendants survive at Wandsworth. In the Mount Nod buryingground there is a monument to "Peter Bordes, died 12th July, 1775 ; and Mary Esther Bordes, his wife, who died 18th November, 1786. Also E. M. Bordes, died 6th June 1796, aged 60.

BULMER, RENÉ : a French refugee who settled at Lambeg, in Ulster. He had attained much celebrity in his own land as a skilled blacksmith, and also as a professor of the veterinary art. King William, after landing at Carrickfergus, proceeded to join his troops. Bulmer and his wife came out to see the soldiers pass, and William III., seeing them at their door, went forward to ask which of the roads (because five roads branched off from there in different directions) led to Lisburn and Hillsborough. Bulmer answered in French. William entered into conversation with him, and inquired about the circumstances which had led to the exile of the family. After paying a gallant compliment to the young and handsome wife of his informant, the king passed on with his troops towards their destination. The Bulmers still remain in the neighbourhood of Belfast.

CHALON : the first refugee of the family fled from the south of France, and took refuge in Geneva. The late Alfred Edward Chalon, R.A., belonged to this family. He was born in Geneva.

CORTEZ : in 1765, about sixty Huguenot families, accompanied by their pastor, the Rev. Peter Cortez, arrived in Cork in the *Red-Head* galley, and settled at Innishannon. They were induced to come over by the junior representative of the city (Mr. Thomas Adderley), who was anxious to introduce the rearing of silkworms, and otherwise to afford employment to the skill and enterprise of the settlers. He granted leases at low rents, and built houses for them. He planted a piece of ground with mulberry trees for the silkworms to feed upon. But the enterprise did not succeed, the silkworms died, and some of the refugees left for London. The mulberry-field has left nothing but its name. The ruined walls and broken gables still pass current as "The Colony." One or two of the colonists' houses are still to be seen at the southern end of Innishannon bridge. They may be recognized by their semi-lozenge-shaped windows, and the ornamental brickwork enclosing the same.

DE BIGOE, PHILIP : a native of Lorraine, allied to the royal family of France. About the year 1574, being a Protestant, he sought refuge in England shortly after the massacre of St. Bartholomew. He received grants of lands in King's County, Ireland, from Queen Elizabeth ; and a descendant and namesake of his obtained further grants of land in the same county in the reign of Charles II., the names of which were Ballyneshragh, Carrowmore, and Newtown in Lusmagh. One of the De Bigoes was High Sheriff of King's County in 1662. The De Bigoes appear, in addition to their noble birth, to have brought considerable wealth to the country of their adoption. They appear to have known the art of glass manufacture, and some members of the family established considerable glassworks in King's County. It appears from an entry in the rental of Sir Lawrence Parsons (ancestor of the Earl of Rosse), dated 9th October, 1623, that he made a lease to Abraham Bigoe, of the castle tower and part of the plough-land, with a provision that the tenant was " not to set up any glasshouse or glasswork on any other land, or buy wood of any other for his glasswork, but only of the said Lawrence Parsons." The glassworks appear to have quickly attained importance, and are referred to in " Boate and Molyneux's Natural History of Ireland." They say, " amongst the principal was that of Birre, a market town " (otherwise Parsonstown), " and from this place Dublin was furnished with all sorts of window and drinking glasses, and such other as are in common use." The place was burnt by the Irish in 1642, after which the glass manufacture ceased.

DE GENNES: a family which derived its name from the parish of Gennes in the diocese of Rennes, in Brittany. Members of it appear in documents of various periods during the middle ages, the earliest dating either from the eleventh or twelfth century (*vide Hist. de Brétagne*, vol. ii., p. 217). Several members of the family adopted the Protestant faith, and were expatriated in the seventeenth century. Some settled in Holland, and afterwards in Surinam or Berbice, where they possessed large coffee plantations, named Helvetia and De Gennes, which continued in the possession of their descendants until late in the last century. One of the family came to this country and left four sons and two daughters. One of the sons, John Daniel de Gennes, entered the English army, and in 1719 had a commission as major; in 1727 he was lieutenant-colonel of G e n e r a l Read's regiment of Dragoons. In 1720 he married Frances, daughter of Dr. Orval, and by her had four daughters. who survived him—viz.: Judith Susanna, who married George Frazer, of Banaher Castle ; Mary Anne, who married Thomas Fenison, of Castle Fenison, county Roscommon ; Caroline, who married John Lyons, of Ledestown, county Westmeath : Louisa Frances, who married Thomas Nesbit of Lismore, county Cavan. John Daniel de Gennes purchased land in the neighbourhood of Portarlington, and there spent the latter part of his life. One of his brothers was a captain in the 2nd (or Queen's) Regiment of Foot, and was attached to the English embassy at Paris when Lord Stair was ambassador there ; and for a short time he acted as *chargé d'affaires* in the absence of his chief.

DE HENZELL : afterwards

called Henzell. A Huguenot family from, Lorraine, who left France shortly after the massacre of St. Bartholomew. They settled in King's County, Ireland. They intermarried with the De Bigoes several times, and their descendants, with the family of Armstrong, in King's County and with that of Eyre, in county Galway,— the present descendants of the Armstrongs of Garry Castle, and of the Eyres of Eyrecourt Castle, being lineal descendants of the Bigoes and Henzells. A tradition runs in the family that the original Henzell had five brothers who did not quit France, and that one of these discovered the art of making glass as hard as iron, and that he was knighted by the King of France in order that he might not divulge the secret. There was a family of Henzells who settled at Newcastle-on-Tyne, shortly after the massacre of Bartholomew, and were glassmakers. Perhaps they may have belonged to the same family.

D'ESCURY : Huguenot refugees from Quintin in Brittany. The following account is given by Henry La Rive, as communicated to us by J. H. Ryan, Esq., Castlecomer, Ireland : "David Collet d'Escury left his country at the commencement of the persecution. The escape of himself and his family to Holland was thus effected. He had three asses, with paniers on each side, in each of which he concealed a child. Over them he placed oranges, lemons, or such like fruits, for apparent sale. By this means he and his father, who helped to lead the asses, passed through the intendants and guards of the frontier districts, which were always strictly watched ; and thus the convoy reached the Dutch territories in safety." Mr. d'Escury's father obtained a cap-tain's commission in the Dutch service ; while he himself went to England and obtained a company of infantry under William III. He had his arm shot off at the battle of the Boyne. His sons were also in the Dutch and English service. One of them, Simon, was colonel of the Twenty-third Foot in 1738. The La Rives intermarried with the d'Escurys, and hence the MS. memoir of Henry La Rive relating to their history.

DE VAUTIER : afterwards anglicized from De Wautier to Wautie, and finally into Wauty ; a Huguenot family who left France soon after the Massacre of St. Bartholomew. They first settled at Thorney Abbey, Cambridgeshire. A French prayer-book has been treasured and handed down in the family, containing a special prayer for use during the time of persecution. The baptismal register of the French Church at Thorney contains many of the Vautier, Wauty, and other similar names which the members of the family bore. The Wautys intermarried with the Peets, and at the death of Mr. Edwin Wauty, Major Flentham Peet, of Holbeach, Lincolnshire, and Mr. Henry Peet, of Mount Pleasant, Liverpool, became the sole representatives of the family.

DU MESNIL, JEAN CHENIN : A Huguenot refugee who settled in Ireland, and took the oath of allegiance on his naturalization in the Court of Common Pleas, on the 7th November, 1710. John du Mesnil, the only son of Jean Chenin, graduated M.A. at Trinity College, Dublin, in 1728, and took Holy Orders. For some years he officiated at the French church in Peter Street. He afterwards went to Tobago, where he, his wife, and four sons died. Two daughters returned to England; one married Mr. Straton, whose grandson represents the family. The other died unmarried.

DUPRÉ, HENRI MARK : was one of the skilled flaxworkers who settled at Lisburn, in Ireland, under Louis Crommelin, the renovator of the flax trade. In his own country he was famed for his skill as a reed maker. His joining the refugee linen-weavers was a most important matter for the trade at that time,—the reeds then in use being of an inferior description, and unsuited to the manufacture of fine cloths. Under his influence kiddle-striking and other sections of loom gearing were remodelled, and the spinning-wheel was added to the best of the improved machines. Many of the Duprés are still in the neighbourhood of Lisburn.

FONTAINE, JAMES : A refugee descended from the Sieurs de la Fontaine, of Maine in Normandy. They were originally of distinction. James, after his arrival in England, married Ann E. Boursiquot. They settled in Wales, at Cwm Castle, Carmarthenshire ; where their son John married Mary Sabatier. But the daughters of emigrant French were difficult to be had in Wales, and eventually the male descendants of this Huguenot family married Welsh ladies—Howell, Williams, Jones, and Lewis. William de la Fontaine was vicar of Barnby, Newark, Notts, several years ago ; and the father of a numerous family.

FOUBERT : The original family name was " Fabert." The head of the house was Abraham Fabert of Metz, chief magistrate of that city, and director of the ducal printing-press. He was born about 1563, and in acknowledgment of his services and his learning, he was ennobled by Henry IV. His two sons, François and Abraham, entered the army. Abraham's brilliant services secured for him the friendship of Cardinals Richelieu and Mazarin, and he was created marquis and marshal of France by Louis XIV. At the Revocation of the Edict of Nantes, three of his sons had adopted the Reformed Faith. They were soldiers like their fathers ; but now, like thousands of others, who refused to conform to the faith of Louis XIV., they fled from France and entered the service of the Prince of Orange. They accompanied the Prince to Torbay, and entered England. One of them served under Marshal Schomberg ; and was severely wounded at the battle of the Boyne, whilst assisting his general when struck down during the crossing of the river. At the termination of the civil war, they settled at Portarlington, where they had received a grant of land. One of them afterwards removed to London, where Foubert's Place in Regent Street is still called after him. Some of the descendants of the others were officers in the British army. One of them fought at Waterloo, and remembering the persecution of his forefathers he used afterwards to relate his great satisfaction of being present at that encounter with the old enemies of his faith. The descendants of the Fouberts still reside in Ireland.

FULLAGAR : Two brothers of this name fled from France at the Revocation of the Edict of Nantes. One settled in London, the other in Kent. The one who settled in London married Miss Cromwell, of Cheshunt Park, a direct descendant of Oliver Cromwell. The Rev. H. F. Fullagar, rector of Hemsworth, East Dereham, Norfolk, represents this branch of the family. The other brother, who settled in Kent, occupied the Manor House, Gillingham, near Chatham. His last heir was a daughter, Mary Fullagar, who married Robert Mackreth, Esq., of Northfleet, whose descendant represents the Kentish branch of the family. It is probable that the original name was " Foulgier," anglicized into " Fullagar."

GOLIGHTY, C. P.: a descendant of a French refugee. His ancestor, who fled from France, was the son of a physician at Le Vigan in the Cevennes. He remembers the child of the original refugee. He possesses the first watch that ever went upon a diamond, given him by Nicholas Jacio (a friend of Sir Isaac Newton), the inventor of that improvement in watchmaking. He also possesses a copy (dated Rouen, 1576) of the " Edict of Pacification " of Henry III. ; which may be called the first Protestant Relief Bill passed in France.

GROS, LE GROS : this Huguenot family, like many others, changed their name into Grose, or Grosse. In the French burying-ground at Wandsworth, there is a monument with the inscription :—" Miss Sally Grosse, died 21st December, 1764, aged ten years and two months." This Sally Grosse belonged to the family of Captain Grose, the antiquarian, author of " The Antiquities of England," a treatise on " Arms and Armour," and another on " Military Antiquities." He visited Scotland for the purpose of sketching and chronicling its antiquities. While there, he became acquainted with Burns, the poet, who wrote the droll and pithy poem beginning "Hear, land o' cakes, and brither Scots." The following lines occur in the poem :—

" He has a fouth o' auld nick-
    nackets,
Rusty airn caps and jinglin' jackets,
Wad haud the Lothians three in
    tackets,
      A towmouth guid ;

And parritch pats, and auld saut-
backets,
Before the Flood."

Captain Grose lived in one of
the houses called "The Gables"
on Wandsworth Common, in
corroboration of which there
is in the Baptismal Register of
the parish the following entry :
"Harriet, daughter of Francis
and Elizabeth Grosse, baptized
30th May, 1771."

GUÉRIN : the first Huguenot
of this name who took refuge
in England was Jacob Guérin,
who came from Normandy in
1563. He was driven from his
home by the terrible persecutions that followed the massacre
on the 1st March in that year,
by order of the Duc de Guise,
when a number of men, women,
and children, were foully murdered whilst holding a meeting
in a barn at Vassy (see p. 46).
Jacob Guérin, with his wife and
children, was one of the eighteen
families, who, headed by their
pastor, Hector Hamon, landed
at Rye, in Sussex. After a
short stay, they proceeded to
Winchelsea, and afterwards
went to Canterbury, to join the
little flock of refugee Protestants who had made that city
their headquarters. The crypt
of the cathedral was assigned
for their especial use. After
some time the Guérins assumed
the more English name of Gearing, or Garing. At the Revocation of the Edict of Nantes,
other members of the Guérin
family took refuge in England :
Samuel, Daniel (naturalized in
1682), Frances, and Magdalen,
his wife, and their two children (naturalized in 1688), and
Solomon de Guérin and Anne
his wife (naturalized in 1679).
Some of the descendants of
these are said to have settled
in Ireland. There are also the
Guérins of Guernsey, who descended from Jean Guérin, a
native of Clairac, in Agenois,
Guienne. His son, Daniel, escaped from France during the
persecutions which followed the
Revocation. Daniel assumed
the dress of a shepherd, and
exchanged his boots for sabots
stuffed with moss to keep them
on his feet. He made for the
south, travelling by night, and
at last safely crossed one of the
most unfrequented defiles of
the Pyrenees. He travelled
across Spain to Lisbon in Portugal, often doing a day's work
to procure him food and a night's
lodging. When he reached Lisbon, his last sou was spent.
He betook himself to a ship
from which the British ensign
was flying, but his surprise was
great when he heard the sailors
engaged in completing the cargo
speaking to each other in *French*,
On inquiry, he found that the
ship belonged to Guernsey, and
that though the sailors spoke
French, they were all Protestants. He applied to the owner
of the ship, Mr. Peter Marten
of Guernsey, and explained his
circumstances. Mr. Marten
immediately granted his request, and undertook to carry
him to Guernsey ; giving him
also clothes and money. After
reaching the island, he received
employment, married a refugee
lady, Mdlle. Marie Bacon, and
eventually settled in Guernsey.
Many of his descendants still

survive there. They inter-married with the Dumaresques, the Saumarezes (from whom the late admiral descended), the De Lisles, the Prices (from whom comes Bonamy Price, M.A., late Professor of Political Economy, Oxford), and many other distinguished personages. The Guérins of Devonshire are also a branch of the Guernsey Huguenot family. The Guérins of Somerset are of the Champagne, Isle de France, and Auvergne families.

GUÉRIN : a branch of this family emigrated at the Revocation from Clairac, Lot et Garonne. They are mentioned in French history as one of the original noble families of France ; and their arms are now to be seen in the Great Hall at Versailles, erected "to the Glories of France." The eldest son was the owner of the estates at the time of his flight. He married a refugee lady from Falaise in Normandy. One of their descendants visited Clairac some years ago, and found the original family still living there ; and from the archives of the town it appeared that they had resided on the same property without intermission since the year 1505. The refugee's family eventually settled near Bristol.

LA RIVE [*additional memoir*] : The head of the La Rive family was a native of St. Antonin, Rouerge, in the south of France, where he succeeded to his father's estate, called La Prunerarde. The Edict of Nantes having been revoked, he was very much persecuted by the troops of Louis XIV. — the "booted missionaries," as they were denominated. A troop of dragoons was quartered in his house ; and he had not only to feed men and horses, but suplied the former with pay. A plot ruined him. Salt (a contraband article) was put in his house ; on its discovery he was put into gaol, and died. He had three sons : St. Martin, William Maret, and Jean. The first commanded a ship of war in the French service ; and the two last, when the persecutions grew hot, fled to England. They escaped with their sister, accompanied by a young lady, and by the help of the elder brother, who commanded the ship of war, they were safely landed on English ground. But St. Martin got into trouble, and he eventually died of grief and fever. The two sons who landed in England became naturalized. They had little money with them, and suffered a good deal at first from want of food. But Jean eventually married one Mdlle. Duplein, a lady with means, and was appointed to a troop of dragoons ; while his brother, William Maret, got the command of a twenty-gun ship in the English navy, and finally a company of foot. The first served in Portugal, under General Sarlande, and the latter in Canada. Both brothers died in Ireland—William at Dublin in his eightieth year, and Jean at Castlecomer, at ninety-one.

LA TROBE : a correspondent sends the following addition to

the family of La Trobe, already mentioned. F. P. Labillière says :—"I have recently published 'The Early History of the Colony of Victoria,' in which I was born and brought up. It is an interesting fact, which you may like to add to your notice of the La Trobe family, that one of them, Charles Joseph la Trobe, was first governor of Victoria. He was superintendent or deputy-governor of Port Philip, from 1839 to 1851, when, on the separation of the district from New South Wales, and its establishment as a distinct colony, he became its first governor, holding the office at the time of the gold discovery, and during the two or three difficult years which followed. He was an excellent and amiable man. He died in England about three years ago. His father was a Moravian clergyman. Lady Franklin's name was Guillemard. I was acquainted in Australia with a Mr. Peter Paul Labertouche, of a Dublin family, and also with a cousin of his, Rev. Chas. Bardin, son of an eminent Dublin preacher, both of Huguenot descent."

LESTURGEON : members of this family took refuge in England after the Revocation of the Edict of Nantes. Five of them, David, Susan, Francis, John, and Mary, were naturalized by letters-patent in 1682. Anne Lesturgeon was naturalized in 1684; John Lesturgeon, John and David, his sons, were naturalized in 1697; and David Lesturgeon was naturalized in 1700. This shows over what a large extent of time the emigration from France lasted. For the most part, the members of the family came from Caen. For the last three generations they have resided at Cambridge.

PETTIGREW : A refugee family named Pichegru settled in Norwich towards the end of the seventeenth century, after the Revocation of the Edict of Nantes. They afterwards removed to Perthshire, where they changed their name to Pettigrue. Some members of the family went to Ireland, where their descendants still live. There is also a Professor Pettigrew at St. Andrew's.

PLATEL : An ancient and noble family, originally of Lille, in Flanders, also of Chatellerie and Beauvais. Lue Platel du Plateaux was in the service of Rene II., King of Jerusalem and Sicily and Duke of Lorraine, as early as 1465. He distinguished himself, as well as others of his family, during the crusades. One of them had the good fortune to rescue Richard I., King of England, from capture during a skirmish with the Saracens. Sieur Jean Batiste Bertrand Platel du Plateau, was the representative of the family in 1676, when he resided at Erize St. Dizier. During the persecution of the Huguenots by Louis XIV., being a Protestant, he took refuge in England. Some of his descendants entered the Church, while others became merchants and lawyers. Peter Platet, M.A., was curate of Barnet, near London—a place where many of the French silkweavers settled. He was afterwards presented to the living of Ashburton, in Devonshire, and finally to that of Enfield, Middlesex, where he died. He was acquainted with Hogarth, who frequently introduced him in pictures, more particularly in the Idle and Industrious Apprentice series [see Ireland's edition of Hogarth's works]. A portrait of him was given as the clergyman enjoying his soup at the Sheriff of London's feast. A tablet to his memory was to be seen some years ago in Enfield Church. Peter Platel left two daughters and two sons :— William, the eldest, acquired a fortune in India, leaving a son George, who died at Peterborough without issue. William's younger brother John, practised as a solicitor in Lincoln's Inn Fields. He was intimate with Lord Kenyon, Mr. Justice Buller, and the leading judges and barristers of the time. Justice Buller appointed him marshal of his assize court—a sinecure office, since abolished. John, forgetting the trials of his family in France, unfortunately invested his money in the Assignats of the French Republic, and thus greatly impaired his fortunes. The present representative of the family in England is John Platel, Brixham, South Devon. He took much interest in the commemoration of the landing of the Prince of Orange at Brixham, held in 1888 ; two hundred years after the event. The Platels still exist in France.

The correspondent of the *Daily Telegraph,* in the number for the 7th of July, 1887, refers to Baron de Platel as " one of the keenest and most analytical wielders of the pen in Paris."

REBOTIER, REV. ELIAS ; A native of St. Jean de Gardonneuque, in the Cevennes, where he was born on the 3rd of August, 1678. He was one of a numerous Protestant family, and from his earliest years he was designed for the service of the Church, though grievous persecution prevailed throughout his district. To prevent the spread of " the religion," boys and girls were apprehended and confined in nunneries and schools belonging to the Jesuits, where they were educated in what Louis XIV. held to be the " true faith." Rebotier's father sent his son Elias, at the age of eighteen, to a Jesuit College at Nismes, where he met with good treatment. His tutor was Father Tapirier—a man of excellent temper and morals. He heard, with patience, the boy's objections to the faith of Rome, and endeavoured to confute them. But the people of the Cevennes were somewhat obstinate, and nothing which Elias heard altered his views. He remained at the college for three years, and was twenty-two years old when he left it. He then desired to go to Geneva, to complete his education as a minister of religion ; but it was exceedingly difficult to escape from the country, as all the roads out of it were diligently watched by soldiers,

—and the penalty of being taken was death, the galleys, or perpetual imprisonment. At length, however, he was sent to a merchant at Nismes for the purpose of being apprenticed ; but before that could be done, he succeeded in making his escape ; and in the company of another person and a guide, he found his way over the mountains by devious routes, and after great difficulties, to the adjoining country of Savoy. It was midwinter when they fled—the 6th January, 1700—when the mountains were covered with snow. They left France at Les Echelles, on the utmost borders of Dauphiné, now in the department of Isère. "At this place," says M. Rebotier in the description of his escape, "there is a hedge, but it was strictly guarded by a company of soldiers. Leaving, therefore, the common road, we turned to the left hand and came upon the banks of the river two miles below the bridge, and waded through the water on the 12th of January. After a successive march of twenty hours, without any other sustenance than a little bread and some brandy, having passed the river, we felt that our greatest danger was over. Nevertheless, fearing a pursuit, we walked several miles into Savoy in our frozen clothes, before we ventured to rest. As soon as we came to an inn, we had a good breakfast, stript and went into a warm bed, where we slept from twelve to fourteen hours while our clothes were drying." They then proceeded by short journeys through Savoy, passed Chambery, and eventually reached Geneva. There they met with joy many of their Protestant friends who had also succeeded in escaping from France and its persecutions. From this place, Rebotier sent tidings of his safety to his relations at home. He then proceeded northward to Germany, to a place called Scheirbach, in the principality of Anspach, where one of his uncles was first minister in the French church. " In our progress through Switzerland," M. Rebotier says, "we were treated with courtesy,—the Switzers being a kind free-hearted people, of a cheerful pleasant humour ; but when we came to Germany we found the reverse. The Germans are a proud, morose people, despising all nations but their own, using all strangers with a haughtiness not to be found in any other civilized nation." Rebotier, however, was received with much affection by his uncle, and was placed in the way of diligently studying the Scriptures. But before long he was seized by a serious illness. In course of time he recovered, and then he was joined by his father and one of his brothers, who had succeeded in escaping ; though his mother, from illness, was still under the necessity of remaining in France. Rebotier in the following year (1701), proceeded from Nuremberg to Frankfort on the Main, and then down the Rhine, through Holland, to England. He reached London, and was received with civility by M. Duchesnoy, a French Protestant refugee. He was engaged as tutor to two young gentlemen at Barbadoes, and went thither to take charge of them, and bring them home to England. On the voyage out, the vessel in which he sailed was nearly lost in a hurricane, and after they had escaped, they were attacked by a pirate. Fortunately the vessel carried guns for defence (for the seas about England swarmed with pirates at that time), and after beating off the pirate, they eventually reached their destination in safety. After a short stay in Barbadoes, Rebotier returned to England with his two pupils and their father (Councillor Lillington), and arrived in London at the end of August, 1702. He then accepted an appointment as tutor to the family of Mr. Strachey of Sutton Court, midway between Bath and Wells ; and spent three or four years in that position with great satisfaction. After sedulous study, he applied to the venerable George Hooper, Lord Bishop of Bath and Wells, and upon examination, was admitted to the Order of Deacon, in May, 1706. After a year's probation, he applied for Priest's Orders, and was admitted an ordained priest on the 6th of June, 1707. The bishop appointed him his chaplain, and he also acted as tutor to the bishop's sons. Eventually he was appointed to the rectory of Chillwood, on the 13th of

June, 1709, and instituted accordingly. The rectory was worth £50 a year. On the 3rd December following, the bishop appointed him further prebend and rector of Dinder ; and on the 16th of April 1718, he exchanged for the prebend of Henstridge, which was a promotion. While at Dinder he became intimately acquainted with a virtuous gentlewoman of the placs, Miss Margaret Bisse, whom he married on the last day of December, 1713. By her he had four sons and one daughter. The rectory of Axbridge falling vacant, the bishop offered it so him, together with the prebendaryship of Wizilscombe, which he accepted. Axbridge being a corporation town required his presence as resident, and in June 1720, he removed thither from Wells. On the 25th of October 1721, he had the misfortune to lose his wife, as well as several of his children. Eight years later he married again, a Mrs. Elizabeth Chorley, a widow, with whom he lived happily for the rest of his life. He died on the 19th December, 1765, at the age of eighty-eight, and a monument was erected to his memory in the church at Axbridge, Somersetshire. He had been rector of the parish for forty-five years.

RENTOUL : After the Revocation, the Rentouls, or Rintouls, settled in Scotland. One of them became a landed proprietor in Perthshire. His eldest son retained the homestead, while the younger sons became professional men. James

Rintoul became a Presbyterian minister, and settled at Kay, in the north of Ireland. He married Anne Reed of Kay, and their descendants inter-married with the Sandys and Blennerhassets of Dublin, and other distinguished families. It is believed that the first editor of the *Spectator* belonged to the Rintouls who remained in Scotland.

RIMBAULT: another Huguenot refugee, whose origin is unknown, except that his ancestor came over to England at the Revocation. The late Dr. Rimbault's father was for forty years organist of the Church of St. Giles-in-the-Fields. At the age of eighteen, Edward Rimbault supported his mother and five younger brothers and sisters. Till his death, in his sixtieth year, Dr. Rimbault's life was one of constant and fruitful industry. In musical literature and antiquities he was a high authority, and his knowledge of general literature was also extensive.

VENOURS, MARQUIS DE: From this family came the Wyners, or Viners, one of whom was a distinguished lawyer, who founded and endowed a Professorship and Scholarship of Common Law at Oxford.

HUGUENOTS AND THEIR DESCENDANTS IN IRELAND.

A CONSIDERABLE number of the Huguenots settled permanently in Ireland, and many of their descendants achieved distinction in connection with the Church, the Army and Navy, Commerce, and Manufactures. Besides the refugee French who settled in the neighbourhood of Belfast—mostly at Lisburn, Lurgan, and Lambeg,—large numbers settled in other parts of Ireland. Amongst the principal immigrants in Ulster were Crommelin, Dupré, Goncourt, De la Cherois, De la Valade, Du Bourdieu, Goyer, Chartrés, Obré, Rochét, Bulmer, d'Ermain, Du Pré, Bouchier, St. Clair, Perrin, and others.

Waterford—the birthplace of Edmund Kean, Tyrone Power, and Dorothea Jordan—was one of the cities of refuge early adopted by the French exiles, principally because of its nearness to the opposite coast, and the commercial intercourse which had existed between its merchants and those in the south of France. In exchange for Irish provisions and linen yarns, large quantities of Bordeaux wines were imported into Waterford, so that the place long continued to be a centre of the French wine trade.

But the principal number of the exiles settled in Dublin, where many of them began the manufacture of silk, poplin, and other fabrics. Others joined the Church, the Army, or the Law. The late Dr. Letablere, Dean of Tuam, left a list of the French refugees and their descendants, who had achieved distinction in their professions, towards the end of the last century.* Among the clergy, he mentions the Bishop of Waterford, the Very Revs. Deans Brocas and Champagné, the Revs. Dr. Pellissier and Mercier, the Revs. M. Lamié, Samien, Greelier, Columbine, De Villeti, Pelletreau, Skosié, Richou, Beaufort, St. Paul, Stonié, Jervois, Hammond, Dubourdieu, Landes, Roukié, Caillard, Desbocus, Chaigneau, Peter Pellissier, Lamillière, George Gruber, Grubert Lou, Mathurin, Ledeveze, Dabsac, Lefanu, Treneford, Fleury, Viridet, and Gast. Besides these are nineteen ministers of Calvinistic congregations, whose names are also given, —namely, Pomee, Daressier, Delagalimére, Baligeux, Du-

---

* The last has been communicated to us by Edward Litton, Esq., Altmore, county Tyrone.

casse, Hany, Viridet, Cartie, Roitblere, Durand, Pallerd, Ostervold, Caullard, Ladouespe, St. Ferail, Desvories, Bonneval, Lavalde, Jusy (Dios).

Among the descendants of French Huguenots then in the British Army, Dean Letablere mentions the names of two generals, six colonels, five majors, twenty-four captains, and eight subaltern officers. They include Generals Degens and Adleiron ; Colonels Ladeveze, Chenevix, Le Grand du Petitbosc, Labouchtiere, Rochebrune, and Tropaud ; Majors Marceille, Vignole, Nicolas, Alesian, and Vigneau ; Captains Jervois, Debrisey, Daressus, Ed. Corneille, John Corneille, Baucon, Labilliere, Caillead, Comberose, Desberies, Dumeny, Trenouillet, Labartese, Lemelquiré, Lemaldovic, Lemenzottiere, Maritus, Nicholas, Laquettiére, Vigneau, Poucet, Rochebrune, Portail, Ferrot, and Viruzel. Among the lieutenants are Favière, Ladeveze,Adleiron, and Dumas, and amongst the Ensigns are Vignole and the two sons of Captain Debrisey.

Dr. Letablere does not record the names of the Legal gentlemen in Ireland descended from the Huguenots, but A. V. Kirwan, Esq., has supplied us with a few of them. In 1780 the following barristers were practising before the Irish Courts : Henri Arabin, Jean Blosset, Jean Chaigneau, Richard Espinasse, Joseph Huband, F. Hassard, W. Lefanu, W. Saurin. In 1789, Lefroy ; in 1806, W. Bessonet (son of a Calvinistic pas-

tor) ; and in 1814, Fleury, Alexander Castelle, Phillipe Lemaitre, D. Pineau, and Andrew Malin, were amongst those who practised as attorneys and notaries.

Among the nobility and gentry were Labarte, La Billière, and La Feuillade. Du Bédat, descendant of the marquis of that name, was employed by the Bank of Ireland ; and among the other bankers were Latouche and the sons and W. Lafanu.

The Physicians and Surgeons were numerous. Among them may be mentioned Drs. Fleury, Pelissier, Labat, Calonne, and the famous surgeon, Dubourdieu. There were also many professors of French.

The wine trade was principally in the hands of the descendants of the Huguenots ; and after the trade of Waterford had declined, Dublin became the centre of the French wine trade. Among the principal wine merchants in 1780, were Chaigneau,Dechozeau, Gabourin, Laurent, Miot, Nairac, Pache, and Seguin.

There were also numerous men in trade—jewellers, goldsmiths, silk manufacturers, lace-makers, embroiderers, milliners, grocers, sugar bakers, and merchants of all kinds. But their names are so numerous, that it is unnecessary to swell this record with recording them. Many of the more important members of the Huguenot families in Ireland are referred to at length in the preceding Lists of the descendants of Huguenot Refugees.

THE FRENCH REFUGEE.

The following song was composed by the late Dr. Byles, descendant of a Huguenot. He was Medical Officer to the French Protestant Hospital, Victoria Park, E. The song, which he himself used to sing at the Directors' meetings after the Quarterly Courts, was always received with great enthusiasm.

I sing of the noble Refugee,
  Who strove in a holy faith,
At the altar of his God to bow,
  When the road was marked with
    death.

How vain was the flight in the wild
  midnight
To the forest's inmost glade,
When the holy few, to those altars
  true,
On the green sward knelt and
  prayed !

When the despot's sword and the
  bigot's torch
Had driven him forth to roam,
From village, and farm, and city,
  and town,
He sought our Island Home.

And store of wealth and a rich
  reward
He brought in his open hand,
For many a peaceful art he taught,
  Instead of the fireman's brand.

And boldly he fought for the land
  he'd sought
When the battle-storm awoke,
In the tented field or the guarded
  fort,
Or on board our " Hearts of Oak."

And dear to him now is the red
  crossed flag,
  (His ancient hate and fear) ;
And well does he love his adopted
  land
  And the Friends who've welcomed
  him here.

Chorus.

Hey ! for our land, our English land,
  The land of the brave and the free ;
Who with open arms in the olden time
  Received the Refugee !

INDEX.

[For Proper Names, see List of Huguenot Refugees.]

Printed by Hazell, Watson, & Viney, Ld., London and Aylesbury.

Lightning Source UK Ltd.
Milton Keynes UK
04 January 2011

165153UK00003B/3/A